INFORMATION SYSTEM CONCEPTS:
An Integrated Discipline Emerging

IFIP - The International Federation for Information Processing

IFIP was founded in 1960 under the auspices of UNESCO, following the First World Computer Congress held in Paris the previous year. An umbrella organization for societies working in information processing, IFIP's aim is two-fold: to support information processing within its member countries and to encourage technology transfer to developing nations. As its mission statement clearly states,

IFIP's mission is to be the leading, truly international, apolitical organization which encourages and assists in the development, exploitation and application of information technology for the benefit of all people.

IFIP is a non-profitmaking organization, run almost solely by 2500 volunteers. It operates through a number of technical committees, which organize events and publications. IFIP's events range from an international congress to local seminars, but the most important are:

- The IFIP World Computer Congress, held every second year;
- open conferences;
- working conferences.

The flagship event is the IFIP World Computer Congress, at which both invited and contributed papers are presented. Contributed papers are rigorously refereed and the rejection rate is high.

As with the Congress, participation in the open conferences is open to all and papers may be invited or submitted. Again, submitted papers are stringently refereed.

The working conferences are structured differently. They are usually run by a working group and attendance is small and by invitation only. Their purpose is to create an atmosphere conducive to innovation and development. Refereeing is less rigorous and papers are subjected to extensive group discussion.

Publications arising from IFIP events vary. The papers presented at the IFIP World Computer Congress and at open conferences are published as conference proceedings, while the results of the working conferences are often published as collections of selected and edited papers.

Any national society whose primary activity is in information may apply to become a full member of IFIP, although full membership is restricted to one society per country. Full members are entitled to vote at the annual General Assembly, National societies preferring a less committed involvement may apply for associate or corresponding membership. Associate members enjoy the same benefits as full members, but without voting rights. Corresponding members are not represented in IFIP bodies. Affiliated membership is open to non-national societies, and individual and honorary membership schemes are also offered.

INFORMATION SYSTEM CONCEPTS:

An Integrated Discipline Emerging

IFIP TC8/WG8.1 International Conference on
Information System Concepts:
An Integrated Discipline Emerging (ISCO-4)
September 20-22, 1999, University of Leiden, The Netherlands

Edited by

Eckhard D. Falkenberg
Germany

Kalle Lyytinen
University of Jyväskylä
Finland

Alexander A. Verrijn-Stuart
University of Leiden
The Netherlands

KLUWER ACADEMIC PUBLISHERS
BOSTON / DORDRECHT / LONDON

Distributors for North, Central and South America:
Kluwer Academic Publishers
101 Philip Drive
Assinippi Park
Norwell, Massachusetts 02061 USA
Telephone (781) 871-6600
Fax (781) 871-6528
E-Mail <kluwer@wkap.com>

Distributors for all other countries:
Kluwer Academic Publishers Group
Distribution Centre
Post Office Box 322
3300 AH Dordrecht, THE NETHERLANDS
Telephone 31 78 6392 392
Fax 31 78 6546 474
E-Mail <services@wkap.nl>

Electronic Services <http://www.wkap.nl>

Library of Congress Cataloging-in-Publication Data

IFIP TC8/WG8.1 International Conference on Information System Concepts (4th : 1999 : University of Leiden)
Information system concepts : an integrated discipline emerging : IFIP TC8/WG8.1 International Conference on Information System Concepts : an Integrated Discipline Emerging (ISCO-4) : September 20-22, 1999, University of Leiden, The Netherlands / edited by Eckhard D. Falkenberg, Kalle Lyytinen, Alexander A. Verrijn-Stuart.
p. cm. — (International Federation for Information Processing; 36)
Includes bibliographical references and index.
ISBN 0-7923-7806-7
1. Database management—Congresses. I. Falkenberg, Eckhard D., 1942- II. Lyytinen, Kalle, 1953- III. Verrijn-Stuart, A.A. IV. Title. V. International Federation for Information Processing (Series) ; 36.

QA76.9.D3 I163 1999
005.74—dc21 00-022054

Printed on acid-free paper.

Printed in the United States of America.

CONTENTS

Editors' Preface

This volume contains the invited paper, the reviewed research papers, the discussants' comments on the latter, and the workshop memoranda of the fourth IFIP WG 8.1 International Working Conference on "Information System Concepts", with the subtitle "An Integrated Discipline Emerging" (ISCO4). It was held in Leiden, The Netherlands, 20-22 September 1999.

The previous three ISCO conferences were subtitled "An In-depth Analysis", "Improving the Understanding", and "Towards a Consolidation of Views". Their proceedings were published in 1989, 1992, and 1995, respectively. The ISCO conferences were instigated by the former Task Group FRISCO (an acronym for "FRamework of Information System Concepts"), charged by the IFIP Working Group 8.1 with the task of proposing a conceptual framework for the information system field. Its report, entitled "A Framework of Information System Concepts" (the "FRISCO Report" for short), is available on the World Wide Web via the address:

http://www.wi.leidenuniv.nl/~verrynst/frisco.html

or may be downloaded directly as a condensed Word-6 file from:

ftp://ftp.leidenuniv.nl/pub/rul/fri-full.zip

The FRISCO Report forms a significant contribution to the long-lasting quest of our community towards developing a scientific outlook on the field of information systems. Clarifying the varied nature of many diverging views - some of which may not easily be reconciled - the report does propose a coherent, consistent and partially formalised framework of concepts. While its coverage may not be complete, its line of reasoning may be helpful in resolving (or at least bringing out into the open) a considerable range of issues and problems addressed by the information system research community. In particular, it advocates that cognizance be taken of the scientific, engineering and social angles.

The previous three ISCO conferences were intended to accompany and stimulate the (at that time ongoing) FRISCO task and to debate possibilities and approaches to further advance our field into a scientific discipline. ISCO4 on the other hand was intended not only to further debate these possibilities and approaches, but also to review the FRISCO Report. For a better understanding of the review aspects in this volume, it is recommended to read (parts of) the FRISCO Report first.

There is no section in this volume called "A Review of the FRISCO Report". Rather, a review spirit will be encountered througout the proceedings. Several research papers and in particular the three workshop memoranda contain reflections on and/or criticism of the FRISCO Report as a whole or of specific aspects thereof.

The research papers in this volume were selected in a blind-reviewing process. They can be classified broadly into the following categories:

- Reflections on and criticism of conceptual frameworks (such as FRISCO)
- Fundamental and generic information system concepts
- Novel information system design approaches
- Approaches to integrate and synthesise information system design methods

These papers appear in the same order as presented at the conference. Each is followed by the comments of at least one invited discussant.

The workshop themes were:

- The conceptual foundations of information systems
- Innovation and standardisation in the information system field
- How do our concepts shape our practice, and vice versa?

We do hope that this volume will indeed help to develop the information system field into an integrated discipline.

We wish to thank Zheying Zhang and Matti Rossi, University of Jyväskylä, for their support during the reviewing process, Hans van Bemmel, manager of the Lorentz Center, for his support concerning the local arrangements before and during the conference, Arnold van Ittersum, director of the sponsoring organisation SERC, for his support regarding the financial arrangements, and for the financial support of the European Espinode Program.

Eckhard D. Falkenberg
Kalle Lyytinen
Alexander A. Verrijn-Stuart

Conference Officers and Committee Members

GENERAL CONFERENCE CHAIR:

Eckhard D. Falkenberg
Germany

PROGRAM COMMITTEE CHAIR:

Kalle Lyytinen
University of Jyväskylä, Finland

PROGRAM COMMITTEE MEMBERS:

David Avison, United Kingdom
Sjaak Brinkkemper, The Netherlands
Jan Dietz, The Netherlands
Terry Halpin, Australia
Brian Henderson-Sellars, Australia
Wolfgang Hesse, Germany
Hannu Kangassalo, Finland
John Krogstie, Norway
Frederick Lochovsky, China
Ojelanki Ngwenyama, USA
Andreas Oberweis, Germany
James Odell, USA
Klaus Pohl, Germany
Colette Rolland, France
Motoshi Saeki, Japan
Ronald Stamper, The Netherlands
Burt Swanson, USA
Jon Turner, USA
Yair Wand, Canada
Richard Welke, USA
Trevor Wood-Harper, United Kingdom

PROGRAM COMMITTEE SECRETARY:

Zheying Zhang
University of Jyväskylä, Finland

ORGANISING COMMITTEE CHAIR:

Alexander A. Verrijn-Stuart
Leiden University, The Netherlands

ORGANISING COMMITTEE MEMBERS:

Hans van Bemmel, Lorentz Center, University of Leiden
Arnold van Ittersum, SERC, Utrecht

Information Systems as a Social Science

An Alternative to the FRISCO Formalism

Ronald K. Stamper

MEASURE Ltd, 29 Dartmouth Road Park, London NW5 1SU
Tel: +44 0207 813 7359 Fax: +44 0207 ***482 2968***
Email: rstamper@compuserve.com
University of Twente, P.O. Box 217, NL-7500 AE Enschede
Email: ***r.k.stamper@sms.utwente.nl***

Abstract: The FRISCO Report has initiated an important debate on the discipline of information. Chapters 1, 2 and 6 contribute ideas for all shades of opinion, a Broad View contrasting with Chapters 3, 4 and 5, "the core of the report". This paper presents a Social View as an alternative to this Core View, which it criticises in two ways. Firstly, it limits the scope of information systems by treating it as an adjunct to software engineering, having no place for key properties of information in organisations and society. Secondly, it does not satisfactorily link its framework of concepts to the empirical world, but relies on the mentalistic notions of 'perceptions' and 'conceptions' in the mind of some, unspecified interpreter. The strength of the Core View lies in its formal precision. But a Social View can lead to an alternative formal framework that can place a much wider range of information systems concepts on a firm empirical basis. Thus provides a foundation for information systems as a social science, rather than a branch of applied mathematics. The Core View includes the belief in an objective reality to which we have direct access via the supposedly transparent languages of words, numbers and diagrams, whereas the Social View, without rejecting that position, requires us to explain how we come to construct such knowledge. It also compels us to examine all the other functions we perform with information, especially our construction of social reality. Forced to examine these questions, we have to address many elusive problems, such as the creation of meanings, the role of intentional communication, the construction of time, and the systems of norms we call 'organisation'. Finally, the paper re-works the Japan Wines case study used in the FRISCO Report. This shows that the Social View leads to a more detailed analysis of the business problems than the Core View, with as much formal precision, which lends itself to computer interpretation, while also yielding models that are easier for users to interpret.

If the FRISCO Report has a lasting contribution it will result from the debate it has provoked about the central concepts of Information Systems, and its effort to place the subject on a scientific foundation. The initial hope that we would produce a stable framework of information systems concepts turned out to be far too ambitious. The people who are working in this field now have a duty to make positions clear and to discuss them in a rigorous, critical, constructive and open way.

AN IMPORTANT DEBATE

FRISCO did not consider seriously, or present in its report all the views deserving attention. Nevertheless, it presents a broad, discursive treatment of information systems concepts in chapters 1, 2 and 6, which succeed in bringing together most of the key ideas that should inhabit any framework of IS concepts. I shall refer to this as the Broad View. On the other hand, one view is given priority. It is asserted on p. 14 that "the core of the report is formed by chapters 3 and 4". So I shall refer to this as the Core View.

Many ideas carefully articulated in the Broad View find no place in the narrowly focused Core View, which I was tempted to might call the Formal View. It has the major virtues of precision, formality and consistency and it strives for clarity. However, I prefer not to suggest that formality is the preserve of the Core View. Indeed, every worthy alternative must aim for such formal clarity so that it can be subjected to constructive criticism in ways that, for instance, the Broad View does not invite. I shall focus my discussion on the Core View and attempt to keep my criticism as constructive as possible by drawing together more ideas from the Broad View, into an alternative also capable of precision, formality and consistency. This alternative I shall refer to as a Social View of information systems.

In Chapter 7 of the Report, my co-authors and I expressed personal positions. Some favoured the Broad View and indicated a little dissatisfaction with the Core View. Wolfgang Hesse emphasises on p. 175 the value of a framework "ranging from the physical level through the linguistic levels up to the social level [for dealing] with all the relevant aspects of information systems." Paul Lindgreen on p. 183 puts his finger on the danger of the formal approach in the Core View by quoting its definition of a language as, "A non-empty set of permissible arrangements of symbols taken from an alphabet.", remarking "For me a language is a social convention." Björn Nilsson comments on the narrow definition of "the information in a message [as] the new knowledge gained by an interpreter thereof." He points to three relevant missing part of the definition, which relate to intentions, meanings and effects of the message. Alex Verrijn-

Stuart, though content with the Core, points out, on p. 196, that the semiotic ladder reveals a different meaning of "meaning" on each level, something which the formal Chapter 4 fails to achieve.

On the contrary, semiotics provides a precise, formal and consistent basis for a discipline of information systems. The FRISCO group never examined this question. My own contribution to Chapter 7, "A Dissenting Position" attempted in the allotted six pages to sketch an answer. As the member responsible for introducing *six* semiotic levels (Stamper 1973 and 1989), I feel obliged to take this discussion further. Hence one of my objectives in this paper is to explain how to handle the three, more problematic, non-technological semiotic levels - semantic, pragmatic and social – in to the formal and precise standards that I share with my colleagues.

Two positions

My motivation for applying semiotics to information systems, besides removing vagueness about our basic concepts, has always been to bridge the gap between the technical and social orientation to information systems problems. This gap appears to me not only to be damaging to our scholarly community, but also to our problem-solving ability, and, most of all to our attempts to create a science of information systems. There still appear to be two, somewhat antagonistic communities representing these two approaches. During the 1970s my research programme was funded by two research councils, one on each side of the divide. We were trying to be precise about organisations using the concept of a norm and using legal norms as empirical materials, to define information requirements for computer applications,. The reviewers on the science and engineering side said, "This isn't real science, it has something to do with the law." Those on the economic and social side said, "We must not fund this because the computer should have nothing to do with the law, which is not just a system of rules." In the debate, which we shall embark upon, I hope that this sterile set of attitudes will not be visible.

The Social View I shall present does not exclude the Core View of FRISCO but incorporates it as a special case. It is also overcomes the inadequacy of treating information systems as a branch of applied mathematics: a formal discipline without empirical foundations. Machines and formalisms for handling information are human artefacts and they should be incorporated naturally into a social model of information systems. This approach gives us a far better chance of building an empirically based science instead of a formalism that has only a rather nebulous connection with reality.

When I became involved in information systems, first in practice then academically, we taught methods and notations, supported by a wealth of practical experience, to enable people to define computer applications in the business world. There was no engineering because there was no supporting science. We were, and still are, the blacksmiths of the information age. The time has come to choose whether to continue that way or to re-discover information systems as a science that can stand comparison with any other in the quality of its theories and the stringency of the empirical tests they have to pass.

Therefore, this paper has three main parts. *First* it explains why the Core View, despite its excellence from a formal perspective, fails as a basis for an empirical science. It lacks the conceptual richness to tackle many of the issues introduced in the Broad View. *Second*, it presents an alternative solution that, while capable of achieving a level of formality comparable with the Core View, also handles the broader subject matter of information systems. *Third*, it applies methods derived from this alternative Social View to the analysis of the Japan Wines case study used in the FRISCO Report, producing a more thorough requirements analysis that is also easier to understand and implement.

THE CORE VIEW OF FRISCO – FORMAL BUT NOT SCIENTIFIC

At the end of the 20th century, the study of information systems is regrettably not yet a scientific. It does not even study information systems in any broad sense. Rather, it subsists as the handmaiden of software engineering, consisting of notations and methods to serve that end. The Broad View of FRISCO moves us towards an empirical science but the Core View, while correctly embracing formality, leaves the empirical questions aside. In effect, Chapter 4 treats information systems as a branch of applied mathematics, closely allied to software development.

Software engineering is important but far more important is the shaping of our information society, for which we need an empirical science that can link software to the social processes it should serve. We have the opportunity to create one of the most exciting and important disciplines for the next century.

What is essential to an empirical scientific discipline?

A massive literature (including Popper 1959 and 1963, Lakatos 1970, Feyerabend 1975) deals with the question of how to draw a line between science and non-science. All the authors relate their answers to the methods of enquiry adopted by the discipline. These range from the strict demarcation line Popper imposes with his refutationist method to the tolerant Feyerabend slogan that "anything goes". However, on one point the philosophers of science do agree. *They all expect scientists to check their theories, their universal laws, against particular empirical observations* ("The only pressing reason for changing a theory is disagreement with the facts." Feyerabend p. 38). To achieve this they must state their theories clearly and unambiguously, using a terminology that allows one to deduce statements that can be tested operationally. Unless a theory or a model or a computer program can meet these conditions, there can be no way of checking it against experience of the real world.

There are two conditions to consider. The first is the standing of the discipline as a deductive system. It must be formulated in a language that allows unambiguous logical conclusions to be drawn from statements of theory and fact. Formality is necessary for exposing and eliminating *syntactic ambiguity*. However that does not deal with *semantic ambiguity* which is achieved by meeting the second condition, that of making operationally reliable connections between reality and the language of the theory. "Ambiguity" is itself ambiguous. In his commentary on FRISCO Alex Verrijn-Stuart (1998) falls into this trap when implicitly he claims that formality is sufficient: "formal, that is to say, unambiguous and precise . . .". Unfortunately formality is only a protection against ambiguity and guarantee of precision in their *syntactic* senses.

Logicism

Logic, understandably, has a high standing in any field associated with computing. Pre-eminently, the computer is a machine for automating logical operations, so logic has, inevitably much to contribute to computing theory, and, one might expect, also to information systems. It has to play a central role in any alternative approach.

But logic inspired a tradition of thought over this century, originating in the works of Frege and of Russell and Whitehead who were convinced that the best way of placing mathematics on a sound foundation would be to show that it arises from logic. Logicism, as this line of thinking is called, is still influential and appears to have inspired the Core View. The goal of Chapter 4 appears to be a kind of "Principia Informatica" intended to give our subject a secure foundation. Its aim is to derive all the essential concepts relevant to information systems by building a logical edifice on some self-evident and totally reliable assumptions. Is this approach likely to succeed?

Logicism as a strategy is loosing its hold. It was shaken by Gödel in the 1930s. Lakatos (1976) examined the creation of mathematics as a social process, contributing to a growing body of opinion (for example, Kitcher 1984, Hersch 1997, Ernest 1998) which favours empirical activity and social constructivism as alternative and more reliable foundations for mathematics. This new line of thinking about the formal disciplines bears some affinity with the Social View of information systems.

Although, at first sight, it may seen reasonable to hope that one formal discipline, mathematics, might be given foundations in another (logic), it is doubtful that any messy, complex empirical discipline can be rooted in logic without loosing touch with reality. Physics appears to be an exception. Newton's laws encode much of our knowledge of the field with astonishing economy. But what those laws encode is a vast amount of concrete knowledge of relevant domains, from everyday mechanics to astronomical observation, knowledge that was accumulated and assimilated long before the formalised summary in modern physical theory was conjectured. The Core View of FRISCO shows less evidence of being based on vast knowledge of organisations and human information systems, than upon deep familiarity with computers and software engineering. Whatever logic may be discovered in organised behaviour should arise from the study of organisations rather than imported from computing.

Logicism assumes that the particular form of logic being used is necessarily a sound instrument, quite free from any pre-suppositions, and capable of guiding our thinking through purely rational deductive arguments. Logic, as any formal system, functions mechanically and can do a wonderful job in the right circumstances. What are the circumstances where classical logics are appropriate? They evolved to deal with problems in the natural sciences and related forms of engineering. We should at least be cautious about applying to the study of information systems forms of logic that evolved to serve disciplines that regard the information in everyday discourse and scientific discussion as a transparent medium through which to 'see' the natural reality that interests them. We can safely adopt the same attitudes of natural science and mathematics when we study the physics, empirics and syntactic aspects of information. But we also have a professional duty to examine those aspects of information that any natural scientist can take for granted. We have no obligation to do more natural science but one of our tasks, for example, is to understand how natural scientists and mathematicians use information to explain their success. We cannot take for granted the informal meta-languages that others use unconsciously, because they are our what our subject is about. Therefore we should be cautious about being trapped within the limits of a formalism that evolved for totally different purposes from our own. I shall return to this issue later, because an alternative approach arises from a critical questioning of the assumptions behind classical logic.

A framework of information systems concepts can be held together *internally* using logical methods but it will only stand up to external, empirical testing if the foundations are well chosen and the framework firmly fastened down. Thus it will only serve its purpose if it is based on all the key concepts relevant to our discipline and if it also links its treatment of them to reality (begging the question about the nature of reality, which natural science can also usually ignore).

The link with reality

Formal systems do not necessarily have any connection with reality. Anyone using information of any kind should be careful to check out its connection to reality. This applies just as much to theories and models as to any other information. Such connections may be irrelevant because all we want is a self-contained formal system that will stimulate the imagination – computer games are like that. Sometimes the link to reality is implicit, as I hope it is with systems to control nuclear power stations or run social security. We just hope we can rely on the intuition of the designers and programmers in the absence of any explicit treatment of that link: the semantics of the data and programs. Surely, any information systems professional should always be able to advise on the quality of the relationship between information and reality.

To set up its links to reality, the Core View uses a sequence of definitions, which, after getting lost in some circularity, eventually lead us back to some primitive notions. The choice of primitive notions is crucial. There is no point in defining everything in words because that process has no end. At some point we have to say, "Well, beyond these definitions we rely on a few primitive terms that anyone can understand by learning to operate with them in practice." Physics uses notions of a physical body and the simplest phenomena involving them. Newton's laws talk of bodies, their motion, change of motion and forces applied to them. A child who has spent time kicking a football on the street will have an *operational* grasp of those concepts *and a way of demonstrating them convincingly to other people.* Physics is an ideal paradigm for a science built upon well-founded, primitive notions. How does the Core View of FRISCO fare in this respect?

Unfortunately, when we reach the primitive notions, they are 'perceptions' and 'conceptions' linked to things in the real domain by processes within the minds of unspecified individuals. The inaccessibility of these mental processes is admitted and dismissed in the same breath, on p. 35: "While,the conceptions, as such, are not accessible, indirectly they are available for discussion and hence operationalisable." If information systems were no more than the discipline of manipulating character strings or other sign-tokens, we could have formulated the Core View without invoking 'perceptions' and 'conceptions'. The physical tokens and their syntactic types can all be observed accurately and handled by operations that can be demonstrated reliably. In that case, information systems would be firmly within the domain of computer science, and would continue to lack the capacity to say anything about people and organisations.

By introducing 'perceptions' and 'conceptions' and declaring that they can be treated operationally, simply because we can discuss them, we have admitted that information systems does raise problems that a computer scientist can safely ignore. But all we are offered to see and work with empirically by examining "any available discussion" will be representations, the signs that our information system will manipulate. We are back in a world that can be handled solely in terms of manipulating tokens, signs, representations, data and so on – the world of computing. We have not begun to get to grips with a real world in any sense. When one designs an information system, one has to be careful how the sign-tokens and sign-types are linked to reality. The Core View would allow us to operationalise astrology and physics in just the same way. Astrologers can discuss their 'perceptions' and 'conceptions' equally convincingly as physicists but they easily bamboozle anyone who is satisfied by the operational criterion expressed in the Core View. Modern science is a huge practical success because the physicists do more than discuss their perceptions and conceptions. They impose the strict criteria of operational meanings on their theories, which must imply particular statements that can be tested empirically.

Meaning

"Meaning" is a word with many meanings, as noted at length in FRISCO's Broad View in Chapter 6. A relationship between a representation and what it represents provides one meaning of that ambiguous word. A general account of how such relationships are formed constitutes a *semantics*. Computer scientists use a completely formal semantics which defines the meaning of one formal structure (eg: a program) as a representation of another (another program or a set-theoretic structure). They inhabit a world of pure symbolic expressions in which their meanings can be defined by rules translating them into other expressions. Their world is tightly controlled and, within mathematically clear limits, uncertainty can be totally eliminated. The world studied by information systems, as envisaged in the Broad View, is quite different; it is full of people and uncertainty, unlike the limited world studied by computer science.

Meaning, in a sense adequate for a science of information systems, must account for three things: for *reality*, the things we represent using information, for the *signs* that do the representing and for the *link* between them. Each of these three components of the semantic model:

sign --------------------------- MEANING -------------------------- thing
(representation) (link) (reality)

It is no good lamenting that the subject matter of information systems is "fuzzy" and complaining that semantics is one of the "nebulous" levels of the semiotic ladder and, therefore ignoring it. Semantics is one of the central issues for a science of information systems and any relevant theory must come to grips with it. Unfortunately, FRISCO's Core View clearly fails to do this. Firstly, it contains no clear commitment concerning the nature of reality. Secondly, instead of the excellent, ostensibly definable primitive, 'sign', on which semiotics is based, it uses 'representation' (defined as an 'actand' (defined as a 'thing' (defined as a 'conception'))). So, thirdly, the only link between the sign and reality we are given is some process in a mind. We are not even told how to identify the relevant mind in any situation. Should we do so, the link between sign and signified is accounted for by private, subjective processes of perceiving and conceiving, processes that are inaccessible except by introspection.

Incompleteness of the Core View

Although semantics is an issue of central importance to anyone using information, the Core View has nothing relevant to say on this subject. It is also unable fully to handle issues on two other semiotic levels: pragmatic and social.

Newton's laws apply equally well to the motion of Mars round the Sun as to the motion of a boot hurled by an angry spouse at a partner. The intention behind the throwing is irrelevant to the motion of the boot, so physics rightly ignores it. However, if nothing more than a verbal insult were hurled, the intention would be highly relevant to understanding this message, as the Broad View makes clear on p. 22. Any framework of concepts that cannot deal with *intention* is not going to be relevant to information systems involving people. The Core View deals with *intension* (the set-theoretic counterpart to an extension) but does not mention "intention". The notion of a "goal" is a partial substitute. On p. 72 "communication" is defined as "an exchange of messages" with an explanation that it may involve several human agents in many transactions "and the goal of the communication is made present in all communication partners." This final proposition is not clear, but it talks of "*the*" goal, implying that one goal alone can govern such a complex process. Often each participant has several goals in mind and changes them in the course of the conversation. The claim that this approach to communication "corresponds to the reasoning applied in speech act theory" is false. The use of goals and omission of intentionality make the Core View unable to treat the separate motivations behind each transaction in a conversation. It cannot therefore handle the analysis of the detailed pragmatics of an information system. This is confirmed by the explanation of the goals in the case study, on p. 132. A science of information systems must be able to accommodate the rich details of speech act theory. Again the Core View of FRISCO is irrelevant to an essential part of the subject.

Now we ask whether the Core View is relevant to the social aspects of information. Assumption [h] on p. 84 acknowledges that "inter-subjective reality" depends on agreement across a society. This idea is basic to a science of information systems. The information, representations, messages, signs we deal with – call them what you will – do not grow on trees. They are normally social products that fall beyond the scope of natural science. We only have information when we have something (a representation) that can stand for something else (what it represents). Such linkages have natural origins in part-whole relationships and in similarities but are now almost entirely products of human cultures. Society is necessarily a core concept of information systems but not only because it is the origin of information. Society is also the product of information. The Broad View, on pp. 17 and 18, makes clear that a science of information systems should account for the value that communication adds through its consequences for society. If we ask what information gives us, it is clear we cannot eat it, wear it nor travel about on it. Indirectly it helps us obtain food, protection and transport, but only by virtue of disposing people to serve us and act in a co-ordinated fashion. Information has no other immediate value than the social effects it causes. Its secondary consequences may be physical and economic. The notions of transition and state, on p. 86, are relevant but they do not relate to changes of a social kind. The Core View has only a treatment of state-transitions lifted directly from computer science, a special version of cause-and-effect relationships in the physical world. An extension is possible. The effect of a communication is to change the propositional attitudes of the people who have some responsible role to play. In the realm of information and society, transitions always entail responsibility on the parts of the players. Responsibility is *mentioned* in the Core View but not *used*. No theory of information systems can be complete if it does not include an adequate means of treating responsibility.

Shortcomings summarised

The Core View of FRISCO belongs in the tradition of the formal disciplines, including computer 'science', which studies the mechanical manipulation of formal structures. I am using "science" in the sense of an empirical discipline that is grounded in the experiences we share in the public domain that our information strives to represent. Empirical sciences can benefit by using formal methods but only if the formal language is firmly linked to the reality being studied. For this link, the Core View relies on empirically inaccessible mental processes.

Logical formality is desirable because it helps us to eliminate *syntactic ambiguity*. In this, the Core View succeeds. But the kind of logic employed still leaves the problem of *semantic ambiguity* untouched. Good definitions rooted in simple, operationalised, primitive notions can solve this problem. We are given definitions of such key terms as "information", "communication" and "knowledge" based on the primitive concepts of "perception" and "conception". Moreover, these fail to distinguish the multiple meanings of these terms that are acknowledged elsewhere in the FRISCO Report..

Users of information are generally indifferent whether the information they receive has been produced by computers or by paper and pencil. But they do want to know that it is *meaningful* and be able to anticipate any semantic problems that may arise. They need to know the true *intentions* and any hidden ones lurking behind the messages they receive. They want to know its *effects on people,* who can only respond by adjusting their values, beliefs, obligations, expectations and so on, before using the information to guide their own actions. And, if pressed to account for those actions, they will try to explain their degree of *responsibility* as well as the responsibilities of any others implicated with them. The Core View does not provide adequate tools for handling these semantic, pragmatic and social aspects of information.

AN ALTERNATIVE FRAMEWORK

To criticise is one thing but to propose an alternative is altogether more difficult. For any alternative worth considering one must ask a number of questions. The Report, p. 159, raises some relevant criteria related to "expressiveness", "arbitrariness" and "suitability".

1) Does it deal adequately with the relevant IS concepts identified in the Broad View, including meaning, intention, responsibility and society?

2) Does it handle the multiple meanings of key IS concepts such as information, communication, meaning and knowledge?

3) Does its structure of definitions lead back to operationally sound primitive notions so that its propositions can be tested empirically?

4) Does it lend itself to a formal method for modelling or describing information systems that ensures internal consistency?

5) Does it lead us to draw distinctions and investigate problems central to information systems that are now overlooked by the Core View?

6) Does it support the continual accretion of testable knowledge of the information systems domain, as we would expect of any other modern science?

7) Does it enable us to do the routine work on information systems conveniently and effectively?

I shall present an alternative and demonstrate that it meets these criteria. Detailed, critical assessment of this alternative will be welcome.

To make the transparent visible

The people working in the natural sciences aspire to discover the eternal laws of nature that have governed the world since its creation and will continue to do so whether or not there are any people around. Relativity and quantum theories recognise the role of the observer but, in general, natural science would become unnecessarily over-complicated if it introduced human observers and experimenters into their explanations at every point. They want to look at the natural world *through* their theories and observational records without having to enquire about all this information as well. For natural scientists, the information systems they use should be transparent.

However, the opposite should be true for us as students of information systems. Interesting though they are, the natural sciences fall outside the scope of our discipline. Of central importance to us are questions about how those natural scientists know anything, how they communicate their knowledge to others, how they justify accepting what anyone says, and indeed, what is the nature of their knowledge and information. Moreover, we must ask similar questions about business people, lawyers, politicians and citizens, concerning how they use information, how they create the kinds of knowledge they need and how they justify the ways they use information and knowledge. We must make the transparent visible.

Transparency is achieved by a mental trick. Asked to explain how we know anything, the person studying the natural world would tell us to open our eyes and look at the world where we shall find the individuals things that compose it. We can mentally order them and place them into sets to define properties, relationships and other predicates that we can assert about the individuals. This is the familiar objectivist position.

The Broad View in FRISCO adopted a radical solution on p. 10. "The constructivist approach rejects the objectivist assumption that reality simply exists as ready-made individual things and replaces it with a reality that is built through the operations of the members of a community through the social consensus about subjective conceptions that serve their culture." However, the Core View retreats from this subjectivist position on p. 28: "**Constructivist:** somebody who also believes that 'reality' exists independently of any observer, . . ." and clings on to the old way of thinking. By introducing the perceiving and conceiving mind, it does not reject objectivism. Rather, it provides an excuse for maintaining the orthodox view of reality.

Reluctance to abandon the security of established habits of thought is understandable, especially as they have served the natural sciences so well. For information systems to be studied scientifically, however, we must bring the old tacit assumptions to the surface because they beg exactly those questions that lie at the heart of our subject: they are assumptions about meanings and how we obtain and represent knowledge of the world. To analyse the transparent layer:

signs ---------- MEANING ------------ real things

we have to have to think very carefully about what we understand by signs, meanings and, perhaps most difficult of all, real things. This last problem can only be solved by adopting an *ontology*, a solution to the kind of metaphysical question we would prefer never to ask.

Ontological assumptions accompanying predicate logic and set theory

Our duty as information systems professionals includes that of making clear and explicit the relationship between information and reality. This applies to the hidden assumptions on which a theory may be based. Examining the Core View reveals several assumptions:

1) An objective reality exists independently of anyone, so that, despite differences of opinion, it is always the same reality that we experience.
2) That reality is composed of individual things.
3) The expressions of a language are always references to individuals or sets (or, recursively, sets of sets and individuals).
4) These true meanings are independent of anyone, despite the possibility of individuals having muddled perceptions and conceptions.

These are accompanied by constructivist caveats cautioning us that different people might have rather different views of this one reality and have to negotiate a shared view, but without realising that the nature of these negotiations is a proper subject for a science of information systems.

Nevertheless, subject to that negotiation, they take for granted one *real* reality about which we can express facts using propositions in the form:

predicate (individual, individual, . . .)

This is the basis of the formalism used in Chapter 4. Although it has the virtues of formality, it allows us to ignore two of the most obvious assumptions that govern any enquiry into how we know anything or represent what we know.

Those two assumptions are rather certain.

1) We know nothing without a knowing agent being involved.
2) That knowing agent has to do things to acquire that knowledge.

They are the basis of what I call an "actualist" ontology because it assumes only the actual world to which we have access via our actions. As far as information systems studies are concerned, predicate logic and set theory are not neutral. They embody assumptions. These do not *prevent* our referring to knowing agents and their actions, but they fail to *ensure* the agents are included in the picture. We could introduce propositional attitudes, predicates applied to propositions, that specify that someone knows [believes, sees, thinks, . . .] that some proposition is the case, but this strategy creates all kinds of difficulties that ruin the mathematical elegance of first order logic.

If we look just a little more carefully at how we know things, we find two routes. The knowing agent can get involved directly to obtain substantive knowledge of the world, alternatively the agent can know something semiologically, by vicariously using the information that others supply about their direct experiences. These correspond to working with the two ends of the line:

signs ----------- MEANING ------------- real things

We can get to know real things directly or vicariously through the use of signs (information). This distinction is basic to any science of information systems which must explain how we use information (signs) to know about the world and order our lives, and where the knowledge comes from in the first place.

Affordances – reality as invariant repertoires of behaviour

Every animal can acquire direct knowledge by encountering the world through its own actions. Human beings learn even more about the world through the use of signs. Signs are also real things with the additional property that they stand for other things. So we should begin by thinking about direct knowledge, first.

Such knowledge we can represent using an alternative to the well-formed-formulas of predicate logic, I proposed in 1984 (Stamper 1985) a wff with two terms:

Agent behaviour

This involves none of the tacit assumptions of an objectivist ontology. No one has any operational knowledge of reality more basic than of himself or herself, as the real thing that does the knowing (excluding some possible doubts about dreaming). Making operational sense of the 'behaviour' term is more challenging. (For a more detailed explanation see, Stamper 1996.) We can start with James Gibson's Theory of Affordances, which he developed, in his new account of perception. He pointed out that the objectivist, opening her eyes to see the world, looks at something and forms an inverted image on her retina; to perceive this image, another, inner eye must do something similar, beginning an infinite regress that succeeds in explaining nothing about perception. Gibson rejected the idea that animals perceive a ready-made world. Instead, they have to make it up by discovering, within the limitless flux of signals impinging on them, whatever can help them to survive, preferably in comfort and without experiencing harm. What every organism has to discover are the useful *invariant repertoires of behaviour* that its own physiology combined with the structure of the environment afford them. Appropriately, Gibson termed these invariants that we perceive "affordances". Affordances are the only real things we can perceive directly. A rabbit, as Gibson points out, must learn where to obtain the repertoire of behaviour we call 'hiding' if it is to escape from predators, some kinds of terrain, with trees, bushes, deep grass or soft earth afford this repertoire of behaviour and others do not.

To understand adequately the notion of an affordance may take some while initially. If you want to see an animal acquiring them, just watch your babies creating their own reality. A baby, given a cup, will do everything imaginable with it, from pouring a drink all over the floor, throwing the cup at Mummy, banging itself on the head with it, and, at some point, if you are lucky, drinking with it. The cup is not a ready-made objective thing, sitting there waiting for the baby to see it as a cup, but it is the full repertoire of behaviour she discovers. Social forces will lead that all-too-rich affordance, the baby's notion of a cup, to be limited within the bounds that the rest of the family will countenance – but that is to run ahead of our story. Everything we recognise constitutes an invariant repertoire of behaviour; I have found no exception, so far. You will find plenty of examples of affordances in the work of Gibson himself (1979) and a useful work by Michaels and Carello (1981), or you can make up your own.

[In this formal system nothing simply *is the case*, as propositional logic would allow us to say, but everything is made or observed to be that way by some responsible agent or agents doing something, most basically, discovering the relevant affordances. (I emphasised this point in my dissenting reflection in the FRISCO Report by writing it without using the verb "to be". Anything with an operational meaning that is worth saying can be said in this constrained language by writing about what agents do, with no assumption that things "are" as they are, of their own accord.]

How does society create reality? An information systems problem

The recognition of affordances can be handed down genetically, as instincts, but all animals will also learn some by themselves (especially our human babies). Humans are unusual because we only construct a very small part of our reality independently. Most of the reality we know has been created by our enveloping cultures over the course of centuries or millennia. The affordance we call a 'cup' is a human artefact and the way it can be used is not only a matter of what behaviour it makes possible physically but also of what it affords us socially. The baby will learn that, in general, you do not throw cups at people or tip them over when full except to pour the contents to another vessel. In later life she may find that cup throwing is permitted in some fairground side-shows or has its use in a dispute with a drunken husband. The world we create is as much social in character as physical. Even the physical world known to natural science is predominantly a social construct, and science is the social activity constructing it.

Moreover, the social construction of reality takes place, not in the way baby first learned the affordance we call 'cup', but in the context of our information systems. We may learn the *name* of a well-established affordance, long before we obtain sufficient direct knowledge of it. I had certainly heard of a reef knot before I learned to tie one and language and diagrams played a significant role in my acquiring the ability to realise that affordance. Many social affordances are constructed with the aid of that most important information system, the legal system: marriage, copyright, and insolvency, for example. Rules, but not legal rules give us football and etiquette. But first class football, which calls for more than sticking to the rules, and courtesy, which goes far beyond etiquette, involve tacit norms of a subtlety that no explicit rules can capture, and we learn them too. These are all products of our social use of information. For these reasons, we should take Society as the ultimate agent at the root of all our common sense knowledge of reality.

Whenever I have advanced this radically subjectivist position, I have provoked two principal kinds of objections. Some arguments have an ideological basis and others are of a rational nature.

Information systems are central to the effective functioning of society

The mention of Society has often elicited the most intemperate reactions, apparently for political reasons, ever since Thatcher and Regan gave Society a bad name, Thatcher even went so far as to assert that it does not exist. Perhaps I should not bother to counter this irrationality, as their outmoded ideology is losing its power to distort perceptions. My argument requires no more than a common sense acceptance that society, represented by the culture in which we are raised, contributes hugely to our perception and understanding of the world. Indeed, today the progress of the natural sciences depends increasingly on social mechanisms.

Even the perception of many important phenomena is beyond any individual. Openness and sharing information gives us enhanced, collective powers of perception. Consider some of the things no single person could possibly perceive without massive contributions of observations and theories from other people – the hole in the ozone layer, a large computer operating system and tectonic plates, for example. Only groups of people supported by sophisticated information systems can experience these huge repertoires of behaviour. If you have difficulty accepting that without society we should be puny things, try to find an individual able to perform these perceptual tasks alone with no prior relevant knowledge. We may credit an individual with discovering the hole in the ozone layer or tectonic plates but they certainly did not perceive them, their achievements were the synthesis and analysis of masses of information generated by large numbers of their colleagues. Without their scientific communities they would have been 'blind'. This does not diminish their achievement in fitting the last piece of the jigsaw-puzzle.

The rational arguments are prompted by a desire to maintain our faith in an absolutely objective reality. I am arguing that we shall not begin to investigate the central scientific problems of information systems until we drop the pretence that all we need do is open our eyes to see the objective world that surrounds us. To admit that we are making a huge assumption brings us face to face with such problems as the following. *How should we use information so that, collectively, we can form reliable perceptions and understanding of the world on a scale and to a degree of detail that surpasses the abilities of even the most able individual?* If we are concerned with scientific information this is often a central issue, and one that calls for our specialist information systems expertise. When we can produce information systems that are reliable in this sense, we can safely resume our simplifying assumption that we can look out upon an objective reality. Objectivity is socially constructed by a consensus that meets certain criteria of clarity and honesty.

There are similar problems where information is used in other fields. Unfortunately we are currently, and for obvious historical reasons obsessed with only one of the many central information systems problems: *How can we be more efficient in office and factory?* Important though this problem may be, it should no longer be our principal or sole professional purpose. The way we are employed or funded, the common reluctance to confront issues with an ethical flavour, as well as the history of our discipline, all conspire to keep our noses on the purely economic grindstone. But we have responsibilities to the wider society, not only to the accountants. We should enquire: What information systems can make us feel safe when living on the lee side of a nuclear power station? In health care we should ask: What information systems enable us to make (economically, ethically, . . .) sound choices when given limited finance but faced with unlimited demands for expensive treatments and drugs? In the law, our use of information is critical for implementing policies democratically arrived at, rather than any arbitrary and prejudiced decisions of those administering them. The list could be extended, and contemplating it should prompt a reappraisal of our subject.

Although we remain responsible individuals, the starting point for our perceptions, cognitions, values and customary behaviour is found in society where they evolve, are maintained and put to use through the communication of information. Our discipline should elucidate both the healthy and pathological functioning of the necessary information systems.

Note that I am not suggesting that an information science should attempt to make the choices governing our knowledge and culture. Everyone should be involved in making these decisions aided by the insights from the fields of epistemology, jurisprudence, ethics, and so on. Our task is limited. It is a task that scarcely existed before the 20th century brought its rapid development of electronic information technologies. Our limited task is to examine how best to give effect to the choices society makes, given the available information technology.

Justifiable and unjustifiable social relativism

Strong rational objections to my position come from opponents of relativism. No better example may be cited than the widely read and powerful attack by Sokal and Bricmont (1998) on the epistemic relativism propounded by a number of leading, French post-modernists (Lacan,

Kristeva, Irigary, Latour, Baudrillard, Deleuze, Guattari and Virilio). At first sight, it will appear that their criticisms apply to the position I am adopting, especially as those under attack are, to varying degrees, writing on semiology.

Sokal and Bricmont attack the post-modernist claim (p. 50) "that the truth or falsity of any statement is relative to an individual or to a social group." They also complain (p. 2), of relativism, that "after mocking the old-fashioned 'dogma' that 'there exists an external world, whose properties are independent of any individual human being and indeed of humanity as a whole', it proclaims categorically that 'physical "reality", no less than social "reality", is at the bottom a social and linguistic construct." Obviously, I have some explaining to do in this paper!

In fact, personally, I support Sokal and Bricmont in their criticisms of lax relativism. I am just as ready as they (and my FRISCO colleagues) to trust that a single reality does exist independently of us all. But they also accept, along with everyone since at least the 18th century, that *absolute knowledge* of the natural world is not available because fallible observers are always involved, their senses being less than perfect and what they see being influenced by all kinds of presuppositions. The difference between their position and mine lies in their absolute belief that, despite all the difficulties, an objective reality does exist, whereas I want always to emphasise that *belief* in an objective reality is just that, a belief, no matter how sound it appears. If I were working on a natural science, I would probably have little interest in this 'quibble'. But I am not. As an information systems scientist, I want to focus our attention on questions about those beliefs. Why and how do we acquire them? How do we *justify* such beliefs? How we can we create a body of knowledge we are prepared to treat as "independent of any individual human being and indeed of humanity as a whole."? Questions of this kind are further core issues for a science of information systems.

Take only our contribution to the natural sciences. In this era of electronic information technology we should be concerned to build and maintain the quality of information systems that will give both scientists and the ordinary citizen confidence that claims to have scientific knowledge are justified. We have enough examples of relevant problems today: mad cow disease, genetically modified organisms, global warming, to mention only three. We are not dealing with 19th century scientific work conducted by individuals or small teams in single laboratories, placing their findings before learned societies many of whose members could subject them to informed criticism. No. We are dealing with teams of various experts scattered over the globe, some working in the open, but many in highly confidential projects in commercial organisations. The openness and informed criticism typical of earlier science is loaded with political and economic pressures which often find their expression in the designs of information systems to gather, select, interpret, propagate, keep secret, publicise etc, not only facts and theories but also funding proposals. The lax relativists would seem not object to each chemical company, each ecological pressure group, each religious group, and each ethnic community, having a diversity of incompatible opinions on the scientific knowledge pertaining to problems of the kinds cited above. Our job, while working on the information systems employed in these domains, is to ensure that the information is being used in ways that can be *justified*. And, of course, understanding what *justification* and its close relative, *responsibility,* should mean are further problems for us to investigate.

Of course, mentioning responsibility brings us back to the ideological distaste some people have for the notion of Society. They usually claim that talk of Society allows people to evade personal responsibility. Indeed that may happen with sloppy political argument, but we are here concerned with scientific argument about information systems, and from that point of view, society and responsibility are closely linked. If, as I argue, it is wise to accept that knowledge is socially constructed, its justification depends on our being able to make people answerable for their contributions towards creating it, maintaining it and using it. A society with coherent perceptions, beliefs, patterns of behaviour and values depends on the exercise of responsibility. The objectivist is tempted to take too much for granted. The notion that knowledge of a world can be "independent of any individual human being and indeed of humanity as a whole", underlies the impersonal style required of us when at school we reported our laboratory experiments. Good science comes from constant testing by those observers and experimentalists responsible for maintaining it, and from the rest of us checking up that they are exercising their responsibility.

Perceptual norms operationalised

The view I present is a rejection of the Core View and its definition of a "**thing** [as] any part of a <u>conception</u> of a <u>domain</u> (being itself a "part" or "aspect" of the "world")." 'Conception' is a vague, mentalistic term and incapable of operationalisation. Instead, by adopting an actualist ontology, the radically subjectivist position I recommend, we can be far more precise. In this case, things, entities, properties, relationships, attributes, everything indeed, is an instance of an affordance. Real things (in this sense of being invariant repertoires of behaviour) can be understood in operational terms – you can take someone by the hand and introduce them to the behaviour, demonstrate it to them, talk about it and test their competence in applying it. We dispense with the inaccessible processes of perception and conception. It is all in the public domain and open to empirical study (though not always without difficulty).

The term 'norm' is also mentioned but not used in the Core View: "**Norms** are socially agreed rules affecting and to a large extent directing the actions within an organisational system." This suggests that norms are built using more primitive components. Sometimes this is the case, but many of our perceptual norms, especially the physical affordances we distinguish, are basic components of our constructed reality. Some legal norms, which are expressed by explicit rules, create parts of our social reality, copyright and marriage, for example. When certain things are done, instances of these come into existence. If a couple makes specified vows in an appointed place before a recognised person and some witnesses, a marriage will start. If a literary work is published, subject to a few conditions, a copyright will start together with the ownership of it, usually by the author; the copyright will finish its existence 70 years after the death of the author, by virtue of another rule. Thus we can extend Gibson's notion of affordances by adding norms which define the invariant repertoires of behaviour that constitute our social world.

There are other kinds of norms beside the perceptual ones. Even more fundamental than perceptual norms are the evaluative norms, which determine whether or not some invariant repertoire of behaviour is worth recognition. The temporal boundaries to the existence of a cup will be fixed by our judgement whether or not it serves its valuable role as a drinking vessel. (Note that a curator of ceramics will still regard an antique Wedgewood cup as a cup, even when broken, because her criteria concern no the use of the cup for drinking now but its having been used that way so that now it tells us about those historical times. The curator's meaning for 'cup' is thus different from the restaurant manager's meaning.) If the link between sign and reality belongs in someone's mind then it may be crucial to know which mind is involved. We shall look at some other kinds of norms later because they play a central role in this alternative framework of IS concepts.

Whose values? Authority and responsibility

The new formalism I am offering, called "Norma" as it represents norms and affordances, is built on the structure

Agent behaviour

This makes it clear that an agent is responsible for the world constructed by recognising useful repertoires of behaviour. The ultimate agent is Society. If we want to operationalise a common sense meaning then we can appeal to

Society to instruct us. The law has to be interpreted ultimately in terms of common sense meanings and who better to provide them than 'the man on the Clapham omnibus', to use the words of in a famous dictum by an English judge. If we can employ a dozen, representative, ordinary members of society to demonstrate what some expression means, there is no need to introduce perceptions and conceptions into our theory.

Of course we often need meanings that are far more precise than any random passenger on the Clapham omnibus can furnish. When a person is sick, an insurance company may need the judgement of a qualified medical practitioner to determine the start of this period, so we use the judgement of a person trained for ten years in this skill to provide it. In this case we cannot find explicit rules; we have to rely on the norms that have been internalised by someone. Different people, with different values, may give us different meanings. Indeed only when we know well enough the agent responsible for making the judgement behind the choice of a term or governing its interpretation, can we grasp the exact meaning being employed.

Sometimes the judgements of several people will be needed. For example, the start of a contract will require the consent of both parties. In other cases, we use explicit rules to determine when things start and finish: copyright, for example. These norms have conditions that refer to many other affordances, which, in turn, depend on the judgements of other agents or other norms, which, in turn, . . . This recursive pattern spreads responsibility for meanings over many individuals. For example, copyright law depends on the notions of a literary work and of publication and other norms help to define them, but ultimately we have to turn to the passenger on the Clapham omnibus, perhaps in the role of a jury member. The meaning in such cases also depends on those who framed the laws and those who administer them. What is so important in a this formalism for modelling information systems is that the structure:

> Agent behaviour
> and its associated start and finish events,

compels us to be explicit about the temporal boundaries of everything, and about the agents who are responsible. The formalism used in the Core View does not even raise these issues, let alone provide a solution.

The start or finish of an affordance may be determined by a person, a group or a norm. This we call the start or finish authority. If we want an explanation for any state of affairs we should turn to these authorities and question them or those who made them because they are responsible or answerable. In more complex cases, an affordance established by a norm can involve many other affordances. The agents determining *their* starts and finishes also carry some responsibility for the collective meaning. The making of reality and its representations is far more complex than the Core View suggests, nonetheless these complexities can be analysed with formal precision.

Time

Time has been introduced into the discussion. The importance of knowing when an affordance starts and finishes, has been noted. If one wants to be clear about the meaning of a term, then think of it as naming an invariant repertoire of behaviour, and next ask what conditions determine its start and finish. In the case of a cup, I suggested two different meanings, one for a museum curator, and another for a restaurant manager. The approach allows us to be as precise about meanings as we require for a given purpose. If you examine a piece of legislation (copyright law will do) then you will find that a large part of it will be concerned with providing clear, operational semantics, and consist of norms that specify when things start and finish. Time, as we know it, is bound up with our perception of affordances.

This observation is important because the analysis of affordances does not produce a static model but it also includes the dynamics. Everything, but everything, has a finite period of existence. Some things may last a very long time but they have a start and a finish in every case. This is evidently true of numbers and other, supposedly eternal mathematical concepts, once we remember they are socially constructed. We may produce *theories* about eternal things but those theories belong to a socially constructed reality which, therefore, cannot exist outside the existence of the society which has constructed them. We are so accustomed to thinking that the natural world is eternal and subject to laws that never change that this notion will be a strange one. I am quite as ready to adopt this belief about the natural world as anyone. However, as someone even more interested in information systems, I am also prepared to admit that all the science I know is a symbolic structure with a history of how it was made, maintained and changed, including the discovery and recording of facts, and the conjecture and refutation of theories. These are information system issues that fall within the scope of our scientific field. Having to be clear about time makes us consider important issues that otherwise escape our attention.

Ontological dependence

Norma, the formalism I am introducing, provides us with another powerful instrument for understanding time. It is the logical relationship of ontological dependence, which, as far as I have been able to ascertain, has no place in any other formalism. It arises because certain affordances are only available when others have been realised. Thus being upright makes possible a range of affordances such as walking, shuffling about, running, jumping, none of which is available if one is seated. But being seated allows one to take one's feet off the ground for extended periods, an affordance denied to an upright person. So we can elaborate our simple wff:

(Agent behaviour) behaviour

where the original agent is modified by the first affordance to become a different kind of agent for whom the second behavioral repertoire is available. Thus we can write

Stamper upright walk

We also have some affordances that depend for their existence on the coexistence of two others. Thus I may separately realise the affordances of paper and of pen but by having one while I have the other available, I have the affordance of writing

Stamper (paper *while* pen) writing

Using a comma as an abbreviation for *while*, we can specify the well-formed structuref as

Agent (behaviour, behaviour) behaviour

The behaviours to the right are ontologically dependent on the antecedent affordances to their left. (It may seem strange, until one is accustomed to the idea, that ordinary objects such as paper and pen can be regarded as behaviours. Remember that every single one of the affordances we discover or learn is an invariant repertoire of behaviour. The categories of entities, attributes and relationships, beloved of database people, vanish, subsumed under the one category of invariant repertoires of behaviour.)

When an affordance goes out of existence, so do all its dependants. These dependencies express important time constraints that can be expressed in predicate logic but only with notational clumsiness. The relationship of ontological dependency applies recursively, of course, so quite complex structures can arise, and in the case of social reality they usually do. But before taking this concept further, it will be convenient to introduce another.

Universals and particulars – the model includes the meta-model

On a particular occasion one may stand. On another one may sit. When one is seated one still has the *ability* to stand and when standing there is the prospect of sitting once again. The *ability* to realise some repertoire of behaviour is itself a repertoire of behaviour, having its own start and finish, each with its own responsible authorities.

An ability relates to a realisation as a universal relates to a particular, or, in data-processing terminology, as a type to an instance. If we want to construct a universal model for an information system, then we do so using types. Similarly, we can introduce a simple notation for ontological dependencies between abilities or universals that are inherited by their particular realisations.

Put these two ideas together. First, an ability is an invariant repertoire of behaviour just like any other affordance. Second, a universal is the ability to realise its particular instances. The result is a unification of all the levels of a meta-model hierarchy as deep as one requires.

This is best explained by an illustration. Take the social institution of mariage.

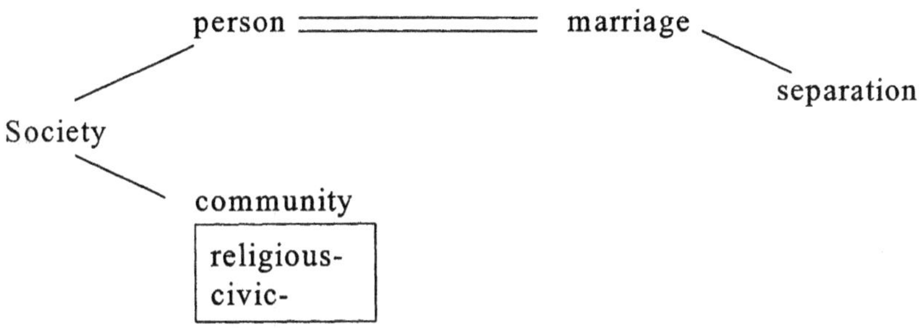

Figure 1: The elements of the marriage institution

The graph is directed with the implied arrows representing the ontological dependencies being left-to-right. Note that marriage requires two persons as antecedents (two antecedents is the maximum permitted) and that they can be identified, in that relationship, by role names. If one partner dies, the marriage finishes its existence. There is also the notion of a separation, which, as well as its common sense meaning, has acquired a number of others, through a series of common law judgements and Matrimonial Acts, which created and evolved the legal concept of being judicially separated. This universal affordance came into being in the 19th century in the UK. There are many other universals that have recognisably finite lives, created not only by the law but by science and technology, as well as by inventors, artists and the flux of fashion. Many of these can be precisely and formally distinguished by specifying the relevant authority.

The time constraints of ontological dependency apply at both the universal and particular levels. Take any affordance and trace through all its antecedents back to Society at the root, and one will have a lattice, called its 'stem'. For the chosen instance of the affordance to exist, appropriate instances of every antecedent and the corresponding universals must also exist. This complex set of temporal constraints is a powerful check on the meaningfulness of data supplied according to this model.

Notice that, when reading this diagram, one should keep in mind that associated with every universal and every particular are start and finish times and start and finish authorities. These can be provided separately and play a role in a social system analogous to a program for a computer. Indeed, we have taken such a model of a social system and derived directly from it a computer system to handle relevant data and support the functioning of the social system. This model though not devised for software engineering, turns out to be suitable for that purpose. As a by-product of modelling social behaviour, one also carries out the information engineering.

There is also a generic-specific hierarchy showing the various communities that have their own meanings for 'marriage' supplied by exercising their authority over the start and finish of that relationship. It is quite feasible for a couple to have multiple marriages. For instance I have friends who have three different marriages, two under the authorities of the different religious communities they come from as well as a UK civil marriage. Thus, Christian marriages cannot predate the 1st century, Islamic marriages, the 7th century and the different kinds of UK civil marriages, the various Acts of Union with Scotland, Ireland and Northern Ireland.

Thus semantics is not a "nebulous" idea. When approached in this manner, any desired degree of semantic detail and precision can be achieved and expressed formally. Although it would be easy, I have not bothered with the superfluous, space-consuming task of translating these specifications of meaning into an impressive mathematical symbolism. I approve of formality but mere formalisation is only decorative. Chapter 4 adds nothing to Chapter 3, beyond a final check on its formal potential.

Here and now

Look again at the model of the marriage institution. You will notice that the elements on the right can only exist during a period of time that falls within the existence of elements to their left. If we use this model to give ourselves a picture of the world that actually exists, it can tell us only about the here-and-now. Although we can use the model to organise data about the past and the future, the model, with its strict temporal constraints given by ontological dependencies, allows us to say nothing about how the past and future are related!

This dreadful limitation appears, at first, to be a defect in the modelling method. In fact the opposite is true, as it forces us to attend to a central problem in the science of information systems: the creation of time.

The Core View's notation has no problem dealing with times past and future. Times, they would say, are either instants or intervals, which we can include with other objectively existing individuals in predicate expressions. For example, the two-place predicate

born (Matthew Stamper, 10 January 1987)

relates my son to an interval of a day. Days exist in possible worlds if not here and now. Objectivist semantics gets into trouble otherwise. For example, what is meant by 'person' is given *extensively* by the set of all persons, so if we do not also count those persons who exist in possible worlds but only those in the present world, the exact meaning of 'person' continually changes as individuals are born and die. As one who always demands an empirical foundation for a science, I feel uncomfortable trying to explain meanings in terms of a purely imaginary domain of possibilities.

The actualist alternative I am offering has no place in its reality for anything except the here-and-now. The past and the future, and indeed things over the horizon, do not exist here-and-now. *We have to create them using signs to represent them in the here-and-now.* This is the most miraculous, magical thing about information! It is our job to explain the processes involved. Rather than to copy the natural scientists who can remain contentedly working with the old illusion of a real, physical time-dimension, which they "see" through the transparent lens of information systems they use, we must investigate the "optical" properties of the information lens.

We construct time by imposing an order on the names of events. For example: I know my son, Matthew, and I know he had a start, so I can construct an expression, "the start of Matthew". This is a name for an event. Many such expressions representing start and finish events can be combined into an ordered pattern. Obviously a collection of these expressions would be a hideously obscure way of talking about time in most circumstances, although you will often find yourself among family and friends talking about time this way ("When X cut his first tooth, just before we moved to York." etc). For general communications about time, we use a calendar and chronometer to generate a stream of conveniently named events or intervals such as "10 January 1987". Today, my knowledge of the past depends upon my being able, here and now, to construct such marks on paper or in memory (neurological notepaper) as, "the start of Matthew" or "10 January 1987". To obtain the time dimension we use in physics, we arrange those events or intervals in an order or partial order, with the appropriate mathematical properties. That is how we construct time. We can have no knowledge of time unless we use signs to represent the starts and finishes of what we know here and now. We cannot experience an event as an affordance or repertoire of behaviour. Once it is here, it is gone!

Quite different are the processes of beginning and ending. These can be experienced, as I witnessed, and his mother experienced, Matthew's birth, the beginning process that successfully started him. This raises the issue of causality.

Causality

Before tackling this subject, let me remove a common misunderstanding about the schemas illustrated in Figures 1, 2, 4, 5, 6 and 7. These do not represent causal relationships but existence dependencies. The affordances on the left do not cause those on the right. Take any affordance, and you will see that it makes *possible* those to its right, while those to its left are *necessary*. People working with computers, who are raised on a diet of flowcharts, dataflow diagrams, logical sequences and so on are in greatest danger of falling into this error.

"So where does causality fit into this schema?" you may ask. Causality, quite different from, but related to time, is another semiological construct. Our familiarity with physics tempts us to believe that causality is quite a simple, physical notion. In physics causal connections take place in the here-and-now, governed by simple physical laws.

Causality is a complex notion in the social world. Social cause-and-effect depends upon information (signs) to link the past to the future. For example, when we look for the cause of an accident, we do so in order to avoid similar harm in future by changing the behaviour of people and their environment, and often to recover payment for the damage done. Consider the judicial enquiry that found a Swiss chemical company so negligent that it caused the escape of dioxin and a tragic loss of life Seveso. Far more was required than tracing chains of physical cause and effect; such a decision called for an investigation of who knew what when, what assumptions should have been made by reasonable persons, who was responsible for training those who controlled the industrial plant and others who handled emergencies. Causality in the social domain goes beyond physical variables into the problems of human responsibility.

Returning to physics, we should note that it deals with causality by formulating laws of a universal kind. A particular cause and its particular effect (one billiard ball setting another in motion) can never be experienced again. We can only create a similar situation and predict the consequences by applying the law. Physical laws and theories are signs. So, even physical causality is a semiological construct.

In our everyday struggle to make sense of causality, we use our experiences of processes that can result in things starting or finishing. We learn to relate the *beginning* and *ending* processes to the *start* and *finish* events. We must be careful not to confuse the processes of change with their results. But we must learn to relate them in order to develop a notion of causality. The birth was the beginning process that successfully concluded with the start of Matthew, his mother experienced it and others witnessed it. That birth process also started and finished, and had its own beginning and ending. Beginning and ending are common sense ideas that enable us to talk about everyday causality. Clearly the beginning of Matthew was a cause of his existence. But note that if we count his existence starting with the finish of his birth, he never coexisted with his birth process. So common sense causality cannot be captured in an ontological dependency schema such as that in Figure 1. The theory needs to be extended.

Let me reiterate that such a schema represents only what exists at present. Unless a cause and its effect coexist, they cannot be treated as the antecedents of a causal relationship. This is because *the schema defines only existence dependencies.* Sometimes there is a moment of coexistence but in general there is none. "So how do we deal with causality?" you may ask, "How do we link the past to the present and the present to the future?"

Making sense of the real world certainly requires a notion of causality. The ontological theory outlined here succeeds in forcing us to recognise the central role played by signs (information) in creating a notion of causation. Whenever we talk about a cause, even a common sense cause, we construct a little theory. The natural sciences consist, to a large extent, of theories of causality. In physical laws, cause and effect coexist. But in a social context, the recognised cause and effect seldom do coexist. For example, causality is often a legal issue, as in the notorious Seveso case. Just as we can take an affordance, x, realised, here and now, and name its start, "start-of-x", so we can name a process, the "beginning-of-x". This enable us always to satisfy our common sense belief that every effect has a cause. You will find that this analysis in terms of signs, whether legal findings or physical theories, removes much of the mystery of causality by forcing us to look carefully at how we use information.

For anyone constructing an information system, this analytical device is a great help. The making and changing of the social world is accomplished by information. Indeed, the only thing that information produces is a change in one or more person's disposition to act, and normally this amounts to a social change. More often than not, this is accomplished by a conversation.

Pragmatics – time and intention

Pragmatics comes higher on the semiotic ladder than semantics, even so it is far from nebulous, being capable of precise analysis. We have seen how we can understand time and causality in terms of our use of signs. Now let me show you how the pragmatic properties of signs are essential for creating the past and the future and binding them together.

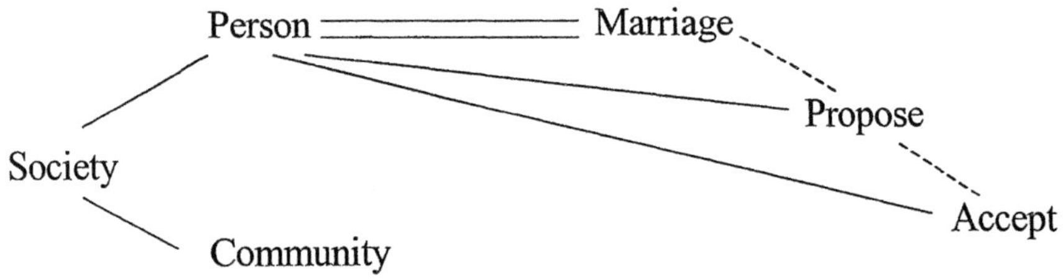

Figure 2: A future created by intentional acts making use of meaningful signs

Take the marriage example. Marriage is not spontaneous and random, unlike the mating of rabbits. Someone has to propose that a marriage takes place and one or more appropriate persons have to accept the proposal. So we have to extend the diagram to include these "communication acts".

This shows marriage as an antecedent to a proposal but linked by a broken line. This is because the marriage itself is not the antecedent (there is no point in proposing an existing marriage!) but the antecedent is a sign representing a possible future marriage. The future marriage exists here and now only as information. The various intentions are expressed by existing persons uttering actual words, such as "I propose that John and Mary should get married.". The antecedents are the speaker and a *sign* representing the marriage. We must be careful to distinguish the speech act, which is a process, from the intention that it begins. The proposal remains on the table until, continuing its existence until, perhaps, withdrawn by another speech act. The proposal forms a small but significant element of the social world. It represents an intention on the part of the person who created it. The nature of this intention is highly sensitive to the social role of the maker – John, Mary, one of their parents, another relative, a marriage broker, a friend. The existence of the proposal may well bring into existence all kinds of other attitudes of expectation, obligation and evaluation, which have not been included in the analysis. All these details could be formalised as norms if that is the point of your analysis.

An acceptance, or a number of acceptances, will be necessary before a wedding is arranged. A proposal and acceptance by youngsters under 18 would require acceptances also by their parents or guardians. This is typical of how, in the here-and-now, we plan, to create, some future world. It is not accomplished by natural processes nor by passing meaningless, intentionless messages from computer to computer. It necessarily involves responsible people using signs that have meanings that only groups of people can supply. It is a social process. Information is the instrument we use for making, preserving and using our social reality. To study information systems scientifically is to engage in a social science. Interestingly, we can make it quite formal and precise, just as precise as anything in FRISCO Chapter 4.

The social level of the semiotic ladder

Now we come to the social level where Falkenberg thinks we are most at risk of being nebulous. Let us test this opinion.

I propose that we adopt a formal and precise definition of society as people and groups of people behaving according to shared norms. Most norms are shared. Even when norms govern the behaviour of individuals, other people have to know about those norms. For example, a head of state may be the only person subject to certain norms, but that role only functions because it is widely understood and taken into account by everyone else.

Norms only exist when they govern the behaviour of people. They can be represented by rules but, remember: the map is not the territory. So, although some norms may be explicit, as in rules and laws, others are implicit, unspoken and even incapable of being expressed but, nevertheless, observable in use. We assume that they all have the common structure:

IF condition THEN norm subject
ADOPTS attitude TOWARDS some thing or proposition

The condition specifies the knowledge of a state of affairs that triggers the norm. At such a point the person or group agent subject to the norm will adopt a direct or indirect disposition to act towards a thing or proposition about the world. Based on the formalism I have introduced, we can express any norm quite precisely and formally, as though we were writing a logical version of a legal rule. But less formal precision may be substituted by greater clarity if a person, rather than a machine is the subject of the norm.

There are four important categories of norms of which we have so far encountered two. *Perceptual norms* generate the attitudes of deeming or accepting the existence of something (contract, copyright, marriage etc). *Evaluative norms* require attitudes of liking, disliking, hoping, fearing and so on. *Cognitive norms,* like those of science or our common sense ideas of how the world functions, generate attitudes of belief or expectation. *Behavioral norms* dispose the subject more directly to act by the attitudes of obligation, permission, prohibition and liberty.

There is also the subcategory of norms having no condition and a fixed attitude. These are called 'attitudes', quite simply. "Everyone abhors murder." for example.

Society is very complex and subtle. So is the physical world, as any engineer will tell you. The elegant simplicity of physical theories can help us to solve engineering problems but more goes on in everyday reality than a physicist can model. Similarly, I would not pretend that whole, real societies could be modelled using norms, as I outline here. However, certain problems can be elucidated using this kind of model, especially in cases where it is normal to use explicit rules, as when we design legal or contractual systems or when we want to apply a computer. Typically such limited social systems we call 'organisations' or, in their more general form, 'institutions'. As information scientists, in addition to formulating broad and general theories about information, it is our duty to identify interesting and instructive institutional phenomena, by analogy with the work of physicists. We can then apply these results to engineering particular organisations in which computers and other technology may be able to play a useful role.

Information fields and knowledge

We are now in a position to replace the vague, unoperationalised, definition of knowledge in the Core View: "**Knowledge** is a relatively stable and sufficiently consistent set of conceptions possessed by single human actors." by one that is operationally clear and precise.

Instead: **Knowledge** comprises norms and attitudes, whether explicit or tacit. This includes knowledge of what exists, what is right or wrong, good or bad, of what to believe about the world, and of how to behave.

This definition is far broader than the philosophers' "justified, true belief". Otherwise it will not serve the purpose of an information systems science..

The Core View has the definition: "**Information** is the knowledge increment brought about by a receiving action in a message transfer, i.e. it is the difference between the conceptions interpreted from the received message and the knowledge before the receiving action." This indicates that we probably need one meaning for "information" that relates it directly to norms (alias knowledge). There are many other precise meanings of "information" (Stamper 1973) but they cannot be found using notions as vague as "conceptions". Instead, following the Broad View, we prefer the notion of a sign as a primitive because it can be defined ostensively. Signs interact with norms, as this figure shows:

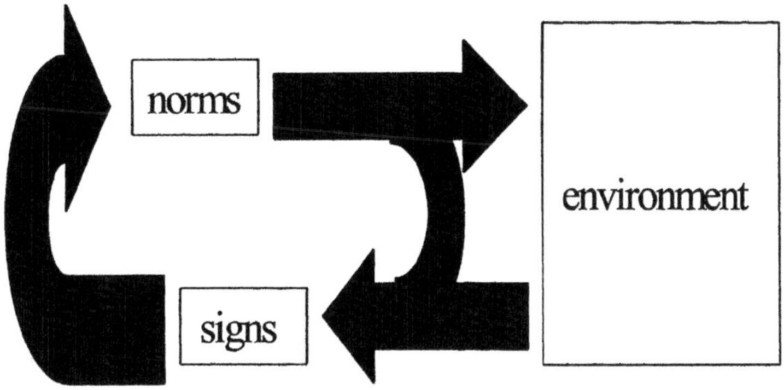

Figure 3: Information field - the interplay of norms, signs and environment

To recognise when a norm should be triggered, the subject needs information (signs) relating to the condition. The resulting attitude may not produce an immediate outcome but sooner or later will be revealed in words or comportment, or sometimes translated eventually into action. In either case the result will be more signs. In addition, observation of the environment (the application of perceptual norms) will also generate a stream of signs. As an analogy, we might consider knowledge or norms as a form of potential semiological energy and signs as the kinetic form, constantly being transformed into one another.

This observation is of major importance to the engineering of information systems. It allows us to introduce the notion of *information fields*. We normally use models of messages flowing between operating nodes, or the dual models of data-structures, which we use to scan storage media. An information field is a social group governed by a system of norms. The norms determine what should happen in that domain and they, in turn, determine what signs are required to fire them and what signs they produce. Thus the information flow is just a logical consequence of the norm structure.

The fields are more fundamental to the information system than the information flows. For any given information field, there may be thousands of different but adequate solutions to the message flow and record search problems. The typical information systems model produced to define the requirements for a computer-based system will tend to reproduce or closely resemble an existing dataflow, often one that has evolved to suit a different technology, and, most likely containing all kinds of irrelevant features for historical reasons. The information field approach cuts through the accumulations of time to capture the essence of what is required to do the job, making it far easier to find innovative solutions to suit whatever new technology is available. Better still, we can generate supporting IT systems directly from the norms specified in the field model.

Summary and comments on formalisms and nebulous ideas

This alternative to framework of information systems concepts in Chapter 4, forming FRISCO's Core View, could have been expressed with as much formality. However, striving at symbolic niceties does not add to the content. The Social View leads to an alternative because it tackles head on the difficult ontological and epistemic issues which the Core View evades. The ontology adopted is that the only world to which we have access consists of the invariant repertoires of behaviour (affordances) we recognise. The epistemological principle is that our knowledge is founded on direct perception of some basic affordances, supplemented by an understanding of many others that Society has discovered over the centuries. The adequacy of such knowledge depends on its practical effectiveness. To know anything we must act. The only world directly accessible to us is the here-and-now. Information allows us to construct the rest.

The following syntax governs most of an ontological structure, or a realisation, based on these assumptions:

1) realisation = Agent | Agent affordance

2) affordance = (affordance *while* affordance) | realisation *sign* | affordance *ability*

The concatenations defined in 1) are the ontological dependencies. The ontological antecedent can be derived from others, as expressed in 2). It may be restricted to the joint existence of two antecedents, it may be anything that functions as a sign for a realisation, or it may be the universal or ability to realise a type of affordance. When we draw an ontology chart, we work with the universals or abilities.

This syntax does not cover the generic-specific hierarchy, which consists of cognitive norms, nor the determiners, indicated by the prefix #, which must have an ability as an antecedent. To extend this syntax to cover the construction of norms requires other functions in addition to *while*. These include *orwhile*, *whilenot*, *before*, *after*, *whenever*, for example. That topic lies outside the scope of this paper.

However, we must note that every realisation has a number of mappings to realisations. These are

sort that maps to the corresponding ability or universal
antecedent 1 that maps to one ontological antecedent

antecedent 2 that maps to a second ontological antecedent, if there is one

start that maps to a realisation simultaneous with the affordance's start event

finish that does the same for the finish event

start authority that maps directly to the responsible agent(s) or indirectly via norm

finish authority that does the same to identify the responsibility for the finish

One point of great importance that has been mentioned deserves to be stressed again. There is a maximum of two ontological antecedents. This constraint is very demanding and the principal reason for the ontological structure being a kind of "semantic normal form" or canonical form for a given problem. It is canonical, not in the sense of a mathematical or logical canonical form, but in a way that can only be justified empirically in the final analysis.

I trust that the above account of the framework arising from the Social View will shoot out of the sky the *canard* that the semantic, pragmatic and social levels of semiotics are nebulous. Admittedly they are frequently discussed in a rather woolly terminology, but that is not the case when we employ this formalism that captures the ontological dependencies among norms and affordances. The case study helps to illustrate this point.

A REWORKING OF THE JAPAN WINES CASE

The Core View of FRISCO concludes, in Chapter 5 9 (q.v.), with a case study. It is now be reworked on the basis of the Social View to demonstrate the practical advantages of the new method. You will notice several improvements. First, for the information system theorist, the new approach models the meanings and the intentions of the messages as well as the relevant norms used in running the business. Second, the solution, while including models of data-structures and dataflows that the Core View produces, also captures, in a very compact form, the minimal, substantive organisational requirements, which helps users to understand their problem in information terms. And third, in the realm of software engineering, the specification is precise and formal enough for it to generate the necessary computer system directly.

The problem statement you will find in Chapter 5, section 1 of the Report. Its formulation betrays a mind-set that treats a business as message-passing system, paper-based in this instance. To avoid the presuppositions this implies and use the information field approach, we need to distinguish between substantive and semiological affordances. The substantive things are what the messages are about, while the semiological things tell us about them – they are representations. For example, the wine in *stock* (which people drink) is substantive and we signify it using an *inventory* (which people read). Another substantive would be a retailer's need for a quantity of wine (based on his assessment of the customers' desire to drink) which he will represent in on an order-form. The contract is a substantive component of the social world, a mutual commitment to exchange wine for money, which will probably also be represented in a document confusingly also called a "contract". Briefly, the map is not the territory, and we want to model separately the business of dealing in wine and its associated paper-chase.

We have a bad habit of confusing the substantive and the semiological. Anyone trained in "inventory management" when they really mean "stock management" is likely to overlook this distinction. The case description includes this misunderstanding in S2: "The business of this centre is to manage the inventory of products and to distribute products to retail shops corresponding to their orders." Thinking is casily confused by sloppy semantics.

The affordances

We begin by listing, in no significant order, some of the obvious, relevant, substantive affordances appearing or implied by the problem description:

#Japan Wines Inc. (a particular, while the rest are universals)

company	nation	distribute	wine	winery	shop
product	stock	item	quantity	warehouse	deliver
place	truck				

Next we make a list of affordances concerned with passing messages and operating on them:

phone	inventory	order	process	check	item
file	orderline	delivery ticket		back order	

Order may need justification for its inclusion in this second list, but statements 4 to 11 make it clear that they concern a document having a syntactic structure (composed of lines or items which refer to products) and a physical representation. There is a quite different substantive notion of order as an intention expressed by a communication act.

The information flow or message logistics

If we turn to the solution in Chapter 5, beginning on p. 126, we find an analysis entirely in terms of flows. Flow charts 5.2-1 and 5.2-2 give vague outlines of the logistics of goods and messages but chart 5.2-3 eliminates the goods. The partial nature of these models is explained as a way of circumventing "modelling uncertainty", in other words, the arbitrariness inherent in the modelling method. As you will note, the new approach leaves hardly any room for arbitrariness. The vagueness appears in descriptions of actions such as "Stock administration" or "Orders-to-wineries handling". We find mention of actors such as "Stock handlers", "Truck drivers", "Order handlers". However, when we come to the detail, supplied by entity-relationship chart 5.2-5 plus the definitions of relationships, these actors have vanished. The messages themselves are not defined but are implicit in the details of the relationships. Nowhere can you see who is responsible for anything. The only place time appears in the model is the date of an order.

The result is a rather vague impression of the logistics, mainly concerning the various documents. Even my business were some kind of document handling (banking, for example), I would at least want to know who sends them, who receives them and where they are at any time. The response I would expect to this complaint is "Go and look in the order file if you want to know where the order is!" Of course, this is a valid implementation detail but a model of the information system at this level of logistics should include an implementation-free specification of document location. This is missing from the Core model.

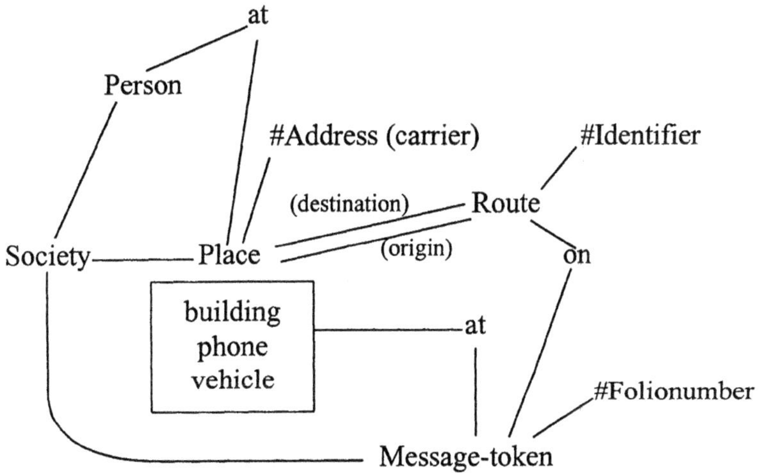

Figure 4: Message logistics

To build the alternative model based on Norma, we construct an ontological schema using the above list of affordances concerned with messages and their flows. There are three levels of analysis we need to include. The most obvious concerns the movements of the physical message-tokens, as shown in figure 4, which omits some obvious details.

Some of the affordances are places, such as a phone, to which I have added other specifics such as building and vehicle, but also person. Places do not have to be fixed. We need to know when a delivery note is on a vehicle just as we need to know when a person has pocketed a message. The arrow from person to place indicates a specific-generic relationship. The name of a place is an address or an equivalent identifier; note the antecedent "carrier" in parentheses, the antecedent agent responsible for assigning the address. We also need to know routes, which are fixed by two places as antecedents with many identifiable alternatives. Sufficient identifiers may select a carrier such as post / courier / email / fax etc. Every message (order, delivery ticket etc.) can be registered as at a place or on a route. It also has a unique identifier, the folio number. "Sign-token" would have been technically a better term to use than "message" because it treats files as large messages, including inventory, back-order file, order file.

When reading the schema in figure 4, one must remember that it represents the universals only, the equivalents of the headings in FRISCO figure 5.2-4 of Chapter 5. You must imagine the sample data for some particulars. Every universal and particular also has its start and finish times and start and finish authorities. So, this Social model pins down all times and responsibilities (such as when a delivery note was raised and by whom). Unlike the perceptions and conceptions of the Core View, this tells us exactly who is making the relevant interpretations.

Also when reading the schema, do not expect that the words should fall into certain syntactic categories. It is not a verbal schema but a pattern of repertoires of behaviour, which are linguistically neutral. The labels attached to the nodes can be in any language or in several. The structure of the graph contains enough information to disambiguate the chosen labels. It is, we believe, an interesting point of departure for research into a semantic grammar.

Syntactic structures of the messages and records

After modelling the message logistics, we have to specify the structures of the messages, stating the syntactic-type (order, delivery ticket) and the components they include (item, order line, company details and so on). See figure 5. The dotted line leading from syntactic-type to message-token is a universal to particular relationship, which their own particulars inherit, so that a particular syntactic-type, such as an order, is the universal to a subset of message-tokens. Finally, the terminal elements in these structures also have to be specified. Notice that the company is the antecedent for its own syntactic structures, although increasingly inter-organisational standard message formats are being agreed. Formats are not completely specified because this level of detail omits the spatial sequences of the types and the syntactic 'pictures' of the elements. These should be treated separately as implementation decisions.

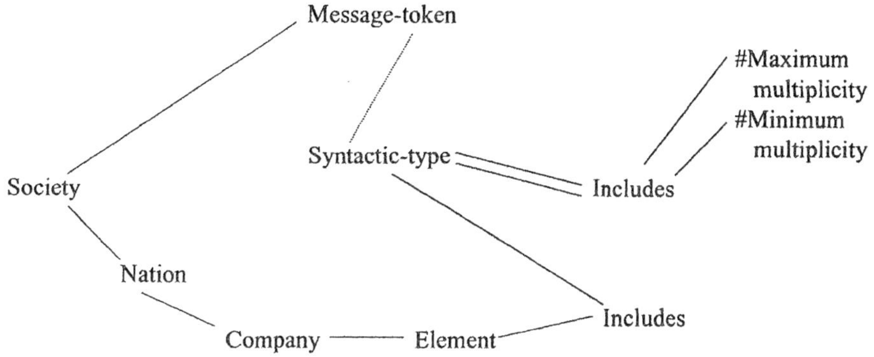

Figure 5: Composition of messages

We could also specify all the processes (check, duplicate, and so on) that have to be performed on the messages, making use of their syntactic structures. All this lies at the implementation level, so it needs to be separated from the core of the specification. Moreover, using this new method, the processes are specified in a different and more fundamental way when we model the substantive system.

The information flow paradigm as used here draws attention to the physical and syntactic levels. We could add a specification at the empiric level by modelling the frequencies of messages of different kinds, the probabilities of errors and so on. Norma and the information field model accommodate all levels of the semiotic properties of a system. However, running a business is more concerned with the semantic, pragmatic and social levels, which are the main focus of the information field paradigm.

The substantive information fields

The Core View models the message logistics but says little or nothing about the core of the business, which is the purchasing, sale and distribution of various products and the management of stocks of them (*not* inventories of them, of course). Any message transactions should be purely a logical consequence of having to perform these substantive tasks. The Core View has no way of modelling them. It relates to selling a computer application to automate the existing message flow, rather than to the more serious problems of making and discharging of unambiguous contracts that concern the a person running this business. Let us now develop the schema of ontological dependencies for these fundamental, substantive business affordances.

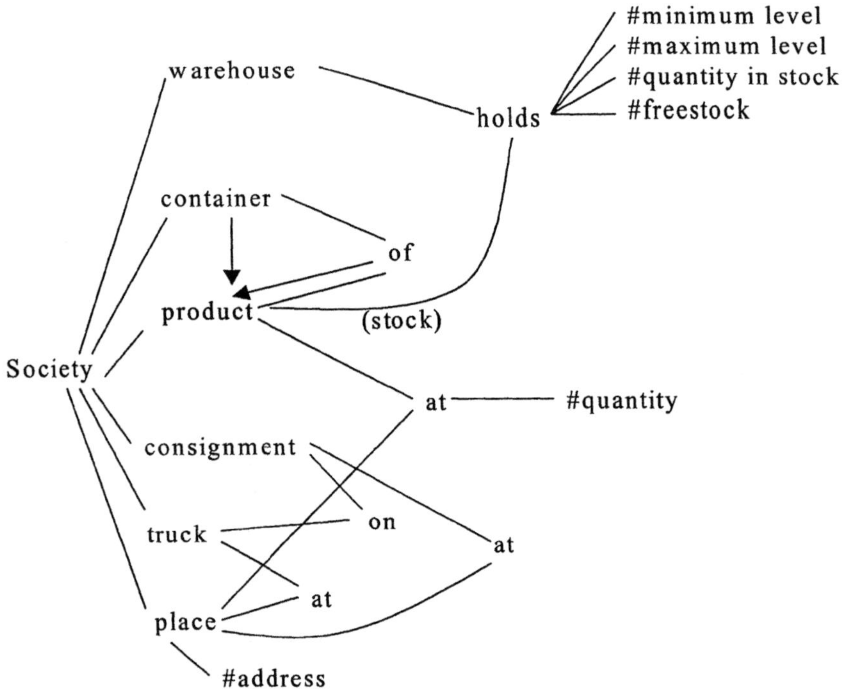

Figure 6: Some substantive logistic affordances

A draft for such an ontology chart is shown in Figure 6. While attempting to construct it, we are forced to recognise the existence of some additional affordances. For example, *product* may mean a type of object (a liquid in the case of wine) which no one can handle unless gathered into an identifiable batch by some form of container. The Core solution on p. 130, says "A specific product, e.g. a brand/vintage of wine, is an elementary thing." which is an example of dangerous semantic vagueness. Once you are forced to explain meanings in terms of affordances or repertoires of behaviour, you are driven to realise that in this business, your products have to be discrete objects that your warehouse staff can handle. They need information at that level of precision. One cannot simply buy and transport Bordeaux. One has to deal in actual, identifiable barrels or bottles of the wine, otherwise the store worker or driver will not know what to do, and no court would ever be able to resolve a dispute over a contract about anything so vague as "Bordeaux wine". Hence the schema shows containers of the product. You can have a bottle of 1995 Chateau Fourtanay, or a one-dozen case of those bottles or a twelve-case pallet of them. You might purchase by the 1000litre cask and bottle it for the retailers. Incidentally, the arrows from container and container of product indicate that these are also specific forms of product.

Goods have to be gathered together as batches or stocks or consignments (three quite different invariants) in order to handle them. Note that a stock or a consignment will remain invariant, although its contents may change. In the despatch bay, a consignment may be built up during the course of a morning as goods are retrieved from their bins and then packed for lifting onto one or more trucks. The schema shows quantities of various products in a consignment at a place, so that the precise composition of the consignment can be handled. The consignment, as delivered, may not be what was sent or loaded. The Core model seems to use "delivery" as meaning consignment in this sense, but it cannot account for partial and incomplete deliveries. Note that a consignment is not a natural thing but a social construct.

On closer inspection, a number of other socially defined invariants become evident, such as *assign* when a quantity of a stock is assigned to a contract, prior to the warehouse adding it to a consignment. The transport company can *present* a consignment at a certain place with the intention to *deliver* it but it may have to try again. The consignment will be consigned (a communication act) by a company to be at a certain place, even before the consignment is made up. The consignment will go through a cycle from being made up to delivered with redeliver as one other status in the cycle. Of course, the 'redeliver' status should appear on one of the documents in the Core model, but it is far more important that the warehouse and transport staff know this status.

Now let us turn to the non-physical aspects of the job. Contracts have to be made and discharged. This always involves making an offer/order and having it accepted. The order will be for the supply of a quantity of a product at some place (and time, implicitly) but always under a contract containing many, often complex rules and conditions in addition to the payment details. So the order will be a sign of all those semantic essentials used by the company placing the order, the party standing in the role of purchaser in relation to that contract. All those semantic structures are shown in the schema.

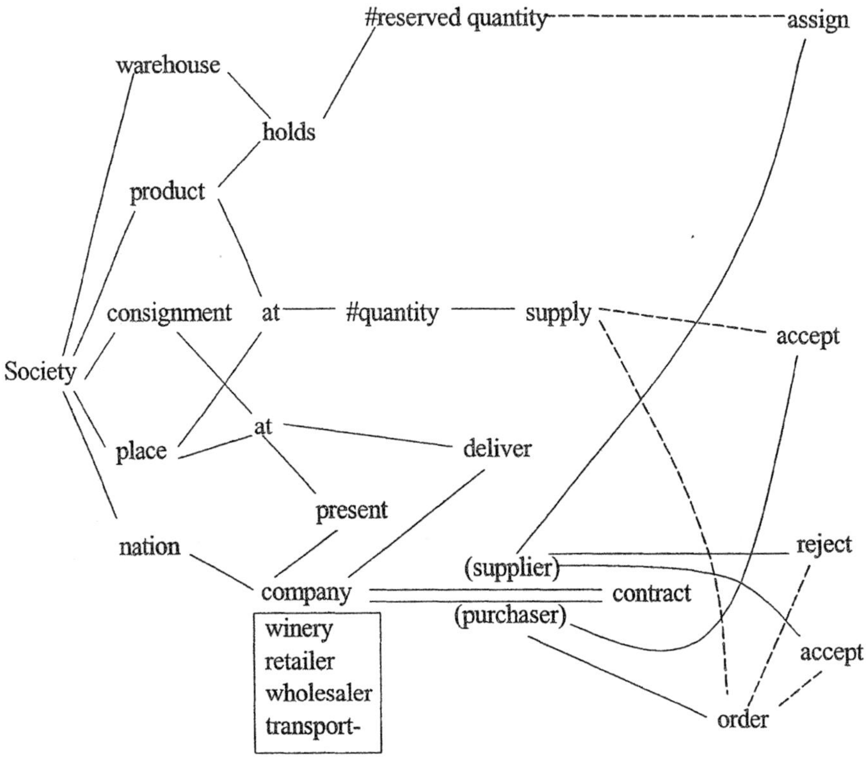

Figure 7: Some legally significant pragmatic affordances

Another sign, referring to that order has to be used by the supplier to accept the order. Then, under provisions of the relevant national law of contract, a contract will come into existence. Notice that this model supplies all the start and finish times and their related authorities that are of importance legally. The FRISCO Core model contains no means of handling these social constructs explicitly. One must have the relevant legal knowledge and apply it implicitly to the messages. In all but the most trivial cases, this is a dangerous strategy.

This analysis of *order* and *accept* transcends the restriction of reality to the here-and-now. For each of these, a broken line leads to one of the antecedents, indicating that it should be interpreted as a sign with that meaning. An order is made using a sign representing some future supply of a batch of a product to a specified place under some contract, an act that does not but belongs in a possible future. On this, substantive level of analysis, we need pay no attention to the physical sign-tokens that represent these communication acts, however, they can be related to the various messages which appear in the Core model. The Social model enables us to design messages that express the essential business intentions unequivocally, and be quite explicit about their roles as authorities for starting and finishing social constructs, such as contracts or consignments. The Core model has nothing to say about these business issues and, instead, concerns itself with the syntax and the flow of documents or their electronic equivalents.

Note some further details: the box headed *company* defines a generic-specific hierarchy. Measurements, prescribed quantities and identifiers, which we call 'determiners' have an initial #. In the context of a certain dependency, an element can have a role name such as *purchaser* or *supplier*, which serves to select the relationship instance (the contract in this case) with the role occupant singled out for attention. Note that *stock* is the role of a *product* that a *warehouse holds*.

A canonical semantic form

The re-working of the case has already illustrated that the new method, based on Norma, is far more expressive than conventional models such as the Core View yields. Take one example of the kind of semantic problem that the new method can handle. There are two related notions: *deliver* and *supply*. In the first case, a company or other agent can *deliver* a batch of a product at some place without there being any legal significance to their action, but in the case of *supply* a contract is an antecedent because the goods are being delivered under its legal provisions. One possibility would be to have *deliver* as an antecedent to *supply*. The behaviour involved in making a delivery is essentially one of physically relocating the goods. *Supply*, it might be argued, may be achieved by the purely legal, communication act of asserting: "The goods at that place are now yours." a step in transferring ownership rather than relocating material things. Incidentally, the point at which tax is collected will probably depend critically on this distinction. Other subtle distinctions come to the surface as one analyses the ontological dependencies, whereas they would be undreamed of, by anyone using the modelling methods of the Core View. Some important innovations in electronic commerce depend on distinguishing logistic delivery from legal supply. If a meta-model prevents our perceiving such things it will block creative thinking about organisations rather than encouraging it.

Far from being 'nebulous' the schema treats semantics with a degree of precision that other methods cannot enforce. The Core View focuses, as do other orthodox methods, on the syntactic level where hundreds of legitimate data-flow solutions for any business problem may be offered. Where the systems designer is trying to devise ways of using computing resources economically, she should be free to use any strategy. However, on the semantic level we are not dealing with computers but with the repertoires of behaviour relevant to the business and how we name them. These are not things an analyst or programmer can dream up; usually they will have evolved over decades or centuries or even millennia, in some cases. Semantics cannot be toyed with by every imaginative systems analyst. Meanings do not belong to the computer industry but to society and its many communities who make them. The importance of the concept of ontological dependency is that it makes it possible to get to grips with the core of a semantic structure quite rigorously. By adding the norms that define start and finish times, the semantics can be expressed in refined form to any desired level of detail. If the analysis is faulty, careful testing should reveal this so that it can be improved. Orthodox modelling methods usually accept indifferently any number of arbitrary solutions, so they cannot ensure a process of cumulating improvements. The precision is achieved by asking whether something can exist, in the sense of the actualist ontology, finding its ontological time constraints, and then checking that it corresponds to the repertoires of behaviour employed by the people acting in the problem domain. In this way the Social View can generate a cumulative and continually improving corpus of semantics, as objective as our corpus of botanical knowledge, for example.

The enforced rigour is probably (judging by practical experience) enough to result in a canonical form which independent analysts should all reach if they are modelling the same system. This contrasts with the high degree of arbitrariness or "modelling uncertainty" permitted by the Core View. Identifying the socially constructed, canonical, stable, semantic core to the information system brings huge reductions in system costs in several ways. Establishing the semantic core makes it easier to maintain a system in line with continually changing, organisational requirements (again confirmed empirically). The stable semantics must remain invariant whatever syntactic, computer-orientated solution is selected. Hence it serves as a 'hinge' around which we can reconfigure an organisation or a collection of legacy systems when we are re-engineering them. The ever-shifting demands placed on organisations make this work continually necessary and costly. The most important re-usable component of any information system consists of the painstakingly negotiated meanings that make the electronic signs and signals useable. Given a few days of tuition, any person of average intelligence can put together plausible looking ER, Niam, Relational or other orthodox data models. Unfortunately, these students are given the impression that they are discovering the semantics of the domain. Genuine semantic analysis is far more intellectually demanding and costly an exercise. But the effort is worthwhile. Huge savings can be obtained if we share a solid and accumulating corpus of re-usable semantics from which to begin the design of each new system. Finally, as we have found in practice, the uniformity of this analysis (every affordance has the same attributes) makes it far easier for users who have no technical interest in computers. They can understand the ontology charts quite easily and use them to formulate precise information requirements to suit their needs.

A caveat: although I am confident that we are approaching a canonical semantic form, more theoretical work and empirical testing are called for.

Building a computer system to support Japan Wines Inc.

The ontology charts introduced above are rather easy to implement directly. However, an interpreter is of little value unless one can construct high quality semantic schemas. Operations on data held under bad schemas with nonsensical time constraints will only generate semantic garbage. On the other hand, good semantics can be profitably implemented with any systems software.

To read a chart and build a computer system to interpret it, one must remember that the arcs are directed from left to right and represent constraints on existence *not* causal dependencies. This applies both to the universals shown in the figure as well as to the particular instances of them. Any element on the right can only exist if relevant individuals exist on the whole of the stem, the lattice leading back to the root Society at the root. The computer system we have built to interpret this schema (called a Semantic Temporal Data Base, STDB) automatically checks the temporal consistency of new data and draws the logical conclusions from the finishing of any element by finishing also its ontological dependants. These time constraints are enforced by the meta-model, whereas conventional methods require one to supply them in additional documentation.

Behind every element, whether universal or particular, there stands a list of attributes, including the start and finish times and authorities. This information enables us, if necessary, to trace the responsible agents who can give operational definitions of the meanings of the elements and account for the data we hold. Unlike the Core model, which depends on some taken-for-granted, shared understanding about the conceptions in the inaccessible minds of unspecified persons, this schema pins responsibility for meanings on identifiable individuals or groups who can be required to account for their observations, choices and actions. It also imposes the exacting semantic discipline of knowing the temporal limits on the existence of each element. A maxim anyone can adopt is: If you cannot account for the start and finish of the existence of things you name, you cannot be sure about the meanings of you terminology.

The STDB, of course, can operate on these start and finish times and authorities. Powerful temporal operators such as *while, orwhile, whilenot, before, after* and so on can be invoked to retrieve and manipulate data and formulate norms. The authorities may be norms, which the computer can interpret as program modules (eg: rules to compute the stock parameters or to assign a part of a stock-holding to a particular contract). But they may be agents with whom the computer can communicate to obtain data or decisions (individuals may be appointed to consign goods or accept orders, for example). It would be far more difficult to drive a computer interpreter from the Core model in chapter 5.

Is the Social View better than the Core View?

I offered some criteria for judging any alternative view with its theory and modelling methods. Let us check that it measures up to them.

1) Does it deal adequately with the relevant IS concepts identified in the Broad View, including meaning, intention, responsibility and society?

Yes. It provides rigorous, operational definitions of all these concepts and methods of accounting for them in the models created using the new approach.

2) Does it handle the multiple meanings of key IS concepts such as information, communication, meaning and knowledge?

Yes, but there is not space to examine all these concepts in detail in this paper. On pp. 141-146, the Report notes the different meanings of "meaning", "communication" and "information" that apply on each of the semiotic levels. These were demonstrated in ontological analyses that I provided for information systems concepts that belong on each level. A published version of these ontology charts you can find in Stamper 1996. All these definitions depend on each semiotic level confining our attention to a different repertoire of behaviour that signs make available to us. "Knowledge" is defined quite precisely in terms of norms, which are then used to give formal precision to what we understand by society.

3) Does its structure of definitions lead back to operationally sound primitive notions so that its propositions can be tested empirically?

Yes! The primitive notions can all be experienced directly and in the public domain where empirical tests can be applied. They include persons, Society, reproducible repertoires of behaviour called 'affordances', including the complex ones, norms, and signs. Norms are the regularities in behaviour that we can observe in the conduct of the norm subjects or elicit from them as the rules they endeavour to follow, often specified as laws. Signs are affordances that can be demonstrated to stand for other affordances in relationship to which people can behave appropriately given only the sign-tokens representing them.

4) *Does it lend itself to a formal modelling with such advantage as ensuring systems are logically complete and internally consistent?*

Probably yes! The new method employs the novel logical concept of 'ontological dependency' and a syntax based on a wff that forces us to recognise the agent responsible for any knowledge. The ontological structures enforce a high degree of consistency on any model. I conjecture that Norma, the new formalism has the potential to become a logic of social action, better suited than the predicate logic used in the Core model for representing social systems. Whereas predicate logic has had the benefit of the research work of a vast academic industry over almost a century, Norma is embryonic. I suspect that the mathematical methods needed to develop it fully will be found in category theory. In a practical sense, Norma is formal enough for generating directly the computer system needed to support the system being modelled.

5) *Does it lead us to draw distinctions and investigate problems central to IS that would otherwise be overlooked by other methods and theories?*

Yes! Overwhelmingly, this is the special advantage of the new approach. Whereas the Core method does not distinguish computer games from systems for running social security or controlling nuclear power stations, the new approach does so by making the locus of responsibility explicit and by differentiating fiction from fact. Dungeons and dragons have totally different semantic standing from contributions and benefits or from reactor activity and control parameters. The Core View does not distinguish clearly beliefs, obligations and values nor draw attention, as the Social View does, to the problems of justifying the information we handle in our systems. Time has no special significance in the Core View whereas the Social View forces us to look at how we create it along with past and future worlds through the use of information. The Core View confines itself to the syntactic level of analysis whereas the Social View provides the means of exploring all semiotic levels, including those most important for users: the semantic, pragmatic and social levels.

6) *Does it support the continual accretion of testable knowledge of the information systems domain, as we would expect of any other modern science?*

Yes, at least in some areas. It treats the human systems of organisations, institutions and communities as the prime object of study. These have evolved for as long mankind; indeed human nature would not be possible without them. The formal models and theories of behaviour (norms and affordances) that we can create can be subjected to rigorous testing, not only of their internal consistency, but of their empirical validity. This takes us out of the non-scientific mode of methodological practice, in which information systems has been confined so far, into a scientific age where engineering is more than a kind of best practice, just as physics transformed the accumulating methodological knowledge of the blacksmith into mechanical engineering.

7) Does it enable us to do the routine work on information systems conveniently and effectively?

Yes, as the reworking of the Japan Wines Inc. case study indicates. Experience with real commercial applications confirms this. The new approach can drastically reduce the costs of system development, support and maintenance. Documentation shrinks by at least a factor of 10. The canonical substantive schema supports re-engineering processes. The apparent disadvantage is that the rigorous semantic analysis, imposed using the new approach is difficult compared with orthodox styles of modelling, but the resulting, rigorous solutions are re-usable. The new methods, by dealing rigorously and explicitly with the problems of meanings, intentions and social knowledge, greatly increase the likelihood that the users' actual needs will be met, and reduce the risk of the organisational failures that have plagued information systems work to date.

Industrial Testing

An essential test to apply to any framework of information systems concepts is to see how well it works in practice. In the case of the Core FRISCO framework, it has never been used to solve any industrial problem. Looking at the definitions and notations in Chapters 3 and 4, one suspects that it never will have an industrial use unless it is hidden in methods that are easier to read. But the Core View is not far removed from the many conventional systems analysis and specification methodologies in use today. In systems development work, these have not saved us from building a high proportion of systems that are organisational failures, however well they run as computer systems. Either way, FRISCO's Core View has not yet scored a high mark in industry.

The Social View has not yet been promulgated to a wide audience of systems developers. We have held back from doing so while the ideas were being tested. Those tests, of course, have included numerous industrial applications. It is very difficult, unless you are already a leading consulting firm, to introduce radically new ideas to systems development from initial study to final implementation. Hence most of our tests have been in the analysis stage and, so far, only two have gone right through to the working system. Analysis based on the Social View forces attention on the business problems and almost invariably unarticulated problems were brought to the surface, clearly articulated and usually solved.

The two systems fully implemented on the basis of the Social View were successful. One of these was a software package being implemented in the conventional way. The documentation was vast and impenetrable to the professional experts whose ideas were being embodied in the package. When they adopted the concepts of the Social View explained in this paper, the user documentation shrank by about a factor of twenty and the professionals regained control of the work, extending the functionality of the package and advising on bad features. The structures produced were easily implemented using a multi-media, object-oriented database. The other system is of medium size and administers a university with rather complex, course-unit degrees. Ades 1999, describes some interesting aspects of this system. It has about 200 affordances in its ontological structures, that means, counting a minimum of four attributes per affordance, that it is equivalent to a system with at least 800 conventional elements. This system was created quickly and has been running for nearly 10 years with hardly any need for revision despite a rapidly evolving set of business requirements. One person deals with all the modifications, support and training. The rigour of the ontology structures explains the economy. They give us a semantic normal form (SNF) if the constraints are applied strictly. Interestingly, these constraints were relaxed at the outset, in the spirit of conventional systems development. The fact that standard relational normal forms were applied did not prevent the system being infected by a few "malignant features" – "malignant" in the sense that they could only be eliminated with the rewriting of application programs. The rest of the system conformed to the SNF and never required any program to be rewritten as requirements changed. Over the 10 year life of the system, the maintenance costs not arising from straightforward augmentation, all resulted from the struggle to eliminate these malignant features. We do hope that others will be interested in adopting the Social View that is set out in this paper.

If information systems is to become a science

I have deliberately courted controversy. That is because controversy, conducted in the right spirit, is essential for science to exist. I have also tried to be precise and clear enough to invite effective criticism, for without criticism applied to theories that cannot escape it through slippery vagueness, there can be no science.

The views expressed here are at variance with nearly all the orthodox approaches to information systems practised in business at the turn of the century, though not entirely lacking academic support (Hirschheim *et al* 1995, for example). I should like these views to be given your time and open-minded attention and then subjected to your detailed critical scrutiny. Belief in a subjectivist position is only a belief, after all. Time and open-minded attention are essential because, all too often, I have had these ideas misinterpreted as some minor variation on an orthodox methodology. Perhaps the critical test that one has grasped the unusual point I am making is that one can appreciate the shift of ontology. One has to relinquish a belief in an objective reality (even one seen through the veil of an unspecified person's perceptions and conceptions) in favour of the radical belief, found in in FRISCO's Broad View, of a socially constructed reality, a world where there is no time but *now*, and no place but *here*. Only having made this leap of imagination can one see that a science of information systems has the exciting task of explaining how we construct this greater reality. Instead of taking information for granted as the transparent lens through which we see the 'real' reality, we begin to examine the lens and its rather magical 'optical' properties that depend on people expressing their intentions to create past, future and distant worlds. We do not take these processes for granted in an unrestrained relativism but we ask how our information systems can make sure our social constructions are justified, through the demand for, and exercise of responsibility by individuals and groups of people. This prospect of a true science, which FRISCO's Broad View opens for us, is a far cry from the old methodological information systems.

Even modern science is the product of information technology. It depends on open, critical discussion of clearly stated and testable facts and theories. Science could not come into being until the technical infrastructure was capable of reproducing factual and theoretical reports with sufficient accuracy and circulating them openly among a sufficiently large community of critical scholars. Criticism and openness are essential to the growth of scientific knowledge. Politics can easily intervene to prevent ideas circulating. In the past, churches and secular authorities often intervened and they continue to do so today wherever it is to their advantage. Institutional science and technology can also be politicised where it suits large corporations, governments and professional groupings. In a spirit that challenges any politics of information systems, I offer this extension of my dissenting reflections in the FRISCO Report.

References

Ades, Yasser, 1999, "Semantic Normal Form: Compliance" in *Proc. Workshop on Organisational Semiotics*, Almelo October 12-14, University of Twente.

Ernest, Paul, 1998, *Social Constructivism as a Philosophy of Mathematics,* New York, State University of NY.

Falkenberg, Eckhard, et al,1998, *A Framework of Information Systems Concepts*, International Federation for Information Processing, ISBN 3-901882-01-4 .

Feyeradend Paul, 1975, *Against Method,* London, Verso.

Gibson, James, J., 1979, *The Ecological Approach to Visual Perception*, Houghton Mifflin, Boston

Hersh, Reuben, 1997, *What is Mathematics Really?*, London, Vintage.

Hirshheim, Rudy, Heinz Klein and Kalle Lyytinen, 1995, *Information Systems Development and Data Modelling: conceptual and philosophical foundations*; Cambridge University Press, Cambridge.

Kitcher, Philip (1984), *The Nature of Mathematical Knowledge*, Oxford University Press.

Lakatos, Imre and Alan Musgrave, 1970, *Criticism and the Growth of Knowledge,* Cambridge, CUP.

Lakatos, Imré (1976), *Proofs and Refutations*, Cambridge, Cambridge University Press.

Michaels, Claire F. and Claudia Carello, 1981, *Direct Perception*, Prentice-Hall, Englewood Cliffs, NJ.

Popper, Sir Karl, 1959 (original 1935*), The Logic of Scientific Discovery*, Basic Books, New York.

Popper, Sir Karl, 1963, *Conjectures and Refutations*, Routledge and Kegan Paul, London.

Sokal, Alan and Jean Bricmont, 1998, *Intellectual Impostures,* London, Profile Books.

Stamper, Ronald, 1973, *Information in Business and Administrative Systems,* Wiley, New York and Batsford, London.

Stamper, Ronald, 1985, A Logic of Social Norms and Individual Affordances, in Gilbert, N. and G. Heath (eds), *Social Action and Artificial Intelligence*, Gower Press, Aldershot.

Stamper, Ronald, 1989, *Information Management*, Enschede, University of Twente.

Stamper, Ronald, 1996, Signs, Norms and Information Systems, in Holmqvist B. *et al* (eds), *Signs at Work*, De Gruyter, Berlin.

Comments on "Information Systems as a Social Science" by R.K. Stamper

Kalle Lyytinen

Department of Computer Science and Information Systems, University of Jyväskylä
P. O. Box 35, 40351 Jyväskylä, Finland
Email: kalle@jytko.jyu.fi

Ronald Stamper's paper presents a well-written and systematic account of the subjectivist and social-constructivist view of information system concepts, which is enjoyable to read. It should be read by anyone interested in theoretical discourse around information system phenomena.

The paper offers a theoretically strong, but not necessarily a unique, or only alternative to the realist position of information system concepts. The paper, though not intentionally, builds often a strawman position against the realist position in the sense that the 'Broad View'//FRISCO 126 does not content or claim to be a complete or *only* alternative to formalise a comprehensive set of information system concepts. The value of the 'Core View'//FRISCO126 is its rigor and in the manner in which it tries to develop the set of concepts and their relationships formally by starting from some basic and fundamental concepts underlying a state-based interpretation of an information system. In this narrower context it may be well equipped to clarify the self-understanding of a technically based (or logically based) view of information systems. I do not think that anyone in IS field would argue that this specific set of formalised concepts is capable of catering for all theoretical needs we may have about information system phenomena.

Though being clearly articulated in a compelling and crisp writing style the "information systems as social science" advocated in Stamper's paper is still far from being adequately and clearly defined at the same level in terms of its basic concepts.

This could have been overcome by developing the alternative view using the same axiomatic and rigorous specification, or in the minimum- by developing the approach using the same principles suggested in the approach i.e. by defining concepts like information, information system, action, norms and their analytic relationships using the ontological dependency charts suggested by Stamper. This type of approach would have also eased the comparison and analysis of differences.

An additional difficulty in reading Stamper's criticism is that it introduces another complicated vocabulary on top of the currently complicated vocabulary introduced in the FRISCO report. In particular the paper does not explicitly clarify to what extent these concepts are suggested as alternatives that *should replace* those residing in the 'Broad View'//FRISCO123 (or the 'Core View'//FRISCO345) report, or are they meant to be *supplementary* that are useful to analyse information system phenomena in a broader social context. This makes a systematic comparison and analysis of their possibly combined usefulness extremely difficult. For example, the union of all concepts advocated in both FRISCO report and Stamper's alternative is clearly too large for any practising IS professional. Therefore, I would like to see some type of convergence and discussion of a *minimal set of concepts* needed to get the work done.

Another issue which naturally flows from Stamper's behaviourist analysis is the lack of behavioural implications that different sets of IS concepts may have for *the practice of system development.* I am to some extent puzzled by the fact that *if* the "information systems as a social science" concept set is truly radically different in the sense that it implicates different semantics for notations and system models thereby necessitating different "sets of affordances" for system developers, there is very little in the paper about how this would take place and what those differences would be. I would imagine that this set of concepts would have radical implications for ISD practices which people are not necessarily willing to adopt and carry out. Moreover, if the approach is so superior as outlined in section "Is the alternative better than 'Core View'//FRISCO345?" a natural question to ask is why the approach has not been taken into widespread industrial use? One explanation is that people are plainly dumb. Another one is that people do not believe in its value in the short term in comparison to the costs and risks involved in adopting it. For example, due to its conceptual obscurity and lack of clear behavioural implications it is not clear how the approach would scale to industrial strength. How would one apply these concepts to different types of computer applications and for different sized computer applications? Are decision support systems, CSCW applications (workflow, organisational memory), document management applications, ERP systems, so similar in terms of underlying "semiotic principles" that we need only one overarching set of concepts to specify and analyse them from a social perspective (this question applies of course to FRISCO concepts and approach overall)? In the same manner, is a social science based approach that is indifferent to technologies that are used to implement the system viable? For example, would distributed object oriented platforms (e.g. CORBA) that may introduce concepts like responsibility based computing, service agreements etc. provide a more natural link between the social specification and the technical implementation.

Another reason for slow uptake of the socially based theory relates to the fact that the theory embodies *a radical change in the positioning of IS research and practice* which people are not willing to take. In short, my reading of the social view suggest that the fundamental agency dynamics within system development must be changed- the system as a technical analyst would change into a system analyst as a policy maker and organisational designer. These role changes are not implied in the Core View which still views IS models and resulting high level conceptual models of IS as contracts for a sustained responsibility in a more limited technical domains. There is a natural reluctance to "cross the barrier" in the community because systems people must after this change enter into the change domain as principals and involve themselves as political agents in the development games. They do not form anymore a part of the solution but part of the problem. In consequence, the borders of IS discipline may have to be drawn anew. Yet, it is not clear what criteria and rules should we apply (not clear from Stamper's paper) in making these decisions. For example, how can we draw relationships between explanatory, constructive and economic activities within the field of IT and what is the role of IS and its views of the domain in this game?

Like in all system development theory the proposed metalanguage to specify information system phenomena implies its own metalanguage and forms of life that "dictate" how one should go about in applying it. But how neutral and clear are these rules that determine effective modelling and design practices? To what extent does the suggested "method" depend on a previous precalibration of forms of understanding. For example, in order to understand charts in figure 7 and to really appreciate the differences between a verb "deliver" and the concept of "supply", it is clearly not so that one can make sense of what is going on in this figure just by reading it? The understanding of the figure implies a shared "lifeworld" of being embedded in trading and transportation practices which have emerged during the last few hundred years. But how can one create such a shared lifeworld as a precondition to use the method and to what extent one can build up such a lifeworld through modelling exercises is not totally clear.

To conclude, any attempt to develop concepts for the practical field of information systems must face the following question. Don't look into the name: look into the cognitive capabilities and skills that these concepts and associated practices bring along.

Comments on “Information Systems as a Social Science” by R.K. Stamper

Eckhard Falkenberg

Germany
e.falkenberg@efsystems.fn.shuttle.de

This is a very good paper for this conference, because it lends itself quite well for triggering lots of discussion and debate. I found so many debatable issues relating to the FRISCO Report [Fal96] in the paper, that I had to give up the idea to discuss all of them in my comments. Therefore I would like to concentrate on just a few points which I consider the most important ones.

1. Philosophical Positions

The philosophical position advocated in the paper is labelled "radical subjectivism". A relationship between things in "reality" and signs or representations is assumed, carrying the "meaning" of the signs. The author rejects the notion of conception because conceptions are "empirically inaccessible". Rather, he advocates to work with the notions of "affordance", "pattern of behaviour" and/or "repertoire of behaviour".

Let me try to compare this view with the FRISCO constructivist position. According to FRISCO, some assumed "reality" is believed to exist, and parts of it (domains) eventually may be observed and represented. This process is stuctured into three sub-processes, viz. perceiving, conceiving and representing actions (ignoring the process of inner inspection and reflection for a moment). Conceptions may be communicated among people via representations, eventually leading to shared conceptions and shared knowledge.

When the author speaks about "reality", he certainly does not mean "reality" in the FRISCO sense, I rather suspect he means "inter-subjective reality", in a many-to-many relation with signs ("meaning"). Otherwise it would imply a naive-realistic position, and I don't assume that the author is a naive realist. Now, what is "inter-subjective reality"? According to the FRISCO position, it is closely related to shared conceptions and shared knowledge. In the FRISCO Report [Fal96 Section 3.8 Definition E38], the following is stated about this issue: "When communication has resulted in shared knowledge regarding some domain, those sharing that knowledge may be said to have achieved "inter-subjectively negotiated conceptions" concerning an "inter-subjective reality"."

Thus, if one follows the author's view that conceptions are "empirically inaccessible", this inaccessibility applies inevitably to "inter-subjective reality" and to its relation to signs ("meaning") as well. Furthermore and even more importantly, it applies to "affordances", "patterns of behaviour" and "repertoires of behaviour" too, since they are subject to perceiving and conceiving processes as well, like anything else. It seems to me that the author tries (and of course fails) to escape from a principally inescapable dilemma.

Let me mention an important issue, which the author seems to ignore. I mean the peculiar human capability of inner mental inspection and of reflecting on its results. I think that this capability has been crucial for the development of human language, science and philosophy, thus I cannot see any reason to ignore it.

How does now the omnipresent notion of "meaning" (of representations) enter the picture? I think the process of inner mental inspection and reflection is the key to answer that question. An observer, perceiving a representation (being a special domain) with his senses, has to apply this process in general not only to this actual perception, but also to previously constructed conceptions or perceptions, for interpreting the actual perception in a proper, "meaningful" way. These previous conceptions may include all sorts of things, such as knowledge about the world at large or about a particular situation or event, knowledge about the rules of a language, or knowledge about other human conventions. When applying these mental processes to a representation and eventually coming to a conclusion, he will or could think or speak: "Aha, that's what it means!" Thus, "meaning" is certainly not a type of thing like any other, it comes about, at least in my view, as a result of more or less complex mental processes. To ignore these processes as a basis for any conceptual framework in general (as the author seems to do) would be quite counter-productive. These issues are highly important for grasping the meaning of "meaning" and for understanding "understanding".

In this context, let me quote the linguist C. Goddard [God98]: "[The semiotic approach to meaning] ... holds that it is a mistake to become preoccupied with "what meaning is", as though "meaning" were a thing of some kind. Since our whole lives are infused with meanings, since we are communicating in meanings even as we try to speak about them, we can never (on this view) escape from language and find a vantage point from which we can look back and describe what it is we have been doing.". Neither the author, nor the FRISCO authors, nor anyone else is or will probably ever be able to escape from that dilemma.

2. The Semiotic Ladder

It is good that the author gives a concrete example, marriage, to illustrate his distinction between the "semantic layer" and the "pragmatic layer". Let's look at it for a moment, from the viewpoint of the FRISCO approach, or any other (according to the author, "orthodox") approach:

In the first model (the author's paper, figure 1), persons are part of a community (during some time), which in turn belongs to a society (not necessarily forever). Persons may get married and divorced (at some time). Thus, we have a number of (time-stamped) relationships. Furthermore, numerous rules and constraints apply, in particular various temporal constraints and dependencies.

In the second model (the author's paper, figure 2), the first model is extended by some additonal (time-stamped) relationships, viz. that a person may propose marriage to another one, and that the latter may accept that proposal. Numerous rules apply here as well, possibly more than in the first model.

It is quite obvious that the second one is a model of a somewhat larger domain than the first one. From a practical point of view, that is all there is to it.

However, there is more to it according to the author, who claims that the first one is on the "semantic layer" while the second one is on the "pragmatic layer". On what grounds is this claim made? Well, I suppose it is made on the grounds that in the second model, there is a predicator in the model ("propose") suggesting some sort of intention, which in turn is related to the orthodox linguists' notion of "pragmatics". I suppose the claim that there is an even "higher" layer, the "social layer", is made on analogous grounds. Since the author doesn't provide a concrete example for that, I refrain from commenting on that in detail.

My view on this issue is that these distinctions (semantic vs. pragmatic vs. social layer) aren't clear in every application case, and furthermore, and more importantly, they don't contribute to the art of modelling. This does not imply that if you have a domain where a lot of "intention" has to be considered, such as in planning systems, you aren't allowed to create a purpose-specific meta-model whereby the predicator "intent" appears in the meta-model, and where the associated rules about "intentions" are incorporated there as well. But this is quite a different issue (see section 3 on modelling and meta-model hierarchies below).

I guess I'm not the only one to critisise these orthodox linguistic distinctions. Let me quote C. Goddard once again [God98]: "...Distinctions like [semantics vs. pragmatics] may sound clear enough in theory, but when it comes down to practical applications there is often disagreement about where the line should be drawn... Some linguists, such as Filmore, Langacker, and Lakoff, argue that it makes no sense to draw a hard and fast distinction between semantics and pragmatics...".

3. Modelling and Meta-Model Hierarchies

Whether you design a simple database, or construct a business system, or set-up social norms or laws, or even indulge in philosopical investigations, a major and crucial part of what you are doing is modelling a domain. So does the author when setting up his "ontological charts", which are just some special models. I fully agree with the author that models need to be precise and clear, and I am pleased to read that he advocates and aims at "canonical" models, which I guess are the same as "deterministic" models (see e.g. the DETERM approach [Fal93a, Fal93b]) (although I'm not sure when reading the paper).

It is a pity that the author ignores the approach concerning meta-model transformations and hierarchies [Fal96 Section 6.3, Oei95, OF94], which is by the way the basis for the step-by-step extentions and refinements of the FRISCO framework. Otherwise he would have recognised that his meta-model is nothing but a node in a meta-model hierarchy. The claimed observations about the effectiveness of his approach are probably due the fact that the applications he has in mind deal quite a lot with aspects emphasised in his meta-model. Thus we have here a case of a more or less purpose-specific meta-model, situated somewhere in a meta-model hierarchy. Whereabout it is, I cannot tell, since the author's meta-model is only very informally sketched in the paper.

It is a general (and somewhat trivial) trade-off rule, that universal meta-models support all sorts of applications, but not necessarily in the most adequate way, while purpose-specific meta-models support some applications very well, and others not so well (or not at all). I doubt that you can escape from that rule by inventing yet other and perhaps more sophisticated meta-models. However, in case you have a complex and large application domain with various special and diverse sub-domains, you can "bend" that rule to your advantage by allowing different purpose-specific meta-models in your overall application, whereby all meta-models are linked by appropriate meta-model transformations.

4. Conclusions: An Alternative to the FRISCO Formalism?

Although the author's approach is presented quite eloquently, I doubt very much that it has the potential to become a serious alternative or challenge to the FRISCO approach.

The author advocates that one should use his meta-model ("ontological charts") as a basis for a conceptual framework, without attempting to link his meta-model to other, existing meta-models. Thus, the author's approach is based on "singular-view" thinking.

If you read the FRISCO Report carefully, you will recognise that the FRISCO approach is a significant and important step ahead of the wide-spread "singular-view" thinking, by advocating a "multiple-view" thinking in the form of meta-model transformations and hierarchy. Although it is not an easy task, I have no doubts that the various existing meta-models (including the author's one) can be arranged in a meta-model hierarchy and thus linked to each other, provided they are sufficiently well-defined.

Of course there are always detailed aspects which can be improved or refined in a large conceptual framework like FRISCO, but unfortunately the author's paper doesn't really contribute in this way, since his way of thinking appears to be radically different from the way of thinking underlying the FRISCO approach.

Whether FRISCO could be a good basis for a "Principia Informatica", I cannot tell. It certainly would be great if it were so. I do hope that the discussion triggered by the author's position regarding FRISCO will help deeper insights to emerge.

References

Fal96 E.D. Falkenberg et al.: *A Framework of Information System Concepts*, Report of the IFIP WG8.1 Task Group FRISCO, 1996

Fal93b E.D. Falkenberg: *DETERM: Deterministic Event-Tuned Entity-Relationship Modeling*, in R.A. Elmasri, V. Kouramajian and B. Thalheim: Proceedings of the 12th International Conference on the Entity-Relationship Approach, Arlington, Texas, December 1993, Lecture Notes in Computer Science, No. 823, pp. 230-241, Springer-Verlag, Berlin, Heidelberg, 1994

Fal93a E.D. Falkenberg: *An Approach to Deterministic Event-Tuned Information Analysis*, in Proceedings of the International Conference on NIAM-ISDM'93, Utrecht, The Netherlands, 1993

God98 C. Goddard: *Semantic Analysis: A Practical Introduction*, Oxford Textbooks in Linguistics, Oxford University Press, New York, 1998

Oei95 J.L.H. Oei: *A Meta-Model Transformation Approach Towards Harmonisation in Information System Modelling*, in E.D. Falkenberg, W. Hesse and A. Olivé (eds.): Information System Concepts: Towards a Consolidation of Views, Proceedings IFIP WG8.1 Conference ISCO3, Marburg, Germany, March 1995, Chapman & Hall, 1995

OF94 J.L.H. Oei and E.D. Falkenberg: *Harmonisation of Information System Modelling and Specification Techniques*, in A.A. Verrijn-Stuart and T.W. Olle (eds.): Methods and Associated Tools for the Information System Life Cycle, Maastricht, The Netherlands, pp. 151-168, IFIP/North-Holland, 1994

Conceptions are Social Constructs

Towards a Solid Foundation of the FRISCO Approach

Hubert von Braun, Wolfgang Hesse, Urs Andelfinger, Hans-Bernd Kittlaus and Gert Scheschonk

Hubert v. Braun: Allen Systems Group, München/Germany, email: hubert.vbraun@uumail.de

Wolfgang Hesse: FB Mathematik und Informatik, Philipps-Universität Marburg, D-35032 Marburg/Germany, email: hesse@informatik.uni-marburg.de

Urs Andelfinger, Hans-Bernd Kittlaus: c/o Informatik-Zentrum der Sparkassenorganisation (SIZ), Bonn/Germany, email: urs.andelfinger@siz.de

Gert Scheschonk: C.I.T. Communication and Information Technology, Berlin/Germany email: sheshonk@tfh-berlin.de

Key words: Information systems, Conceptual framework, Semiotics, Conceptual modelling, System theory

Abstract: In this article we revisit some core concepts of the FRISCO report related to semiotics and the philosophical foundations of FRISCO. Starting from some earlier versions of the semiotic triangle we focus on its top corner labelled "conception" in its FRISCO version.

The notion of conception (which is most fundamental for the whole framework) has been (and still is) a source of many controversies. It is indeed problematic when it is seen from a pure mentalistic point of view or introduced via terms of perception psychology. However, if we apply the constructivist principles in a systematic way and associate conceptions rather with social groups than with individual observers, they become "social constructs" and thus objective and operational, i.e. verifiable or at least reconstructable by applying laws and rules. As a consequence, some circular definitions in the present report can be removed and the FRISCO basis be stabilised.

1. INTRODUCTION: THE FRISCO WORLD – A UNIVERSE BASED ON CONCEPTIONS

In its report [FRI 98] the FRISCO group intended to establish a framework of information system concepts, i.e. a consistent network of terms and concepts which can form a sound basis for the field of information system development and use. The overall approach of the group is based on language and semiotics, but psychology–related terms like observations and perceptions play a fundamental role in the definitional framework as well.

Information systems are human products which are formed to support the communication and co-operation of human beings living and working together. The essence of these activities is exchange of signs and its principal medium is language. *Semiotics* is the scientific field dealing with signs, their form (syntax), meaning (semantics) and use and effect (pragmatics).

Like many authors in the history and presence of semiotics, the FRISCO authors have used a triangular graphical representation to depict the different aspects of a sign and their relationships. The three corners of their figure stand for the *domain* of a sign (its *referent* or *pragmatic* aspect), the *conception* of a sign (its *meaning* or *semantic* aspect), and the *representation* of a sign (its *syntactic* aspect). However, the FRISCO authors have extended the triangle by a fourth point in the centre thus forming a pyramid or tetrahedron rather than a simple triangle (cf. fig. 1). This central point annotated by *"actor"* emphasises the essential role of the entity or group of entities which is responsible for forming, communicating, interpreting and using signs.

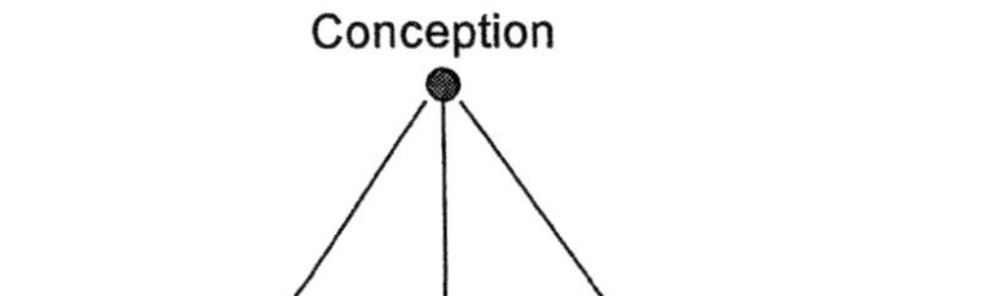

Fig. 1: The semiotic tetrahedron of FRISCO

By emphasising this central role of the actor the authors have expressed their belief that there is no direct connection between representations of signs and their referents but that this is always mediated by something which they called "conceptions" – placed at the uppermost corner of the semiotic pyramid and inseparably linked with the actor in the centre. A closer look to chapters 3 and 4 of the report shows that the term "conception" is in fact fundamental for the whole terminological framework: Essentially, it assumes a "world" to be composed of "things" (and their states): "A thing is any part of a conception of a domain (being itself a "part" or "aspect" of the "world" [FRI 98, p. 36]). This way, the whole framework is based on conceptions and there is no way to understand or "re-construct" the world without understanding (and accepting) what the authors have called "conceptions".

According to the FRISCO report, a conception is "a special actand (i.e. a thing involved in a post-state of an action) resulting from an action whereby a human actor aims at interpreting a perception in his mind, possibly in a specific action context." ([FRI 98], ch. 3, def. E 20)

Ron Stamper has focussed and severely attacked this approach in his reflecting paper "A dissenting position" [Sta 98]. According to his arguments, conceptions are not an appropriate basis for a theory on Information Systems since "we cannot observe the 'conceptions' locked inside our skulls ...". Further, for defining the 'meaning' of a sign he advocates for a "definition by ostention" and claims that this "does not work for the inaccessible conception which one can only 'see' in a metaphorical sense by introspection. ..". His counter-proposal basically implies to replace "conception" by *"repertoire of behaviour"* thus avoiding the explicit reference to mental states and results of introspection.

Other critical arguments on the fundaments of the FRISCO approach are concerned with its "ontology" starting with the sentence "The world exists, independent of our own existence, or of our cognitive or intellectual capabilities:" [FRI 98, assumption [a], p. 31]. Stamper calls such a world a "ready-made reality" [p. 193] and argues that it "defies observation because the observer involved always gets in the way." [p. 191]. As a conclusion, he classifies the FRISCO approach (in its "formal" parts) as "mentalistic with a touch of naive realism." [p. 194]

Our group (as a whole) came across the FRISCO approach while trying to study and clarify the terminology of the so-called object-oriented approach of Informatics. Of course, this is a task which has to start with the concept of "object" itself and has to base it on a sound and consistent philosophical basis. Here the same questions arise: Does an "object" exist independent from our own existence? What is an object at all? Is it something "just for the picking" [Mey 88] or is it a "conception" we have to negotiate with others? This has led us to what we consider the crucial point of the whole FRISCO approach: What, after all, is the nature and essence of conceptions? Are they the missing link between representations and their referents? Or are they some sort of mentalistic magic we should rather avoid to touch?

2. A TOUR D'HORIZON ON THE SEMIOTIC TRIANGLE

In order to answer the above questions, we will start with a closer examination of the semiotic triangle and, in particular, with its uppermost corner (cf. [Fer 98]).

Three Versions of the semiotic triangle

At a first glance one might ask whether we need a triangle at all. Ron Stamper's reflection paper suggests that meaning is a "relationship established by people in a language community" relating one *thing-A* to another *thing-B* it *"stands for"*.

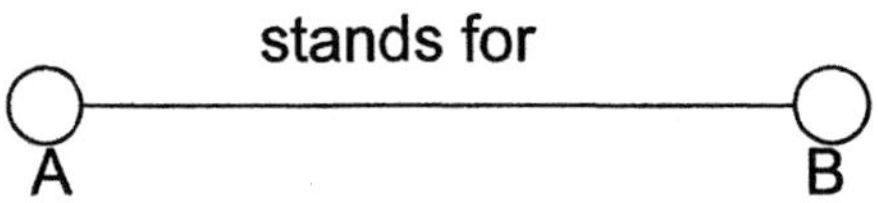

Fig. 2: The "meaning" relationship

But already Aristotle claimed to have good reasons to pose something in between which he called "Imagined thing" in order to express what we might call the n:1- (or n:m) relationship between *words* and their *references* (things they refer to).

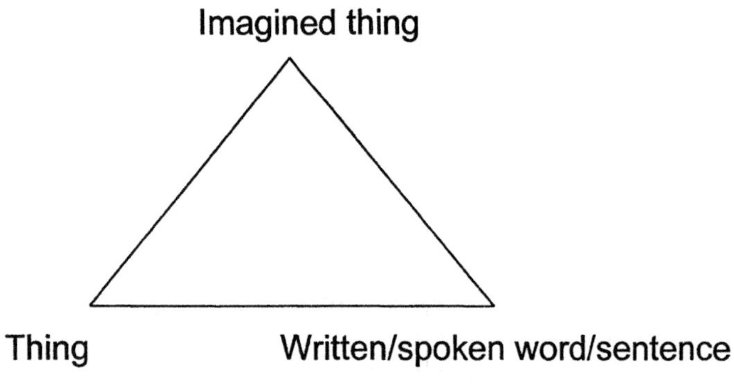

Fig. 3: Aristotle's triangle

For Aristotle "...spoken words are the symbols of mental experience and written words are the symbols of spoken words. Just as all men have not the same writing, so all men have not the same speech sounds, but the mental experiences, which these directly symbolise, are the same for all, as also are those things of which our experiences are the images..." (Aristotle, on interpretation).

This way, the meaning of words is understood as a mental state resulting from what is imagined when words are spoken or written. This mental state is said to control speech in an unambiguous way.

About 2000 years later we find a slightly different version of the triangle used by the German philosopher G. Frege:

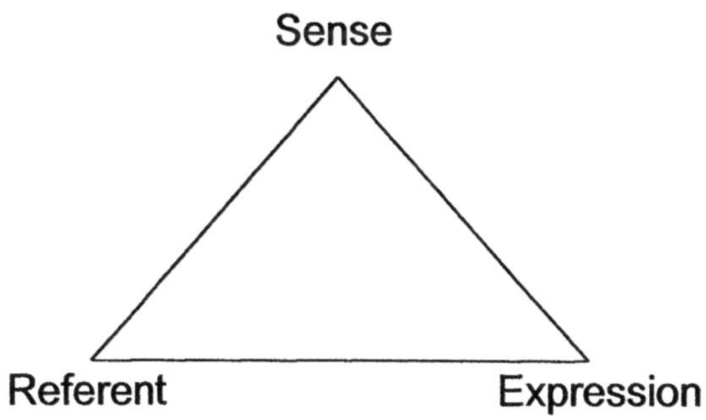

Fig. 4: Frege's triangle

Frege argued that imagined things depend on a medium like a human being whereas the referents are independent from any medium. According to Frege, the meaning of an expression cannot be based only on imagining because mental states are private and understanding cannot work on such subjective grounds. Thus he extended the model of meaning by introducing *sense* as "the way things are given". As the sense of a thing, like the thing itself, is the same for all people, it serves as an objective criteria for understanding. Thus, for Frege "meaning" consists of both imagining and sense. Frege's explanation of meaning catches the argument of objectivity but it depends on a sort of metaphysical realm populated with sense-entities.

Another, quite different approach is taken by Wittgenstein (cf. fig. 5). For Wittgenstein, it is neither imagining nor sense that provides meaning to an expression. "The meaning of a word is *its use*". To speak is nothing more than performing speech acts by following certain rules. Sharing the same meaning results from following the same rule. Only if the rules have been internalised beforehand, something like imagining can occur or the sense of a thing can be projected as "the way it is given". We apply the rules blindly, without any mental pre-dispositions, in the same way as we apply the rules of a game. The meaning of words and sentences is nothing more than the restrictions, rules, and regularities that govern their use. As the same holds true also for all kinds of games, Wittgenstein introduced the notion of language game. For him, the question "What is a word at all?" is analogous to "What is a piece in chess?".

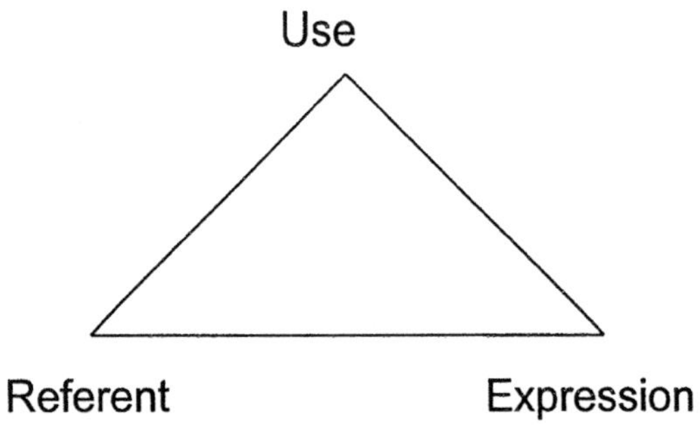

Fig. 5: Wittgenstein's triangle

The further development of the *use theory of meaning* is well known. Its most prominent result is the so-called *speech act theory*. Austin and later on Searle offered a systematic classification of the variety of speech acts. According to them, to *say something* is to *do something*, and what one does in saying something is typically indicated by a particular performative verb prefixing the "normal form" of the utterance. These verbs, such as "state," "request", "promise", "judge, "warn," "apologise," and so on, mark the illocutionary role of the utterance in question.

For our purposes - i.e. for a closer examination what conceptions really are - it is useful to see that a speech act like an assertive consists of two parts, namely an illocutionary role in the first place (e.g. judge, doubt, being afraid of, etc.) and a proposition which follows that role. While the illocutionary role evidently refers to a private mental state, the proposition is insofar constructed in a public way as the applied construction rules are everybody's rules.

The intuitively used construction rules and intuitively applied construction acts can be made explicit by pointing out the logic of the relations existing between terms, between referents, and between terms and referents of a proposition. As an example for the equivalence and dependence relations the following types of construction acts and their propositional expressions have been suggested by E. Ortner (cf. fig. 6, adopted from [Ort 83]).

This exposition of the construction acts and the relations founding these acts demonstrates how objective and how public everybody's rules are, even if applied only intuitively after having internalised them. Applying these rules ends up in a construct which owes its objectivity to the fact that it can be reconstructed in public at any time.

Abstraction (based on equivalence relations)

Construction act	Propositional expression	Relationship type	Example
Identification	$x \equiv N$	Identity	John is client no. 4711
Predication	$x \, \varepsilon \, P$ $x \, \nu \, P$ $x \, \pi \, P$	Subsumption	John is a CLIENT John has CREDIT John does ORDER
Inclusion	$Q \subset S$	Subordination	CLIENT is BUSINESS_PARTNER

Composition (based on equivalence relations)

Construction act	Propositional expression	Relationship type	Example
Attribution	$x \, \nu \, A$	Participation	John has a CLIENT_NO
Possessive Integration	$Q \succ A$	Possession	ASSEMBLY has WHOLE_NO and PART_NO
Participative Integration	$Q \prec A$	Participation	ASSEMBLY has QUANTITY
Connection	A1 <<->> A2	Interdependence	Combination WHOLE_NO and PART_NO serving as denotation

Fig. 6: Construction acts and their propositional expressions following (cf. [Ort 83])

3. CONCEPTIONS: THE ESSENCE OF OUR ASPECTS OF THE WORLD

After this tour d'horizon we will try to summarise our understanding of the semiotic relations with a particular focus on what the FRISCO authors have named "conceptions":

(1) Any attempt to draw a link between a *representation R* and its *domain (referent) D* has to start with an *observer A* who is forming or recognising a representation. This justifies the central position of the observer in all sign

processes which the FRISCO authors have highlighted in their version of the semiotic figure. However, in the FRISCO report, no distinction is made between the observer (a sort of "meta-actor" used to explain the philosophical background) and the concrete actors occurring in the context of every specific information system. We consider this distinction essential (also to end up with better layering of the FRISCO report, see below) and therefore have deliberately chosen the term *observer* for the first kind of FRISCO "actor" and restricted the term *actor* to the second one.

Thus, for any closer examination of the "meaning" relationship, its relativity with respect to the observer A should be emphasised: We prefer to say: *"R represents D for A"* or *"R is interpreted by A as representing D"* instead of just *"R stands for D"* (cf. fig. 2).

(2) To form or to interpret representations are often complex processes. Since we cannot grasp a domain in its totality while representing it and we do not (re-) create that domain in its totality while interpreting its representation we have to distinguish the considered domain from those *aspects which are relevant for an observer* while representing it or analysing its representation. Thus we prefer to extend the above sentence to its final, more comprehensive form:

> *"For observer A, the expression R represents the aspect(s) C of some domain D".*

With this interpretation, we are now able to (re-) explain the four corners of the semiotic tetrahedron and – in particular - to find a satisfying explanation for the "conception" corner:

(2A) Again we start with the central point of the figure: the *observer*. Above we have already emphasised his/her importance for the whole sign process. Essential for the flexibility of the whole approach is the fact that we can consider individual observers as well as groups or even whole societies. Whenever more than one individual is involved, only those statements (on representation or interpretation) are accepted as "valid" which are shared by all individuals of the group or society or at least by a substantial majority of those individuals. Such statements are the result of negotiations and can be summarised by collections of (written or unwritten) rules and laws.

(2R) *Representations are* symbolic, graphical, depictive, auditive or otherwise (by observers through their senses) perceivable expressions or signals for which corresponding references exist.

(2D) The *reference* of a representation may be any "something" or *domain*: The whole or any part of the concrete or abstract world, perceived or imagined by the observer, including him- or herself, his or her physical components or thoughts (self references), and other representations or their parts (mediated references).

(2C) The *conception* at the top of the triangle reflects the aspect character of all recognition which is an epistemic prerequisite: a referent can never be recognised and then represented as a whole but only in the form of *aspects* the observer is able to perceive. Note that *"aspect"* in this sense does *not* imply previous full knowledge of the referent but on the contrary may be used as a means to "approach" the referent, i.e. to get more knowledge on it. The normal form of its statement points it out: Some D is *recognised as* a C. Thus "conception" or better "collection of aspects" is *"that as what the observer has recognised the subject of his/her reference"*.

In other words, "conceptions" are collections of aspects of things which are relevant for an observer while forming or interpreting representations. Note that with this explanation, a conception is always an abstract entity. It is neither the subject of reference (which may be concrete or abstract) itself nor a representation (which is always concrete). But it can be represented: for example by listing the relevant aspects, stating rules, drawing graphics or pictures, filling data bases ...

If we try to define the term "entity" such an approach can be helpful: In a narrower sense, an *entity* can be defined as a "conception", i.e. as a collection of aspects - which we normally call *attributes* and represent by *data elements* in the IS field. In a broader sense, constructing an entity starts up by building a "conception" in the above sense, namely by collecting aspects but eventually an *entity* will cover all three corners of the triangle including one or several representation(s) and a domain, i.e. something in the real or imagined world it refers to.

What is considered to be an entity and which of its aspects are considered relevant is determined by the observer(s), i.e. the system analysts in our case. In a more general sense, it is the society which has determined, delimited and named its entities through continuous use and communication – a process which continues and will continue as long as human beings are able to do so. In this view, conceptions are *social constructs, formed by a language community through common use and shared understanding*. Thus they are a *product of social agreement* and may vary if such agreements change in time. They might, for example, be represented by collections of rules which are acknowledged and agreed on in that community or in terms of a standardised "norm language" common for (most of) its members. It is important to note, that not the rules by themselves bring conceptions into existence, but it is their common use by a language community that *dynamically* produces conceptions and meaning. So, if the underlying rules and/or the language community varies, the resulting conceptions and meaning may vary as well, even if their representations remain the same.

Whether the term "conception" is the most appropriate wording to express this view, is still a matter of dispute. As an alternative, we have discussed the terms "construct" or "social constructs" but the first seemed to be too wide and the second too narrow to us.

4. CONSEQUENCES FOR THE FRISCO LINE OF REASONING

What have we achieved with this explanation and what are the consequences for a possible revision of the FRISCO outline of concepts?

- We have given an explanation of "conceptions" which is rather based on the results of cognition of an (individual or social) observer than on psychological dispositions like perception. Depending on whether the observer is an individual one or a group of observers we might call such conceptions *subjective* or *objective*, bearing in mind that agreements of groups or even societies may change in time and therefore this kind of "objectivity" is a relative one.

- We have given an explanation which is *operational* in that sense that an individual itself or an independent deputy of a group or society is able to prove or at least reconstruct - for example, *by applying certain given rules* - whether a given interpretation of a representation is correct or not. In fig. 6 we have sketched how existing formal mechanisms can be used to formulate concepts and their relationships in an reconstructable way.

- The term *thing* (if useful at all) might be identified with the term *conception*. That means: Everything what an observer has "recognised as a C" (for example, by analysing its aspects) deserves to be called a "thing". This approach circumvents (and thus avoids) one of the most problematic circular definitions in the FRISCO report concerning the *terms "thing"*, *"actand"* and *"conception"* (cf. definitions E1, E20 and E15). With this interpretation, "things" are social constructs as well: they are the result of social communication and consensus achieved by a group. Such a consensus is achieved when "things" are treated in the same way or at least in an expected way (i.e. following the same rules) by the people involved. This corresponds to Stamper's "repertoire of behaviour" and helps making things "operational".

A further consequence of such an approach would be a better layering of the whole framework of FRISCO definitions: Semiotics including observers and their cognition would form *the base layer* including terms like *observer, domain, representation, conception*. Neither of these terms must occur in the now following first layer of defined terms – thus circular definitions like the mentioned ones can easily be avoided. In particular, most of the definitions E19- E23 should be (re-) moved to the base layer.

The *kernel layer* would start (as in the original report) with *things* (explained as *conceptions*) and build terms like *entity, relationship, type, state, action*, etc. on it. This works quite well with the exception of *"set membership"* where FRISCO tries to redefine basic terms of mathematical set theory. This has to be removed (to avoid another source of circular definitions) or better to be replaced by something like "composed thing".

On a third layer, terms like *model, system, information system* etc. can be added as has been done in the original report. A list of proposed modifications of the conceptual framework (which would essentially affect chapters 3 and 4 of the report) is given in the appendix.

In our view, such a modification of the FRISCO report could remove some severe sources of dispute including flaws like circular definitions while maintaining the overall line of reasoning which we appreciate as a very important contribution to an evolving theory of the Information Systems field.

A future version of the FRISCO report revised along these lines and exhibiting a clearer, layered structure might well be used in the practice of Information Systems design since it could provide a well-founded compendium of basic concepts and a line of reasoning for professional designers. This way they can build their models on top of the FRISCO framework instead of inventing general basic concepts each time when a specific application domain has to be modelled. Such a standardisation might help the practitioners to save much work and the whole community to reduce inconsistencies and sources of misunderstanding.

5. REFERENCES

[FRI 98] E. Falkenberg, W. Hesse, P. Lindgreen, B.E. Nilsson, J.L.H. Oei, C. Rolland, R.K. Stamper, F.J.M. Van Assche, A.A. Verrijn-Stuart, K. Voss: *FRISCO - A Framework of Information System Concepts* - The FRISCO Report. IFIP WG 8.1 Task Group FRISCO;
Web version: *ftp://ftp.leidenuniv.nl/pub/rul/fri-full.zip* (1998).

[Fer 98] R. Ferber: *Philosophische Grundbegriffe. Eine Einführung.* Beck-Verlag, München 1998.

[Mey 88] B. Meyer: *Object oriented software construction*, Prentice Hall 1988.

[Ort 83] E. Ortner.: *Aspekte einer Konstruktionssprache für den Datenbankentwurf* (Aspects of a construction language for database design), Darmstadt 1983.

[Sea 79] J.R. Searle: *Expression and meaning. Studies in the Theory of Speech Acts.* University Press, Cambridge 1973.

[Sea 83] J.R. Searle: *Intentionality. An essay in the philosophy of mind.* University Press, Cambridge 1983.

[Sea 95] J.R. Searle: *The construction of social reality.* Penguin Press, London 1995.

[Sta 98] R. Stamper: *A dissenting position.* In: [FRI 98], chapter 7: Reflections: Committed positions on the report by individual FRISCO members and associates.

Appendix: Proposed modifications and error corrections in the FRISCO tutorial and formalisation (chapters 3 and 4)

The FRISCO authors have chosen a two-level approach for explaining concepts:

. Base level: Concepts introduced by assumptions (ch. 3.1)
. Definition level: Concepts introduced by definitions (ch. 3.2)

There are terms introduced in the base level (i.e. by assumptions) which occur again as defined terms on the upper level. This contradicts to a fundamental principle of the definition process. The base level forms a "platform" for the following definitions. All terms introduced in the base level are taken for granted and are used as a prerequisite for the following definitions. The distinction between base level and definition level must be clear and unique.

Any attempt to (re-) define terms introduced in the base level necessarily ends up in a circular definition ("petitio principii"). A necessary consequence is: Concepts to be formally defined must not be introduced earlier by informal "assumptions", or vice versa: What has been introduced by an assumption, must not be (re-)defined in the definition part. In the present version of the report, these rules are violated at the following points:

(1) *Perception/conception:* introduced in assumption [b] and [c], p. 31 and then in definitions E 19 and E20, p.48

(2) *Actor:* introduced as the originator and interpreter of conceptions on pp. 30/31 (there sometimes called "human being"), in assumption [f] on p. 31, but also in definition E 13, p.43, and again – now as a "human actor" - as "capable of

performing perceiving actions, conceiving actions, transforming actions" (p. 48), and as "representer" (p. 50).

(3) *Predicator/predicated thing:* Explicitly these do occur only on the definition level (def. E2, p. 37), but they are already implicitly used (and necessary!) on the base level: "A thing is any part of ..." (def. E1, p. 36), "A predicator *is a thing* ..." (def. E2, p. 37) is not admissible since *"is a thing"* is already a predicator!

(4) *Set membership:* In chapter 3 (def. E4, p. 38) "set membership" is defined as a FRISCO concept, but basic knowledge of (mathematical) set theory is assumed throughout the report (including definitions where "set membership" is based upon - e.g. " ... the set of all things", def. E1, p.36). The corresponding definition in ch. 4 (def. D4, p. 97) suggests (by identifying the notation) that the "set membership" relation defined here is identical to mathematical set membership (cf. the "usual abbreviations" in def. D4). This would, however, lead to an inadmissible definition circle. The problem can be solved by replacing "set membership" by a concept of "composition" or "aggregation", which in fact is required as a FRISCO concept. On the other hand, set membership is a (different) basic concept from mathematics which need not (and must not) be redefined.

Most of these problems can be solved by a better separation of the layers:

- Base layer: It starts with an explanation of the overall constructivist approach which has to be based on an *observer* (in the sense explained above). This *(general) observer* has to be newly introduced and to be well distinguished from the "actor" on the following definition level. The base level has to comprise *basic ontology (assumptions), semiotics, linguistics (language, predicators etc.), perceptions (if still needed) and conceptions. Set theory* is assumed to belong to the underlying basic knowledge like any other used concepts of mathematics, logic or philosophy.

- Kernel layer: The pivotal definition which links this layer to the base layer is that of *"thing"* - explained as some sort of *conception* (but not vice versa!). The kernel level basically covers the main part of chapter 3 of the FRISCO report (def's. E1 - E29), but without the *semiotics* part (section 3.4), *"per/conceptions"* and with the *"actor"* reduced to his role in def. E13 (p. 43), i.e. *not identical* with the (world) *observer* introduced in the assumptions at the beginning of chapter 3. *"Set membership"* should be replaced (and reduced to) *"composition"* or *"aggregation"* or be replaced by definitions of *"composed"* or *"aggregated things"*.

- System layer: This level covers all system- and organisation-related concepts. It contains the material of sections 3.6-3.10 of the original FRISCO report (def's. E30 - E41).

Comments on "Conceptions are Social Constructs" by H. v. Braun, W. Hesse, U. Andelfinger, H.-B. Kittlaus and G. Scheschonk

Hannu Kangassalo

University of Tampere, PO Box 607, FIN-33101 Finland
hk@cs.uta.fi

The FRISCO report aims to form a comprising and consistent system of terms and concepts which could be applied to handle issues, problems and solutions in the information systems field. The overall approach used is based on language and semiotics illustrated by the use of a variant of the semiotic triangle extended by adding an *actor* at its central position.

In more general terms, the report concerns the notions, views, and rules planned to be used for designing, understanding, and evaluating information systems, i.e. the notions, views, and rules for description, subsumption, explanation, prediction, and retrodiction of information available for describing the domain and informational constructs deducible from it. The issues in the report concern partly with the nature of knowledge and the structure of it, and possibility, scope, and general basis of knowledge. They also deal with a question on which grounds knowledge about the domain, views, concepts, rules, and facts in information systems are based, and which kind of justification we can have for that knowledge.

In the paper of "Conceptions are social Constructs - ..." the authors analyse the use of the (tetrahedron) variant of the semiotic triangle. They concentrate on the notion of *conception* which they recognise to be important but problematic. They propose that the interpretation of the notion of conception should be revised.

First, the notion of conception should rather be based on cognition of an observer than on psychological disposition of perception. Second, they give an explanation of the notion of conception which is operational in the sense that a given interpretation of a representation can be reconstructed or even proved to be correct or not. Third, they propose that the term *thing* might be identified with the term *conception*. Fourth, they reveal some deficiencies and circular constructs in the structure of the concept system presented in the report, and they propose how these "problematic" constructs could be corrected or removed.

In information systems design we are constructing models about the domain, and knowledge based on them. This approach turns our point of view into issues of scientific methodology; how can one develop models or theories that are better than competing models or theories? That question is a fundamental problem in the area of theory of knowledge or epistemology. We have to pay more attention to the *epistemology of information systems*, which is a branch of research that studies knowledge in information systems, especially questions, e.g. how that knowledge is or should be synthesised, and how can one develop models or theories that are better than competing models or theories?

There are different approaches to epistemology of information systems. These approaches are not necessarily coherent with each other, and it may be that they can not be harmonised into one system of concepts to form a coherent theory. In the FRISCO report the main part of the work is based on one epistemology, but there is also a dissenting position expressed which indicates that a quite different ontology and epistemology could be applied, too. Also the authors of the paper of "Conceptions are social Constructs - ..." seem to support some of the views in this other epistemology. Research on this direction should be continued, and also other possible epistemologies should be searched for.

The main epistemological approach in the report is constructivism, about which there are different branches, e.g. individual constructivism and social constructivism. These branches are not recognised in the report. The first one assumes that an individual attempts to reach coherence among the different pieces of knowledge. The second one sees consensus between different subjects as the ultimate criterion to judge knowledge. 'Truth' will be accorded only to those constructions on which most people of a social group agree.

The authors say that conceptions as "social constructs" are objective and operational, i.e. verifiable or at least reconstructable by applying laws and rules [see abstract]. That is an ideal, but very often constructs seem to be more or less biased, on the basis of erroneous assumptions of the group. Later the authors discuss about *observers* and say that "essential for the flexibility of the whole approach is that we can consider individual observers as well as groups or even whole societies." That is true, but from it follows that both individual constructivism and social constructivism must explicitly be taken into account. That has not been done. All individuals have originally their own conceptions, and even in communication situations the receiver tries to understand an incoming message from his own point of view. There are methods how communicating parties may try to improve their mutual understanding but complete understanding can hardly be achieved. Learning and extensive education systems tend to standardise some of the conceptions, but not all of them. The authors also emphasise that conceptions are a product of social agreement and they may vary if such agreements change in time. However, in the analysis of changes the identity of conceptions and naming relations used in the language must be taken into account, too.

The authors say also that "The intuitively used construction rules and intuitively applied construction acts can be made explicit by pointing out the logic of the relations existing between terms, between referents, and between terms and referents of a proposition". They propose a logic of construction acts. Is it the same thing than a conceptualisation process in formal ontology?

It seems that authors' proposals direct the work into a right direction, but the research on deep ontological and epistemological aspects of information systems should be continued, especially on applied principles of information system epistemology, formal ontology, and construction and use of conceptions and also specific concepts.

An Organizational Theory of Information

Anatol W. Holt and Felice Cardone

DISCo, Università di Milano-Bicocca, Via Bicocca degli Arcimboldi 8, I-20126 Milano, Italy
e-mail: anatolholt@popmail.iol.it, cardone@disco.unimib.it

Key words: Information, Organization, Plan.

Abstract: This paper briefly presents a new technical and philosophical approach to "information" as relevant to computerized society. Our definition of "information" makes no reference to computers, but makes extensive reference to organized activities within a society affected. Specific problems that particularly impact computer use are indicated. The subject concept "information" is compared to others that have had influence in the past. The paper is less a contribution to an established direction in practice and research than it is direction setting.

1. INTRODUCTION

For half a century it has been clear that computers are, above all, "information machines"; as users we let information flow in and out, store it, transform it, search, discard and view it. Nevertheless — although information is so important to computers, and computers are so important to our society — no new concepts of "information" have guided users or designers into the future. A theory of information taking into account the variety of information-relative operations that can be performed with the hclp of computers is likely to have to the computer the same relation as thermodynamics to the steam engine. This can hardly be the case for classical information theory, as developed originally by Shannon (Shannon and Weaver, 1949), motivated by the needs of telephony and focussed essentially on the (efficiency of) transmission of information.

In our culture people assume (consciously or unconsciously) that information is objective — simply there, like the center of mass of the solar system (to borrow an example from Frege). This attitude is supported by current theories of information, that disregard the fact that information is produced, sold, stored, maintained and used, i.e. that it behaves as a *commodity*. (In particular, this implies that information is a resource, as appears from the fact that — as all resources — it may become scarce.) We claim that treating information like the center of mass of the solar system rather than as a (new) type of commodity has a number of serious negative social consequences, especially where computers are concerned.

Most serious is the implied failure to understand that effective information depends on effective social agreements which bind people together in organized activities. Like everything in society, these only last for a while, and so the information they generate also has a limited life.

Secondly: all goods call crimes into existence (but, it seems, not the center of mass of the solar system). If information — including computer information — is basically like commodities, there will be "information crimes" (as in fact there are). Therefore the popular prejudice about information militates against a truly basic attack on the computer crime problem.

There is also the issue of maintenance. If lumps of information are commodities then they must be maintained if stored (unlike the center of mass of the solar system, it seems). Note that computers make realizing the need for maintenance effort especially difficult: computer information that might be useful to someone sometime is produced in enormous quantities; decay does not make it smell (like decaying vegetables), and it hardly takes visible space.

All this is closely related to the essential modifications that have taken place in the relation of computers with their users: while they were originally designed to perform numerical calculations on behalf of *single-person users*, computers have gradually been turned into processors of information of any kind on behalf of *many-person users*. As a result of this shift, computer systems designers have now to face such issues as decision support, authentication and information maintenance.

The word "computer" seems more related to "number" than to "information", and this is historically accurate. But with hindsight we can say: numbers in a computer are always informations, even if this is not the case in mathematics. It is one thing to consider the properties of the number 11, no matter how it is written (for example the fact that it is a prime); it is another thing to design adequate procedures for dealing with 11 million dollars at a bank — or for that matter, 11 pounds of potatoes bought at a market. (In particular, in these latter contexts it does matter how '11' is written or spoken; because, if a translator is needed, the organized activity is changed.) On the one hand, numbers are (an important) part of the subject of pure mathematics; on the other hand, numbers naturally arise in the context of organized activities — as information, with or without computers. (Numbers also play an important role in applied mathematics as a middle ground between organized activity and mathematics.) Numbers in computers are always information (and never "pure", even if a computer is used by mathematicians for mathematical purposes). Thus we claim: information is the link that ties all computer applications together — including classical computation, a fortiori.

The rest of this paper contains:

- a review of a theory of organized activity which serves as a basis for our definition of information;
- the above mentioned definition of information;
- an indication of practical problems that may be solved with the help of this definition; and finally
- an indication of the relationships between this view of information and other views that are known to us, and some comments on how this view of information impinges on the content of the FRISCO report.

2. SUMMARY OF A THEORY OF ORGANIZED ACTIVITY

What is "organized activity"? According to us, it is a human universal, perhaps even more so than language (for, to communicate by language requires organized activity, but not vice versa). Organized activity can evolve within a society, or it can be artificially created — by design and implementation. Organized activity always presupposes a society, but can be carried out by very few or very many persons. The following "equivalences" will help convey the idea:

2.1 Organized activity is present if and only if coordination (of action) is present.

2.2 Organized activity is present if and only if repetition (of something) is present.

Organized activities, while possibly for fun or for profit or for both, are always motivated — necessarily so since they always require effort, and consequently time. Organized activities characterize all human societies, whether primitive or technological. That information always functions in the context of organized activities hardly needs to be stressed in the context of the community of readers of this paper. But our approach to its definition and analytic use depends on a few notions summarized below and exposited more fully in (Holt, 1997).

2.1 Units, realizations and criteria

Organized activities depend on agreements between the participants as to what is what and who is who. In the theory of organized activity this is vouchsafed by UNITS which, in their turn — as a social phenomenon — only arise in the context of organized activities and point to an order of reality which stands in between the usual dichotomy subjective/objective and that we call, for lack of a better term, CONJECTIVE.[1] In many cases units are similar to concepts, being denoted linguistically by common nouns, but much more belongs to the realm of conjective than just concepts. There are units that can only be defined operationally, like e.g."double-click the mouse button", or "clean glassware" in the chemical laboratory, and it would be in harmony with the present view to argue that, in fact, all units are so defined (within a particular organized activity). Units are designed to model the "conjective world" associated with the execution of plans within a community of cooperating performers.

Units of special kinds have received much attention in the social sciences, notably in linguistics and anthropology as for instance phonemes in the sense of structuralist phonology (Trubeckoj, 1939). The whole system of oppositions that defines the phonological structure of a language is produced and maintained by the collective action of the community of speakers. In anthropology, notions like *mana* and *hau*, both studied by Mauss (Mauss, 1950), cannot be understood outside those particular organized activities that are the relevant magical rites and ceremonies for the exchange of goods, respectively, and are units in the communities involved. The same dependence of meaning on social practices is highlighted by Malinowski in his analysis of the record of a trading expedition in the Trobriand Islands (Malinowski, 1923). But, of course, it is in Wittgenstein's later philosophy that organized activities (in the form of "language games") are shown to be pervasive and conjectivity is fully recognized as playing a central role even in so formal a practice as arithmetic (Wittgenstein, 1956, 1976).

Each unit is associated with a CRITERION to judge whether some thing or event, real or only imagined, is or is not one of its EXAMPLES. Two units are different if and only if their criteria are different.

We can distinguish between two types of units:

2.1.1 Those for which the occurrence of disagreement represents a plan failure, and those for which it does not. We will call the first type of unit and its criterion DEFINITE; the second type (and its criterion) INDEFINITE.

[1] This term is formed from 'cum' (together), and the verb 'iacere' (to throw) which provides the common root to 'subjective' and 'objective'.

Thinking in terms of units (and their criteria) makes it important to be clear about the relationship of units to their examples. Suppose we set up a clerk to sort forms that arrive at his desk into two piles — pink ones on the right, blue ones on the left. In this plan two units play a fundamental role: pink forms and bluc forms. Even if this clerk as a matter of fact never sees a blue form, "blue form" is a unit of basic importance to this plan. To handle the resulting distinctions, we introduce the following vocabulary:

2.1.2 A REALIZATION of a unit is an historically real (and therefore irrepeatable) example.

2.1.3 An INSTANCE of a unit is an imagined example; the community may or may not believe that the unit criterion can be met in reality.

The role of set inclusion is played in the present setting by the following intensional notion:

2.1.4 Unit *Y* is a CASE of unit *X* if: satisfying the criterion of *Y* implies satisfying the criterion of *X*, but not vice versa.

In particular, if Y is a case of X, then every instance of Y is also an instance of X. The following concept will be instrumental later on, in our definition of information.

2.1.5 Unit *X* has (a set of) CASE ALTERNATIVES if: there is a finite set Y_i of two or more cases of *X* such that every instance of *X* is an instance of one and only one Y_i. If unit *X* has case alternatives, both *X* and its case alternatives are definite.

2.2 Bodies and actions

The theory of organized activity assumes that the reality of organized life can be captured in two types of lumps and their relationships: lumps of effort, called ACTIONS, and lumps of material, called BODIES.

2.2.1 The actions as well as bodies must be conjects for the potential performers, and therefore are instances of units (these units may be called ACTION and BODY, respectively).

The exertion of human effort always "takes time"; similarly every material lump — whether a piece of furniture, a building, or a human body — always "takes space", where "space" and "time" are meant in the sense of ordinary experience. The following notions are motivated precisely by the fact that *all* units are lumps:

2.2.2 Unit *Y* is PART of *X* if: every instance of *X* includes (as a part) an instance of *Y*.

2.2.3 Unit X has a DECOMPOSITION if: there is a finite set Y_i of two-or-more parts of X such that every instance of X contains one, and only one, instance of each Y_i; every part of X is included.

These definitions, together with those relative to case alternatives, are helpful in the study hierarchies and classifications. In particular, in many important examples classifications are just a way of establishing mappings between case alternatives and decompositions: think of a computer menu (whose items correspond to case alternatives of an action) or a map of a public transport network, that displays (as its parts) all possible alternative routes.

The effects of an action on a body involved in it is part of the definition of both — the action as well as the body. The effects are various, but two types in particular are especially relevant to the present theory:

2.2.4 PRODUCTION AND CONSUMPTION. An action may CONSUME or PRODUCE a body. These two are mutually exclusive: an action cannot both consume and produce a body. (A fortiori, an instance of an action cannot produce as well as consume an instance of a body.) A body consumed by an action is called an INPUT of the action; a body produced by an action is called an OUTPUT of the action.

Instead of producing or consuming a body, an action can change the *state* of the body: our definition of a state relies ultimately only upon the notion of case alternatives of a unit.

2.2.5 STATE CHANGE. A STATE S of a body B is a case of B that belongs to a set of case alternatives (2.1.5). A change of state of a body is an action that consumes one case of a body and produces another case of the same body. Thus the body B is present throughout a change of its state; but the action causes B in its input state to vanish, and B in its output state to be born.

2.3 Plans and exceptions

A fundamental aspect of the theory of organized activity is this:

2.3.1 Performing an organized activity means: following its PLAN while countenancing EXCEPTIONS.

Thus the theory says: every organized activity is described by a plan, but its actual performance can (and usually does) involve deviations from the plan.[2] Obviously, practices for the creation, management, change etc. of an

[2] Petri nets may be considered as a graphical language for the expression of plans; so can Diplan (Holt, 1997) and others.

organized activity is an organized activity itself. Within this latter, PLAN is a unit, whose criterion — of course — must be consistent with 2.3.1. This division of the reality of organized activity into plans and exceptions is of far-reaching importance. It allows us to develop precise analyses based on plans, knowing full well that "real life" is never precise.

Additional units, that relate actions and bodies, play a role in the study of organized activity — namely two types of persons: flesh-and-blood PERSONS and ORGANIZATIONAL ENTITIES — akin to "juridical persons" but more inclusive.

2.3.2 The performance of any action is driven by the INTERESTS of its performers.

2.3.3 Persons are considered to be driven by personal interests; organizational entities by organizational interests.

For a given action, the number of flesh-and-blood persons involved (and their flesh-and-blood identities) may vary from execution to execution of the same plan; it can even vary within a single execution.

3. INFORMATION

3.1 What is it?

With the help of the above we can now construct a new notion of information. To begin with we assume:

3.1.1 INFORMATION is always carried by a body (the body which carries it being called its CARRIER).

When does a body *B* carry information *J*? The form of this question suggests several matters of importance.

3.1.2 Whether body *B* carries information *J*, depends on an organized activity within which *B* has its definition.

Thus, the same physical body may carry information *J* in one organized activity context, and not in another; similarly, in different contexts it may carry different information.

3.1.3 That information — and even what information — is carried by a body can be part of the criterion of a body.

And now, the answer to the question:

3.1.4 (a) *J* is the information carried by a body *B* if and only if *J* corresponds to a state of *B*.

(b) The body in this state is operated upon in a manner which one expects of a body carrying information.

To reiterate: it is not enough that *B* have a state (which might be interpreted as information); the plan must foresee operations performed on *B* characteristic of information carriers. As far as 3.1.4(a) is concerned, any body might be interpreted as carrying information. So:

3.1.5 INFORMATION (as a unit) is the same as: a body which carries information.

3.2 Information and meaning

Claude Shannon (Shannon and Weaver, 1949), helped to develop a technical notion of "information" that is radically divorced from meaning, against the naïve conception. Our own position is quite different from his, but certainly not its opposite.

Information being plan-relative, it simply inherits its relationship to meaning from plans. So: once we understand how plans relate to meaning, we will have understood how information does.

Consider as an example the plan *C* for a game of catch: I throw, you catch; then you throw, I catch. Although this plan abstracts from many details of particular games of catch (such as the height and sex of the players) still, the criteria of *C* call for two people throwing a ball back and forth — and this last statement is part of its meaning. Now there are many other types of back-and-forth exchanges that are similar to a game of catch, yet obviously different — for example, a normal type of conversation: I transmit a message to you which you receive (analogous to throw/catch); you in your turn, transmit a message to me which I receive (catch/throw) — and so on, into the indefinite past/future. All of these — including the game of catch — can be covered by *another* plan *A*, of which *C* is a case. *A* calls for two people passing an object back-and-forth indefinitely.

So what about *A* and *C*'s relationship to meaning? Both plans call for two people (really!); both plans call for a something that is passed back and forth between them, but in *C* this something must be a ball (really!). But: although in ordinary parlance one would call *A* "more abstract" than *C*, they are — in our view — both bound to real world meanings in the same way; exactly the way in which — in our view — "information" is bound to meaning.

3.3 Information equivalence

It is enough to ask (and answer): when — relative to a plan — are two body instances equivalent (whether or not they carry information).

3.3.1 The bodies b_1 and b_2 are EQUIVALENT within a plan if and only if: for any unit B within the plan, b_1 is an instance of B if and only if b_2 is an instance of B.

Therefore:

3.3.2 Two instances of INFORMATION are equivalent within a plan if they satisfy 3.3.1.

That is about all that there is to it. Yet, to really understand this, it is necessary to internalize the idea that "information" is treated as relative to an organized activity — perhaps represented by its plan.

For example we may ask: do two ways of writing the same number "give the same information"? If the two ways of writing call for two different modes of reading, then the answer must be "no".

Lewis Carroll, in *Through the looking glass*, makes this point wonderfully:

"Can you do addition?" the White Queen asked. "What's one and one and one and one and one and one and one and one and one and one?" "I don't know," said Alice. "I lost count."

While in the set-theoretic definition of numbers the White Queen's question would be pointless (because 10 is defined essentially as the unary numeral $1 + 1 + 1 + 1 + 1 + 1 + 1 + 1 + 1 + 1$), Alice is vindicated by the present account of the use of numerals in plans, as she is by the remarks of Wittgenstein (Wittgenstein, 1956; II 3, 2) on calculations with long numerals and the surveyability of mathematical proofs:

"Now let us imagine the cardinal numbers explained as 1, 1+1, (1+1)+1, ((1+1)+1)+1, and so on. You say that the definitions introducing the figures of the decimal system are a mere matter of convenience; the calculation 703000 × 40000101 could be done in that wearisome notation too. But is that true?—'Of course it's true! I can surely write down, construct, a calculation in that notation corresponding to the calculation in the decimal notation.'—But how do I know that it corresponds to it? Well, because I have derived it from the other by a given method.—But now if I look at it again half an hour later, may it not have altered? For one cannot command a clear view of it. [...] I want to say: if you have a proof-pattern that cannot be taken in, and by a change in notation you turn it into one that can, then you are producing a proof, where there was none before."

Thus, the difference between notations is seen here, quite appropriately, not as a subjective matter related to the psychology of perception, but as a conjective fact on which is based the execution of a plan.

3.4 Commodities and information

Commodities are relevant to information because information is often packaged as a commodity, and therefore is subject to commodity-relative operations — such as trade, transfer from owner to owner, storage and (ultimately) use. Computers are used extensively to support such commodity-relative operations as applied to packages of information. It follows that computer implementation of information handling must also address commodity-relative operations, as we shall now try to illustrate concretely.

Take as an example the problem of AUTHENTICATION — a problem that: (a) is very real, especially in the context of computers; (b) makes no sense if information is deprived of its market setting; (c) is also a problem for non-informational commodities.

Why does the authentication problem exist? Because, under most modern circumstances: (a) the commodity passes through many intermediate hands so variable with time and user location, that the user cannot keep track of the intermediaries; (b) there are many possible producers, ingredients, and methods for any given commodity as it presents itself to the user. Thus:

3.4.1 The package of the commodity may carry features which identify the producer and/or the ingredients and/or the methods of production. These latter we shall call IDENTITY FEATURES of the commodity.

3.4.2 User and producer — who after all depend on each other — are interested in binding the identity features to the contents so that: (a) the binding can be performed without a lot of expense and trouble; (b) a potential criminal would find tampering with this binding too expensive to be worth the trouble.

3.4.3 The identity features should make it easy for the user to contact the producer, or to judge if the ingredients and methods suit his purposes.

Computers were never designed to facilitate the binding of identity features to information packages (3.4.2); nor were they designed to ease the use of identity features in allowing the user (of information) to contact its producer (3.4.3).

3.5 Operations characteristic of information

We have seen in 3.1.4(b) that a defining feature of information is the set of operations that can be performed on a body that carries information. These are of the following three kinds:

3.5.1 MATHEMATICAL TRANSFORMATIONS, of the sort used in logic, copying and coding.

3.5.2 DECISIONS, like those needed to answer questions like "is the variable *x* greater than 0?" or "To what place should this letter be sent?"

3.5.3 CONVERSIONS, like those performed in operating numerically controlled machines, or in producing visual images from computer programs.

While mathematical transformations produce information out of information (except for copying from a medium to another one, in which case one should rather speak of a conversion), decisions take information as input and produce actions. On the other hand, conversions normally rely on peripherals (for typing and display) and can be regarded as special kinds of decisions, because they rely essentially upon them. We shall not dwell in detail upon these operations, but illustrate here the kind of problems that arise in connection with two especially important examples, namely copying and deciding.

While it is true that many physical objects (such as houses) can be copied, copying is particularly effective (mechanizable, and therefore made fast and cheap) in the case of information. In all copy operations — whether of information or of houses — there is an "original" which is not destroyed as input, and one or more "copies" which are produced as output, of the copy operation. The framework for a theory of organized activity set up above naturally raises the question: does one copy a unit or a realization of a unit? We assert: only units can be copied (or transmitted), and not realizations.

As an illustration of how the argument runs, consider copying a document page by means of a fax. Since bits are units, so is a bit stream. There is no doubt, therefore, that a new instance of the stream of bits created in a fax sender can be recreated in a fax receiver. But a stream of bits — no matter how many they are — can at best specify a unit of which the document page is a realization. Therefore, the page to be transmitted will certainly have properties that the stream of bits will not characterize. Assume that we produce the page with a machine that exercises dimensional control over the characters beyond the capabilities of normal fax printers. Suppose, further, that use is made of this dimensional control to encode a secret message that does not depend on the character content of the page. The meaningful "information" on such a page obviously cannot be transmitted by fax. Now, it is enough to get a fax with finer resolution, so we can put the message on a page over which it is possible to exercise humidity control; the degree of humidity is not encoded. Could it be theoretically? Yes. But we claim that it is not theoretically possible to list in advance *all* properties that might matter, so that these too can be encoded.

And now deciding: it is a fundamentally important reason for the intimate tie between information and organized activity; it is also an important part of the reason why computers are so crucially important to our society.

We will call an action a DECISION if one of its consequences is choosing one of several possible next actions — whatever other consequences there may be. A decision always resolves a choice between several next action alternatives. Thus a restaurant customer, on reading the menu (input information) does not — technically speaking — choose between steak and lobster, but chooses to order steak, or to order lobster. As in the case of all actions, decisions take effort (on the part of some actor), and they require one or more packages of information as input. Decision is an end use of information; a decision may or may not consume its informational inputs. Whether something is, or is not, a package of information that enters a decision may depend on relatively sophisticated considerations — as illustrated by the following contrastive examples.

At some point in time, a door is locked, or left open. After this, actor *X* comes by.

a) *X* may push on the door: if the door is not locked, *X* goes through; if the door is locked, *X* is prevented from advancing;
b) *X* may try the door to decide whether it is, or is not, locked; choose his next action accordingly.

In case a) the state of the door is not informational (relative to *X*); in case b), it is.

As a (somewhat) elaborate illustration, suppose *A* in city *X* sends a letter to *B* in city *Y*. *A* puts the letter in a mailbox. The letter is an information package. At the first step — that of transporting the letter from the mailbox to the post office, all of the information that the letter carries exercises no influence. At the next step a rough-sort of letters takes place according to general destination. At this stage a part of the address on the envelope contributes to a decision; the rest of the address (name and street address of recipient) and the content continue to have no influence. The mail delivery person decides on how to handle this letter based on the rest of the address which, at this stage, is input to his decision; the recipient who opens the letter and reads it, uses the informational content of the letter in some combination of ways which is hard to specify. The sender's address and the cancellation stamp affixed by the post office may serve to control the letter source, and the time of its mailing. If this becomes necessary, they too will be input to decisions made at a later time.

At the dawn of modern science, a French schoolman, Jean Buridan, took a serious look at human decision, in the form of the following question:

> If a hungry man be placed at equal distance from two equally attractive dishes, will he starve to death?

Contrary to common sense, Buridan thought the right answer was "yes" (he would starve to death). As we read his answer, it should be taken to mean:

- The choice of dish should depend on the two dishes, and on nothing else.
- In all relevant respects, the two dishes are assumed the same.

- Therefore, given that the hungry man only looks at the two dishes, the combination offers him no information on the basis of which to make a choice (make a decision) — and a decision cannot be made without information, the very same assumption that we make.

We want to emphasize that decisions taken in the context of a computer program are not the same as decisions taken by persons. For example: a person may, in the eyes of others, make a wrong decision; others will decide that his error was due to inattention, willful sabotage, etc., and he will be reprimanded, or otherwise punished, accordingly; a computer program is not judged in the same way, nor will the computer program be reprimanded or punished. Nevertheless, everything we have said above applies with equal force to decisions carried out by persons pursuant to their roles, or decisions carried out in programs on behalf, and under the responsibility, of some actor.

4. RELATED WORK AND CONCLUSIONS

The organizational theory of information sketched here has several points in common with the work described in the FRISCO report (Falkenberg et al., 1998): in particular, it aims at the same thing by related means; yet there are fundamental differences that are worth stressing. Both approaches emphasize the need for a general philosophical outlook, but a first divergence appears already in the choice of the subject matter: while information systems are the defining concern of the FRISCO project, we believe that 'system' is not necessary to the analysis of information. Rather, the place of systems in our approach is held by organized activities that, as we have suggested, are the environment in which most naturally information is produced and consumed. Also the theory of information described in the FRISCO report points, though implicitly, to a theory of organized activity — via the definition of such terms as *organisational system*, *actor* (as a responsible *thing*), *goal*. In fact, the conceptual framework of the theory of organized activity overlaps to a large extent with that of the FRISCO report, though the underlying ontological assumptions seem to differ substantially. For example, "social reality" is construed there as the result of communicating (representations of) *conceptions* that are based on individual cognitive activity (Falkenberg et alii, 1998; Assumption [h]). For us, organized activity underlies the formation of units, which in their turn, *create* the conjective world. (Observe that even the term 'inter-subjectivity', used in FRISCO with a meaning often similar to that of 'conjectivity', implies a prior understanding of 'subjectivity', while conjectivity claims to be a primary fact — more basic than either objectivity or subjectivity.)

Because of this more operational attitude, our views are perhaps closer to the position of Stamper, sketched in (Falkenberg et alii, 1998) and in related publications (Stamper, 1985, 1996). He emphasizes the social aspects of information systems, and its ontology, uses Gibson's notion of *affordance*, an invariant repertoire of behavior, that seems to have a conjective flavor. Social affordances, those that make up social reality, arise then as the invariants of organized behavior. Also, his proposal to root the study of information in the notion of *sign* seems to make signs similar to the units of the theory of organized activity sketched above.

Another far-reaching alternative to traditional theories of information is that described in (Goguen, 1996), where the prominence given to the social (and ethical) aspects of information is accompanied by the recourse to concepts and techniques taken from the social sciences, in particular ethnomethodology. There, the slant on conjectivity shows up in the need for a social semiotics, as opposed to the traditional logical semiotics that lies behind either the statistical theory of information (Shannon and Weaver, 1949) or descriptive theories based on model-theoretic semantics, like (Barwise, Perry, 1983) and (Barwise, Seligman, 1998). (This is also a main concern in (Stamper, 1996), appearing in the upper levels of his "Semiological Ladder" and motivating the fundamental role played by the concept of a *norm* in his account of information systems.)

A leading unifying theme in all these views is a natural consequence of the fact that information is always situated in a group involved in an organized activity of some kind: namely that *responsibility* enters the processing of information. The members of such a group are responsible for maintaining the criteria for judging whether something is an example of some unit (Holt, 1997); signs have to be interpreted by someone, who becomes responsible for that interpretation (Stamper, 1996); the members of the group are held *accountable* for the interpretation of signs as describing an item of information, as for the *Principle of Accountability* in (Goguen, 1996), derived from ethnomethodology.[3]

This paper has focused mainly on those aspects of the theory of organized activity and of information that may be useful to information system designers, rather than users. The concepts that the present theory helps to formulate can, however, also be applied by system users in many cases of practical interest. In particular, there is a theory of hierarchies (and classifications) based on the first principles of the theory of organized activity, that relates *bodies* with *interests*, and provides a new view of the organization of computer storage. There are other delicate topics in the study of information that we haven't directly addressed in this paper. Notably, all

[3] A closer investigation of this discipline is needed in order to see whether the notions of *category* and *method* used there are coextensive with those of *unit* and *criterion*.

uses of information in *documents* (especially contracts) are of great importance for computer applications used in banking and electronic commerce. In part these uses are accounted for by viewing information as a resource, and by putting it in the framework of an economic process, but a smoother treatment of these problems needs a detailed study that will be pursued elsewhere.

5. REFERENCES

Barwise, J., Perry, J.: *Situations and Attitudes*, MIT Press, Cambridge (Mass.), 1983.

Barwise, J., Seligman, J.: *Information Flow*, Cambridge University Press, Cambridge (UK), 1998.

Diamond, C.: *Wittgenstein's Lectures on the Foundations of Mathematics, Cambridge 1939*, The University of Chicago Press, Chicago and London, 1976.

Falkenberg et alii: *A Framework of Information System Concepts*, 1998. Web edition available at: ftp.leidenuniv.nl/pub/rul/fri-full.zip.

Goguen, J. A.: Towards a social, ethical theory of information, in *Social Science Research, Technical Systems and Cooperative Work: Beyond the Great Divide*, edited by G. Bowker, L. Gasser, L. Star and W. Turner, Erlbaum, 1997, pp. 27–56.

Holt, A. W.: *Organized Activity and Its Support by Computer*, Kluwer Academic Publishers, Dordrecht, Boston and London, 1997.

Kripke, S. A.: *Wittgenstein on Rules and Private Language*, Basil Blackwell, Oxford, 1982.

Malinowski, B.: The problem of meaning in primitive languages, Supplement I to: Ogden, C.K. and Richards, I. A., *The Meaning of Meaning*, Harcourt, Brace and Jovanovich, San Diego, New York and London, 1923.

Mauss, M.: *Sociologie et anthropologie*, Presses Universitaires de France, 1950. (A collection of essays, including *Esquisse d'une théorie générale de la magie*, 1902–3, and *Essai sur le don: Forme et raison de l'échange dans les sociétés archaïques*, 1923–4.)

Shannon, C., Weaver, W.: *The Mathematical Theory of Communications*, University of Illinois Press, 1949.

Stamper, R. K.: A logic of social norms, for the semantics of business information, in *Knowledge and Data*, edited by T. Steel and R. Meersmann, North-Holland, 1985.

Stamper, R. K.: Signs, Information, Norms and Systems, in *Signs at Work*, edited by B. Holmqvist, P. B. Andersen, H. Klein and R. Posner, De Gruyter, 1996.

Trubeckoj, N. S.: *Grundzüge der Phonologie*, Travaux du Cercle Linguistique de Prague, VII, 1939; Vandenhoeck & Ruprecht, Göttingen, 1958^2.

Wittgenstein, L.: *Bemerkungen über die Grundlagen der Mathematik*, edited by G. H. von Wright, R. Rhees and G. E. M. Anscombe, Basil Blackwell, Oxford, 1956. English translation by G. E. M. Anscombe.

Comments on "An Organizational Theory of Information" by A.W. Holt and F. Cardone

Ronald K. Stamper

MEASURE Ltd, 29 Dartmouth Road Park, London NW5 1SU
Tel: +44 0207 813 7359 Fax: +44 0207 ***482 2968***
Email: rstamper@compuserve.com
University of Twente, P.O. Box 217, NL-7500 AE Enschede
Email: ***r.k.stamper@sms.utwente.nl***

This paper is rather tough reading. Like FRISCO Chapter 4, it is dense, abstract and somewhat formal. The reader is advised to populate its abstractions with concrete instances. It would also be interesting to visit the corpus of raw material that inspired this approach to information systems. The authors have an abundance of varied practical experience to draw upon. One can often appreciate a theory better when its roots are visible, at least this guides one's choice of concrete illustrations.

Its style forces the reader to take a personal route into its meaning. For me, that route lies naturally enough through my semiotic framework. Every information system that functions successfully must be functioning on each of these levels. (See Section 6.1 of the FRISCO Report.) Thus, one way of interpreting this paper is to check how it handles each level.

Cardone and Holt begin with the *physical level.* The theory is grounded upon the notion of Organised Activity, OA, which developed among our biological ancestors, preceding language.

Thus they provide us with an escape from the circularity of verbal definitions. Information and its phenomena can be brought into empirical relationships with aspects of OA.

In the original version of their paper, the version I was invited to discuss, they go rather too far, in my opinion, in relating information to physical phenomena, when they claim information as a commodity. But information is fundamentally unlike goods that may be scarce commodities. For a trivial cost in material resources, any information can be reproduced. Information is only like a good and in limited supply when we conjure it to be so by means of the laws creating copyrights, patents, etc. This observation breaks the syllogism leading them from information being a commodity *plus* "all goods call crimes into existence" to the problem of the misuse of information. The same conclusion is reached directly if one adopts Eco's definition of a sign (and therefore information) as anything with which one can tell a lie. Information is the instrument for making and manipulating the social domain (=OA?), hence its value as a criminal instrument.

The authors capture a key to the *empirics* level neatly. By their assertion that OA always entails co-ordination and repetition. Co-ordination can only occur when there is some communication channel linking the co-ordinated elements. The central problems of empirics concern the transmission of signals through channels. This notion of co-ordination takes us further than the familiar model of

source > encoder > channel > decoder > receiver

because it forces us into an awareness of the completion of the cycle of transmission, if only via an observer. Within that transmission cycle, the empirical study of the properties of signs requires one to count the frequencies of the tokens sent and received, and their random transformations (= lack of co-ordination). The existence of countable sign-tokens is only possible when they are recognisably repeated forms falling into a classification. Hence, I am content that their conceptual framework is sufficient for this level of analysis.

They capture the core ideas of the *syntactic* level in at least two ways. Neatest of them is illustrated by the White Queen metaphor. Alice is confronted with syntactic alternatives for integers. On the semantic level they are the same. On the syntactic level they are different, as Alice indignantly points out. The thread of a syntactic invariant links them together and that link is a suitable notion of validity, preserved by deductive rules.

The basis of the *semantic* properties of information is rooted the authors' notions of a unit and the relations of *realisations*, *cases*, *parts* and so on. These enable the universal / particular, the generic / specific and the part / whole structures to be developed. The production and consumption processes and the changes of state are handled in the spirit of classical physics without addressing the problem of explaining how we know of the connections between past and present, except through the use of information. Here, I think too much is taken for granted.

Pragmatics concerns intentional commitments, which are treated by the authors in terms of authentication. They emphasise the importance of identifying the communication, the maker and the receiver. Their notion of a plan also relates to pragmatics but this is embedded in the notion of the conceptual units, especially those constituting our social reality. Information, in their analysis, has to be understood in its context, a key component of which is the social activity and its associated plan. This is an excellent way of making sure (transformed into my perspective) that we insist that any phenomenon that embodies information must function correctly on every level of the semiotic framework. Eco's definition of a sign similarly captures its essence at the pragmatic level.

The *social* level constituted from the organised activity basis to this theory is the central idea. Language games are recognised as instruments for creating the 'units' in which the world is conceived. However, I am not convinced that "every organized activity is described by a plan". This would rule out those organised patterns of activity that are performed without conscious planning but express the norms which a community has evolved for those activities, such as those regulating behaviour in a crowded shopping centre, for example. If the plans do not have to be conscious, then perhaps they equate with norms.

My few remarks cannot begin to capture these authors' many challenges to our views and theories about information. The absence of the notion of a 'sign' is notable and was a subject of long discussions during the conference. I suspect that, once I can reinterpret their theory of organised activity in terms of norms and signs, I shall discover many more congruencies than conflicts. I recommend other readers to bring to this serious work their own co-ordinate frameworks, not necessarily mine.

A Semiotic Approach to the Design of Agent-mediated E-commerce Systems

Samuel Chong and Kecheng Liu

School of Computing, Staffordshire University, Beaconside, Stafford ST18 0DG

Key words: E-commerce, Agents, Agent communication language, Organisational semiotics, Semantic analysis, Norm analysis

Abstract: The emergence of the Internet and electronic commerce (or e-commerce) has opened up a new dimension for conducting business. Incorporating agent technology into e-commerce systems has brought even more potential to the improvement of efficiency and effectiveness of business systems. While the work and technology of agent-mediated e-commerce starts to benefit the industry and economy, much research in the theory, methods and technologies is needed to achieve the return of value of e-commerce in a larger scale. In agent-mediated e-commerce systems, issues such as the delegation of authorities from a human user to a machine agent need to be dealt with. Also, for agents to communicate with one another, there is a need for techniques for specifying a common vocabulary of terms to be used.

This paper presents a semiotic approach to evaluating and addressing these problems. It presents a set of methods for the design of agent-mediated e-commerce systems. A case study of an online bookstore is described to demonstrate how the design of an agent-mediated e-commerce system can be conducted using the semiotic approach. The approach offers a way of identifying the information that should be shared by agents. It also offers a method to represent and handle propositional attitudes and make explicit link between the attitudes and intentions, beliefs, perceptions, acts and values.

1. INTRODUCTION

Electronic commerce (or e-commerce) is already considered to be a multi-billion dollar industry, as the emergence of e-commerce has brought in a new and effective means of conducting business and reaching potential customers.

New paradigms and theories of business have provided frameworks for conceiving and designing e-commerce systems, such as virtual organisation (Mowshowitz, 1997) and distributed enterprise (Liu *et al.*, 1999). Emerging technologies such as software agents have enabled the implementation of these systems, especially the agent mediated e-commerce systems. These systems have their special features because they have direct impact on the business processes and practices within an organisation, and they are open systems interacting with a broad range of users. Methods and techniques for e-commerce systems development therefore are needed to cope with these features.

The uniqueness of agent-mediated e-commerce makes it complex to use existing requirements analysis methods. For example, an agent has roles and intentions and we need a formal method that is able to specify that. Our research adopts the semiotic framework and semiotic methods for requirements analysis and systems design for agent-mediated e-commerce.

In section 2, agents and e-commerce and the problems of agent-mediated e-commerce will be discussed. Section 3 and 4 discuss the theoretical foundations such as organisational semiotics and speech act theory. The former is to be adopted for critical analysis of agent communication; while the latter serves as a conceptual ground for current work and future development of agent communication languages. In section 4, we evaluate a widely used agent communication language, KQML, using the semiotic framework. We also look at the inadequacy of KQML to be used in an agent-mediated electronic commerce setting. Section 5 presents the semiotic methods for the design of an agent-mediated e-commerce system with an illustration of a case study. This section also highlights the possibility of identifying the internal mental states of agents such as beliefs and intentions using norm analysis. Section 6 summaries the work and indicates some directions for further work.

2. AGENTS AND E-COMMERCE

In this section, an introduction of e-commerce and agents will be given. The main objective is to identify the problems in designing an agent-mediated e-commerce system.

2.1 Electronic Commerce

E-commerce has been defined as the ability to share a wide range of communiqué and data with trading partners (Adams, 1994).The components that make up e-commerce could be the Internet, the e-mail networks such as MCI Mail, Compuserve, groupware systems such as LotusNotes , Wordperfect Office and many others (Adams, 1994). Some of the technologies that make up e-commerce are Electronic Data Interchange (EDI), bar coding, fax, imaging and smart cards (Spence, 1994). Business data sent in e-commerce consist of both structured and unstructured data such as electronic memos send via e-mail (Fisher, 1996).

E-commerce is emerging as an important avenue for companies to reach their prospective buyers in the world of business today. One reason for its attractiveness is its low cost (Lederer, *et al.,* 1996). It is having and will continue to have a dramatic impact on business into the 21st century (Hornback, 1995). E-commerce can be seen as an important means for companies to implement business strategies. In this aspect, productivity, cash flow can be increased, inventory can be decreased and relationships with customers can be enhanced (Boynton, 1994).

The fast emerging technologies have widened the scopes of electronic commerce. When the scopes expand, there is also an increased need for agents to support the processes. Agents-mediated electronic commerce needs to interpret a wider range of meanings. Kimbrough & Moore (1997) called this 'the requirement for expressive felicity'. This means that the semantic meanings in the interaction between different parties or agents in an electronic commerce setting needs to be sent and encoded in an unambiguous way. The next section will discuss the definition of agency and their workings.

2.2 Definition of Agency and Agents

One of the most influential researches in Agency theory is due to the work of Cohen and Levesque (1990a, 1990b). Their contributions have been used to develop a theory of intention (as in 'I intent to..'), which forms the pre-requisite for applying the theory of speech acts (Searle, 1969).

The fundamental aspect of agency theories is the delegation of duties and responsibilities to a person or machine whom we call an *Agent*. It is almost impossible to know where to look for things when we need it, especially information that is available across global computer networks. Therefore agents are created to help us find information that we need as quickly as possible.

Over the past years, there has been a lot of interest in agent systems (Shoham, 1993). There is an increased need for agents to support both customers and suppliers in electronic commerce. "Agents are important because they let software components interoperate within modern applications like electronic commerce" (Singh, 1998). However, it is not easy to reach a common consensus on the definition of agents. As with object technology a decade ago, it is difficult for anyone to agree even on the basic question of what an agent is (Nwana and Wooldridge, 1996). According to Finin *et al.* (1997), anything might qualify as an agent these days. Several definitions coexist and each definition has different emphasis on the properties of agents. The definitions found in Michael *et al.* (1994), Shoham (1997) and Hayes-Roth (1995) are some examples. There are a lot more definitions on agents. Each definition specifies different properties that an agent should have.

Many authors defines agents as software entities, which we think is inappropriate. Though agents are normally software entities, hardware devices and humans may also be seen as agents, if they act on someone else's behalf, with proper delegation and authorisation. Generally speaking, an agent acts on the behalf of someone else who has the right to delegate their job functions to agents, without transferring their responsibilities. We define an agent as follows, which will be used in our work:

An agent is a software entity, hardware device or human, that have been delegated job functions and limited authorities from someone else, and is within or part of an environment that senses on that environment and have the ability to react on the environment or cooperate with other agents to reach a common goal, based on its internal state.

2.3 Problems in Agent-Mediated E-commerce

In a collaborative system, people have responsibilities and commitments, some of which can be delegated to machine agents in many roles, which then perform actions, interacting with other agents on the user's behalf (Liu and Dix, 1997). The first problem here is that agent designers tend to develop agent applications without a clear distinction between the responsibilities and roles of agents. There is also lack of techniques to determine the responsibilities of the machine agents delegated by the human users. As a result, agent designers find it hard to specify the unique intentions and beliefs of an agent at a higher level. There are currently no formal methods that designers can use for these tasks.

Another key issue in agent-mediated e-commerce is the shared meanings of the terms and concepts used in a business domain. Agents need to share a common vocabulary of the terms for their communication to be effective.

There is not enough attention been given on this area, though some work addresses this problems, for example, Ontolingua (Gruber, 1991). A metaphor to use is to imagine two workers trying to build a computer. They must share the same understanding of the terms such as "hard disk", "CPU", "mother board", etc. Only then will their communication gain value.

There are many other problems such as security issues, interoperability issues and language compatibility in e-commerce, though they will not be addressed in this paper.

3. ORGANISATIONAL SEMIOTICS FOR ANALYSING AGENTS BEHAVIOUR

3.1 Organisational Semiotics

The organisational semiotics approach is helpful in dealing with the problems we intend to address. It is derived from semiotics, the study of signs, human communication and meanings (Pierce 1931/35, Locke, 1960). The organisational semiotic framework (Stamper, 1998), provides guidance of information analysis at six layers: *Physical, Empirics, Syntatic, Semantic, Pragmatic and Social layers*. The framework offers the aspects that are required for designing agent applications in both technical and human dimensions. As Stamper (1998) puts it, "the semiotic framework serves as a basic checklist for every information system problems, for if the system do not function correctly on every level of the framework, it will fail to deliver value".

Interaction of information at a technical dimension includes the agent application being able to provide accurate and reliable physical signals at the *physical* layer. Then at the *empirics* layer, when transmitting the signals across the network, noise must not make the signals equivocal. When we have reliable signs, the receiving agent across the network can then build elaborate and formal structures at the *syntactic* layer.

The human and social dimensions of the framework helps agent designers to analyse business processes at a business level rather than at a technology level. This level of the semiotic framework is concerned with how signs are used for communicating meanings, intentions and also the effect through the usage of signs. It views the communication of agents in a social context. Firstly, meaningful signs at the *semantics* layer are created by agents based on the formal structure formed at the syntactic layer. With meaningful signs, agents can then express their intentions and beliefs at the *pragmatic* layer. It can also interpret other agents' intentions and beliefs. The resulting communication then creates a commitment, judgement, expectation, beliefs and so on at the *social* layer. The semiotic framework can be used as a guidebook for agent designers to broaden their understanding of the signs that will be generated at different layers which will contribute to effective communication between agents. It will also aid in requirements studies of agent applications. The semantic analysis method has the potential to be used for such requirements studies in the design of agent applications, which will be discussed in more detail in the next section.

3.2 The Semiotic Methods

Semantic analysis has been developed as a method for systems requirements analysis. Semantic analysis is a process of finding the meanings of the problem at a business level and expresses them in a graphical form called a semantic model. The method of semantic analysis studies the repertoires of behavior for requirements elicitation and representation (Liu, 2000).

3.2.1 Semantic analysis to identify shared meaning

As mentioned, agents need to create meaningful signs at the *semantics* layer. For other agents to be able to interpret the meaning of that sign, they must have a common understanding of that sign. For example, in human communication, a shared vocabulary is needed for that communication to gain its value. Likewise, all agents involve in a communication should have a common understanding of the terms used. This vocabulary is called an Ontology (Gruber, 1991), though we think it is more appropriate to be called conceptual models or semantic models. A semantic model is a conceptualization of a subject domain. With semantic models in place, agent designers can be informed of the vocabularies and terms that is available for communicating with other agents and the meanings that are ascribed to them.

Tools for conceptual modelling of agent systems such as the Ontolingua (Gruber, 1991) and ZEUS (Collis & Lee 1998; Collis *et al.* 1998) are already being developed. However, they are simply tools for representation and do not provide a formal ground for domain clarity. They are inadequate in conceptualization of a domain at a business level. Agent designers need to be able to specify the domain from a business level rather than at the development level. The resulting semantic model from the semantic analysis enables designers to build a conceptual model of that domain where meaning of the term and the dependency between each term are formally defined. Designers can then use an implementation language such as Ontolingua to translate the conceptual model into an execution format in a seamless transition. Semantic analysis also helps designers to identify agents and the roles they play.

3.2.2 Semantic analysis to identify roles of agents

When agents function together, they negotiate with one another to determine the best course of actions in a particular context. Negotiation involves the ability to express its intentions, deduce what is being communicated and interpret the intentions of other agents at the *pragmatic* layer. The interpreted intention then creates a commitment or belief at the *social* layer. Agent communication language therefore must be flexible enough to accommodate such negotiations. However, such flexibility will make it difficult to determine the semantic meanings of a communication. To facilitate such ability, agent designers have to promote internal mental states in agents. Singh (1998) suggest that this internal state includes:

- beliefs- determines what an agent imagines its world state to be
- goals- describes what states an agent would prefer
- desires- describes the agent's preferences
- intentions- determines the goals and desires of the agents

Semantic analysis enables agent designers to specify the roles of agents. When roles are determined, it is not difficult for agent designers to analyse the internal states of an agent during norm analysis, which is another method in the semiotic approach.

3.2.3 Norm analysis to specify intentions and beliefs of agents

Norm analysis is used for studying an organisation from the perspective of agents' behavior which are governed by norms (Liu, 2000). When agents behave in an organised way with certain regularities, they are known as norms. Norm analysis is normally carried out based on the resulting semantic model from semantic analysis. The semantic model describes the primary area of concerns surrounding an agent application. The pattern of behavior such as the ontological relationship between agents and actions are part of the fundamental norms. Normally, norm have the following structure (Stamper, 1998):

IF condition **THEN** subject attitude consequent

When a *condition* is met, it will lead the *subject* (agents) of that norm to adopt a certain attitude towards some *consequent* (a reference to something). The attitude is reflected in a speech act or a situation which results in a disposition in one's internal state of the world. By specifying norms, agent designers can specify the intentions, beliefs, expectations etc. of agents, depending on the different roles that they play. For example, consider the following norms:

IF one throws an apple up, **THEN** one will expect that it will fall down.
IF one say "It is too expensive", **THEN** his intention is to hope that the price can be lowered down.
IF one makes a commitment to sell an item at a price **THEN** he is obliged to do so.
IF two persons are declared married, **THEN** they are recognised as husband and wife.

In the first example, the norm reveals that there is an expectation or belief from an agent. In the second example, an agent is revealing an intention. In the third example, an agent is obliged to do something that he had promised. In the fourth example, an agent has a status that is acknowledged by others. Stamper *et al.* (2000) suggests there are a number of categories of norms. Norms govern humans to behave in a certain way in perceiving, recognising and assessing things, which are perceptual, cognitive and evaluative norms. Norms are also associated with power, based on which one can make decisions or delegate duties (Krogh & Herrestad, 1996). In an agent-mediated e-commerce system, norms are important because they help agent designers to identify the attitudes that agents will adopt. These attitudes in turn reveal the beliefs, intentions and goals of an agent, which are so important to facilitate the internal states in agents. Table 1 shows the type of disposition of an agent that can be revealed simply by studying the norms and the attitude that agents will adopt:

Attitudes	**Disposition**
Know, expect, imagine, think, suppose, assume, believe, convinced, conclude……	*Beliefs*
Aim to, plan to, intent to, mean to, plead, to persuade, want to……	*Intentions*
Like, deplore, hope for, desire, dislike, hate, disgusted……	*Values*
Be obliged to, be permitted to, be forbidden to, be indebted to, be bound to, be prohibited to, entitled to……	*Acts*
Acknowledge, deem, recognise, admit, declare, proclaim……	*Perception*

Table 1. Dispositions that can be revealed by attitudes of agents

4. FOUNDATION FOR AGENCY AND COMMUNICATIONS

4.1 Speech Act Theory (SAT)

Work in the area of language and communication has emphasised on the role of inference and context. Following the publication of Austin's (1962) 'How to Do Thing with Words', the speech act theory has been developed by Searle (1969). It has been further developed and used continually by linguist, philosophers, psychologist and cognitive scientist alike (Kimbrough & Moore 1997). The strength of the theory lies in its ability to classify each sentence or utterance into its corresponding act.

To illustrate the theory, consider the following example:
If John were to say:
"I promise to give you ten dollars tomorrow"
John had made a promise by the words that he used. The promise was made according to the choice of words that he used. The context which the words are used also makes a difference. Consider the following sentence:
"There's a tiger in the jungle"

- Under the context of describing the jungle, that sentence is a statement or assertion.
- However, if you tell me that you intend to take a short cut through the jungle, then under this context, that sentence is a warning.
- If you tell me that you are going hunting, that sentence then becomes a piece of advice or suggestion.

Communication languages tend to be based on speech act theory. The best known work on agent communication language is that by the APRA knowledge effort (Patil *et al.*, 1992). This work has been devoted to developing KQML, which will be discussed next.

4.2 Knowledge Query and Manipulation Language (KQML)

KQML is a communication language designed for software agents to exchange high level information and knowledge. It was conceived both as a message format and a message-handling protocol to support run-time knowledge sharing among agents (Finin *et al.*, 1997). KQML is an evolving standard Agent Communication Language.

The communication function of KQML is divided into three layers: the content, message and communication layer as shown in figure 1.

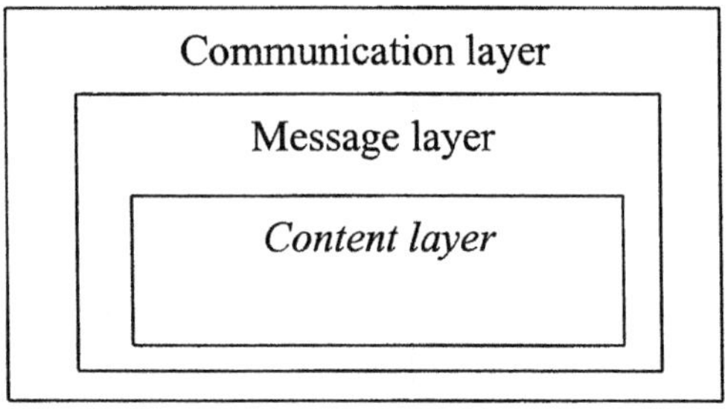

Figure 1. An abstract view of the KQML language (Nwana and Wooldridge, 1996)

4.2.1 Communication layer

The communication layer is based on the current network technology such as TCPIP, HTTP etc. It encodes low level parameters for communication such as specifying the sender and receiver of a message, the message ID (e.g. *in-reply-to*) and a unique identifier of a particular speech act. However, sometimes the communication will not involve network usage. Such communication occurs when agents reside in the same machine.

4.2.2 Content layer

The content layer specifies the intended content of the message expressed in a certain language and ontology. The ontology here refers to a shared vocabulary of terms. KQML is indifferent to the format of the content. In fact, the KQML standard itself has nothing to say about this. Therefore, a KQML content could be expressed in Prolog code, C code, Java code, KIF, SQL, LISP or whatsoever language, as long as it is ASCII representable.

4.2.3 Message layer

The message layer forms the core of KQML language. This layer of abstraction tells the receiver what actions should be executed. Most of the elements, called performatives, are used to communicate attitudes about information. There are 36 performatives and they can be classified into nine main categories which are shown in table 2. This layer also specifies the protocol for transmitting the message and the content. By protocol, we mean the rules that must be used when agents initiate an exchange and maintaining that exchange. There are several protocols in KQML (Nwana and Wooldridge, 1996).

Category	Reserved performative names
Basic informational performatives	tell, deny, untell, cancel
Basic query performatives	evaluate, reply, ask-if, ask-about, ask-one, ask-all, sorry
Multi-response query performatives	stream-about, stream-all
Basic effector performatives	achieve, unachieve
Generator performatives	standby, ready, next, rest, discard, generator
Capability definition performatives	advertise
Notification performatives	subscribe, monitor
Networking performatives	register, unregister, forward, broadcast, pipe, break
Facilitation performatives	broker-one, broker-all, recommend-one, recommend-all, recruit-one, recruit-all

Table 2. Performatives of KQML

4.2.4 Performatives

Besides being a message carrier, the main function of a performative is to say something about that message. It informs the receiver whether a message is a question, assertion of a fact, an answer, request, or a denial to a previous question. The protocol is also specified in the performative (e.g. what response is required? A single answer or a series of answer, an instant response to a question or a delayed answer but a guaranteed one?)

4.3 Evaluation of KQML using Organisational Semiotics

As KQML is still an evolving standard ACL, there will inevitably be some shortcomings in it. Organisational semiotics (Stamper, 1998) provides a powerful approach for us to evaluate KQML. In this section, KQML will be evaluated using the upper three layers of the semiotic framework and its shortcomings will be discussed. The lower three levels will not be considered as they are more concerned with the physical properties of signs, how signs are organised and transmitted and how signs are structured and used in language. The focus of this evaluation is on the use of KQML to communicate meanings, to communicate intentions and the social effects through the use of KQML.

Firstly, let us consider the *semantic* level of the semiotic framework. For a successful communication to take place, the people involved in that communication must have a common semantic meaning of the terms that are used. KQML, like all programming languages, does not have a formal and precise semantic meaning of the performatives. The only way to describe the intended semantic meanings of the performatives and their use are currently restricted to natural language descriptions (Finin, 1997). As a result, agent designers do not have a common understanding of the language, its performatives and protocol. Cohen and Levesque (1995) expressed this concern by stating that agent designers cannot be certain whether the same interpretation that they give to a performative can be unambiguously understood by other designers.

Secondly, at the *pragmatic* level, intentions, beliefs, etc. can be communicated with the existence of a shared body of knowledge or meanings at the *semantic* level. Since no one is clear how to give the performatives a precise definition at the semantic level, intention and beliefs cannot be communicated unambiguously at the pragmatic level. For example, the interpretation that a designer gives to the ask-one performative may be different from the interpretation of another designer, which will then cause confusion. It is therefore not possible to determine whether any agent application is KQML compliant. As Singh (1998) puts it, "if you cannot determine compliance, that standard is useless".

When intentions can be unambiguously communicated at the pragmatic level, it creates a commitment or belief at the *Social* level. However, due to a lack of performatives in KQML, designers cannot create the kind of beliefs that he intend the receiving agent to have. The following section in this paper also argues that KQML misses a few important classes of performatives.

Singh (1998) states that there are seven main categories of communicative acts:

Assertives- the speaker informs or states a fact and he is committed to the truth of that fact. Example: "It is hot"

Directives- the speaker attempts to get the recipient to do something for instance request, ask, and command. Example: "Open the door".

Commissives- the speaker is committed to a certain course of actions that was uttered. Example: "I promise to go home before 5.00pm"

Permissives- the speaker gives permission for the recipient to do an act. Example: "You may go".

Prohibitives- the speaker bans the recipient to do an act. Example: "You may not leave the office before 5.00pm"

Declaratives- the speaker attempts to alter the external status of an object or circumstance and cause event solely by uttering the act. Example: "I declare you husband and wife".

Expressives- the speaker expresses emotions and physchological attitude about a state of affairs. Example: "Thank you for coming".

First of all, before evaluating whether the performatives in KQML are adequate for use in an agent-mediated e-commerce system, let us consider the basic phases that will be involved in a simple deal in e-commerce. There are four basic phases (see figure 2), which form a co-ordinated process between two agents, the buyer and the supplier. In the first phase, the buyer requests for some products or services from the supplier. In the second phase, the buyer and supplier negotiate on the terms of the deal such as delivery dates, prices and so on. In the third phase, the supplier commits on the deal, for instance the prices and performs the work. In the fourth phase, the supplier has to provide support of their products to the buyer. These four phases give a very general description of a business deal. One does not have to take all the four phases to complete a deal. In an actual business deal, there may be more phases like raising a purchasing order, sending an invoice and so on. But these are the four main ones. Table 3 shows the associated speech acts in these phases.

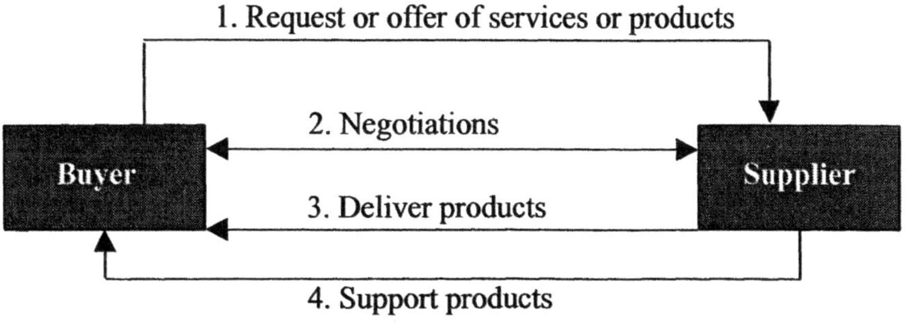

Figure 2. The main phases of a deal in electronic commerce

To illustrate the inadequacy of the performatives in KQML, we want to particularly comment on phase two. At the end of a negotiation process, the seller may promise to sell the products at a price that the buyer agree upon. Likewise, the buyer may also promise to buy from the seller if that price remains unchanged. KQML needs to support this characteristic of making commitments and promise but the performatives in KQML have limited coverage. All performatives, as Singh (1998) argued, are either assertives or directives. With only a limited and small set of performatives, there is a possibility that overloading may occur at the content lever.

Phases	**Agent**	**Speech acts**
Phase 1: Request	Buyer Seller	Request, Ask Offer
Phase 2: Negotiation	Buyer	Request, Insist, Suggest Promise/Commit, Refuse
	Seller	Offer, Insist, Suggest, Promise/Commit, Refuse
Phase 3: Delivery	Buyer	Acknowledge
	Seller	Thank
Phase 4: Support	Buyer	Satisfied, Unsatisfied, Request
	Seller	Apologise Offer

Table 3. Four phases of a deal and their corresponding speech acts

While we do not deny that providing an overly extensive set of performatives will results in narrowing down the distinction between different performatives, we argue that performatives like commisives, prohibitives etc. should be included for agents to be able to engage in a more complex social relationship especially in e-commerce.

5. SEMIOTIC METHODS FOR DESIGNING E-COMMERCE SYSTEMS

To illustrate how semiotic methods can help in designing an e-commerce system, the case of an online bookstore will be used. The analysis begins with a problem description as follows:

"A bookstore, employing a number of staff, offers many books to be sold online. The online bookstore has a Web address where the online catalogue is stored. Customers have the ability to search for books, using the online catalogue. The search can be done in various options such as book title, ISBN, author. Customers can then know the price of the books. If he wishes to buy that book, he submits his credit card number and the details of the book. This transaction then initiates a transfer of funds from the customer's credit card company to the bookstore. The bookstore is committed to deliver the book within three days of ordering. Prices indicated are inclusive of delivery charges."

5.1 Architecture of Agent-Mediated E-Commerce System

The proposed architecture of the e-commerce system is shown in figure 3, on which the rest of the discussion will be based. In figure 3, we show the relationship between conceptual model, agents and the dynamic aspect of agent behaviour (norms). All agents will refer to the conceptual model and be subjeted to the norms for their behaviour.

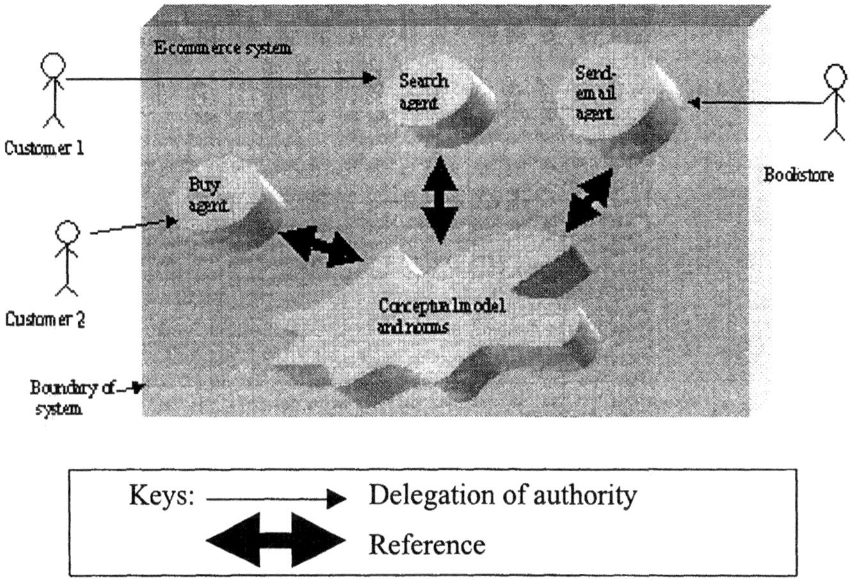

Figure 3. Proposed architecture of agent-mediated e-commerce system

5.2 Conceptual Model Shared By Agents

The method of semantic analysis is applied at this stage to obtain a conceptual model that is shared by all the agents. Semantic units are identified from the problem definition and grouped. Words or phrases are singled out as candidate semantic units. Every word in the problem definition is important as they may carry some information to a concept, a relationship or an intention. As a result, the following lists are some examples of the candidate entities that are obtained:

Bookstore, Employee, Shipped, Address, Books, Buy, Sell, etc.

After the functions of candidate entities are listed and studied, they are classified into a list of entities, patterns of behaviour, role-names and attributes. Some examples are shown in table 4. At this stage, we may have developed sketches of piecemeal semantic structure as shown in figure 4.

Bookstore:	Legal entity of business which owns and sells books
Employer:	A role name of an agent who employs staffs
Invoice:	An patterns of behaviour of Bookstore
Price	An attribute of books

Table 4. Some semantic candidates

Some candidate entities did not appear literally in the list, for example, "seller" and "buyer" are incorporated into the representation implicitly by introducing a pattern of behaviour called "trade". Some new terms such as society, person, buyer and seller are introduced in the grouping in order to construct a sound semantic structure.

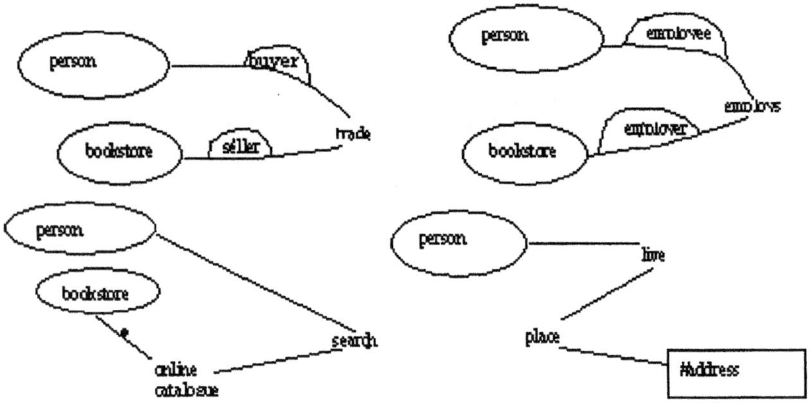

Figure 4. Piecemeal of semantic structure

The fragments in figure 4 will be assembled into an integrated semantic model as shown in figure 5. The semantic model is a conceptual model in a given domain. Entities and patterns of behaviour are nodes in this model and society is the root agent which defines the boundary of the study. The entities are normally human actors or organisations that have authority and can delegate responsibilities to machine agents. As seen in figure 5, the Society has three patterns of behaviour, books, person and bookstore and all three are ontologically dependent on the Society. That means if Society does not exist, bookstore, person and book will also become undefined.

The model shows clearly the roles of person. Role names are in semi-circles. For example, in this domain, the entity person can have the role of a buyer or an employee of the bookstore. When we can identify the roles that each agent have to perform, it is not difficult to also specify the beliefs and intentions in the next phase which is known as the norm analysis.

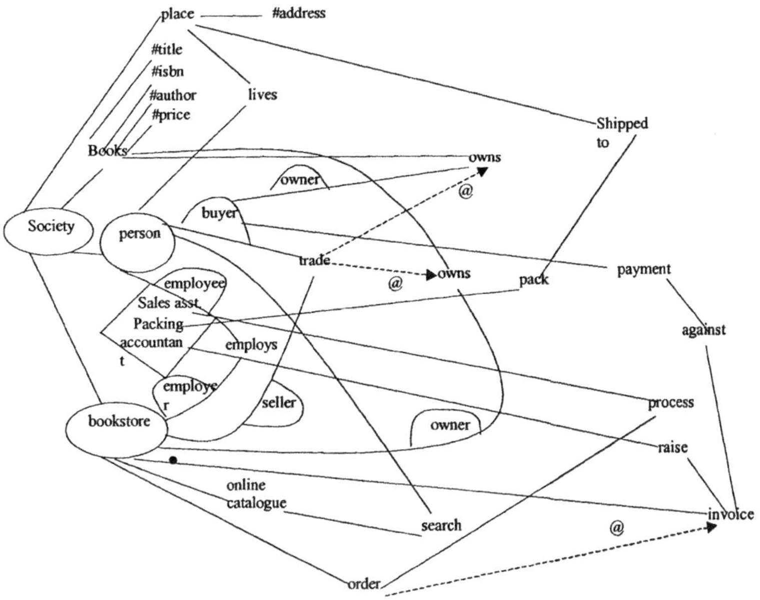

Figure 5. Semantic model of online bookstore

Using the semantic model that we already have (see figure 5), we attempt to find out the disposition of the agents based on their different roles.

5.3 Capturing the Dynamics of Agent Behaviour in Norms

In this section, we capture the norms and derive the attitude and disposition of agents. The attitudes are reflected in a speech act or a situation which results in a personality, called disposition, in one's internal state of the world. Table 5 shows some examples of the norms governing the behaviour of agents in the bookstore case study.

The norms specify conditions and constraints for certain events and actions. Agents are normally involved in these events and actions with attitudes and dispositions in their internal state of the world. Once these norms are elicited, they can then be specified further for execution.

5.4 Implementation of E-Commerce Systems

As displayed in figure 3, the semantic model and norms will be the conceptual model for designing the e-commerce system for the bookstore. All agents that serve the bookstore will share the same semantic model and the same set of norms.

Agent	Norms	Attitude	Disposition
Buyer	**IF** buyer wish to buy a book, **THEN** he will plan to search for that book	Plan	Intentions
Buyer	**IF** buyer has ordered a book, **THEN** he is obliged to make payment	Obliged	Acts
Owner	**IF** bookstore owns a book, **THEN** he is permitted to sell it	Permitted to	Acts
Seller	**IF** seller has promised to sell the book at a price, **THEN** he is obliged to sell at that price	Obliged	Acts
Buyer/seller	**IF** a trade is successful, **THEN** the transfer of ownership of books between seller and person can be acknowledged	Acknowled -ged	Perception

Table 5. Disposition revealed by norms

These provide the unifying basis for agents to communicate at the semantic and pragmatic levels with shared meanings and concepts. To validate this hypothesis, an experiment is being carried out by prototyping the agent-mediated system using an agent-building CASE tool ZEUS (Collis et al. 1998).

6. DISCUSSION AND FURTHER WORK

Firstly, we showed how agents are involved in agent mediated e-commerce applications. The definition of agents and their properties were discussed. Secondly, we showed the problems of agent-mediated e-commerce. The semiotic framework was introduced and was used to evaluate KQML. Also, the shortcomings and inadequacy of KQML was discussed.

Thirdly, semiotic methods were presented for designing agent-mediated e-commerce systems. Using a case study of a bookstore, we showed how semantic analysis enables system developers to identify agents and specify its roles. The norm analysis was use to identify the norms, the agents involved, the attitude that they will adopt and eventually, the disposition of an agent so that the internal states of agents can be properly and accurately coded.

Many opportunities for future work exist. This may lead to an extension of KQML so that it can be used by agent mediated e-commerce systems to specify a more complex relationship. Applying semiotic methods into analysis and modelling agent behaviour within the constraints of responsibilities and authorities set by human users in e-commerce is an important follow-up that will be carried out in the near future. Another task is to develop a formal syntax and semantics for specifying norms and disposition to facilitate analysis and design of internal states (beliefs, intentions) of agents.

References

Adams, E.J. (1994) *"Electronic Commerce Focusing On Success"*, Chain Store Age Executive.

Austin, J.L. (1962) "*How to Do Things with Words*", Oxford at the Clarendon Press, Oxford, U.K.

Boynton, A.G. (1994) *"Electronic Commerce Focusing on Success"*, Chain Store Age Executive.

Cohen, P.R. and Levesque, H.J. (1990a) "Intention Is Choice With Commitment", *Artificial Intelligence*, 42, pp. 213-261

Cohen, P.R. and Levesque, H.J. (1990b) "Rational Interaction As The Basis For Communication". In Cohen, P.R., Morgan, J., Pollack, M.E. (Eds.), *Intentions in Communication,* The MIT press: Cambridge, MA, pp. 221-256

Cohen, P.R. & Levesque H.J. (1995) "Communicative Actions for Artificial Agents", In *Proceeedings of the First International Conference on Multi-Agent Systems*, San Francisco, Cambridge: AAAI Press pp. 65-72

Collis, J.C. & Lee, L.C. (1998) "Building Electronic Marketplaces with the ZEUS Agent Toolkit", *Proceedings of the Agent Mediated Electronic Trading (AMET) Workshop*, May, pp. 17-32

Collis, J.C., Ndumu, D.T., Nwana, H.S. & Lee, L.C. (1998) "The ZEUS Agent Building Toolkit" *BT Technology Journal,* 16(3), pp. 60-68

Finin, T., Fritzson, R., McKay, D. & McEntire, R. (1994) "KQML as an agent communication language", In *Proceedings of 3rd International Conference on Information and Knowledge Management (CIKM)*, November, New York: ACM Press.

Finin, T. Labrou, Y. Mayfield, J. (1997) "KQML as an agent communication language". In J. Bradshaw (Ed.) *Software Agents*, MIT Press, Cambridge.

Fisher, J. (1995) "Electronic Commerce, A Definition", *AIIA/ECA Publication on Electronic Commerce*, February

Gruber, T. (1991) *"Ontolingua: A Mechanism to Support Portable Ontologies"*, KSL-91-66, Stanford University Knowledge Systems Laboratory

Hayes-Roth, B. (1995) "An architecture for adaptive Intelligent Systems" *Artificial Intelligence: Special Issue on Agents and Interactivity*, Vol. 72

Hornback, R. (1995) "Electronic Commerce in the 21st Century", *Journal of Systems Management*, May/June, pp. 28-33

Kimbrough & Moore (1997) "On Automated Message Processing in Electronic Commerce and Work Support Systems: Speech Act Theory and Expressive Felicity", ACM Transactions on Information Systems, Vol. 15(4), pp. 321-367

Krogh, C. & Herrestad (1996) "Getting Personal: Some Notes on the Relationship Between Personal and Impersonal Obligation", in Brown, M.A. & Carmo, J. (Eds.) Deontic Logic, Agency and Normative Systems, Springer

Lederer, A.L., Mirchandani, D.A., Sims, K. (1996) "Electronic Commerce: A Strategic Application", SIGCPR/SIGMIS, Denver Colorado USA, pp. 277-287.

Locke, John (1960) "Essay Concerning Human Understanding", Unabridged edition 1959, Dover, NY

Liu, K., Apers, P., Chattopadhyay, S., Cheng, A., Fox, M., Greene, T., Klein M. & Stamper, R. (1999) "Enterprise Information Systems: issues, challenges and viewpoints". In J. Filip (Ed.), Enterprise Information Systems, Kluwer Academic Publishers (in press).

Liu, K. (2000) "Semiotics in Information Systems Development" Cambridge University Press (in press)

Liu, K. and Dix, A.(1997) "Norm Governed Agents in CSCW", 1st International Workshop on Computational Semiotics, University of De Vinchi, Paris.

Mowshowitz (1997) "Virtual Organisation", Communications of the ACM 40(9), pp. 30-37

Michael R., Genesereth, Steven P. K. (1994) "Software Agents", Communications of the ACM 37(7) pp. 48-53

Singh, M P. (1998) 'Agent Communication Language: Rethinking the Principles', Computer: Innovative Technology for Computer Professionals, December, pp. 40-47

Nwana H. S., Michael Wooldridge (1996), "Software Agent Technologies", BT Technology Journal. Also available from: http://www.labs.bt.com/projects/agents/publish/papers/sat_report.html

Collis, J.C., Ndumu, D.T., Nwana, H.S. & Lee, L.C. (1998) "The ZEUS Agent Building Toolkit" BT Technology Journal, 16(3), pp. 60-68

Patil, R.S., Fikes, R.E., Patel-Schneider, P.F, McKay, D, Finin, T., Gruber, T., and Neches, R. (1992) "The DAPRA Knowledge Sharing Effort: Progress Report." In Rich, C., Swartout, W. and Nebel, B., (Eds), *Proceedings of Knowledge Representation and Reasoning*, pp 777-788

Pierce, C.S. (1931/35) *"Collected Papers of C.S., Pierce (1931-35)"*, edited in 1960 by Hartshorne, C. & Weiss, P., Cambridge, Mass

Searle, J.R. (1969) "*Speech Acts*", Cambridge University Press, Cambridge, U.K.

Shoham, Y. (1993) "Agent Oriented Programming" *Artificial Intelligence,* Vol. 60 pp.51-92

Shoham, Y. (1997) "An Overview of Agent-Oriented Programming", *Software Agents,* Bradshaw, J.M.(ED), AAAI Press, Menlo Park, CA, USA

Spence, M.A. (1994) 'Electronic Commerce Is The First Beneficiary of The Information Highway', *CAM Magazine*, June, pp. 6

Stamper (1998) "Organisational Semiotics". In John Mingers & Frank Stowell (Eds.), *Information Systems: An Emerging Discipline?,* The McGraw Hill Companies, pp.267-283

Comments on "A Semiotic Approach to the Design of Agent-mediated E-commerce Systems" by S. Chong and K. Liu

John Krogstie

Andersen Consulting and IDI, Norwegian University of Science and Technology (NTNU), Norway

In the nineties, several new technologies and technological possibilities have been established, such as ERP-systems (e.g. SAP and Baan) and internet-technology spawning increasing possibilities in areas such as eCommerce. In general, the academic world is rather slow in addressing the problems and opportunities of new commercial concepts and technologies, although the general frameworks and ideas developed in the scientific community often have a lot to offer for understanding the development and use of new technologies in practice. The paper by Chong and Liu is an attempt on such cross-fertilisation, using the academically devised organisational semiotics in connection to eCommerce-systems, systems that are of increasing importance in most modern organisations.

ECommerce can be defined as any interaction over an electronic network between two or more computers or electronic interfaces, where:

- Information/media, services or physical goods are traded for financial or other consideration.
- Payment is accomplished electronically either through the same or a parallel network

The paper addresses (requirements) analysis (*not* design) of eCommerce systems, with particular emphasis on the effective use of agent-technology. Agents are one of many useful (but not mandatory) technologies that are applied as part of an eCommerce-solution. The "agent" label is stuck on many different kinds of software processes or systems to the point that it is now difficult to give a precise definition of what an agent is.

A common idea is that an agent is software that acts on a user's behalf and achieves tasks a user could achieve if he had enough time. Although delegation is mentioned in the paper, it is not included as part of the definition of the term, giving a definition of agent that can be used for almost anything. It could be useful for the further work of the authors for them to define which agent characteristics and agent types they are supporting.

I use ideas of organisational semiotics and the semiotic ladder in many circumstances myself, but have some comments on the way it is used in the paper. When evaluating KQML only the three upper levels (semantics, pragmatics, and social) are addressed. I understand that this is a conscious decision by the authors, but think that this a sub-optimal way of using the semiotic ladder.

The critique of KQML at the semantic level (and indirectly pragmatic level), can be summarised with: 'KQML, like all programming languages do not have a *formal and precise semantic meaning* of the performatives..... As a result agent designers do not have a common understanding of the language, its performatives and protocol." A KQML-message is usually one piece of dialogue, consisting of a communications type and one or more KIF expressions. KIF is an enhanced version of the language of first-order predicate calculus, which does have a formal (mathematical) semantics, which is quite well known and used in practice. Obviously, using a language with mathematical foundations only addresses the semantical issues when dealing with simple problems where the people involved share a well-established consensus about the task at hand. This is not the case when taking about eCommerce systems, were systems that eventually will need to communicate can be developed anywhere in the world. On the other hand, it is very difficult to see how the work described in the paper can help in this regard, since it present a language for which not even a formal syntax is developed for important parts of the language.

More interesting then is the discussion on language appropriateness linked up to the social level, i.e. to what extent it is possible to express what one would like to express in connection to the development of agents. This is used partly on the basis of an extended list of communicative acts (the traditional five from Searle extended with two deontic notions, 'permissives' and 'prohibitives'), and partly using the ideas of speech acts in the similar way as they are used in Action Workflow. Although pointing to some weaknesses in KQML, it is not spelled out in detail how the proposed 'semiotic' methods address these and other needs. It is generally difficult to see to what extent the proposed language is adapted to agent and eCommerce-systems. Another open point is how to sensibly formalise the proposed framework, which include fuzzy concepts such as 'attitudes' and 'dispositions'.

The Quality of Business Process Modelling Methods

Illustration of a Framework for Understanding Modelling Quality

Bart-Jan Hommes and Victor van Reijswoud

Bart-Jan Hommes: Delft University of Technology, Faculty of Information Technology and Systems, Department of Information Systems and Software Engineering, PO Box 356, 2600AJ, Delft, The Netherlands, email: hommes@is.twi.tudelft.nl

Victor van Reijswoud: Devote Institute of Technology, Devote nv, PO Box 73, 3980 CB Bunnik, The Netherlands, email : vreijswoud@devote.nl

Key words: Business process modelling, Quality, Evaluation of modelling methods

Abstract: The conceptual modelling of business processes is becoming popular. The number of methods and tools is growing fast. At the same time, an appropriate framework for understanding the quality of these modelling methods is lacking. In this paper we report upon the development of a framework for understanding the quality of business process modelling methods, called the Q-Me framework. The framework defines the elements that constitute a modelling method and presents a number of quality properties as well as ways to operationalise them. In this paper, the framework is illustrated by studying the quality of the Unified Modelling Language (UML) for the purpose of business process modelling. Conclusions are drawn both on the quality of UML and on the application of the framework to study UML.

1. INTRODUCTION

The modelling of business processes is becoming increasingly popular. Both experts in the field of Information and Communication Technology (ICT) and in the field of Business Engineering have come to the conclusion that successful systems (re)engineering starts with a thorough understanding of the business processes of an organisation: a business process model.

Conceptual modelling of business processes is deployed on a large scale to facilitate for instance Business Process Reengineering (BPR), ERP system implementation [Dav98], [Post96], Total Quality Management and Workflow Automation [Bar98].

The increasing popularity of business process modelling results in a rapid growing number of modelling methods. This increase in methods makes the process of selection and/or assembling a modelling method (e.g. method engineering [Har97]) more and more complex and time-consuming. Indicative for the huge range of different tools and methods is the overview of [Ket97]. An analysis of the Internet by the authors reveals approximately 350 business process modelling tools, all claiming to support 'effective', 'comprehensible', 'compact', 'suitable' etc. conceptual business modelling (see http://is.twi.tudelft.nl/~hommes/tools.html for this overview).

In fact, methods are seldom tested on these claims, since there is no framework available for assessing the quality of methods for conceptual business modelling. Existing frameworks for evaluating quality, focus on the quality of software- and information systems modelling methods, rather than on business process modelling methods. Apart from the fact that these frameworks do not have a business focus, there is criticism about the 'vagueness' of quality properties and the lack of operationalisation [Lind94], [Gil92].

The lack of appropriate means to assess (evaluate) the quality of this rapidly growing number of business modelling methods, and the dominant role these methods and tools can have in, for instance, Business Process Reengineering, ERP system implementation, Total Quality Management and Workflow Automation, justifies the development of a conceptual framework for understanding and evaluating the quality of these methods.

This paper reports on the first steps in developing a Quality-based Modelling Evaluation framework, called the Q-Me framework. The aim is to provide a set of well-defined quality properties and procedures to make an objective assessment of these properties possible. In section 2, a general framework for describing modelling methods will be presented. As an extension of this framework, quality properties for business modelling methods are identified in section 3. In section 4 the extended framework is illustrated by evaluating the quality of the Unified Modelling Language (UML) and its potential for business process modelling. After this, conclusions are drawn and directions for further research are presented in section 5.

2. MODELLING BUSINESS PROCESSES

Although the usage of modelling methods for understanding the information and business structure of organisations is increasing, the evaluation of these methods is a poorly developed scientific field. Some high-level frameworks have been proposed for the description of the elements in an information systems development methodology [Sel89], the evaluation and engineering of methods [Har97] and the application information systems methodologies in practice [Jay94]. However, these approaches do not focus in detail on the modelling methods used in a particular methodology. In this section we first introduce a general framework for describing modelling methods. In section 2.2 the area of business modelling methods is highlighted more specifically.

2.1 Framework

Based on the Method Theory as developed in [Gold98] and the general description of elements in an information systems methodology as described in the Framework for Understanding in [Sel89], we propose a framework that allows the description and evaluation of modelling methods. In line with [Sel89], we identify a *way of modelling* and a *way of working* in a modelling method. The Way of Modelling describes the models that are used in a method and the Way of Working describes the procedures by which these models are constructed. This division corresponds with the distinction between conceptual product method fragments and conceptual process method fragments as described in [Har97].

In the Way of Modelling we describe models by their constituting modelling concepts. The constituting modelling concepts are characterised by their notation and their meaning. We also describe the relationships between the different modelling concepts in one model and the notation of this relationship. The individual models are described by their mutual relationships as well as by their goals or purposes.

The Way of Working of a modelling method is described as a related set of activities together constituting the modelling procedure. Within the framework the procedure is specified at the model level. A complete overview of the way of working is achieved with the description of the mutual relationships between the procedures. Together the Way of Working and the Way of Modelling represent the perspective of the modelling method. By perspective we mean the view and purpose that guides the conceptualisation of the real system into the conceptual system. The framework for evaluation is depicted in Figure 1.

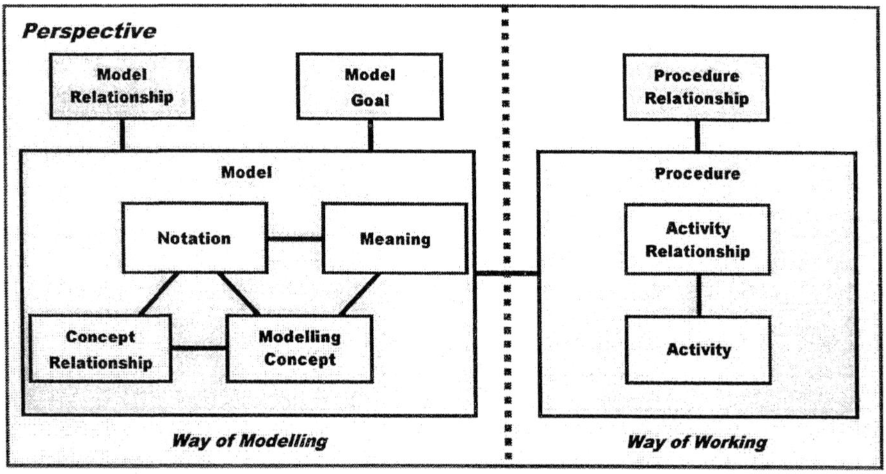

Figure 1. Framework for evaluation

For a detailed description of the four elements that constitute an individual model, we introduce a *modelling concept table.* In this table, each modelling concept is described together with its meaning and notation. The last column of the table describes the concept relationship by means of a meta model. The modelling language used to construct these meta models is similar to the ORM modelling language. A comprehensive overview of ORM (Object Role Modelling) can be found in [Hal98]. Other approaches, such as an ER approach [Chen77] or an object-oriented approach [Rum91] may also be used for meta modelling. As an example, the modelling concept table of a simple flowchart diagram is shown below.

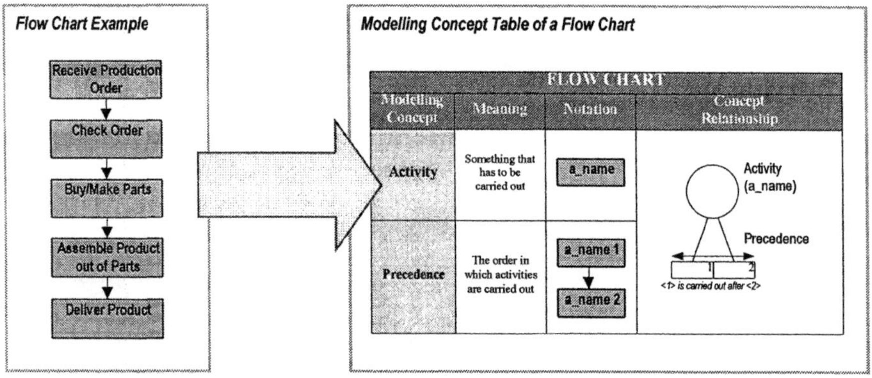

Figure 2. Simple Example of a Modelling Concept Table

A detailed description of the three elements that constitute the way of modelling is achieved by means of a *model table*. This table is drawn in the same fashion as the modelling concept table. It contains two columns specifying the models and their goals. The last column describes the model relationship by means of a meta model. The model table will be illustrated when the UML is described in section 4.

2.2 Modelling Business Processes

The interrelated set of modelling concepts that constitute the way of modelling represents an application domain. In the case of business processes modelling, this application domain is the business process. This section is a reflection of the existing consensus about what 'business processes' are and thus to what application domain the modelling concepts of the method should correspond. This is the *perspective* element of the framework presented in figure 1.

In the literature, a 'business process' is commonly defined as a chain of organisational or inter-organisational activities that are necessary to accomplish a product or service. Examples of this definition are "an ordering of work activities across time and place, with a beginning, an end, and clearly identified inputs and outputs" [Dav93] or "A set of activities that, taken together, produce a result of value to a customer" [Ham93]. We will refer to these definitions as definitions of a 'process' in general. The term 'business process' is reserved for a more specific class of processes.

Founded in [WiFl86], [Med92] and [Die94] we classify processes according to the nature of the activities that are carried out. If the nature of the activities is physical, such as assembling a product, then we speak of a *material process*. If their nature is about processing information, such as calculating the price of a product, then we speak of an *information process*. If the nature is about doing something with information, such as making a commitment to a supplier to pay for a product, then the corresponding process is called a *business process*.

Often 'core' and 'supportive' business processes are distinguished. A core (or primary) process is initiated from outside an organisation, e.g. the chain of activities that realises the delivery of a product to a customer. A supportive (or secondary) process is initiated from inside the organisation to provide support for core processes, e.g. buying new stock from a supplier.

A business modelling method should provide means to describe the dynamic aspects of the functioning of an organisation as well as the static characteristics of the information space on which the dynamic aspects build. Also the distinction between organisation and environment should be modelled, in order to distinguish between core and supportive processes.

3. THE QUALITY OF BUSINESS PROCESS MODELLING METHODS

This section addresses the quality of business process modelling methods. After a general definition of quality is given, quality properties specific to (business) modelling will be assigned to methods (section 3.1). Some attention to the operationalisation of these properties is paid in section 3.2.

3.1 Quality Properties of a Business Modelling Method

Quality has been defined in many ways, ranging from extremes as 'conformance to requirements' [Cro79] to 'fitness for use' [Jur79]. The International Standards Organisation (ISO) has attempted to unite the different views on quality in a general definition stating that quality is "the total of properties and characteristics of a product or service that are relevant for satisfying specific requirements and obvious necessities". This definition is taken as a starting point for a refinement of the definition of quality. Since the nuance between the meaning of the term 'property' and 'characteristic' is slight, we will not distinguish between them and use the term 'property' in the remainder of this paper. The 'product or service' under consideration is the business modelling method.

A common way to understand the quality of something is to subdivide quality in a number of quality properties that each address a particular aspect of quality. The evaluation of software quality by [Boe78] is an example of this approach. [Boe78] decomposes high level quality properties into lower level properties, resulting in a 'tree of quality properties'. This approach is adopted in this paper.

Three quality properties that provide a good basis for the evaluation of modelling methods are the properties particular to meta models of modelling languages as presented in the FRISCO report as formulated by the IFIP8.1 Working Group [Frisco96]. According to the FRISCO report, the following quality properties are important:

- *Expressiveness* - the degree to which a given modelling method is capable of denoting the models of any number and kinds of application domains;
- *Arbitrariness* - the degree of freedom one has when modelling one and the same domain;
- *Suitability* - the degree to which a given modelling method is specifically tailored for a specific kind of application domain.

The first two properties, viz. expressiveness and arbitrariness, are properties that are applicable for any modelling method, regardless of the domain that is modelled. The latter one, viz. suitability, is a property that is specific for the business process domain. Suitability for this business process domain is referred to as 'business suitability' [Bar98].

Both expressiveness and (business) suitability are quality properties of the way of modelling in particular. The properties are not orthogonal, they influence each other in such a way that an optimum has to be found [Frisco96]. A modelling method that is highly expressive contains modelling concepts that are generally applicable. Therefore, it has low business suitability. On the other hand, a modelling method that is highly suitable for business modelling contains concepts that are specific for the business domain. Therefore its expressiveness is low.

Arbitrariness is a property of the way of working in particular. Low arbitrariness limits the degree of freedom one has while modelling a domain. A low degree of freedom during the modelling process results in a way of working with results that are reproducible. Since particularly low arbitrariness is a quality of a way of working, we will use the opposite term '*determinism*' in stead of arbitrariness in the remainder of this article.

Due to the fact that the three properties that were mentioned above specifically address the meta model of the modelling language, their contribution to the overall quality of a modelling method is restricted to the *modelling concept*, *meaning* and *concept relationship* elements of the framework. In order to cover all the elements that constitute a method, other properties are necessary. Other properties that are proposed in literature (e.g. [Bar98], [Har97]) are:

- *Comprehensibility* - the ease with which the way of working and way of modelling are understood by the participants;

- *Coherence* - the degree to which the individual sub models of a way of modelling constitute a whole;
- *Completeness* - the degree to which all necessary concepts of the application domain are represented in the way of modelling;
- *Efficiency* - the degree to which the modelling process utilises resources such as time and people;
- *Effectiveness* - the degree to which the modelling process achieves its goal.

The properties are summarised in figure 3. First of all, product quality and process quality are distinguished. They refer to the quality of respectively the way of modelling and the way of working of a modelling method. For each property, its area of application and the knowledge that is required to study the property is presented. The figure is a reflection of the informal introduction of the properties in the previous paragraphs, combined with the framework for modelling methods as presented in section 2.1. Note that 'arbitrariness', as mentioned in [Frisco96] has been replaced with its opposite 'determinism'.

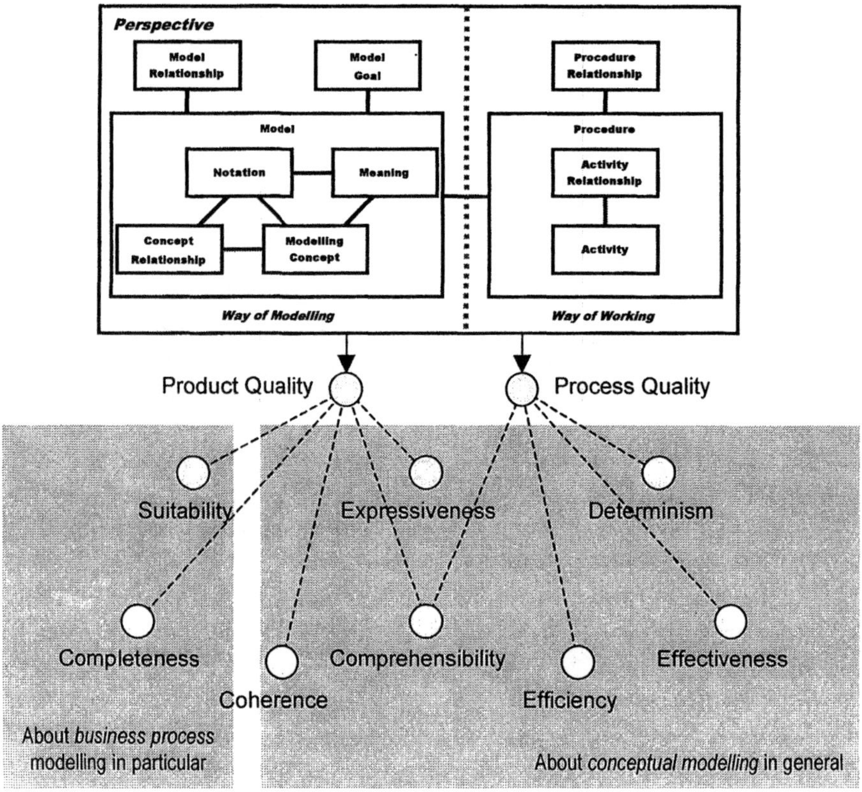

Figure 3. The Quality of a Business Modelling Method

3.2 Measuring the Quality Properties

In this section we discuss the operationalisation of the quality properties that were presented in the previous section. We will discuss how the quality properties relate to the elements of the framework that was introduced in section 2.1 and how the proposed *modelling concept table* and *model table* contribute as means for the measurement of the quality properties.

Suitability, Completeness - The operationalisation of the properties that have a business focus, viz. suitability and completeness, comprehends a comparison between the modelling concepts of the method that is evaluated and the consensus that there is about the concepts that should comprise the business domain, as was discussed in section 2.2. As such, the elements *modelling concept* and *meaning* of the framework provide the basis for doing this. This shows for instance that the flow chart example of figure 2 is *suitable*, since it is able to express a process as activities and some form of interrelation between them. It is however *incomplete*, since it lacks the appropriate concepts for distinguishing between core and supportive processes, material-, information- and business processes, etc.

Coherence - The two elements in the framework that provide a basis for the operationalisation of the coherence property are the elements that refer to the structure of the way of modelling, viz. the *concept relationship* and the *model relationship* elements. The concept relationship is described by means of a meta model in the last column of the modelling concept table. A model is coherent when there are no isolated parts in its meta model. The overall coherence of a way of modelling is described by a meta model that combines the meta models of the individual models. The way of modelling is coherent when this overall meta model does not contain isolated parts. Furthermore, a meta model of the way of modelling is the basis for an understanding of how the individual models constitute a coherent whole.

Expressiveness - Expressiveness is the degree to which a modelling method is capable of modelling any number and kinds of application domains. The specificity / generality of the *meaning* of *modelling concepts* is an indication for the level of expressiveness. In literature, meta model transformations are mentioned as a measure for expressiveness [Frisco96]. When there is a mapping from a meta model of a method A to the meta model of a method B without loss of meaning, it can be derived that B is at least as expressive as A. Furthermore, the ability of a method to describe its own concepts is an indication for high expressive power.

Comprehensibility - The elements *meaning, notation* and *modelling concept* provide a useful 'triangle' for an operationalisation of the comprehensibility property of a modelling method. Consistency between the notation-meaning and meaning-modelling concept relations is a measure for comprehensibility. The flow chart example is comprehensible in that sense. The notation-meaning relation of the 'flow' concept is consistent because an arrow is a perfect means for sequencing activities. It is obvious that omitting the arrowhead from the arrow notation would make the model very incomprehensible.

Another way of operationalising comprehensibility is to consider the amount of different modelling concepts per model. The lower the number of modelling concepts, the easier the model is to comprehend. This also holds for the deviation in the number of concepts per model.

Determinism - The degree of freedom one has when modelling one and the same domain using a method is reflected in the determinism property. When there is only one way of modelling a domain using a method, the method is said to be *deterministic* or has zero arbitrariness. Arbitrariness is introduced in a method when there are different modelling concepts or structures of modelling concepts in a method that have a same meaning. If this is the case, different models can model the same domain and freedom is introduced. The *meaning, modelling concept* and *concept relationship* need to be evaluated to determine the determinism of a method.

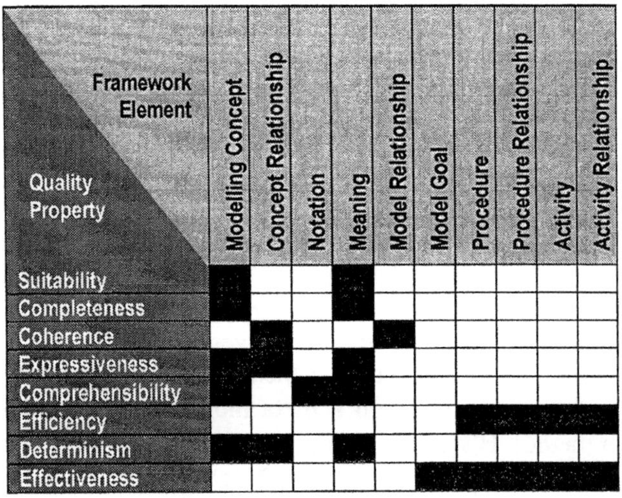

Figure 4. Quality properties and requested elements for evaluation

Effectiveness, Efficiency - Effectiveness on the level of a single model is the extent to which the goal of that model is achieved by means of the interrelated set of activities that constitute the procedure for that model. It is clear that the elements *model goal*, *activity* and *activity relationship* of the framework need to be evaluated in order to operationalise the effectiveness of a method. Evaluation of the effectiveness of the whole method also requires an assessment of the *procedure relationship* and *model relationship*.

In this paper, no attention is paid to the evaluation of effectiveness and efficiency of a method. This is due to the fact that not much is know yet about how to evaluate the framework elements that refer to the way of working of the method. This is not problematic for the evaluation of the UML in the next section. Since it is a modelling language, the emphasis is on the way of modelling rather than the way of working.

Figure 4 shows which elements of the framework need to be evaluated in order to operationalise the quality properties of the framework.

4. THE QUALITY OF THE UNIFIED MODELLING LANGUAGE

In this section, the proposed framework is illustrated by applying it to draw conclusions on the quality of the Unified Modelling Language (UML) for the purpose of business process modelling. Most of the description of UML is based on [OMG99] and [Fow97]. The aim of this section is to illustrate the application of the Q-Me framework.

4.1 UML put into the Framework

In this section, the UML is described using the Q-Me framework that was introduced in section 2.1. Since the UML is a modelling language rather than a method [Fow97], the focus will be on the way of modelling of the framework. First of all, the *model* and *model goal* elements of the framework are presented by means of a model table (table 1). This table describes the most prominent models of the UML and their goals.

WAY OF MODELLING	
Model	**Model Goal**
Use Case	Modelling the interactions between the system that is to be modelled an its environment by means of environmental actors and their use of the system (use cases)
Class	Modelling the static structure of the systems object- and subject world by means of a classification of objects and their interrelationships
Sequence	Modelling the way that the objects interact within one use case
State Transition	Modelling the internal states and transitions of a single object class
Activity	Modelling the overall system behaviour by means of an interrelated set of tasks

Table 1. Model Table of the UML

The framework elements that constitute a model, viz. modelling concept, notation, meaning and concept relationship are set out in detail by means of modelling concept tables. Due to the limited space in this paper, we present the modelling concept tables of three models: the use case-, class- and sequence diagrams, since these models are most often used.

The construction of a *Use Case Model* is often the first step in a project that uses UML as a notation. It is a model that describes system interactions, i.e. interactions between a computer system and its environment. Two modelling concepts are characteristic for the use case model: the concept of an 'actor' and the concept of a 'use case'. According to [Fow97], an 'actor' is a role that a user plays with respect to the system. Actors carry out 'use cases' which can be seen as pieces of user functionality of the system. Furthermore, it is possible to model relations between individual use cases, so called 'extends' and 'uses'. The procedure for identifying actors and use cases is not clear. Fowler describes four alternatives for doing this [Fow97, p.46]. An overview of the use case model is presented in table 2.

The class model is considered to be the core of any object oriented modelling method and as such also for the Unified Modelling Language. In this paper the most important modelling concepts of the class diagram are discussed. An elaborate discussion can be found in [OMG99]. The class model describes the types of objects that are part of the system and their mutual relationships. In order to maintain clarity later on, the table below (table 3) shows only the most important modelling concepts of this model.

USE CASE MODEL			
Modelling Concept	Meaning	Notation	Concept Relationship
Use Case	A coherent unit of functionality provided by a system	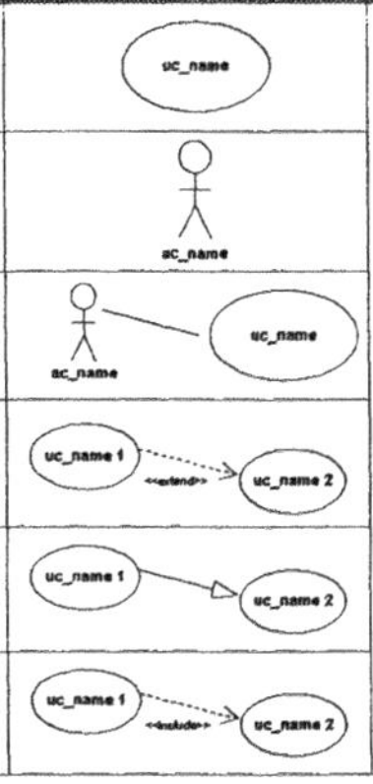	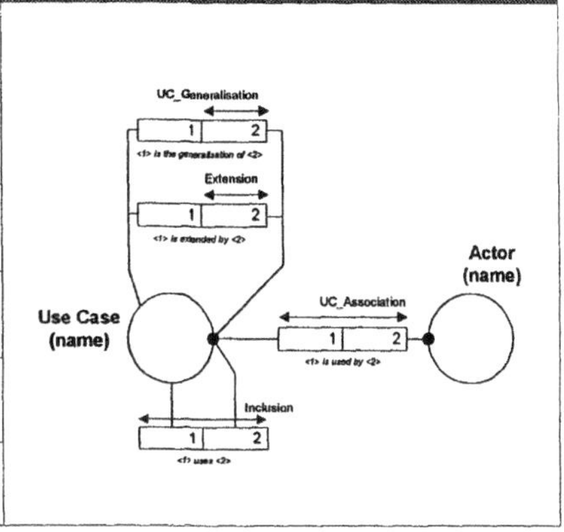
Actor	An interactor in the system environment		
UC_ Association(*)	The participation of an actor in a use case		
Extension	One use case extending the functionality of another		
UC_ Generalisation(*)	One use case being offering more specific functionality than another		
Inclusion	The (re)use of overlapping functionality		

(*) In the OMG standard UML V1.3, the names of modelling concepts are unique within a single aspect model, not within the whole model cycle.' Association' for example, is a modelling concept used in the Use Case Model as well as in the Class Model. We prefer to give modelling concepts unique names within the whole model cycle and added prefixes to conflicting concept names. In general, the names of the modelling concepts correspond to the names mentioned in the OMG standard UML V1.3. However, in the OMG standard. This remark hold also for the modelling concept tables in the remainder of this article.

Table 2. Modelling Concept Table of the Use Case Model

CLASS MODEL			
Modelling Concept	Meaning	Notation	Concept Relationship
Class	A descriptor of a set of objects with similar structure, behaviour and relationships	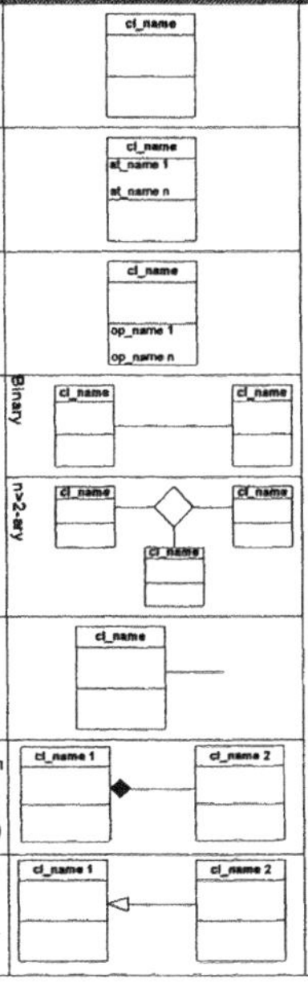	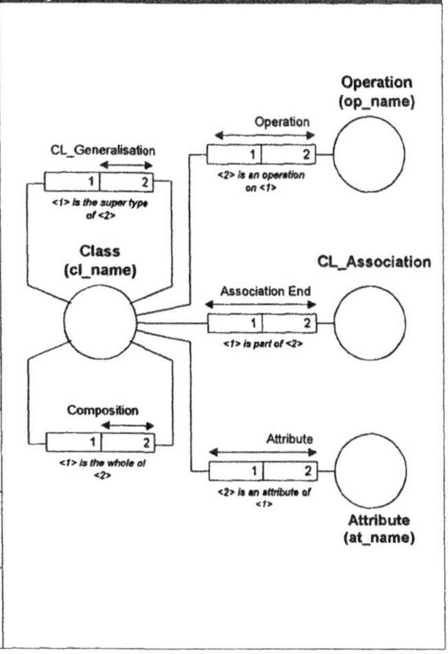
Attribute	A property of a class		
Operation	A service that an instance of the class may be requested to perform		
CL_Association	A static n-ary relationship between classes		
Association End	Identification of a class in an association		
Composition	A form of aggregation with strong ownership and coincident lifetime of the part (2) with the whole (1)		
CL_ Generalisation	Relationship between a generic class (1) and a more specific class (2) with additional behaviour and structure		

Table 3. Modelling Concept Table of the Class Model

SEQUENCE MODEL			
Modelling Concept	Meaning	Notation	Concept Relationship
Time	A point in time	Represented by the Y-axis in the diagram	
Object Lifetime	The instantiation of a class or actor in a specific role		
Activation	A period in time during which an instantiation of a class or actor if performing action	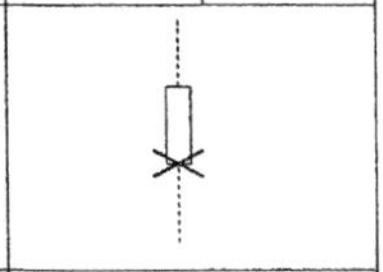	
Message	Specification of a stimulus from a sending to a receiving activation at a point in time	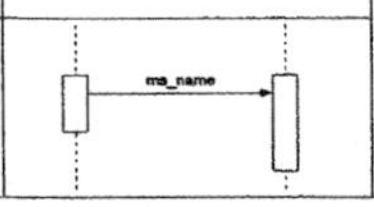	

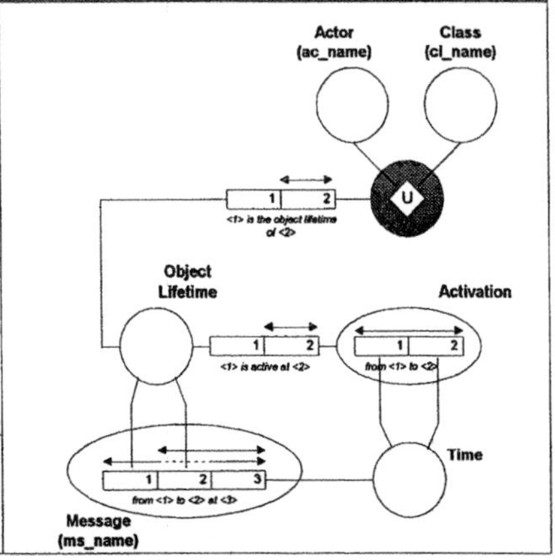

Table 4. Modelling Concept Table of the Sequence Model

A sequence model describes the collaboration between object classes over time. It assumes that objects collaborate by sending messages to each other in a sequence. Messages are represented by horizontal arrows. The time dependency between messages is expressed by the vertical ordering of the horizontal arrows in the diagram. An overview of the main concepts is presented below (table 4).

The description of the *model relationship* element of the evaluation framework encompasses the integration of the individual meta models as presented in the concept relationship column of the modelling concept tables (table 2, 3, 4). This integration results in an overall meta model which is presented in figure 5.

The dotted ellipses in this diagram are an extension to the ORM notation as described by [Hal98]. They can be compared to what is referred to as a 'schema type' in [Hof93]. They group the modelling concepts that belong to one single sub model. The concept itself is a specialisation of the ORM object type concept, identified by its population. Since it is a specialisation of an object type it can participate as a role in new fact types, of which the 'UC/SQ Interrelationship' fact type is an example. It expresses the interrelationship between sequence model and use case model: within UML, a sequence model is drawn for each use case.

The meta model shows that there is no direct interrelationship between the class model and the use case model. The relationship between these models is established by the sequence model. For every use case, a sequence model can be drawn. This sequence model addresses the classes of the class model by means of 'object lifetimes'.

Furthermore, the meta model shows that there is a double interrelationship between the class model and sequence model. On the one hand, the 'class' of the class model is related to the 'object lifetime' in the sequence model. On the other hand, operations on classes are related to messages in the sequence model.

This same double relationship holds for the use case model and the sequence model. On the one hand, a sequence model can be drawn for each use case. On the other hand, the 'actor' concept of the use case model is related to an 'object lifetime' in the sequence model.

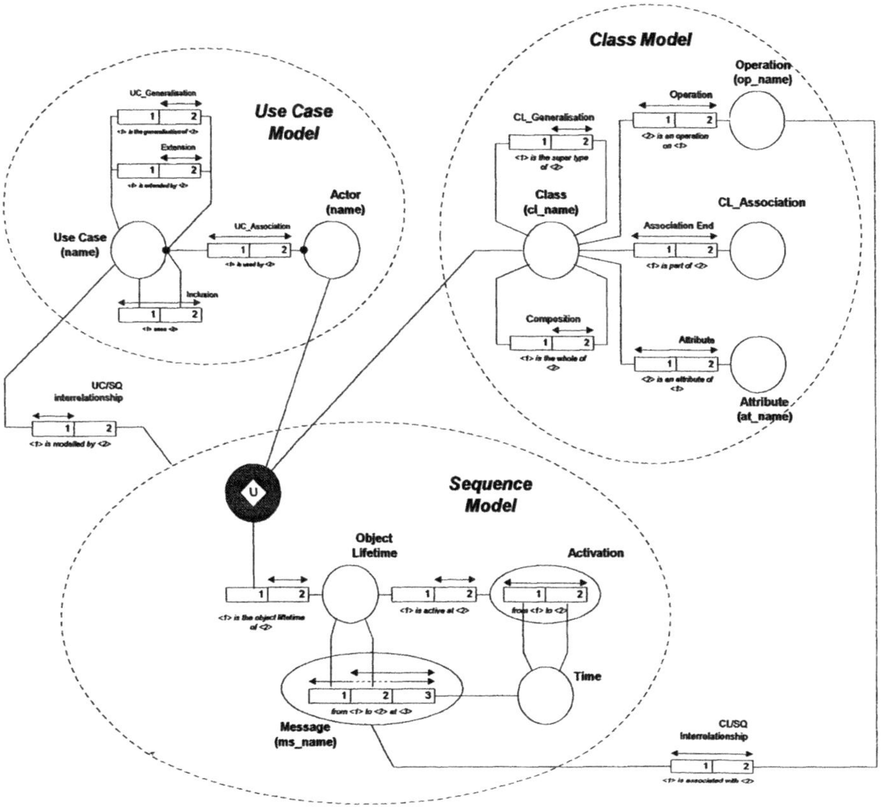

Figure 5. Model Relationship

The activity- and state transition model are not discussed in detail in this paper. When they would have been placed in the meta model it would become clear that there is a strong relation between the state transition model and the class model, since each state transition model describes the states and transitions of one class. Furthermore it would become clear that the activity model is isolated from the other models, since no relationships could be found.

4.2 Business Modelling and UML

Recently, the application of UML for modelling business systems has gained popularity [Pen99], [Hru98], [UML97]. In [UML97], the standard UML extension mechanisms are used to introduce modelling concepts that are more business suitable. The same approach is adopted in [Hru98] to introduce workflow suitable modelling concepts. Since these mechanisms extend the meta model with additional sub types to the existing object types, they do not have a large impact on the general UML that is presented in this paper. The authors do not know the approach adopted in [Pen99], since it was not published during the writing of this paper.

4.3 Conclusions on the Quality of UML

In this section, conclusions with respect to the quality of UML are drawn. In order to do so we will pass the quality properties that were mentioned in section 3.2 in review. For each property, the conclusions are underpinned by the evaluation of the framework elements that are applicable for that property.

Suitability, Completeness - An evaluation of the modelling concepts and their meaning reveals that the UML is a very general approach which is not exclusively suitable for business process modelling. The modelling concepts in the business domain (see section 2.2) are not easily mapped to UML concepts. Some business suitability can be found in use case model and the activity model, with which it is possible to model processes as described by [Dav93] as "an ordering of work activities across time and place". Since it does not for instance distinguish between material-, informational- and business activities, core- and supportive processes, it can be considered *incomplete* with respect to the UML concepts covering the business domain.

Coherence - An evaluation of the individual UML models reveals that the concept relationship of each model forms a coherent whole, i.e. that their corresponding meta models do not show any isolated parts.

The interrelationship between the aspect models of UML is less coherent. There is no direct relationship between the use case model and the class model, which means that it is not possible to keep these models consistent without using sequence models in a modelling project. The double relationship between class- and sequence model as well as the double relationship between sequence- and use case model makes it unnecessarily difficult to maintain consistency.

The activity diagram, which was briefly introduced in table 1, but has not been presented in detail due to the limited space in this paper, does not have any coherence with the rest of the UML models. This is especially regrettable since it is a model with some business suitability as has been concluded before.

Expressiveness - The generality of the meaning of the modelling concepts reveals that UML has a high expressive power. This conclusion is in line with the conclusion on the low business suitability, taking into account the dependency between both properties as discussed in section 3.1. Especially the class model, which is to be considered as the core of any object oriented method is build up out of modelling concepts with a very general meaning. Illustrative is the concept of a 'class'. Another indication of high expressive power is the fact that the meta model of UML can be described in its own class model, see for instance the formal semantics of UML in [UML97].

Comprehensibility - It can be concluded that UML is a comprehensible modelling method. Meaning, notation and modelling concept form a consistent whole. For instance, the notation of the concept 'class' is a rectangle, both in the class diagram and in the sequence model. Arrows represent concepts that deal with 'flows' of something, except for the arrows between use cases in the use case diagram. Another indication for comprehensibility is the number of concepts per model. We can conclude that this number is well balanced over all models.

Determinism - With respect to determinism it can be concluded that there are some weak points with respect to the degree of freedom one has when modelling one domain. An unwanted degree of freedom is present in the class model in which the meaning of the concept 'association' and 'attribute' overlaps (see [Fow97, p. 63]). A 'Colour' is, for instance, a property of a 'Car' but might as well be a descriptor of a group of things that have same properties (e.g. all colours have the property to be perceived by the eye). The difference between 'association' and 'class' is also not clear. 'Marriage' is for instance 'a binary relationship between two persons but also a descriptor for a group of concepts with similar properties (e.g. that they can be happy or unhappy). The result is that several class models can be drawn that represent the same domain correctly, which means that the results of the modelling process are not reproducible.

Furthermore, a consensus about the meaning of the concept 'UC_Association' in the use case diagram is lacking. In [Fow97, p.46] four alternative meanings can be found. This does also not contribute a deterministic modelling process with reproducible results.

Effectiveness, Efficiency - As has been mentioned before, the *effectiveness* and *efficiency* properties are not evaluated here because not much is known about the way of working in UML. This is due to the fact that UML is a language rather than a method.

5. CONCLUSIONS ON THE APPLICATION OF THE FRAMEWORK

In this paper we have proposed and illustrated the Q-Me framework for the evaluation of the quality of business modelling methods. The framework allows an assessment of both the product quality and the process quality of modelling methods, with regard to a set of properties that have been defined in the literature. The increasing usage of business modelling methods for reengineering, ERP implementation, TQM and workflow automation projects requires a framework which allows analysts and users to assess the quality of the vastly increasing amount of available methods.

The application of the Q-Me framework on the UML revealed both some strengths and weaknesses. The most important benefit of the framework is that it provides a set of categories and properties that allows a uniform and formal description of the model elements within one model type as well as the different model types used within one modelling method.

A uniform characterisation of a modelling method forms a precondition for comparison. The meta modelling method used in the Q-Me framework enables a good evaluation of coherence between the modelling concepts and models used in a modelling method. This property is important when designing support for the method. Also, the level of comprehensibility is revealed by the meta modelling method. Large numbers of concepts and relationships between the concepts decrease the ease with which users and analysts master a method.

A major shortcoming of the current status of the Q-Me framework is the lack of a formal definition of the operationalisation of properties and the absence of a quantifiable metric to express the quality of a business modelling method. Although the framework allows a characterisation on the basis of individual properties, the lack of an overall metric makes it difficult to make an objective comparison on the quality of different methods.

Finally, the application of the framework to the UML failed to test the effectiveness and efficiency since the UML has no pre-defined modelling process.

Future research will be conducted to improve the framework. The operationalisation of the introduced quality properties will be studied in more detail. Especially properties that relate to the way of working, such as effectiveness and efficiency will get attention. Furthermore, the theory will be validated by means of the application of the framework to other business process modelling methods. The results of this application will be compared with the opinion of experts in the field of business process modelling.

6. REFERENCES

[Bar98] Barros, A. P., Hofstede A. H. M. ter, *Towards the Construction of Workflow Suitable Conceptual Modelling Methods,* Information Systems Journal, October 1998;

[Boe78] Boehm, B., *Characteristics of Software Quality*, North-Holland, New York, 1978;

[Chen77] Chen, P. P., *The Entity-Relationship Model: towards a Unified View of Data*, ACM-TODS, 1977;

[Cro79] Crosby, P. B., *Quality is Free*, McGraw-Hill, London, 1979;

[Dav93] Davenport, T. H., *Process Innovation: Reengineering Work Through Information Technology,* Harvard Business School Press, Boston, 1993;

[Dav98] Davenport, T. H., *Putting the Enterprise into the Enterprise System*, Harvard Business Review, July-August 1998;

[Die94] Dietz, J. L. G., *Business Modelling for Business Redesign*, In: Proceedings of the 27th international conference on system sciences, IEEE Press, Los Alamitos, August 1994, pp. 723-732;

[Fow97] Fowler, M., Scott, K., *UML Distilled*, Addison-Wesley, Boston, 1997;

[Frisco96] Falkenberg, E. D. *et al, A Framework of Information System Concepts* (IFIP WG 8.1 Task Group FRISCO), Leiden University, Leiden, 1996;

[Gil92] Gillies, A. C., *Software Quality,* Chapman & Hall computing, London, 1992;

[Gold98] Goldkuhl, G., Lind, M., Seigerroth, U., *Method Integration as a Learning Process*, in: Jayaratna, N., Fitzgerald, B., Wood-Harper, T., Larasquet, J-M (Eds.), *Training and Education of Methodology Practitioners and Researchers*, Springer-Verlag, London;

[Hal98] Halpin, T., *Object Role Modeling (ORM/NIAM)* in: Handbook on Information Systems Architectures, Springer-Verlag, Heidelberg, 1998;

[Ham93] Hammer M., Champy, C., *Reengineering the Corporation: A Manifesto for Business Revolution*, Brealey, London, 1993;

[Har97] Harmsen A. F., *Situational Method Engineering*, Ph.D thesis, Moret Ernst & Young Management Consultants, Utrecht, 1997;

[Hof93] Hofstede, A. H. M. ter, *Information Modelling in Data Intensive Domains*, Ph.D thesis, University of Nijmegen, Nijmegen, 1993;

[Hru98] Hruby, P., *Structuring Specification of Business Systems with UML (with an Emphasis on Workflow Management Systems)*, Springer-Verlag, Heidelberg, 1998;

[Jay94] Jayaratna, N., *Understanding and Evaluating Methodologies; NIMSAD, a Systemic Framework.* McGraw-Hill, London, 1994;

[Jur79] Juran, J. M., *Quality Control Handbook,* McGraw-Hill, London, 1979;

[Ket97] Kettinger, W.J., *Business Process Change: A Study of Methodologies, Methods, and Tools*, MIS Quarterly, March 1997;

[Lind94] Lindland, O.I., Sindre, G., Sølvberg, A., *Understanding Quality in Conceptual Modelling*, IEEE Software, March 1994;

[Med92] Medina-Mora, R., Winograd, T., Flores, R., Flores, F., *The Action Workflow Approach to Workflow Management Technology,* CSCW'92 Proceedings, ACM, New-York, 1992;

[OMG99] Rational, UML Standard Version 1.3 Alpha R5, www.rational.com/uml, March 1999;

[Pen99] Penker M., Eriksson, H. J., *Business Modelling With UML; Business Patterns and Business Objects*, John Wiley & Sons, New-York, to be published 1999;

[Post96] Post H. A., Es, R. M. van (Eds), *Dynamic Enterprise Modeling: A paradigm Shift in Software Implementation,* Kluwer, Dordrecht, 1996;

[Rum91] Rumbaugh, J., Blaha, M., Premerlani, W., Eddy, F., Lorensen, W., *Object-Oriented Modeling and Design*, Prentice-Hall, Englewood Cliffs, 1991;

[Sel89] Seligmann, P. S., Wijers, G. M., Sol, H. G., *Analysing the Structure of IS methodologies, an Alternative Approach*, in: Proceedings of the 1st dutch conference on information systems, Amersfoort, 1989;

[UML97] Rational, *UML Extension for Business Modeling* version 1.1, www.rational.com/uml, 1997;

Comments on "The Quality of Business Process Modelling Methods" by B.-J. Hommes and V. van Reijswoud

Pieter W.G. Bots

Faculty of Technology, Policy, and Management
Delft University of Technology
P.O. Box 5015, 2600 GA Delft, The Netherlands
E-mail: p.w.g.bots@tpm.tudelft.nl

Quality matters. Good models are important to our discipline, and Bart-Jan Hommes and Victor van Reijswoud are to be commended for their effort to define what constitutes a good business process model. Their first steps in developing a Quality-based Modeling Evaluation (Q-Me) framework reflect a sincere determination to improve the current practice of business modeling by providing the means for objective comparison of modeling methods. The fundamental questions they must tackle are: 'What is model quality?' and 'Can it be measured objectively?' Quality is an elusive concept, and while trying to capture it in a framework, one is bound to get tangled up in what Hofstadter (1981) calls 'funny loops'. To gain a proper understanding of the approach the authors take in defining and operationalizing model quality, I try to trace the choices they make and assess the consequences of these choices.

Q-Me seems to be founded on three paradigmatic choices:

1. the 'four ways' view on modeling is appropriate to capture those aspects of a business process modeling method that constitute the determinants (in the sense of 'independent variables') for model quality,
2. the classification of processes as material/information/business, and the distinction between core processes and supportive processes, are appropriate to define business processes as an application domain, and

3. the FRISCO quality properties are appropriate starting nodes for a tree that operationalizes model quality as the 'dependent variable' of modeling method evaluation.

These decisions make sense, since they establish an immediate connection with previous work in relevant academic communities. But what biases do they introduce? Within the constraint of a two-page review, I can only point out some potential dangers.

First and foremost, figure 1 on page 116 reveals a blind spot that results from the adoption of the 'way of modeling' and the 'way of working' as looking glasses: for lack of a 'way of analyzing' and a 'way of implementing', the evaluation framework has no concepts to represent the *pragmatics* of a model, i.e., no concepts that can describe how insights are systematically derived from a model, or how these insights are converted to action. The FRISCO quality property 'effectiveness' offers but a fragile handhold for investigation of this vital aspect of model quality: does the model help improving the business performance?

Secondly, the adoption of a classification of processes within organizations in three categories (material processes, informational processes, and business processes) and the distinction between core processes and supportive processes as the standard for 'suitability' and 'completeness' may need reconsideration. If this classification is axiomatic in the sense that it *defines* the business process application area, this axiom deserves a more elaborate introduction and justification. If it is an arbitrary choice, it defies further attempts to *objective* measurement, which would seem to be the ultimate purpose of the Q-Me framework.

The Q-Me framework succeeds in providing the concepts necessary for objective measurement of the FRISCO quality properties 'coherence' and 'expressiveness'. 'Coherence' is operationalized in terms of the *existence* of relations between modeling concepts. However, it does not address the semantics and pragmatics of these relations, although these might make a significant difference in the *strength* of these relations. 'Expressiveness' is defined as a relative measure, since it requires at least two modeling methods to establish its value. Objective measurement therefore would require a standard for the business process domain, similar to the 'Turing completeness' criterion for imperative programming languages. Moreover, such a standard would effectively counter my earlier criticism on the definition of what constitutes the business process domain.

The FRISCO quality property 'comprehensibility' is more slippery when it comes to objective measurement. How to establish the consistency of the notation-meaning and meaning-concept relations in the Q-Me framework? If the arrow in a flowchart is comprehensible because an arrow is a 'natural symbol' for sequence, what about the arrows that model causality in concept maps, or the arrows that model inputs, controls, outputs, and mechanisms in SADT (see e.g., DeMarca)? Apparently, arrows are 'natural symbols' for a variety of concepts; it is the notion of 'natural symbol' is inherently subjective. The second operationalization of 'comprehensibility' – the number of different modeling concepts used in a method – can be measured objectively, but such a count does not take into account that 'loading' of symbols (e.g., four different meanings of an arrow in SADT) *decreases* comprehensibility, whereas a hierarchical structure of a modeling method (e.g., the recursive decomposition of activities in SADT) *increases* comprehensibility

When the relation between modeling concepts and 'reality' becomes more central to a FRISCO quality property, the Q-Me framework obviously needs more work, still. It is doubtful whether 'determinism' is a property that can be measured objectively. Any symbolic notation requires 'correspondence rules' with objects in 'reality', and how are such rules to be expressed? Any language is intersubjective, at best. A similar problem emerges when trying to operationalize 'effectiveness'. The authors acknowledge that a lot of empirical ground needs to be covered here, still. 'Effectiveness' is by definition a measure for goal attainment. But what *is* the goal of a modeling method? If the goal is merely representational, it is attained the moment the modeler states the model is complete. If the goal is to be functional in analysis, the types of questions the model should be capable of answering must be defined more precisely. If the goal is practical, its expected impact on the behavior of people must be defined, etcetera.

To summarize, the current version of the Q-Me framework is successful in operationalizing quality mainly in terms of the syntax of a business process modeling language. Syntax may constitute the structure of conceptual models, but semantics and pragmatics are their heart and life blood. To be a truly effective means in the hands of business modelers, a conceptual model of quality should focus on measuring these aspects. In its present state, Q-Me may be lopsided still, but it has good growth potential.

References

Hofstadter, D.R. (1979) *Goedel, Escher, Bach: an Eternal Golden Braid*, New York: Basic Books.

Marca, D.A. and C.L. McGowan (1988) *SADT: Structured Analysis and Design Technique*, New York: McGraw-Hill.

MODELLING CONCURRENT PROCESS COORDINATION IN WORKFLOW SPECIFICATIONS

Alistair P. Barros
Distributed Systems Technology Centre
The University of Queensland
Brisbane Qld 4072
*Australia**
abarros@dstc.edu.au

Arthur H.M. ter Hofstede
Cooperative Information Systems Research Centre
Queensland University of Technology
GPO Box 2434, Brisbane Qld 4001
Australia
arthur@icis.qut.edu.au

Keywords: workflow, conceptual modelling, formalisation, semantics

Abstract The provision of business services, in practice, exhibits the processes of several organisations, run in parallel for their local stakeholds, with points of synchronisation serving to coordinate the differently executing parts. Current workflow tools restrict business processing coordination to *single* workflows. This means different processing parts are unnaturally coupled into the same unit of modularity, thereby restricting workflow resusability. In this paper, we demonstrate three extensions which serve to coordinate the execution of concurrently executing and interdependent workflows: the adaption of synchronous and asynchronous messaging for inter-workflow communication, the abort of inter-related execution paths for coordinated exception handling and the exclusive, i.e. atomic, execution of nested processes in the context concurrently executing processes. These extensions are applied at the conceptual level

*Part of this work has been supported by CITEC, a business unit of the Queensland Government's Department of Public Works and Housing.

of specification, illustrated through highlights from an industrial case study and assigned a formal semantics.

1. INTRODUCTION

Through workflow management, a number of concepts emerging from the last twenty years of dynamic and process modelling research, are exploited to capture models of business processes such that those models are directly interpreted and executed. Constructs like task sequencing, choice, iteration and parallelisation, combined with mechanisms of data flow and organisational resource models, are now common place in a large number of (production) workflow tools (see workflow technology survey in (Makey, 1996)).

Currently, workflow tools restrict the coordination of business processes to single workflows. While this seems adequate for organisations in fairly early phases of workflow use or where their business processing fits into relatively isolated and single workflows, in practice, single workflow coordination is restrictive. This is because the provision of business services such as insurance claims, property transfers and legal court matters, involves not just customers and service providers, but a whole spectrum of stakeholders (typically external agencies), whose processing occurs in parallel with points of synchronisation "threading" together the workflow.

Of course, constructs like multiple task triggers (e.g. AND splits) and synchronisers (e.g. AND and OR joins) allow the processing of different parties to run in parallel and to be synchronised "downstream". Furthermore, the nested feature of workflow tasks allows entire workflows to be encapsulated into tasks, allowing modular specifications to be built up and reused. Under this construction, however, the workflow is still relatively sequential and one part serves to coordinate the workflow as a whole. For service provision involving truly autonomous and separate parts, for instance domains utilising autonomous agents in E-commerce services, the workflow components may be observed to be inflexibly constructed and quasi-autonomous. What is required is the interoperability of truly autonomous workflows where synchronisation can occur across the different workflows, as opposed to occurring in a single (coordinator) workflow.

Concurrent interaction in conceptual modelling has been has been well-researched when one considers, say, the work done with Petri nets (Aalst, 1996). Petri nets have provided an *expressive* and a *formal* base for technique development, and much of the adaptations of higher order Petri nets have yielded relatively *comprehensive* and *suitable* constructs for commercial domains, e.g. (Ramackers, 1994; Kappel and Schrefl, 1990). On the other hand, two related areas of omission are exception handling (Eder and Liebhart, 1998) and rollback recovery (Alonso et al., 1996) both of which are vital for workflow suitability (Barros and Hofstede, 1998). Currently in techniques, the ramifications of concurrent processing for exception handling are not well understood.

In this paper, we demonstrate how the coordination of a number of workflow components can captured at the conceptual level. In particular, we adapt *messaging* which allows the different components to communicate in an asynchronous and synchronous manner. Our proposal focussed on process control aspects. As shown in (Barros and Hofstede, 1997) the integration with a data modelling technique allows the typing of message tokens which captures the document/data structure they represent. Moreover, data model query languages like RIDL and LISA-D (Hofstede et al., 1993) can be used in detailed task specifications of the workflow to manipulate the passed information - thereby preserving full conceptualisation of the specification.

To complete the workflow treatment, we illustrate how exception handling can be incorporated in the parallel context. For this, we introduce *aborts* which are applied to a related set of processes running concurrently and we indicate how such a construct fits into rollback recovery.

Through the combination of the messaging and parallel aborts, some quite powerful workflow processing situations can be captured - like sending out requests for information to a number of stakeholders, continuing processing, receiving any responses and if any exception arises, aborting processing.

The introduction of such powerful constructs in the face of concurrent workflow execution, particularly the presence of multiple instances of the same type of process and process decompositions, can complicate correct workflow execution. We show how a formal semantics can be assigned for the constructs using a formal language from the Process Algebra family, Algebra of Communicating Processes (ACP) (Baeten and Weijland, 1990) which has had significant applications (Baeten, 1990).

The organisation of this paper is as follows. In section 2, we describe the modelling extensions and their contribution to concurrent workflow coordination. Examples are drawn from an industrial case study, the tenure administration of Road Closures documented in (Barros et al., 1997). In section 3, the formal semantics is presented based on a full formalisation defined in (Barros and Hofstede, 1997). In section 4, the paper is concluded and future research directions are described.

2. CONCEPTUAL WORKFLOW MODELLING: A PRACTICAL ILLUSTRATION

In this section, we describe the workflow extensions (section 2.2) of abstract messaging and aborts to concurrent workflow coordination, within a practical setting. In particular, the proposed constructs are used to illustrate the business processing "patterns" of: remote information polling, deferred exception handling and remote object validation.

The extensions are applied to a conceptual process modelling technique Task Structures (Hofstede and Nieuwland, 1993). Task Structures provide a number of constructs which are characteristic of process-centric workflow specifications (section 2.1). Importantly, Task Structures are integrated with a multi-level, data modelling technique CDM (Creasy and Proper, 1996). This allows for a (schema) typing of information manipulated by the workflow at the conceptual level. The manipulation capturing *detailed* process specifications, is described in a conceptual specification language, LISA-D (Hofstede et al., 1993).

2.1. BASIC TASK STRUCTURES

As depicted in Figure 1, the coordinative mechanism in Task Structures is a trigger (solid arrow) and the chief end of triggering is the execution of a process, also referred to as a task (rounded box). A process may be defined in terms of other processes known as its subprocesses. The execution of a process decomposition follows the triggering structure, starting with its initially executing elements (indicated by bent arrows at the top of the elements). An initially executing element needs to be indicated because iteration, i.e. a trigger looping back to a preceeding element, introduces uncertainty as to what this is.

Decisions (circles) model moments of choice, where each outgoing trigger is associated with a condition. A decision's outcome, i.e. executed trigger, is the one which is truth satisfied. Like guarded commands of (Dijkstra, 1975), decision conditions may overlap, allowing nondeterministic choices to be modelled. Some decisions terminate, meaning that one of their outcomes results in no further processing, thereby terminating the execution path.

Synchronisers (triangle) allow a junction of incoming and/or outgoing triggers. The former models the synchronisation of execution paths (running in parallel), prior to further processing continuing. The latter models a set of execution paths to be started in parallel (this would typically be used in relation to a decision, as multiple output triggers of a task also capture parallel initiation of other task objects).

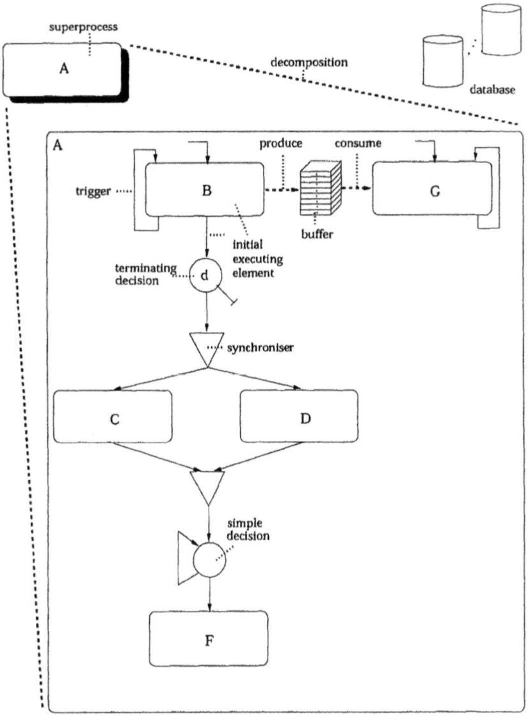

Figure 1 Basic Task Structure concepts

In line with multi-database workflow environments, we allow a set of databases to be associated with a workflow model. Database schemas are captured through CDM data models and detailed specifications of processes (preconditions, actions and postconditions) and decisions (conditions) are expressed through LISA-D. In LISA-D statements, therefore, the databases that they apply to should be qualified. Through abstraction, specialisation and generalisation hierarchies, different types of multi-database configurations can be captured. As we will see through messaging extensions below, this modelling flexibility can also be applied to capture document flow and manipulation.

In addition to the synchroniser, Task Structures allow concurrent parts of a workflow to be coordinated through buffers. By using buffers, e.g. in-trays, pigeon holes and e-mail boxes, different though data dependent processes can run independently, where data produced by one process, is consumed by another, via a buffer. Two special operations, *produce* and *consume*, are available for buffer manipulation and buffers have a *protocol* which defines their order, e.g. a First-In, Last-Out (FILO) or an arbitrarily ordered queue. When a process produces data into a buffer, the value is "appended" to the buffer as part of its termination. When a process consumes from a buffer, the value of buffer's "top" location is removed and allocated to the process as part of its initiation.

To assist in the expressive power of specifications, variables may be defined in decompositions and accessed by processes and decisions in their decomposition hierarchies. Values produced in, or consumed from, buffers are stored in variables (having the same name as buffers).

2.2. EXTENSIONS TO TASK STRUCTURES

Abstract messaging Our application of messaging at the workflow level, namely *abstract* messaging, permits communication between processes running in separate decomposition contexts. In contrast to buffering, messaging involves direct process to process communication.

Like in traditional messaging systems, messaging at the abstract level is characterised by two modes. A *synchronous* mode, also available in object-oriented techniques, e.g. UML (Fowler, 1997), involves a suspension of execution related to a messaging dependency on some other process. An *asynchronous* mode involves no such suspension of execution. As illustrated in Figure 2, these modes are used in three fundamental configurations to capture different message processing requirements.

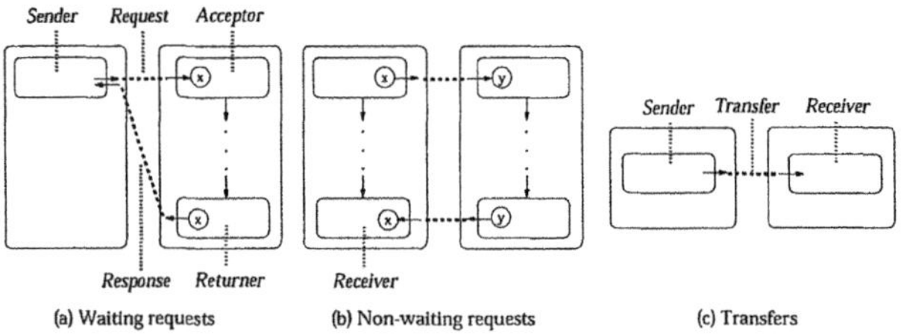

Figure 2 Messaging configurations

Through a *waiting request* configuration (a), a message is passed to a remote source, however further execution of the process is suspended until a return message is received. Hence, we say the configuration embodies a request. The required construct for the initiating request is clearly a synchronous *sender*.

In another decomposition, the request is received by an *acceptor*. As apparent, receiving is inherently synchronous, i.e. the process is blocked from execution until receipt of the message. To return a *response* for the request, we also require a *returner* which simply performs an asynchronous send. For the construction of responses, we allow any general processing to occur prior to the return. This means that the acceptor and the returner should be *correlated*, to ensure that their relationship is preserved and not mixed up with other message constructs in the decomposition.

The configuration of *non-waiting requests* (b) arises through liberating the suspension of execution associated with the request. In this case, the request is issued through an asynchronous sender. A *receiver* which is correlated with this sender is therefore required to receive the request. We describe this pair as a *send-receive* pair, and for reasons which we have just described, a corresponding accept-return pair contributes to the full configuration.

Finally, the configuration of (c) involves one-way communication only, between an (asynchronous) sender and a receiver. Since no other dependency occurs in the communication, we describe this configuration as a *transfer*.

To illustrate the application of messaging for workflows, consider Figures 3 and 4. Together, these illustrate a scenario which we refer to as *remote information polling*. One part of the process model in Figure 3 involves the determination of information from a remote site using a waiting request; processing from the sender's side, only, is illustrated. A message label (Parcel Info) is used to indicate the request and transfer communication between processes. Thus, to specify the receiving side in this example, the same message label would be have to be assigned to an acceptor. The other part of Figure 3 involves the transfer of messages (Notify Stakeholders) based on information gathered from the preceeding search.

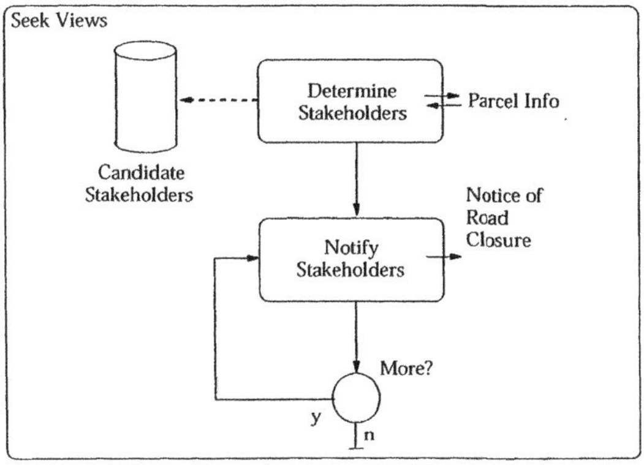

Figure 3 Information polling example: request sending

Figure 4 depicts the receiving of messages, anticipated as a result of the requests which have been issued. A receiver accepts incoming correspondences which are each split up and examined. Note, the cyclic trigger for message receiving, since multiple responses should arrive. In effect, each receipt generates a separate and possibly parallel execution path for subsequent processing. Also note, the parallel processing between the splitting and examination processes via a buffer.

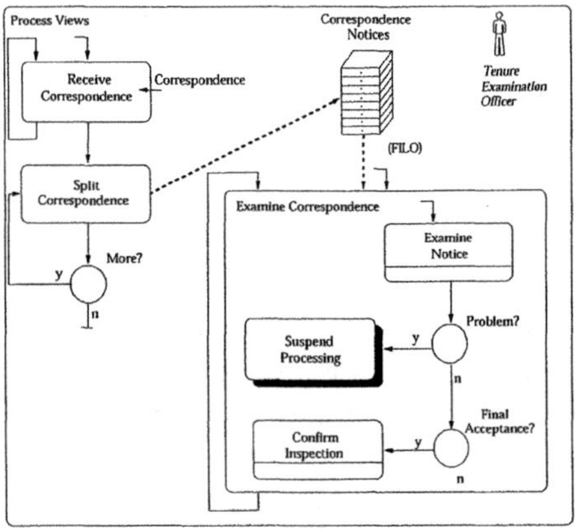

Figure 4 Information polling example: response receiving

Aborts A second extension arises from the existence of parallel (and semantically related execution paths) in a workflow. We have just seen an example of this situation in Figure 4, where process instances are generated continuously through cyclic triggers. An important question is: when does such a process (decomposition) terminate? In general, while constructs are available to initiate multiple execution paths, e.g. through multiple initially executing elements and multiple triggers from a process or synchroniser, no associated construct is available which issues their termination. This can lead to a practice where such a design is avoided or termination is left to programming detail, thereby compromising the conceptualisation of the design.

For this type of situation, we introduce a particular type of trigger, an *abort*, whose function is to terminate related execution paths. To control which parts of a workflow are terminated, we restrict the effect of aborts to decompositions. In general, when an abort is executed, all the processing in a decomposition is terminated and an *abort handler* is executed.

In Figure 5, the use of aborts is combined with messaging to illustrate an efficiency in business processing which we refer to as *deferred exception handling*. In the example, under normal circumstances, customers are required to confirm acceptance and make payments before further processing can continue. An efficiency is introduced by allowing the processing to go ahead on the understanding that customers typically make these provisions, and if the provisions are not made, processing is aborted. Two examples of such deferred exception handling are evident in the figure.

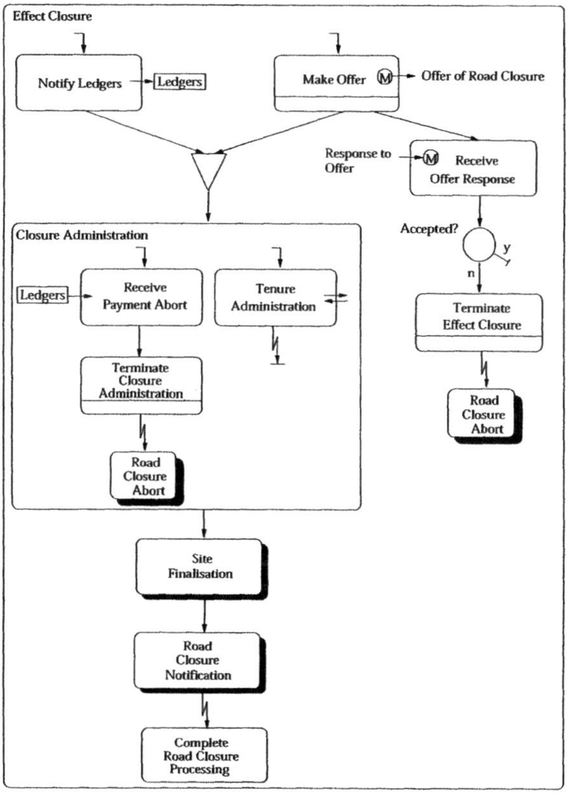

Figure 5 Deferred exception handling example using aborts

Firstly, Make Offer issues an Offer of Road Closure and triggers two processes, one which allows the main processing to continue ahead and the other which waits for the Response to (the) Offer. If the offer is not Accepted?, the whole of the Effect Closure is aborted. The abort (zig-zag arrow) is activated by Terminate Effect Closure, and as a result, the abort handler, Road Closure Abort, is run. This can be used for post-abort processing, e.g. notifying stakeholders about the abort.

Secondly, within Closure Administration the new tenure information is prepared remotely, with another process used to Receive Payment Abort; this might have occurred because payment was not made for whatever reason. There is an assumption that if the Tenure Administration completes prior to any payment abort, then remaining processing continues. Hence, an abort is triggered after Tenure Administration to ensure that no part of the decomposition "hangs" around after its execution. For the same sort of reason, we include an abort of Effect Closure at the end.

Another application of aborts and messaging is a commonly encountered scenario which we refer to as *remote object validation*. Here, validation checks through remote searches, are run in parallel, where the determination of some outcomes might not warrant further processing to continue. Figure 6 illustrates this by incorporating messaging and aborts into a composite decision construct.

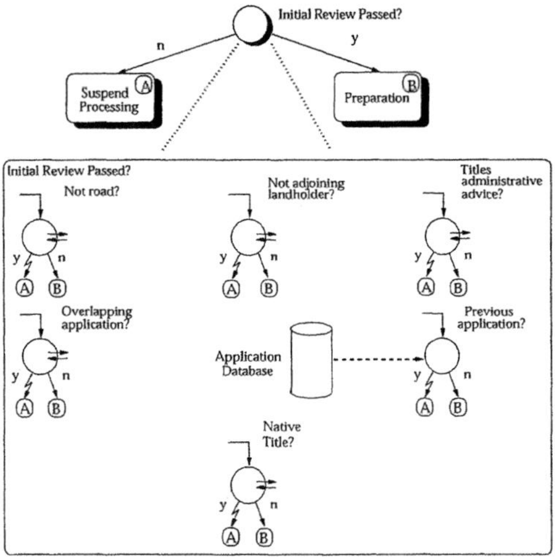

Figure 6 Object validation example: parallel searches in complex decisions

The example involves the validation of a Road Closures Application object to determine whether further processing is warranted. The whole validation is modelled as a complex decision whereby its two outcomes are determined from its internal structure. Each check is modelled as a simple decision running in parallel (hence the initial element symbol). Decisions with synchronous messaging capture the remote searches; note messaging on a decision is a short-hand for a messaging process followed by a decision.

For the requirement that any one decision failing is sufficient to determine a complex decision outcome, we use the abort construct. The triggering of an abort results in the complex decision being terminated (i.e. all its execution paths), and the relevant external outcome (A) being executed. For non-aborting outcomes, we do not want multiple executions of the related complex decision outcome (B), for each of the internal, exiting outcomes, to be executed. Rather, each such internal outcome has the effect of an exit, without terminating the complex decision. The exception is, of course, the last outcome which should indeed trigger the external outcome.

Figure 7 illustrates a modification to the example where prioritisation in the decision processing is introduced. This is useful since object validation in workflow applications can involve large and expensive remote searches which somehow should be prioritised.

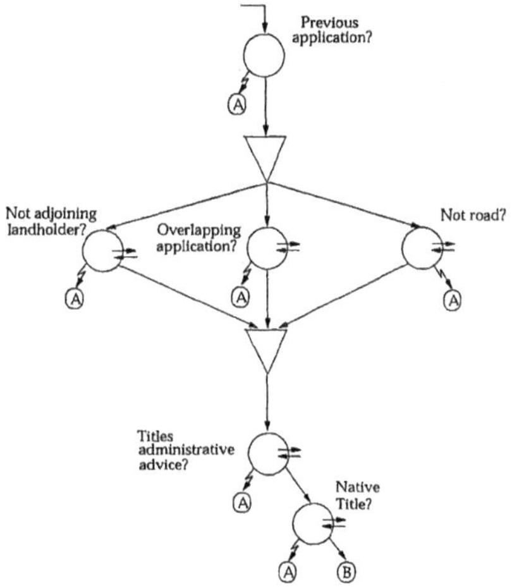

Figure 7 Object validation example: prioritised searches in complex decisions

Combining buffering, messaging and aborts Yet another illustration of buffering, messaging and aborts for concurrent workflow processing arises in the example of a Change of Address service, illustrated in Figures 8 and 9. The intention of this workflow is to provide people on the Web with a flexible mechanism of notifying particular parties (e.g. banks, insurance companies, civil service departments, doctors etc.) of their address changes.

The first part, illustrated in Figure 8 shows the specification of parties by a person through one or more invocations of Change of Address entry/update. Each invocation generates an execution path which determines whether personal authentication is required from a trusted agent and accordingly aborting the service or effecting notifications (based on the supplied parties). Effecting notifications involves a further parallelism - for each notification sent, a corresponding receiver waits for the response from the party.

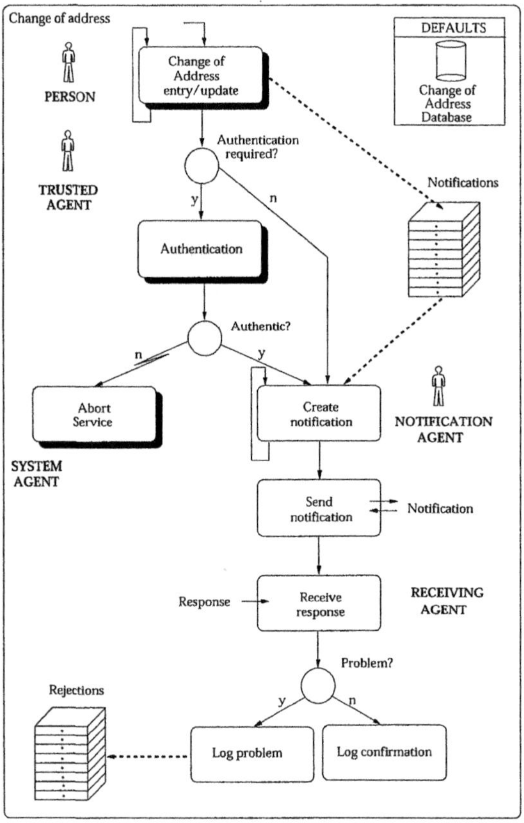

Figure 8 Another information polling example - part 1

The second part, illustrated in Figure 9 shows the specification allowing people to deal with rejections in parallel and converting them into notification, proper. The third part, also in the same figure, caters for service termination. This has to be done explicitly since the flexibility of the workflow activates new invocations of all its parts (specified through cyclic triggers on the initial processes). Such flexibility caters for people using the same service over a "long" duration (which is typically required when people recollect how they have to notify for their address changes).

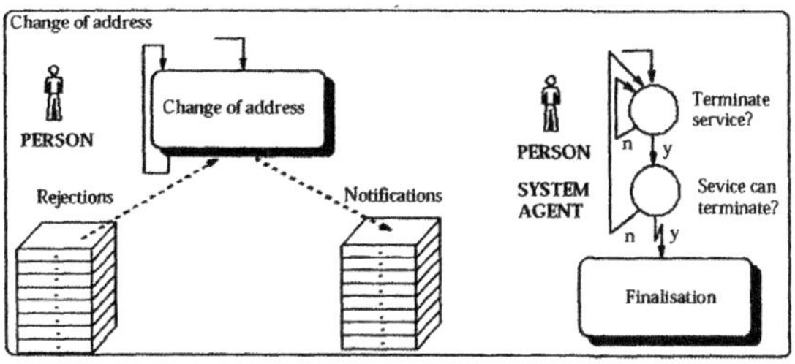

Figure 9 Another information polling example - part 2 and 3

3. FORMAL SEMANTICS

In this section, we demonstrate how the advanced workflow concepts discussed in the previous section can be assigned a formal semantics. Naturally, in the context of concurrent and distributed systems, such as workflows, it is imperative that their specifications are unambiguous and allow for formal reasoning. Hence, such specifications need a formal semantics, which can be achieved through a mapping to a formal system. In this case we have chosen the Process Algebra as our formal domain. Although the name Process Algebra suggests a single algebra to describe processes, it actually refers to a whole family of algebras based on the same principles. Traditionally, only the family member used is presented. As an algebraic theory, Process Algebra belongs to the same family as CSP (Hoare, 1978) and CCS (Milner, 1989) Our translation is based on a particular Process Algebra, the Algebra of Communicating Processes with the empty action (which we will abbreviate to ACP_ε). An in-depth description may be found in (Baeten and Weijland, 1990) with a useful set of applications described in (Baeten, 1990).

It should be noted right from the start though, that this section will not provide the complete formal semantics of the presented workflow specification language (for this, the reader is referred to (Barros and Hofstede, 1997)). Rather, focus is on the formalization of the process control aspects of the three workflow extensions presented in the previous section including three illustrating (abstract) examples, showing how the formal semantics can be manipulated. Data environments, e.g. databases, buffers and messages, are not considered in the formalization. Apart from its importance for e.g. equivalence considerations, the formalization serves to demonstrate that the presented workflow specification language is more than just another drawing convention.

3.1. PROCESS MODEL TRANSLATION

In assigning a formal semantics to workflow specifications, basically each concept will correspond to a process variable with a corresponding ACP_ε equation. Typically, for a workflow object x the corresponding process variable is denoted E_x. For each aborting processes z we also need to introduce a process variable T_z, as such objects need to be initiated differently. As we do not aim at a comprehensive treatment of the formalization, the syntax will be discussed "on the fly" and only as far as needed for a proper understanding of the semantics.

Executing a task t means executing its body, given by its name $\mathsf{Name}(t)$, followed by triggering in parallel its output task objects:

$$E_t = \mathsf{Name}(t) \cdot \mathbf{trigrest}(t)$$

The abbreviation **trigrest**(t) provides the possible triggering paths following the execution of t. As previously mentioned, the translation of triggering and aborting process elements is distinguished. Synchronizers have to be treated differently too. Every process element x which is to trigger synchroniser s, starts an atomic action $\sigma_{x,s}$ after termination. A synchroniser is started when all such atomic actions, related to its input process elements, communicate, noting that communication is not necessarily binary since more than two process elements may be input to a synchroniser. The details of the formal semantics of synchronizers will not be discussed further in the context of this paper, we refer the reader to (Hofstede and Nieuwland, 1993).

$$\mathbf{trigrest}(t) \quad = \quad \left(\mathop{\Big\|}_{\substack{x \in \mathcal{X} \setminus (\mathcal{Y} \cup \mathcal{Z}), \\ \mathsf{Trig}(t,x)}} E_x \quad \mathop{\Big\|}_{\substack{z \in \mathcal{Z} \setminus \mathcal{Y}, \\ \mathsf{Trig}(t,z)}} T_z \quad \mathop{\Big\|}_{\substack{y \in \mathcal{Y}, \\ \mathsf{Trig}(t,y)}} \sigma_{t,y} \right)$$

In the above definition, $\mathcal{X}$ is the set of all process elements, $\mathcal{Y}$ is the set of all synchronizers, and $\mathcal{Z}$ is the set of all aborting processes. The relation Trig defines the trigger relations between workflow objects. If t does not invoke one of the three possible types of execution paths, the relevant merge will be defined over the empty set. This exception is dealt with by defining the merge over the empty set to be the empty action ε as this is the neutral element for parallel composition.

Tasks that have names that do not have an associated decomposition correspond to atomic actions. For names that have an associated decomposition the corresponding equation states that its execution corresponds to starting all its initial items in parallel. Naturally, the usual distinction between aborting and nonaborting processes needs to be made, but we also need to add the brackets for the aborting context (this will be explained in the next subsection):

$$V = \ll \left(\mathop{\Big\|}_{\substack{\mathsf{Init}(x) = V \\ x \notin \mathcal{Z}}} E_x \quad \mathop{\Big\|}_{\substack{\mathsf{Init}(x) = V \\ x \in \mathcal{Z}}} T_x \right) \gg$$

The partial function Init applied to a process element x yields, if defined, the name of the supertask of x. This function is only defined for those process elements that are initial item.

The corresponding equation for a decision d has to reflect the choice for the possible workflow objects involved:

$$E_d = \sum_{\substack{d \,\mathsf{Trig}\, y, \\ y \in \mathcal{Y}}} \sigma_{d,s} + \sum_{\substack{d \,\mathsf{Trig}\, z, \\ z \in \mathcal{Z}}} T_z + \sum_{\substack{d \,\mathsf{Trig}\, x, \\ x \notin \mathcal{Y} \cup \mathcal{Z}}} E_x + \zeta_d$$

where $\zeta_d = \varepsilon$ if d is a terminating decision and $\zeta_d = \delta$ otherwise.

3.1.1 Translation of abort processes. An entire decomposition's execution can be aborted when a process element, specifically a process or decision, in the decomposition is executed. The only processing which follows is an abort handler associated with the aborting element. We saw two significant applications of this, namely messaging interrupts (Figure 5) and complex decision processing (Figure 6).

To provide a general treatment for aborts, we introduce the abort operator which is axiomatised below.

$$\begin{aligned}
\ll \varepsilon \gg &= \varepsilon && \text{(I1)}\\
\ll a \cdot X \gg &= a \cdot \ll X \gg \text{ if } a \notin Q && \text{(I2)}\\
\ll X + Y \gg &= \ll X \gg + \ll Y \gg && \text{(I3)}\\
\ll \langle X \rangle \looparrowright \langle Y \rangle \cdot Z \gg &= XY && \text{(I4)}
\end{aligned}$$

For the translation of aborting process elements, we introduce in I4, an abort expression of the form $\langle X \rangle \looparrowright \langle Y \rangle$, where X denotes the aborting element and Y denotes the abort handler. Since aborting elements and abort handlers may be entire decompositions, X and Y are delimited. The effect of the abort operator is achieved by ignoring everything after the abort handler in an abort context. (The abort context is also removed since the abort expression is removed). The set of all abort expressions is given by Q, and such expressions should be treated as atomic actions in terms of the ACP_ε axioms. Through axiom I2, we can see that atomic actions can be shifted outside abort contexts provided they are not abort expressions.

Since an abort expression already contains the equation denotation for an aborting element, its translation requires an alternate equation denotation to represent the whole equation. This circumvents circularity in the translation. So for an aborting process $z \in \mathcal{Z}$, we have:

$$T_z = \langle E_z \rangle \looparrowright \left\langle E_{\mathsf{Abt}(z)} \right\rangle$$

where $\mathsf{Abt}(z)$ yields the abort handler of z.

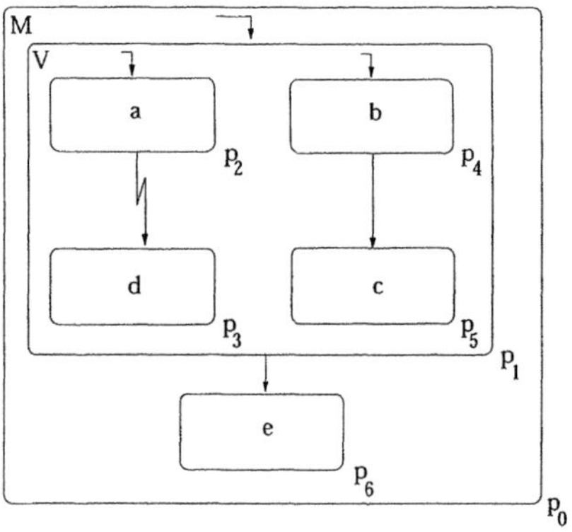

Figure 10 Aborting process example

Example 3.1

In the process model of Figure 10, a decomposition V contains two subprocesses, p_2 *and* p_4*, started in parallel, one of which,* p_2*, aborts processing, triggering the abort handler* p_3 *in the decomposition.*

The previous translations applied to the process model yield the following equations:

$$\begin{array}{lcl@{\qquad}lcl} E_{p_0} & = & M & E_{p_2} & = & a \\ M & = & E_{p_1} & E_{p_3} & = & d \\ E_{p_1} & = & V \cdot E_{p_6} & E_{p_4} & = & b \cdot E_{p_5} \\ E_{p_6} & = & e & E_{p_5} & = & c \\ V & = & \ll T_{p_2} \parallel E_{p_4} \gg & T_{p_2} & = & \langle E_{p_2} \rangle \looparrowright \langle E_{p_3} \rangle \end{array}$$

The abort processing axioms can then be applied to reduce the equation for the process model:

$$E_{p_0} = \ll E_{p_2} \parallel E_{p_4} \gg \cdot\, e$$

$$
\begin{aligned}
&= \ll \langle a \rangle \looparrowright \langle d \rangle \parallel bc \gg \cdot\, e \\
&= \ll \langle a \rangle \looparrowright \langle d \rangle \mathbin{|\!\!\lfloor} bc + bc \mathbin{|\!\!\lfloor} \langle a \rangle \looparrowright \langle d \rangle \gg \cdot\, e \\
&= (\ll \langle a \rangle \looparrowright \langle d \rangle\, bc \gg + \ll b(c \parallel \langle a \rangle \looparrowright \langle d \rangle) \gg) \cdot e \\
&= (ad + b(\ll c \langle a \rangle \looparrowright \langle d \rangle \gg + \ll \langle a \rangle \looparrowright \langle d \rangle \cdot c \gg)) \cdot e \\
&= (ad + b(cad + ad))e \\
&= ade + b(cade + ade)
\end{aligned}
$$

This shows that after executing the abort task named a the tasks named b and c are not executed anymore.

3.1.2 Translation of messaging. All up, we have described three essential types of messaging configurations which may be identified in specifications involving direct (i.e. unbuffered) inter-process messaging. These are *waiting requests* involving a synchronous sender and an accept-return pair (two way communication), *non-waiting requests* involving send-receive and accept-return pairs (two way communication), and *transfers* involving an asynchronous sender and a receiver (one way communication). For communication, processes require the same messaging scopes, and inherent in this is the compatibility of parameter passing. Moreover, accept-return and send-receive pairs require a correlation.

As, from a formal perspective, non-waiting requests and transfers are simpler than waiting requests, just representing variations on a similar theme, only the (simplified) formalization of waiting requests is presented here. The approach is simplified in that 1) individualization of processes (and hence of their messages) is (virtually) not considered, and 2) information passing and how this affects the global state of the system is ignored (again, the reader is referred to (Barros and Hofstede, 1997) for a full treatment of these issues). Our strategy has been adapted from the approach undertaken in a formalisation of messaging for Jacobson's Objectory (Hubbers and Hofstede, 1997).

Synchronous senders cater for situations like *requests* for information or the provision of notifications, where *responses* or acknowledgements (to the sender) are required. Characteristic of this type of communication is the suspension of execution which follows the message sending, until a return message is received.

Intuitively, the translation of synchronous senders $w \in \mathcal{W}$ contains a send and a receive part. The send part requires a messaging scope $\mathsf{MesgScope}(w)$ "within" which, the message occurs, together with parameters $\mathsf{SendPar}(w)$ containing queries from which any associated information can be constructed. The wait part requires parameters $\mathsf{RecPar}(w)$

which will contain any returned data.

$$\begin{aligned} E_w &= \mathsf{send}(\mathsf{MesgScope}(w); \mathsf{SendPar}(w)) \cdot \\ &\quad \mathtt{wait}(\mathsf{MesgScope}(w); \mathsf{RecPar}(w)) \cdot \\ &\quad \mathbf{trigrest}(w) \end{aligned}$$

We allow a number of message parameters for generality, e.g. for multiple documents or the passing of process control data accompanying a document.

As it is possible that multiple instances of the same task are active at the same time, one needs to be able to distinguish between messages sent by these different instances. To this end, a rename operator ρ^α (inspired by the work in (Vaandrager, 1990), where it was used for the formal semantics of the parallel object oriented language POOL) is used that individualises send related statements. This leads to expressions such as:

$$\rho^\alpha(\mathtt{send}(c; q_1, \ldots, q_n) \cdot X) \quad = \quad \mathtt{send}(c; q_1, \ldots, q_n)@\alpha \cdot \rho^\alpha(X)$$

In this equation, α represents a process id, which is incorporated in the send action. This allows other actions to recognize which particular process instance has sent the message. In the context of this paper though, we will not go into further details in relation to process individualization.

Of course, a request cannot be materialised unless the sent message is received by an acceptor a. Its translation involves an `accept` action with its parameters corresponding to the sent message:

$$E_a = \mathtt{accept}(\mathsf{MesgScope}(a); \mathsf{RecPar}(a))$$

A `request` (pending) is generated when individualised `send` and `accept` actions communicate:

$$\begin{aligned} &\mathtt{send}(c; q_1, \ldots, q_n)@\alpha \mid \mathtt{accept}(c; s_1, \ldots, s_n)@\beta = \\ &\mathtt{request}(\langle \alpha, \beta, \rangle; q_1 \colon s_1, \ldots, q_n \colon s_n) \end{aligned}$$

Effectively, the sent and received parameters are associated within a specific messaging context denoted by the pair $\langle \alpha, \beta \rangle$. This enables messaging configuration construction, where α identifies the sender of the request and β identifies the acceptor. The communication function γ restricts `request` actions generated to those which involve compatible message scopes c, i.e. both `send` and `accept` actions have the same messaging scope c. Final materialisation of a request occurs when a state operator passes through the `request` action.

Corresponding to an acceptor is a returner r, which is instrumental in providing a response to requests. It has the following translation:

$$E_r = \mathtt{return}(\mathsf{MesgScope}(\mathsf{Acceptor}(r)); \mathsf{SendPar}(r))$$

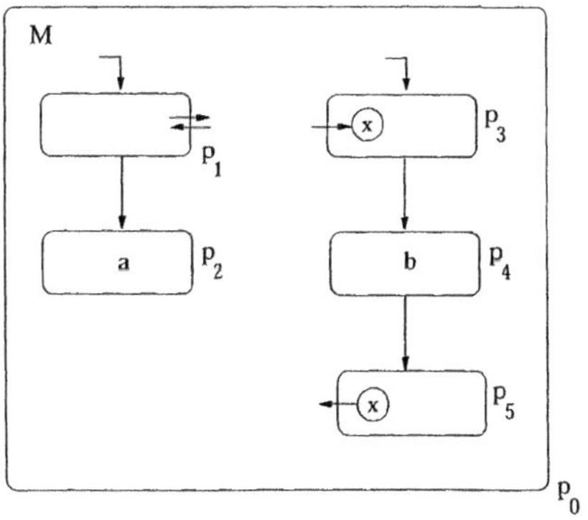

Figure 11 Example of a waiting request configuration

where $\mathsf{Acceptor}(r)$ yields the corresponding acceptor of r. A `response` is generated when a `return` communicates with a `wait`:

$$\texttt{return}(c; t_1, \ldots, t_m)@\beta \mid \texttt{wait}(c; r_1, \ldots, r_m)@\alpha = \texttt{response}(\langle \alpha, \beta \rangle; r_1{:}\, t_1, \ldots, r_m{:}\, t_m)$$

The state operator restricts `response` actions to those where the `return` and `wait` are part of the same messaging configuration.

Finally, it should be remarked that as communications actions are used, the encapsulation operator needs to be applied. Hence, the corresponding equation for the main task becomes:

$$E_{p_0} = \preccurlyeq \partial_H(\mathsf{Name}(E_{p_0})) \succcurlyeq$$

where H represents the set containing all communication actions.

Example 3.2

The process model of Figure 11 depicts a waiting request configuration. The synchronous sender is p_1 and the corresponding accept-return pair consists of p_3 and p_5, with p_3 the acceptor and p_5 the returner. For communication to proceed, the messaging scope is defined as $\mathsf{MesgScope}(p_1) = \mathsf{MesgScope}(p_3) = m$ and we assume no information passing.

Ignoring abort and system contexts (as no aborts or monitors occur), the previous translations applied to the process model yield the following equations:

$$\begin{aligned} E_{p_0} &= M & M &= \partial_H(E_{p_1} \parallel E_{p_3}) \\ E_{p_1} &= \texttt{send}(m) \cdot \texttt{wait}(m) \cdot E_{p_2} & E_{p_4} &= b \cdot E_{p_5} \\ E_{p_2} &= a & E_{p_5} &= \texttt{return}(m) \\ E_{p_3} &= \texttt{accept}(m) \cdot E_{p_4} \end{aligned}$$

The reduction for E_{p0} is:

$$
\begin{aligned}
E_{p0} &= \partial_H(E_{p1} \parallel E_{p3}) \\
&= \partial_H(\texttt{send}(m) \cdot \texttt{wait}(m) \cdot E_{p2} \parallel \texttt{accept}(m) \cdot E_{p4}) \\
&= \partial_H((\texttt{send}(m) \cdot \texttt{wait}(m) \cdot a \mid \texttt{accept}(m) \cdot b \cdot \texttt{return}(m))) \\
&= \partial_H(\texttt{send}(m) \mid \texttt{accept}(m))(\texttt{wait}(m) \cdot a \parallel b \cdot \texttt{return}(m)) \\
&= \texttt{request}(m) \cdot \partial_H(b \cdot \texttt{return}(m) \,⌊\!⌊\, \texttt{wait}(m) \cdot a) \\
&= \texttt{request}(m) \cdot b \cdot \partial_H(\texttt{return}(m) \parallel \texttt{wait}(m) \cdot a) \\
&= \texttt{request}(m) \cdot b \cdot \partial_H((\texttt{return}(m) \mid \texttt{wait}(m)) \cdot a) \\
&= \texttt{request}(m) \cdot b \cdot \texttt{response}(m) \cdot a
\end{aligned}
$$

4. CONCLUSION

In this paper, we argued that more sophisticated forms of inter-process communication are necessary for increased workflow automation. In particular, two extensions which preserve the parallelisation of execution paths were proposed: asynchronous and synchronous messaging across execution paths and aborts of related execution paths. Illustrations from an industrial case study showed that such requirements exist in practice despite the shortcomings of existing WFMS products. By combining these advanced workflow constructs with classical workflow constructs it is possible to capture complex but common themes of business processing.

To precisely impart the ramifications for workflow execution, we showed how a formal semantics can be assigned. In the short term, we see that it is viable to simulate increasingly complex aspects of business processing. In the longer term, specific workflow specification languages, among others as supported by current workflow tools, can be targeted and augmented with such features. The formal semantics guides such extensions.

As the formal semantics was defined in terms of Process Algebra, formal theory developed for Process Algebra, e.g. in the context of process equivalence (bisimulation), can be exploited when reasoning about workflow specifications. Further research will focus, among others, on the formalization of other needed concepts in workflow specifications, such as temporal constraints, actor resource models, and compensation.

References

Aalst, W. v. d. (1996). Three Good reasons for Using a Petri-net-based Workflow Management System. In Navathe, S. and Wakayama, T., editors, *Proceedings of the International Working Conference on In-*

formation and Process Integration in Enterprises (IPIC'96), pages 179–201, Cambridge, Massachusetts.

Alonso, G., Agrawal, D., El Abadi, E., Kammath, M., Günthör, R., and Mohan, C. (1996). Advanced transaction models in workflow concepts. In *Proceedings of the 12th International Conference on Data Engineering*, New Orleans, Lousiana.

Baeten, J., editor (1990). *Applications of Process Algebra.* Cambridge University Press, Cambridge, United Kingdom.

Baeten, J. and Weijland, W. (1990). *Process Algebra.* Cambridge University Press, Cambridge, United Kingdom.

Barros, A. and Hofstede, A. t. (1997). Formal Semantics of Coordinative Workflow Specifications. Technical Report 420, Department of Computer Science & Electrical Engineering, University of Queensland, Brisbane, Australia.

Barros, A. and Hofstede, A. t. (1998). Towards the construction of workflow-suitable conceptual modelling techniques. *Information Systems J.*, 8(4):313–337.

Barros, A., Hofstede, A. t., and Proper, H. (1997). Towards Real-Scale Business Transaction Workflow Modelling. In Olivé, A. and Pastor, J., editors, *Proceedings of the Ninth International Conference CAiSE'97 on Advanced Information Systems Engineering*, volume 1250 of *Lecture Notes in Computer Science*, pages 437–450, Barcelona, Spain. Springer Verlag.

Creasy, P. and Proper, H. (1996). A Generic Model for 3-Dimensional Conceptual Modelling. *Data & Knowledge Engineering*, 20(2):119–162.

Dijkstra, E. (1975). Guarded Commands, Nondeterminacy, and Formal Derivation of Programs. *Communications of the ACM*, 18(8):453–457.

Eder, J. and Liebhart, W. (1998). Contributions to Exception Handling in Workflow Management. In Bukhres, O., Eder, J., and Salza, S., editors, *Proceedings EDBT Workshop on Workflow Management Systems*, pages 3–10, Valencia, Spain.

Fowler, M. (1997). *UML Distilled: Applying the Standard Object Modeling Language.* Addison-Wesley, Reading, Massachusetts.

Hoare, C. (1978). Communicating Sequential Processes. *Communications of the ACM*, 21(8):666–677.

Hofstede, A. t. and Nieuwland, E. (1993). Task structure semantics through process algebra. *Software Engineering Journal*, 8(1):14–20.

Hofstede, A. t., Proper, H., and Weide, T. v. d. (1993). Formal definition of a conceptual language for the description and manipulation of information models. *Information Systems*, 18(7):489–523.

Hubbers, J. and Hofstede, A. t. (1997). Formalization of Communication and Behaviour in Object-Oriented Analysis. *Data & Knowledge Engineering*, 23(2):147–184.

Kappel, G. and Schrefl, M. (1990). Using an object-oriented diagram technique for the design of information systems. In Sol, H. and van Hee, K., editors, *Proceedings of the International Working Conference on Dynamic Modelling of Information Systems*, Noordwijkerhout, The Netherlands.

Makey, P., editor (1996). *Workflow: Integrating the Enterprise.* Report of the Butler Group.

Milner, R. (1989). *Communication and Concurrency.* Prentice-Hall, Englewood Cliffs, New Jersey.

Ramackers, G. (1994). *Integrated Object Modelling, an Executable Specification Framework for Business Analysis and Information System Design.* PhD thesis, University of Leiden, Leiden, The Netherlands.

Vaandrager, F. (1990). Process Algebra Semantics of POOL. In Baeten, J., editor, *Applications of Process Algebra*, volume 17 of *Cambridge Tracts in Theoretical Computer Science*, pages 173–236. Cambridge University Press, Cambridge, United Kingdom.

Comments on “Modelling Concurrent Process Coordination in Workflow Specifications” by A.P. Barros and A.H.M. ter Hofstede

Jan L.G. Dietz

Technical University Delft, The Netherlands

Discussant’s summary of the paper

The topic of the paper is the conceptual modelling of workflows, and the formalisation of these models. A workflow is understood to be a process or task structure.

Four basic constructs, i.e. coordinating mechanisms are distinguished in a task structure:

- *Trigger*. The activation or initiation of the execution of a task by some other task, is called triggering. A trigger is an instance of triggering.
- *Decision*. A decision is a construct that takes a trigger as input and dispatches it in one of a number of output directions, according to some condition being fulfilled. The output directions seem to be mutually exclusive.
- *Synchroniser*. A synchroniser takes a number of triggers as input and produces a number of triggers as output. On the input side it seems to function as an AND gate.
- *Buffer*. A task may produce items (data, values) that are put in a buffer, from which some other task consumes items.

The authors propose to extend these constructs by two new ones: abstract messaging and aborts. Three abstract messaging configurations are distinguished:

- *Waiting request*. A subtask, called the sender, of some task A, sends a request to a subtask, called the acceptor, of some task B, and suspends its execution until another subtask of B, called the returner, sends a response back to the sender.
- *Non-waiting request*. A subtask, called the sender, of some task A, sends a request to a subtask, called the acceptor, of some task B. After some time, another subtask of B, called the returner, sends a response back to another subtask of A, called the receiver.
- *Transfer*. A subtask, called the sender, of some task A, sends a message to a subtask, called the receiver, of some task B.

An *abort* is a special type of trigger. The effect of generating an abort is that the task to which it belongs is terminated. A secondary effect may be that a special task, called the abort handler, is executed.

Discussant's comments

In the list of comments hereafter, the comments are marked with one of three marks: "+", "-", "?". Their meaning is respectively: positive or strong point, negative or weak point, and question or unclear point.

\+ The authors demonstrate that they are well able to provide elegant formal representations of process or task structures.

? It is yet uncertain whether these formal specifications can easily be applied for simulating the dynamics of a task structure, as well as for direct execution.

\- It is not so easy to grasp what the authors exactly had in mind when proposing the extensions. Comments from the reviewers regarding the confusing explanation in section 2 were not taken into account.

? Why didn't they apply more well-known graphical formalisms, like the Petrinet, to explain task structures?

\- Although the models are indeed conceptual in the sense that they abstract from realization issues, the fail to be conceptual in the sense of being purely about work flow or business processes. This holds particularly for the 'informative' communications, like the buffer and the transfer(?).

An Autopoietic View of the Concept 'Information System'

El-Sayed Abou-Zeid

Department of Decision Sciences and MIS, Faculty of Commerce and Administration, Concordia University, 1550, de Maisonneuve Blvd. W., Montreal (Quebec), Canada, H3G 1M8, Email: elsayed@vax2.concordia.ca

Key words: System theory, Organizational communication, Enterprise modeling, Information system architecture, Autopoiesis

Abstract: The system-theoretic concepts of autopoiesis, as a theory of living systems, are used to develop a metamodel for enterprise information systems. At the core of this model are two fundamental conceptual constructs. The first one is the "negotiated meaning" associated with each thing in the enterprise's cognitive domains. The second one is the concept of "situation" which "encapsulates" the data/information and behavioral aspects of the constituents of the enterprise universe of discourse together with the communicative processes needed to continuously conceptualize, maintain, and re-conceptualize them. In this model, enterprise information system is viewed as the realization of the enterprise's autopoieticity in the semiotic situational space. The dynamics of such system is represented through a modified version of an event-driven rule (WHEN...IF...THEN....ELSE). Some of the implications of this approach are discussed in this paper.

1. INTRODUCTION

An Enterprise Information System (EIS) phenomenon is a volatile one. This is because it is, by its very nature, an "**interference phenomenon**" that results from the superimposition of several waves, e.g., business waves, technology waves... Such volatility has revealed in the last few decades in several paradigm shifts in its conceptualization, i.e., function, data, and object-oriented paradigms, and consequently in the debate of what is the basic building block of what so called "Enterprise Information System", i.e., process, data entity/process and object.

Behind these paradigm shifts is the motivation of creating flexible and adaptable IS architecture that is capable to respond to the ever-changing business needs and user requirements. This motivation is usually expressed in different terms such as maintainability and re-usability. However, all of the methodologies based on these paradigms start its conceptualization/modeling process by assuming "snapshot", or "frozen" set of business/user requirements. Therefore, they neglect the dynamic processes needed to re-conceptualize/re-model the constituents of the ever-changing enterprise's universe of discourse. The result is a rigid information system architecture that is poorly coupled to its environment.

Therefore, in order to build an evolving and self-organizing information system, such architecture need not to have a fixed structure built solely by the designer but an evolving internal structure that can be congruently responds to environmental perturbations, i.e., structurally coupled to environment but at the same time "**conserves**" the "**very nature**" of an enterprise. Moreover, the building block of such architecture has to include in an explicit and organic manner the processes needed for re-conceptualizing the constituents of the universe of discourse. The characterization of such architecture as "*self-organizing*" one reflects its ability to re-configure its components structure in response to unexpected and contingent environmental changes (perturbations). The characterization of it as "*evolving*" one has two implications. The first one is the necessity of building-in "*learning mechanisms*". The second implication is the adoption of an "*open system architecture*" design philosophy.

In order to develop such architecture one needs a conceptual framework that:

i. provides common basis for modeling both an enterprise and its information system.
ii. provides a conceptual ground for structurally coupled information system architecture with the enterprise's environment. In other words, this architecture has to take into consideration "**second-order dynamics**" beside "**first-order dynamics**" that already taken care of by the conventional system development [17].

To this end, the main objective of this paper is to introduce the concept of "**situation**" as a building block for enterprise information system architecture. Such concept "encapsulates" the data and behavioral aspects of the constituents of the enterprise universe of discourse together with the communicative processes needed to continuously conceptualize, maintain, and re-conceptualize them.

In order to attain this objective the **autopoietic theory**, as a general form of system building using self-referential closure, is used as potential system-theoretic framework for self-organizing and evolving information system architecture.

In section **2**, the fundamental concepts of the theory of autopoiesis, as a theory of living systems, is introduced. In section **3**, the Luhmann's extension of the theory of autopoiesis, together with Winograd, Flora and Morgan views, have been used as a paradigm for a conceptual framework for modeling an enterprise and its information system as autopoietic systems. The case study provided in section **4** shows how this framework could be used. The paper is concluded in section **5** by discussing some of the implications of this approach together with suggestions for further researches.

2. AUTOPOIESIS SYSTEM-THEORETIC FUNDAMENTALS

2.1 Autopoiesis

In order to find what is the distinguishing feature of living (biological) systems, Maturana and Varela [10] coined the word **autopoiesis** (αυτοσ = self, ποιενιν = creation, production) to describe this feature. In fact, the meaning of this word coveys the very nature of living systems as systems that maintain their identity through their own operations of continuous self-renewal. Moreover, these systems could only be characterized with *reference to themselves* and whatever takes place in them, takes place as necessarily and constitutively determined in relation to themselves.

One of the key concepts of autopoiesis, as a theory of biological living systems, is the distinction between *organization* and *structure*. On one hand, ***organization*** is the capability of a system to re-produce its identity by referring constantly to itself, through the alternate re-production of its components together with the component-producing processes, i.e., the capability of a recursive self-reproduction. In other words, organization is nothing more than *the mode of operation that maintains system unity* [10]. On the other hand, ***structure*** is the realization of a system's organization through the presence and interplay of its components in a specific realization space. In other words, organization provides the formal context within which components, of whatever kind, can interact and still maintain the system's unity, thus it specifies the limits within which structural changes may occur while system unity is prescrved. An actual system requires, for its actualization, the unification of both of organization and structure. While **organization** is necessary to establish system unity, **structure** is necessary because different spaces of its actualization impose different constraints on system's components [10]. By analogy, an algorithm for solving certain problem can be viewed as a description of the system's organization whereas the corresponding computer program can be viewed as the realization of this organization (structure) in a certain space (programming language).

In summary, autopoiesis; from dynamic point of view, is the process of maintenance and self-renewal of a systemic whole and, from static point of view; it is a kind of system **organization** which can be manifested, in principle, in indefinite number of different system **structures** but cannot be identified with any one of them.

2.2. Autopoietic Systems

An autopoietic system is defined by Maturana and Varela as "*a network of processes of production, transformation and destruction of components. These components constitute the system as a distinct unity in the space of its actualization and they continuously regenerate and realize, through their interactions and transformations, the network of processes that produce them.*" [10, p.135]

Among the distinct characteristics of the autopoietic systems, the most relevant ones are:

- **Autopoietic organization (autopoieticity)**, the capacity of autopoietic systems to *establish* and *maintain* their *unity* by means of their own autonomous processes (*autonomy*);
- **Invariance of autopoieticity**, since autopoieticity is the essential and defining characteristic of an autopoietic system, anything to change this would result in its destruction.
- **The simultaneous openness and closure**, Autopoietic systems are **open** with respect to structural interaction with the environment, i.e. *structural openness*, which is unavoidable consequence of the fact that system elements must satisfy the particular requirements of the physical (or conceptual) domain in which they occur, while they are **closed** with respect to their own organization, i.e. *organizational closure*. The recognition of *the simultaneous openness and closure* of autopoietic systems is in opposition to the tradition for which a system is one or the other but not both. This interpretation is possible only on the basis of a clear *distinction between organization and structure* [2].
- **Structural determination**, In spite of its structural openess, the behavior of autopoietic system is constrained by its structure rather than by direct influence of its environment, i.e., **structural determination principle**. The environmental perturbations could

trigger the system's structural changes but can never determine or direct these changes. In fact, the interaction between autopoietic system and its environment is an ongoing process of recurrent mutually congruent structural changes in both system and its environment, i.e., **structural coupling**. Such structural coupling has connotations of coordination and co-evolution.

3. AN ENTERPRISE AS AUTPOIETIC SYSTEM

3.1. Autopoietic Perspective of Enterprises

Enterprises such as companies and public administrations, and consequently their information processing machinery, are by their very nature, social systems. Moreover, "*any cohesive social institution is an autopoietic system, because it survives; its method of survival answers the autopoietic criteria and it may well change its entire appearance and its apparent purpose in process*" [10].

Metaphorically, an enterprise can be compared with the biological cell which "*is a complex production system, producing and synthesizing macromolecules of proteins, lipids, and enzymes, among others; it consists of about 10^5 macromolecules on the average. The entire macromolecular population of a given cell is renewed about 10^4 times during its lifetime. Through their staggering turnover of matter, the cell maintains its distinctiveness, coherence, and relative autonomy.*" [22] Ontologically, "*an organization is a network of intersubjectively shared meanings that are sustained through the development and use of a common language and everyday social interactions.*" [3]. Moreover, Winograd and Flora have viewed of enterprise as ***constituted from networks of recurrent conversations*** that are activated whenever it encounters requests and other external contingencies [20].

However, in order to extend the theory of autopoiesis beyond the realm of biological living systems one has to transcend the physical space of biological living systems into other conceptual spaces that can also meet its requirements. Among of these requirements is the homogeneity of processes and components of the autopoietic system, i.e. its processes and its components must belong to the same physical or conceptual space. To this end, Luhmann uses the formal aspects of the theory of autopoiesis to redefine autopoiesis as "*a general form of system building using self-*

referential closure." [7, p. 2] Based on this (re-) definition, distinction bas been made between two different modes of autopoiesis' realization, namely, life and meaning. **Life** is the mode of **living biological systems**, and **meaning** is that of **meaning-used systems** such as individuals (psychic systems) and societies. Meaning-used systems are further differentiated according whether they use **consciousness** or **communication** as a mode of meaning-based reproduction [7, 8]. Figure (1) shows the classification of systems according to this definition.

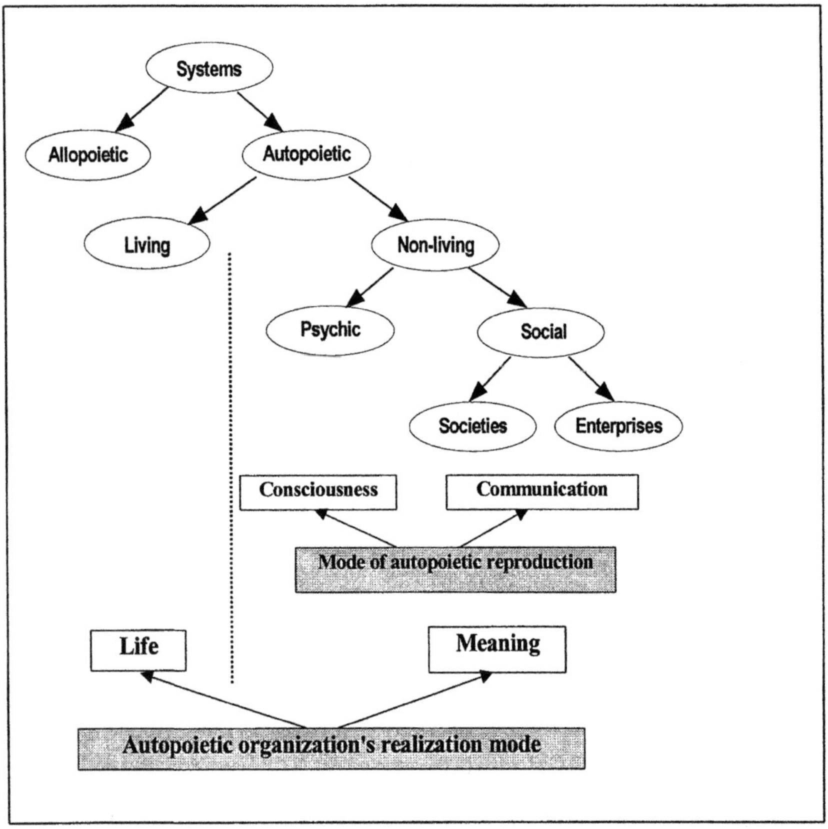

Figure (1): Autopoietic and Allopoietic Systems (revised from references 7 and 8)

According to Luhmann's theory, "*social systems uses communications as their particular mode of autopoietic reproduction. Their elements are communications which are recursively produced and reproduced by a network of communications and which cannot exist outside such network.*" [9] Such organizationally closed network of communication acts results in collective weltanschauung-context of meaning- that is continually sustained by further communicative acts. Moreover, this collective Weltanschauung, includes among other things the system's self-description, defines the system's boundary (system' unity) in the symbolic social domain.

One of the implications of this view is the indispensable role played by meaning in establishing the system's unity. This is because its role in conjoining communicative acts. However, meaning is completely open self-referential structure that excludes nothing, even the negation of meanings. Therefore, meaning-based communication systems are both organizationally closed and structurally open [7]

3.2. An Autopoietic Model of Enterprise

In order to consolidate and formalize these perspectives and to develop a model for an enterprise and its information system as autopoietic systems, the following concepts are introduced. Examples from the case study of section **4** will be used to illustrate each concept.

Concept (1), Thing: A **thing** is the concept that is used to represent a concrete or abstract entity in an enterprise or in its environment toward which thought or action is directed or is communicated about by actors (concept 2) [13]. Enterprise's mission, objectives, policy, invoice, claim, driver, and accident are examples of the relevant things for an automobile insurance company. Each thing is characterized by its state and its behavior. The set of all relevant things is denoted by **O**.

However, the same thing may appear in different contexts, i.e., referential domains or relationships between it and other things. Hence, instead of dealing with *bare thing*, we have to deal with a **contexted thing**, i.e., a thing together with the context it appear in. A contexted thing can be represented as a pair $< \mathbf{o}, \mathbf{c}_o >$ where $\mathbf{o} \in \mathbf{O}$ and $\mathbf{c}_\mathbf{O} \in \mathbf{C}_\mathbf{O}$, and $\mathbf{C}_\mathbf{O}$ is the set of contexts of the things. For example, a claim may appear in different contexts, i.e., in relation to a policy or in relation to accident type.

The set of all contexted things is denoted by **K**. In the autopoietic terminology, the set **K** together with the set of possible relationships between them represents the **enterprise's external cognitive domain** of an enterprise, i.e., "*the domain of all the interactions in which an autopoietic system can enter without loss of identity.*" [10, p. 119]. On the other hand, the set of all contexted things that represents the enterprise's self-image and self-consciousness (e.g., goals, the rules and relations guiding the entry of new components or the termination of component's membership, the rules guiding the associations, roles, functions and positions of enterprise's components, and rules guiding components transformations, i.e., training and organizational learning) is called **enterprise's internal cognitive domain**.

Concept (2), Actor (A): An **actor** is the concept of an active or responsive agent within an enterprise or its environment that is conceived as an ***executor*** of certain activities, a ***governor (decision maker)*** of their execution or as a ***provider/requester*** (***user***) of certain products/services. It could be human, individual or collective (e.g., manager, functional unit, enterprise, DBMS), or artifact (e.g., software component, IT-based system). In fact, an actor can be viewed as "a role that someone or something in the environment can play in relation to the business." [6]

In the case an automobile insurance company one can identify insurance agent, Claim Department and claim database as examples of the internal actors; and Police Department, Emergency clinics and Automobile Repair Shops as examples of the external actors.

Concept (3), Negotiated Meaning (NM): A **negotiated meaning** is the consensual interpretation (or shared point of view) which is constructed by at least two active actors in relation to the state, behavior of the constituents of the enterprise's cognitive domains or the relationship between them. In fact, this meaning is ever changing and has to be re-constructed de novo whenever a new context emerges or circumstance changes [21]. Therefore, networks of recurrent communication (conversation) are needed to establish and maintain the novelty of the enterprise's repository of negotiated meanings.

Figure (2) shows a simple model of the dynamic needed to construct negotiated meaning about a thing X in the enterprise cognitive domains. In this model, which is a modified version of the communication model between two human actors of Reference 5 [Fig. 3.5-1], the process of constructing negotiated meaning starts when each actor forms her/is conception of a thing X and utters its representation

$$\mathbf{R}_{0}^{(j)}.$$

These initial representations serve as domains for the second iteration in which each actor interpret and represents her/is conception of the conception of the other actor, i.e.,

$$[\mathbf{a}_j, \mathbf{R}_k^{(i)}(\mathbf{X})] \rightarrow \mathbf{R}_{k+1}^{(j)}(\mathbf{X})$$

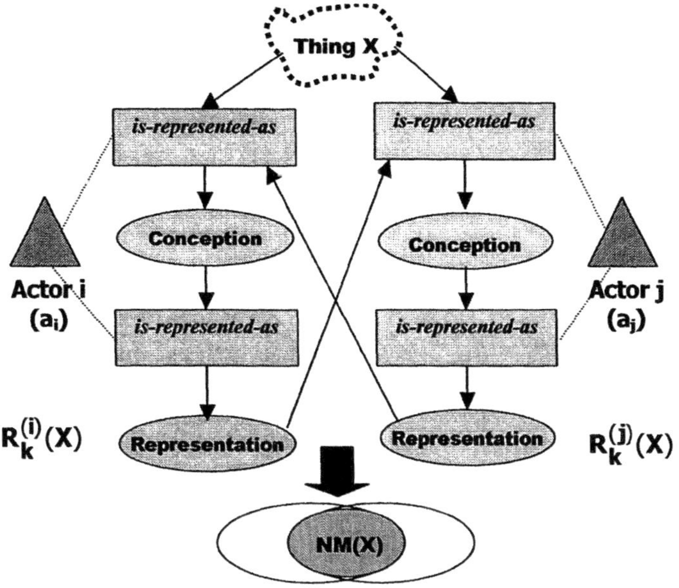

Figure (2): A simple model of the dynamic of constructing negotiated meaning about a thing X

This process will continue until both actors decide that the intersection between their representation can be considered as an agreed upon interpretation and representation of X, i.e.,

$$R_N^{(j)}(X) \cap R_N^{(k)}(X) = NM(X)$$

The description of a negotiated meaning about a thing in the enterprise's cognitive domains is composed of two elements. The first element is the description of the data/information aspects of the thing. This element includes, for example, the thing's relevant properties, the applicable business rules and its context. The data/information content of a negotiated meaning can be represented in many different semiotic constructs and forms. It could be represented as a set of values of the thing properties, or as standard operating procedures, or as enterprise's data/object models, or any combination of them. The second element is the description of the communicative schema that is needed to construct and maintain it (see appendix A-1). Therefore, it can be represented as follows:

<Description of the thing's data/information content, Description of the relevant communicative situation(s)>.

For example, conceptual data model of an enterprise can be viewed as a representation of the description of the data content of negotiated meaning about the things enterprise's cognitive domains. Moreover, this representation is the outcome of a negotiation process between system owners/users and system developers.

Each negotiated meaning can be actualized through many situations (concept 5) depending on its state.

The totality of all negotiated meanings at certain point of time is an instant of an enterprise agreed-upon (negotiated) reality. This negotiated reality forms an organizationally closed space in which an enterprise is identified as a distinct unity. For example, the procedures of providing certain service have to conform (refer) to enterprise's objectives, goals and mission. In turn, enterprise's objectives, goals and mission have to adapt (refer) to the changes in the nature of this service.

Concept (4), Action: An **action** is the concept of the piece of work performed by an actor, or collection of actors, in relation to certain contexted thing and induces a change in the state of enterprise' cognitive domains. This change could be addition of a new thing, removal an existing one, or modifying its state or its context.

Actions can be classified according to two criteria: the realization space; i.e., *physical space* and *semiotic space**, and the nature of their outcomes (Figure 3). Based on the first criteria actions can be classified into two main categories physical actions and semiotic actions. **Physical actions** are deeds performed by an actor, or collection of actors, by means of some material resources. The set of all possible physical actions is denoted by $\mathbf{T}_p$. On the other hand, **semiotic actions** are the actions that handle the semiotic constructs that represent the things in the enterprise's cognitive domain.

Based on the nature of outcome, actions can be further classified into two categories, **performative actions** and **communicative action. Performative physical actions (PPAs)** are those, which change the physical state of a concrete thing (e.g., location, dimension, quantity,). **Performative semiotic actions (PSAs)** are those that generate new semiotic constructs or modifying existing ones to reflect the changes in the enterprise's cognitive domains. On the other hand, **communicative semiotic actions (CSAs)** are the actions of exchanging semiotic constructs that represent things in the enterprise's cognitive domains between, at least, two actors, whereas **communicative physical actions (CPAs)** are the physical arrangement for realizing them. The set of all relevant semiotic actions is denoted by $\mathbf{T}_s$. The set of all actions is denoted by $\mathbf{T}$ ($=\mathbf{T}_p \cup \mathbf{T}_s$).

* The space that composed of all kinds of sign used by human being to communicate and to store their negotiated meanings

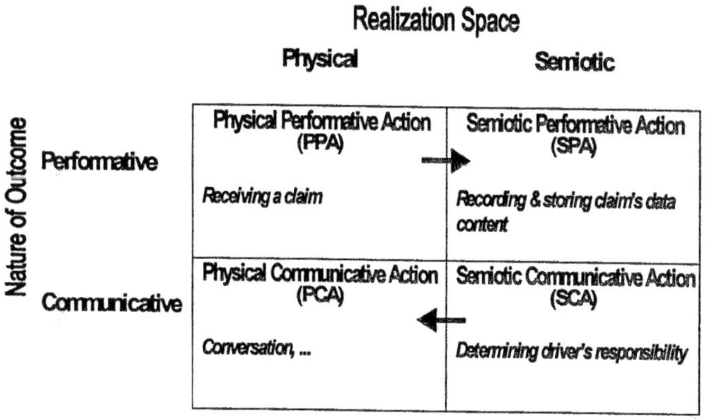

Figure (3): Types of actions

Concept (5), Situation: A **situation** is a dynamic construct composed of collection of actors that is configured and re-configured to actualize certain action. Situations can be classified according to the nature of the action they actualize. Therefore, one can distinguishes four types of situations: physical performative (**PP**), semiotic performative (**SP**), physical communicative (**PC**), and semiotic communicative (**SC**).

Configuring certain situation is based on whether there is a NM concerning the pertinent thing. **Performative situation** is the one that actualizes the existing NM concerning the pertinent thing. On the other hand, **communicative situation** is the one that has to be established to generate a new NM or to modify an existing one.

The set of all possible physical situations is denoted by Σ_p and the set of all possible semiotic situations is denoted by Σ_s. The union of these two sets is the **situational space** (Σ) in which the enterprise's autopoieticity can be realized in many different structures. In other words, an enterprise' structure is viewed as a configuration of situations which is continually re-constructed in response to environmental perturbations such as new market requirements.

A situation can be represented as follows
(see table 1 and appendices A-2, A-3):

$$<\{NM(k_x), S\}, t_y, \{a_z\}, O>$$

where

$NM(k_x)$ is the associated negotiated meaning associated with a contexted thing in the enterprise's cognitive domains ($\in$ K);
S the state of the negotiated meaning (e.g., complete, incomplete, to be modified,..)
t_y is an action ($\in$ T);
a_z is an actor ($\in$ A); and
O is the outcome of the situation

Based on these concepts an enterprise can be modeled as a collection of interrelated and inseparable semiotic and physical situations. These situations are invoked by the events in the enterprise cognitive domains or by other situations. Many of the enterprise's situations can be a priory designed to respond to the expected environmental perturbations, i.e., **recurrent situations**. However, new situations can be promptly constructed to respond to unexpected environmental perturbations, i.e., **novel situations**. Such novel situations are characterized by their open set of actors, incomplete information about the relevant things and the proper action, and by the uncertain outcome.

Now the enterprise dynamics can be represented by the following event-driven rule:

> **WHEN** *<occurrence of event in enterprise's cognitive domain (**K**) is identified>*
> **IF** <there is NM concerning it exists>
> **THEN** <configure the relevant performative situation>
> **INVOLVING** <actors>
> **AFFECTING** <thing(s)>
> **ELSE** <configure relevant communicative situation>
> **INVOLVING** <actors>
> **CONCERNING** <thing(s)>

The WHEN part of the rule is compulsory and initiates the structure coupling mechanism between an enterprise and its environment. The precondition part (IF part) determines the kind of situation to be configured. The THEN part generally represents first-order dynamics of enterprise while the ELSE part represents its second-order dynamics.

3.3. An autopoietic model of information system

According to Pattee's semantic closure principle there is an autonomous closure (self-referent relation) between the physical (phenotypic) aspects and symbolic (genotypic) aspects of any autonomous, self-organizing and evolvable system [14, 15, 16]. In this context, it should be noted that for natural symbols, one couldn't strictly separate their syntax from their semantics [18]. Therefore, there is irreducible complementarity between physical situations and semiotic ones which together realize the negotiated reality of an enterprise.

From autopoietic point of view, enterprise information system can be defined as **the totality of the possible semiotic situations that is configured and re-configured in response to perturbations (events) in the enterprise's cognitive domains**. Therefore, it can be represented by the following mapping:

$$\mathbf{EIS : \{events\}} \rightarrow \mathbf{2}^{\Sigma_S}$$

Based on the aforementioned general event-driven model of an enterprise, the dynamics of enterprise's information system can be represented by the following rule:

WHEN <*occurrence of event in enterprise's cognitive domain (**K**) is identified*>
    IF <there is NM concerning it exists>
    THEN <configure relevant performative semiotic situation>
        INVOLVING <actors>
        AFFECTING <thing(s)>
    ELSE <configure relevant communicative semiotic situation>
        INVOLVING <actors>
        CONCERNING <thing(s)>

One of the important consequences of the autopoietic approach to an enterprise and its information system is that the later is viewed as an "**interwoven**" system with enterprise system rather than viewing it as a "**subsystem**".

4. Case Study

4.1. Background

Grand Prix Automobile Insurance Company (GPAIC) is a small company that sells automobile insurance policies to licensed drivers in the Province of Quebec. The company headquarters are located in Montreal. The company employs about 150 people, most of which are insurance agents located at several different offices throughout the province. GPAIC was established in 1991, and has grown to about 50,000 policyholders today. Last years net profit was $875,000.

Mission

GPAIC is committed to provide value-added and high quality services to its customer, a level of financial security and performance which fully meet their needs, while at all times maintaining its financial strength.

Goals

- Customer focus professional people.
- Excellence in customer service through technology.
- Financial strength.

Objectives

- **Customer**: Maximize the value to GPAIC's customers by providing superior quality services.
- **Growth**: Grow revenue and assets on profitable basis. Increase GPAIC's number of customers.
- **People**: Cultivate an environment with GPAIC's values, develops and retains high-quality people.

Structure

GPAIC does business in three primary locations; the Montreal headquarters, the Quebec city office, and the Sherbrooke office. The Montreal headquarters consist of Policy Department, the Claim Department, Information Services Department and insurance agents. The Quebec city office consists of the Legal Department and insurance agents. The Sherbrooke office consists of the Personnel Department, the Payroll Department and insurance agents.

GPAIC 's Activities

For the purpose of this example only one of its major activities will be discussed, namely, claim handling activity.

Claim mission

GPAIC is committed to amaze its customers with its claim settlement process, while reaching a fair and rapid settlement.

Claim Goal

Immediate initiation of claim settlement with minimal hand-offs and at fair cost.

Claim Procedures

Upon the reception of a claim, it is recorded and stored. Next, the matching policy is found and a determination is made as to whether the claim is covered by the provision (coverage) of the policy. If the claim is not covered, the claim is rejected, the claim status modified, and the policyholder notified of the claim rejection. If the claim is covered, the claim is checked for a minimum of two accompanying estimates. If the estimates are missing, a pending status is recorded for the claim and the policyholder is notified to obtain the necessary estimates. If the estimates are included, the claim type is determined. If the claim involves a collision with another vehicle, a police accident report request is sent to the police department, and the status of the claim is modified. When the accident report is received, it is determined whether the policyholder was at fault (or charged) for the accident. If the policyholder was not charged or the accident did not involve a collision, a claim payment is generated and sent to the policyholder, and the claim is updated. If the policyholder was charged, a claim payment is still made as described above, but also; the policy is updated to reflect an increased rate for the next invoice.

4.2. GPAIC Conceptual Models

GPAIC cognitive domains

The GPAIC's internal cognitive domain includes things such as Mission statement, Goals/Objectives, Organizational structure, Functions, Policy application, Policy, Claim, Invoice, and Accident.

The GPAIC's external cognitive domain includes things such as Customer, Deriving record, Vehicle, Vehicle registration record, Police, Accident, Medical report, Expert witness evaluation report, Weather bureau report, and Repair shop report.

GPAIC Actors Set

Internal actors set includes, for example, GPAIC Management (**MG**), Policy Department (**PD**), Claim Department (**CD**), Information Services Department (**IS**), Legal Department (**LD**), Insurance Agent and Claim database.

External actors set includes, for example, Motor Vehicle Registration Agency (**MV**), Police Departments (**PL**), Automobile Repair Shops (**RS**), Emergency Clinics (**EC**), Weather Bureau (**WB**), Expert witness (**EW**)

Situations

Examples of the conceptual (analysis) situations that are needed to handle collision claims are listed in Table (1). A modified version of activity diagram (Situation Dependency Diagram) is used to depict the situations' dynamic (Figure (4)).

TABLE (1): Conceptual situations for collision's claim handling

	Name	Description ♣,♥	Type ♦
[1]	Recording & Storing Claim	<(NM(Claim), Data Content), Record& Store, {CD, IS, X}, A new claim record>	SP
[2]	Determining Claim Coverage	<{(NM(Claim), Coverage amount?), (NM(Policy), Coverage)},Determine, {CD, PD, X}, Reject/Accept Decision>	SC
[3]	Checking the Estimates	<(NM(Claim), Accompanied estimates?), Check, {CD, X}, Processing/Pending Decision>	SC
[4]	Obtaining Accident Description	<(NM(Accident), Data Content?), Obtain, {CD, PL, EC, WB}, Request for the relevant reports>	SC
[5]	Determining Driver's Responsibility	<{(NM(Accident), Data Content), (NM(Driver), Responsibility?)}, Determine, {CD, LD}, Decision on driver's responsibility>	SC
[6]	Updating Claim's Status	<(NM(Claim), Data Content), Update, {CD, IS, X}, Updated claim's data content>	SP
[7]	Notifying the Customer	<(NM(Claim), Data Contert), Send, {CD, Policyholder}, Notification to the customer>	(S/P)P
[8]	Generating the Claim Payment	<(NM(Claim), Data Content), Generate, {CD, MG}, Payment check>	(S/P)P
[9]	Updating Policy's Data Content	<{(NM(Policy), Data Content), (NM(Claim), DataContent)}, Update, {CD, PD, IS, X}, Updated policy data content}>	SP

♦ SC = Semiotic Communicative, SP = Semiotic Performative, (S/P)P = (Semiotic/Physical) Performative.

♣ ? means that there is no established NM or it is unknown

♥ X stands for any supporting artifact (e.g., claim database)

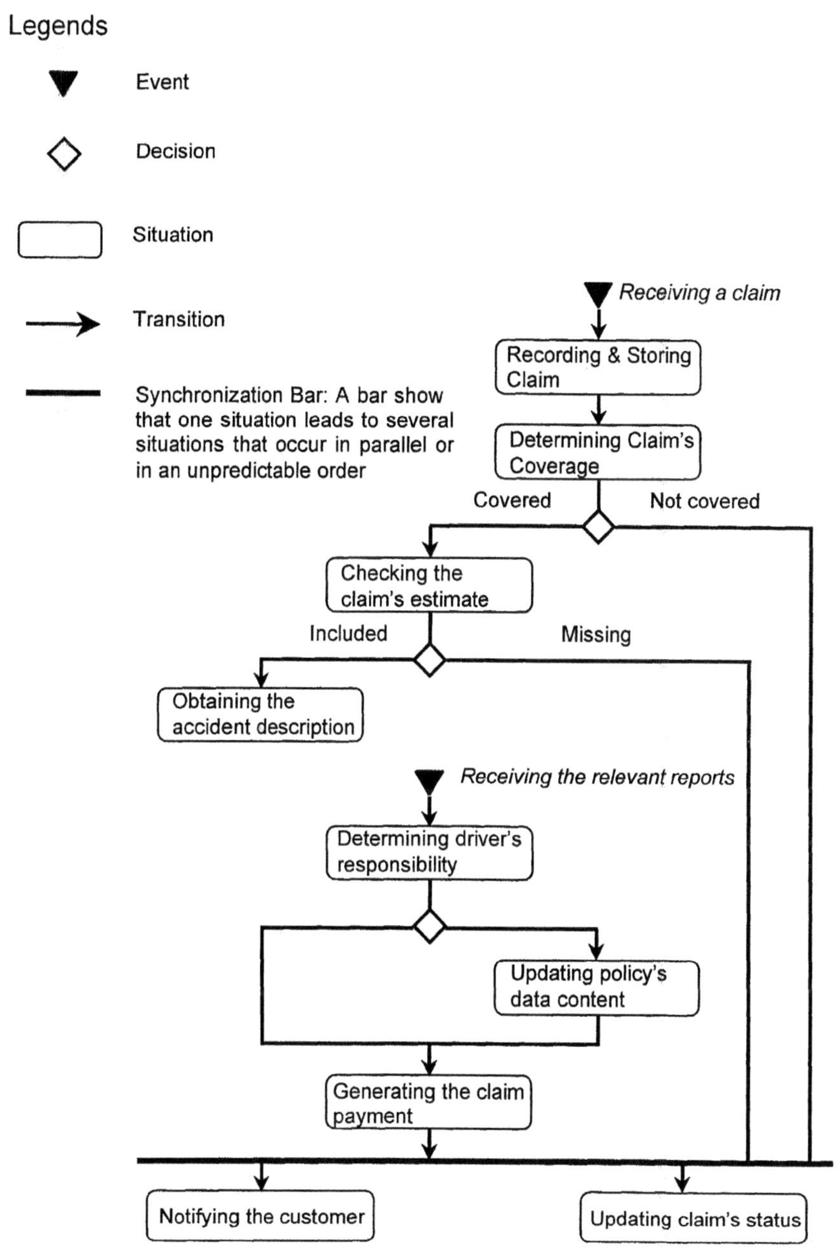

Figure (4): Situation Dependency Diagrams for collision claim handling

5. CONCLUSIONS

The model of enterprise information system that is discussed in the previous section has many implications on the conceptual and practical levels. On the conceptual level, there are five implications. **First** it represents explicitly the "**virtuality**" [12, 19] of information system as it conceptually separates between requests (demands or environmental perturbations), i.e., WHEN part, and their satisfiers (semiotic situations), i.e., IF...THEN...ELSE part. Thus it provides a perspective view to the EIS rather than the conventional descriptive one. **Second**, it emphasizes on the parallelism between the physical reality, i.e., enterprise's physical situation space, and the virtual reality, i.e., enterprise's semiotic situational space. Such explicit display of correspondence helps in narrowing the gap between software design and work design [4] by promoting the notion of "action-enabled-by-information" and by viewing the information system "**interwoven**" system with enterprise system rather than viewing it as a subsystem. **Third**, it introduces the concept of structural plasticity of information system by subordinating its structure to the function required and allowing the information system structure to be seen as an emergent order that is dynamic and constantly changing. **Fourth**, it presents a starting point for communication-based approach to information system conceptualization. Moreover, it shows the role of that communication in system self-organization, through construction and re-construction of the enterprise's negotiated reality. It also provides a conceptual construct, i.e., semiotic communicative situation, for establishing communication infrastructure. **Finally**, it calls for revisiting our existing information system development methods to accommodate the salient feature of autopoietic systems, namely, the simultaneous **organizational closure** of the enterprise negotiated reality and **structural openess** that is manifested in its situation space [1].

On the practical level, the conceptual (analysis) situations, which represent system's requirements, can be mapped into design situations. This mapping process can be accomplished through activities such as: deciding the proper representation of data/information content of the things in the enterprise's cognitive domains, describing the detailed steps of the associated action, and classifying the involved actors with respect to their role in completing the action (executor, governor, provider, requester) and with respect to their type (human, artifact). Once the mapping is completed, each design situation can serve as reusable and/or novel context for component-based application. Moreover, the design situation dependency diagrams can serve as architecture for Web-Based information system. In such architecture each design situation can be implemented as a thick hyperdocument where its nodes can contain the logic and data that support the situation's action beside reference to other hyperdocuments (situations).

In conclusion the proposed metamodel views information system's architecture as an emergent and self-organizing structure that is constructed and re-constructed in accordance to the environmental perturbations and by the interactivity of its components, not as a priory constructed one. It also provides interdisciplinary and unifying approach to "information system phenomena". For instance, one of its core concepts, the concept of "negotiated meaning" and its actualization, are related to different disciplines such as management (e.g., organizational memory), artificial intelligence (e.g., ontology), and cognitive sciences (e.g., cognitive map). Moreover, communications, in its various forms (human-human, computer-computer, and human-computer), is treated as an organic component of the proposed model.

However, a number of topics deserve further research effort is needed to fully operationalize the proposed approach. One of these research topics is to construct and test a system development methodology based on an "inverted perspective", which views an enterprise from within, i.e., one which guarantees the simultaneous **organizational closure** of the enterprise negotiated reality and **structural openess** of its information system as realized in its situation space.

REFERENCES

[1] Abou-Zeid, E., *Autopoiesis as a Conceptual Framework for Information Systems Engineering,* in *Systems Engineering and Public Administration*, IFIP Transactions (A-36), Ed. H.E.G. Bonin, Elsevier Science Publishers (North Holland), 1993, pp. 97-108.

[2] Bednarz, J. *Autopoiesis: the Organizational Closure of Social Systems*, System research, Vol. 5, No. 1, 1988, pp. 57-64.

[3] Burrell, G. and Morgan, G., *Sociological paradigms and organizational analysis*, Heineman Educational Books, London, 1979.

[4] Butler, K. A., Espsite, C. and Hebrone R., *Connecting the Design of Software to the Design of Work*, Comm. Of ACM, Vol. 47, No. 1, 1999, pp. 38-46

[5] Falkenberg, E et al, *A Framework for Information System Concepts*, 1998, ftp://ftp.leidenuniv.nl/pub/rul/fri-full.zip.

[6] Jacobson M. and Jacobson A., *The Object Advantage: Business reengineering with object technology*, Addison-Wesley, Reading Mass., 1995.

[7] Luhmann, N. *Essays on Self-reference*, Columbia University Press, New York, 1990.

[8] Luhmann, N. ***Social Systems***, Stanford University Press, Stanford, California, 1995.

[9] Luhmann, N. ***The Autopoiesis of Social Systems***, in *Sociocybernetic Paradoxes*, F. Geyer and J. van der Zouwen (Editors), Sage Publications, London, 1986, pp. 172-193.

[10] Maturana, H.R. and Varela, F.J. ***autopoiesis and Cognition***, Reidel, Boston, 1980.

[11] Morgan, G., ***Images of Organization***, Sage Publications, Beverly Hills, 1986.

[12] Mowshowitz, A, ***Virtual organization***, Comm. ACM, Vol. 40, No. 9, 1997, pp. 30-37.

[13] Parson, J. and Wand, Y., ***Using objects for systems analysis***, Comm. ACM, Vol. 40, No. 12, 1997, pp. 104-110.

[14] Pattee H., "***Universal Principles of Measurement and Language Functions" in Evolving Systems, Complexity***, Language and Life: Mathematical Approaches, Casti J.L. and Karlquist A. Eds., International Institute for Applied System Analysis. Laxenburg, Austria, 1986, pp. 579-592

[15] Pattee H., ***Evolving Self-reference: Matter, Symbols, and Semantic Closure***, Communication and Cognition-Artificial Intelligence, Vol. 12, No. 1-2, 1995, pp. 9-27

[16] Pattee, H., ***Dynamic and linguistic modes of complex systems***, Int. J. general systems, Vol. 3, 1977, pp. 259-266.

[17] Ramackers, G.T. and Verrijn-Stuart A. A., ***First and second order dynamics in information systems***, in *Dynamic Modeling of Information Systems*, Eds. Sol, H. G. and van Hee, K. M., Elsevier Science Publishers B. V. (North Holland), 1991, pp. 237-256.

[18] Rocha L., ***Artificial Semantically Closed Object***, Communication and Cognition-Artificial Intelligence, Vol. 12, No. 1-2, 1995, pp. 63-90.

[19] Turoff, M., ***Virtuality***, Comm. ACM, Vol. 40, No. 9, 1997, pp. 38-43.

[20] Winograd, T. and Flores, F., ***Understanding Computer and Cognition***, Addison-Wesley, 1986.

[21] Zeleny, M. ***Cognitive Equilibrium: A Knowledge-based Theory of Fuzziness and Fuzzy Sets***, In. J. General Systems, Vol. 19, 1991, pp. 359-381.

[22] Zeleny, M., ***What is autopoiesis?*** in *Autopoiesis, a theory of living organization*, Ed. Zeleny, W, Elsevier North-Holland, 1981, pp. 5-17.

Appendix A

A.1: Claim's Negotiated Meaning

NM(Claim)

Description of data/information content

Definition

A request by customer to pay expenses covered by a policy for a vehicle, policyholder, property, and/or other person.

Data Content

Claim Amount, Claim Date, Claim Description, Claim Number, Claim Payment Amount, Claim Payment Date, Claim Payment Explanation, Claim Rejection Reason, Claim Status (accepted, rejected, pended), Claim Type (collision, theft, windstorm, vandalism), Coverage Amount, Coverage Code, Coverage Description, Estimate Amount, Estimate Company Name, Estimate Description, Driver responsibility (responsible, not responsible).

Business Rules

- Involved parties contact should be made within twenty-four hours of the receipt of the claim by the Claim Department
- Any claim must include, at least, two estimates
- Any claim payment in excess of $10,000 must have GPAIC CEO' authority
- Any claim checks of $2,000 or more must have two signatures of authorized personnel

Context

Policy, Policyholder, Relevant accident reports

Description of Communication Schema

Actors involved in NM(Claim) construction and maintenance (*Type, Role(s), Location(s)*)

- GPAIC Management (human, governor/ decision maker, Montreal)
- Policy Department (human, information provider, Montreal)
- Claim Department (human, governor/ decision maker/requester, Montreal)
- Information Services Department (human/artifact, information services provider, Montreal)
- Legal Department (human, information provider, Quebec City)
- Police Departments (human, information provider, different locations)
- Automobile Repair Shops (human, information provider, different locations)
- Emergency Clinics (human, information provider, different locations)
- Weather Bureau (human, information provider, different locations)
- Expert Witnesses (human, information provider, different locations)

Types of Communication

- Local synchronous (e.g., face-to-face)
- Local asynchronous (e.g., retrieving data from a database)
- Distributed asynchronous (e.g., email)

Accepted Level of Consensus

To be determined in accordance to GPAIC' mission, goals, and objectives (organizational closure's constraint)

Invoking Condition(s)

- Deciding the data/information content elements.
- Updating data /information content.
- Creating a claim record.
- Formulating/modifying business rules

A.2

Situation's Name
Obtaining accident description
Invoking Condition(s)/Event(s)
Processing decision is made
Type
Semiotic communicative
Thing(s) Involved
Accident
Action
Send a request for information to the relevant bodies
Actors involved in the situation (Type, Role, Location)
- Claim Department (human, ***requester***, Montreal)
- Police Departments (human, information provider, different locations)
- Automobile Repair Shops (human, information provider, different locations)
- Emergency Clinics (human, information provider, different locations)
- Weather Bureau (human, information provider, different locations)
- Expert Witnesses (human, information provider, different locations)

Types of Communication
- Local synchronous (e.g., face-to-face)
- Local asynchronous (e.g., retrieving data from a database)
- Distributed asynchronous (e.g., email)

Outcome(s)
Several copies of the information request are sent to the relevant actors.
Related Situations
Pre: Checking claim's estimates
Post: Determining driver's responsibility

A.3

Situation's Name
Updating policy's data content
Invoking Condition(s)/Event(s)
Decision on the driver's responsibility is made
Type
Semiotic performative
Thing(s) Involved
Policy, Claim
Action
Update policy's data content
Actors involved in the situation (*Type, Role, Location*)
- Policy Department (human, information provider, Montreal)
- Claim Department (human, information provider, Montreal)
- Information Services Department (human/artifact, executer, Montreal)

Outcome(s)
Updated policy's data content
Related Situations
Pre: Determining driver's responsibility
Post: Generating the claim payment

Comments on "An Autopoietic View of the Concept Information Systems" by E.-S. Abou-Zeid

Motoshi Saeki

Tokyo Institute of Technology, Department of Computer Science, Ookyama 2-12-1, Meguro-ku, Tokyo 152-8552, Japan, email:saeki@cs.titech.ac.jp

Key words: Autopoiesis, Information system modelling, Reflection

Abstract: The modelling framework that the author proposed has the capability of adapting the dynamic changes of information systems by themselves. In this paper, I analyse the computational aspect of the author's "An Autopoietic View of the Concept 'Information Systems'" and compare it with reflective computation technique.

Information systems frequently change their characteristics such as their structures and behaviour even during their actual operation according to the changes of external environments. It is very important to adapt the systems without stopping their operation if the changes occur. We should model and design the systems so that they can have the flexibility to adapt the changes and to evolve themselves. One of the key techniques to get the flexible and evolvable model of an information system is to make the model have a "self-referential" and "self-updating" mechanism. The model having this mechanism can access its current state and update it by itself. It can change even its interpretation of the model representation.

El-Sayed Abou-Zeid's paper discussed a meta model with "self-referential" mechanism for modelling the dynamics of information systems. The author employed the concept "Thing" to model the structure of information systems and it expresses "Object" that are structural constituents. Furthermore the author introduced the notion of "Negotiated Meaning (shortly NM)" for interpreting the constituents of information systems, and it has various kind of information, e.g. data that the constituent has, the business rules related to the constituent, actions that changes the state of the constituent and so on.

The NM encapsulates the data, the operations (actions) and the constraints (business rules) on a constituent. To generate a new NM and to update the existing NMs, the modelling framework has event-driven rules. The rules generate a new NM or update the information the NM has when an event that causes dynamic change of the information system occurs. This mechanism is similar to computational reflection of programming languages [Maes87]. Programming languages with reflection have syntactic constructs for accessing to their interpreters, for updating computational states of the interpreters and even for changing computation rules of the interpreters. From comparative view with reflection, I listed up the discussion points and the comments to the author's modelling framework as follows.

1. Separating or identifying clearly event-driven rules that create and update NMs from Things. When developers model actual systems with two level architecture; meta level as event-driven rules and object level as Thing, one of the most crucial problems is the methods to separate them.
2. Maintaining reflective consistency between meta level and object level. Suppose that we have two event-driven rules, both of them update the same NM. As the external environments to a system changes, these rules try to change the same NM simultaneously. This simultaneous updating causes semantic inconsistency of the Thing of the NM.
3. Methods or methodologies to model information systems following the author's framework. This topic is closely related the item 1. The methods provide some guidelines, e.g. how to identify Things, for developers to model an information system. The existing methods, e.g. James Martin's Information Engineering, can be extended into the methods that are adapted to two-level architecture (NMs and Things).
4. Possibility of defining all or almost of event-driven rules that can express all dynamics of information systems during modelling a system following the framework. The changes of external environments and the system's reactions to them are unpredictable.
5. Reflective tower problem in programming language community. When we consider dynamic change of event-driven rules on NMs, we should construct meta-meta level where some operational rules that update the event-driven rules of the NMs can be defined. Continuing this consideration, we get an infinite tower. The point is where we should stop the construction.
6. More examples, especially event-driven rules can show more practical benefits of the author's technique.

References

[Maes87] Maes,P., *Concepts and Experiments in Computation Reflection*, In: Proc. of Object-Oriented Programming Systems, Languages and Application (OOPSLA), pp.147-155, 1987

Failure, Identity Loss and Living Information Systems

Panagiotis Kanellis[1], Mark Lycett and Ray J. Paul[2]

[1]*Arthur Andersen, 377 Syngrou Ave. Athens 175 64, GREECE*
E-mail: Panagiotis.Kanellis@gr.arthurandersen.com

[2]*Centre for Living Information Systems Thinking, Department of Information Systems and Computing, Brunel University, Uxbridge, Middlesex UB8 3PH, UNITED KINGDOM*
E-mail: Mark.Lycett@brunel.ac.uk, Ray.Paul@brunel.ac.uk

Key words: Information systems failure, Information systems flexibility, Organizational change

Abstract: Attempting to understand information systems failure is a complex task. Recent approaches described in the literature have sought to reject positivist explanations as being too simplistic, shifting the debate in favor of more 'web-like' explanations based on the interpretation of case studies. This paper seeks to synthesize two well-known explanatory frameworks into an enhanced conceptual model that approach information systems failure through the concept of 'identity loss'. Whilst this synthesis offers explanation, the resulting model also challenges the existing paradigm of information systems development. Utilizing the findings of a case study that investigates the effects of privatization on the systems of an industrial organization, we postulate that, rather than to continue offering palliatives to combat the symptoms of information systems failure, what is needed is a fundamental reconsideration of approach.

1. INTRODUCTION

Numerous 'public' cases abound relating to the failure of information systems: *'Chief of Stock Exchange Quits in Computer Fiasco'* - The Times (12/03/93) describing the collapse of the London Stock Exchange 'Taurus' (Transfer and Automatic Registration of Uncertified Stock) system; *'Home*

Office Slams Met System Delays' - Computer Weekly (09/05/96) reporting on the £4 million Metropolitan Police system in danger of missing its 1997 implementation date; *'Computer flop cost taxpayers £59 million'* - The Independent (10/02/94) raising doubts regarding a system that was about to be implemented in HM Customs and Excise. Whatever the outcomes of the above, if we judge by the past, information systems will continue to fail. Maybe, as they become more and more institutionalized, the 'entertainment value' of such cases will diminish - making them less attractive contenders for tomorrow's front page. To the organization however, this institutionalization means that as its dependence on these systems increases, they will need to be less and less susceptible to failure. Clearly a better understanding of 'failure' is needed, if not of information systems themselves. With the environment getting increasingly complex, and with inter-organizational systems on the rise, this will become an even more significant issue. Beynon-Davies (1995) argues that the importance of the study of information systems failure holds for two reasons: firstly, as is evident from numerous reported cases, information systems continue to fail despite our increasing knowledge of them; secondly, such cases act as an important resource for validating information systems development practice.

Subscribing to these reasons, the paper begins with a brief overview of the literature falling under this theme. Concentration is focused upon an emergent epistemology in information systems research - that of interpretivism (Walsham, 1995). This questions the validity of deterministic propositions in favor of more pluralistic explanations of the phenomena under investigation. The paper builds upon this idea in two ways. Firstly, we reinforce the unavoidable plurality associated with information systems failure. This is achieved through the development of a model, which stresses the relevance of perception at the individual level concomitantly with the influences on perception at collective levels. In the interest of cumulative research in information systems (Keen, 1991), this builds on the work of Ives *et al* (1980), Scarborough and Corbett (1992) and Tricker (1992). Secondly, this is further developed into a conceptual model explaining information systems failure through the notion of 'identity loss'. This seeks to *synthesize* and *extend* two well known frameworks for 'understanding' information systems failure - those of Lyytinen and Hirschheim (1987) and Sauer (1993).

Whilst this model offers explanation, it also highlights a fundamental flaw within the predominant information systems development paradigm - its 'static' nature. Thus the latter part of the paper reports the findings of a case study illustrating the vulnerability of information systems in turbulent environments, concerns itself with the effects of 'identity loss' on development 'understanding', and discusses our own efforts to pragmatically reconsider this understanding.

2. THE TRADITIONAL VIEW OF INFORMATION SYSTEMS FAILURE

There have been numerous attempts documented in the traditional literature that try to identify what causes the success or failure of an information system. The majority of these may be argued to exhibit a positivist view of knowledge and how to obtain it. DeLone and McLean (1992) undertook a literature review of the 'information systems success' thematic and, amongst the 180 references they list, virtually none delve away from the positivist perspective. The sheer volume of this literature makes it impossible to ignore and DeLone and McLean's (1992) work is a good reference point upon which our brief overview is based. This is not intended to be critical but rather to provide the interested reader with a summary of this line of research, and a sample of representative works.

Their extensive survey of the empirical literature resulted in a classification of the existing studies based upon the following variables (used to assess information systems success):

- *System quality*; this refers to the characteristics of the information system itself. This stream of research has been trying mostly to determine system success with respect to how 'good' or 'bad' a system is in technical terms (see, for example: Swanson, 1974; Hiltz and Turoff, 1981; Bailey and Pearson, 1983)

- *Information quality*; the focus here is on the output of the system rather than the system itself. Olson and Lucas (1982) for example, argued for accuracy and the appearance of reports as an indication of information quality. Typical measurement criteria of information quality are precision, timeliness, reliability, completeness, conciseness and relevance (Bailey and Pearson, 1983). Of interest is King and Epstein's (1983) study which attempts to yield a composite measure of the quality and value of information by proposing multiple information attributes such as understandability, decision relevance, sufficiency and freedom of bias.

- *Use*; this refers to a recipient's consumption of the output of an information system. Lucas (1975a; 1975b), most notably amongst others, proposed the 'use of system' as a determinant of information systems success. Similar studies include Benbasat *et al.* (1981); Bell (1984); King and Rodriguez (1981); Fuerst and Cheney (1982); Mahmood and Medewitz (1985); Kim and Lee (1986) and Baroudi *et al.*

(1986). The 'use of system' remains a popular success variable as shown more recently by Markus and Keil (1994).

- *User satisfaction*; this is arguably the most widely used single criterion for measuring the success of an information system. User Information Satisfaction (UIS) is used as a surrogate measure for information systems success, and is defined as 'the extent to which users believe the system available to them meets their information requirements' (Ives *et al.*, 1983; Ives and Olson, 1983). UIS measurement tools usually involve single (Lucas, 1976) or multiple-item rating scales (Bailey and Pearson, 1983). These are divided into two types with one focusing on variables associated with the system itself (e.g. output quality) and the other encompassing issues related to organizational support for development and maintenance (e.g. training) -as well as the system product itself. User characteristics are seen as important to this outcome variable (Zmud, 1979), as are user attitudes and *a priori* involvement (Zanna and Fazio, 1982; Baronas and Louis, 1988; Goodhue, 1988; Melone, 1990).

- *Individual impact*; although it is related to personal and organizational performance, 'impact' can also ". . . be an indication that an information system has given the user a better understanding of the decision context, has improved his or her decision-making productivity, has produced a change in user activity, or has changed the decision maker's perception of the importance or usefulness of the information system" (DeLone and McLean, 1992: 69). Success variables in this category include information understanding and accurate interpretation (Dickson *et al.*, 1986), problem identification and understanding (Lucas, 1981), improved decision analysis and confidence in decisions (Aldag and Power, 1986), and task performance (Benbasat and Dexter, 1986; DeBrabander and Thiers, 1984).

- *Organizational impact*; this refers to the extent of the effect that the systems can have on organizational performance. Assessing information systems against this variable is particularly attractive to practitioners: information system departments, facing budgetary cuts, constantly need to be able to objectively evaluate and justify further expenditure to top management. As a result, 'organizational impact' is an outcome variable that has been prolifically investigated (Hamilton and Chervany, 1981; Keen, 1981; Rivard and Huff, 1984; Strassmann, 1985; Millman and Hartwick, 1987).

3. BUILDING AN INTERPRETIVE VIEW OF INFORMATION SYSTEMS FAILURE

Lyytinen and Hirschheim (1987) arrived at their conceptualization of failure in much the same way as DeLone and McLean (1992) - by reviewing the empirical literature. After an extensive survey and classification, they defined the overriding generic concept of failure as that of *expectation*. This ". . . stresses the importance of understanding how various stakeholders comment on the value of the IS [information system]: failure is the embodiment of a *perceived* situation" (Lyytinen and Hirschheim, 1987: 264, emphasis added). By 'stakeholders' they mean any number of people who have an immediate interest in the information system, be the users or the developers themselves. Such a group is seen as sharing a set of values that define the desirable features of the information system and the ways in which they should be obtained. In those terms, an information system failure signifies a gap between a particular situation that is currently unfolding, and the desired one. Expectation failure is a superset of three other notions that were identified by Lyytinen and Hirschheim (1987), these being:

- *Correspondence failure*; this notion of failure is based on the premise held by the process of stating the design objectives in advance. If consequently these are not met for any reason, the information system is a failure. Although this provides the ultimate rational idea of how failure should be viewed, it is problematic in practice. Objectives are ambiguous and their interpretation is context-driven. At the same time, it is very difficult - if not impossible - to accurately measure the performance of an information system, due to the immense problems related with the verification and validation of the measurement instruments (Hirschheim and Smithson, 1988).
- *Process failure*; this relates to situations where the proposed information system cannot be delivered within a set of given budget constraints. Under this notion, overspending in cost and time is seen as a failure because it eventually limits or negates the global system benefits. In project management terms, process failure ". . . signals management's inability to achieve predicted resource allocations, to develop appropriate costing and budgeting schemes for systems design, or to predict the implementation difficulties of information technology" (Lyytinen and Hirschheim, 1987: 265-266).
- *Interaction failure*; This conceptualisation parallels DeLone and McLean's (1992) criteria of 'information use' (see above).

Lyytinen and Hirschheim (1987) criticized each of these three 'stand-alone' notions as portraying a highly rational image of information systems development, which in essence views the system as a neutral, technical artifact. To compensate for this, expectation failure conveys a ". . . more encompassing, politically and pluralistically informed view, which helps to analyze relationships among the other failure notions and to understand their social origin" (Lyytinen and Hirschheim, 1987: 268).

It is precisely this explicit plurality advocated by expectation failure that Sauer (1993) does not feel comfortable with. By not giving preference to the interests of any particular group, this notion can in principle ". . . accommodate any kind of shortcoming in an information system. However, it is this very flexibility and scope that prove to limit its value" (*ibid.*: 23). For Sauer (1993), any account of failure should indicate both where to look for the causes of failure and how to respond to them. Expectation failure is thus criticized because it gives equal weight to all interests, and does not provide any indication or explanation as to what might be the most problematic inabilities to satisfy stakeholder interests. As a result, no indications as to which problems demand priority can be derived, or indeed what types of action might satisfy them. This provides the basis for three criticisms, these being: (1) that some expectations are more reasonable than others; (2) that expectation failure ignores intention; and (3) that some stakeholders have greater capacities than others.

Based on those considerations, Sauer's (1993) thoughts culminated in a conceptualization of information systems failure that encompasses three components: the project organization, the information system itself, and its supporters. The development of information systems in organizations is seen as an innovation process that is characterized and ultimately governed by the dependencies between the three components (see Figure 1). In order to innovate, the project organization depends on the provision of continuous support in the form of material resources and help in coping with contingencies. In turn, this support will only be provided if the stakeholders see a range of potential benefits that can be obtained via the information system. The information system requires the effort and expertise of the project organization for its continued existence. In this context, failure occurs when ". . . the level of dissatisfaction with a system is such that there is no longer enough support to sustain it. The objective indicator is the cessation of all work whatsoever in the system. This means the termination of all development, maintenance and operation" (Sauer, 1993: 27). Sauer refers to this state as *termination failure*.

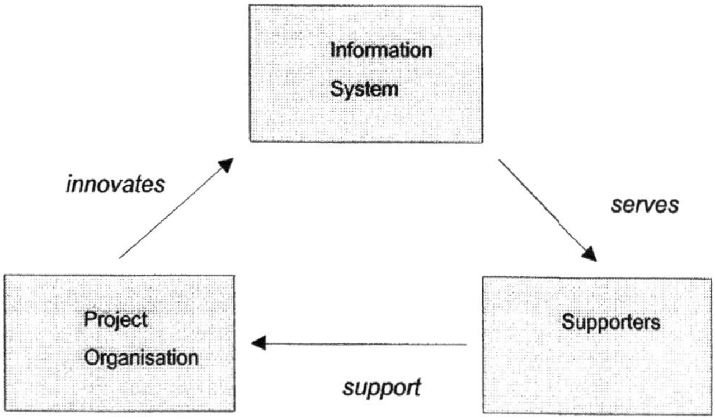

Figure 1: Triangle of Dependencies: System, Supporters and Project Organisation (Adapted from Sauer, 1993)

Termination failure is stricter than expectation failure in the sense that a system should only be deemed as a failure when the development or operation ceases. The distinction between expectation and termination can be understood by considering the concept of flaw. Flaw is akin to dissatisfaction; only termination can be failure. Hence, because of the inherent uncertainty that any innovation process, such as information systems development entails, expectation failures (flaws) are seen and accepted as being normal occurrences. These can be corrected within such a process at a cost, or accepted at a cost. Sauer (1993) correctly notes that flaws describe the perception the supporters hold for an undesired situation, which is waiting to be dealt with. Unless the required support is provided, those flaws will have the negative effect of reducing the capacity of an information system to serve its supporters and, in a domino-effect fashion, may culminate in the introduction of even more faults. Over the passage of time, the volume of flaws may become overbearing and trigger a decision to remove support. This would mean the termination of the project and thus failure.

4. UNDERSTANDING FAILURE THROUGH IDENTITY LOSS

Having discussed these two important frameworks for explaining information systems failure, we now build upon them. The purpose here is to 'add value', through synthesis, by developing a conceptual model that: firstly, shows each framework in a complementary light, enhancing the explanatory strength of each; and secondly, challenges the existing paradigm of information systems development. In the first instance we return to Lyytinen and Hirschheim's (1987) criticism relating to the rational image of information systems as neutral, technical artifacts. This is then expanded to cater for their observation that ". . . a more detailed understanding of the environment in which stakeholders act is required for clarifying why ISs [information systems] fail" (Lyytinen and Hirschheim, 1987: 298).

The past three decades have seen an incredible increase in both the capacity and availability of information technology (see for example, Land and McGregor, 1987). In accounting for this, a study of the meaning attached to information systems may see the evolution of such as moving from their recognition as technical systems to recognition as technical systems with concomitant behavioral and social implications. Land and Hirschheim (1983) argue that this is not the case and that they should be seen, first and foremost, as social systems, which increasingly rely on information technology. However, it is proposed here that the *fluidity* and *interpenetration* between technological and social views makes it increasingly difficult to know, in Scarborough and Corbett's (1992) words, 'the dancer from the dance'.

For the purpose of illustration, it is proposed that this fluidity and interpenetration between technological and social context can be viewed at micro and macro levels. Taking the micro case first, Land (1992) contends that the majority of information systems have three major *information sources:* (1) the real world itself; (2) the designed (or formal) information system - represented as an artifact whose intention is to provide an exact image of the real world; and (3) an informal information system - which may substitute for the formal system, and which is often used to provide qualitative and evaluative information about the real world. How an *individual* employs these sources depends upon a number of *factors* such as cognitive style and preference, knowledge, and memory, and the mode and language of presentation (verbal as against body language for example). In turn, the *operations* of these are often rooted in the individual's culture, education and experience always in parallel with specific environmental and situational factors. We suggest that these factors and operations may be grouped under the heading of *perception*, which the Collins English Dictionary (1994: 1156) defines as "the process by which an organism [the individual] detects and interprets information from an external world [the information sources] by means of the sensory receptors [the factors and operations]".

In moving the analyses of fluidity and interpenetration from the micro to macro, we seek here to extend the work of Ives *et al* (1980) who views an information system as the outcome of three distinct internal environments - those of *use*, *development* and *operations*. In turn, we visualise these environments integrated with three circuits defined by Scarborough and Corbett (1992), these being:

- *Circuits of power*; concerned, in the main, with the political considerations of stakeholder groups. In dichotometric terms, this revolves around the tendency for such groups to use the information system to reproduce or expand their power and influence, set against the loss of such power and influence - via the information system - to a wider range of groups, contexts, and knowledge.
- *Circuits of meaning*; where the objectivity of the material form of the information system may disguise levels of subjective intent and knowledge - intentionally or unintentionally. Thus, on one hand, stakeholders may translate their interests and perceptions into powerful and coherent 'ideologies' whilst, on the other, implicit and protracted use of the information system may 'reframe' the way the real world is perceived - thus reshaping values.
- *Circuits of design*; which can be broadly seen as the flows of knowledge, information and artifacts between the processes of invention, exchange and use (characteristics of the innovation process). This may be seen as the political and ideological 'frame' within which new technologies and new ideas may be evaluated. Within such a frame, the perception of the relative efficiencies and utilities of the information system becomes both the validation of the system and the determinants of its success or failure.

Figure 2 illustrates the fluidity and interpenetration of these micro and macro views. The individual is central to the environments depicted and is an integral part of the information system itself. Whilst an individual may bring preconception to an environment, the interplay between individuals is explained through the circuits of power, meaning and design. It is such 'interplay' that counters Sauer's (1993) criticisms regarding expectation that were discussed earlier. However, we would argue that any particular balance of interest could only be observed in context. In addition, the model

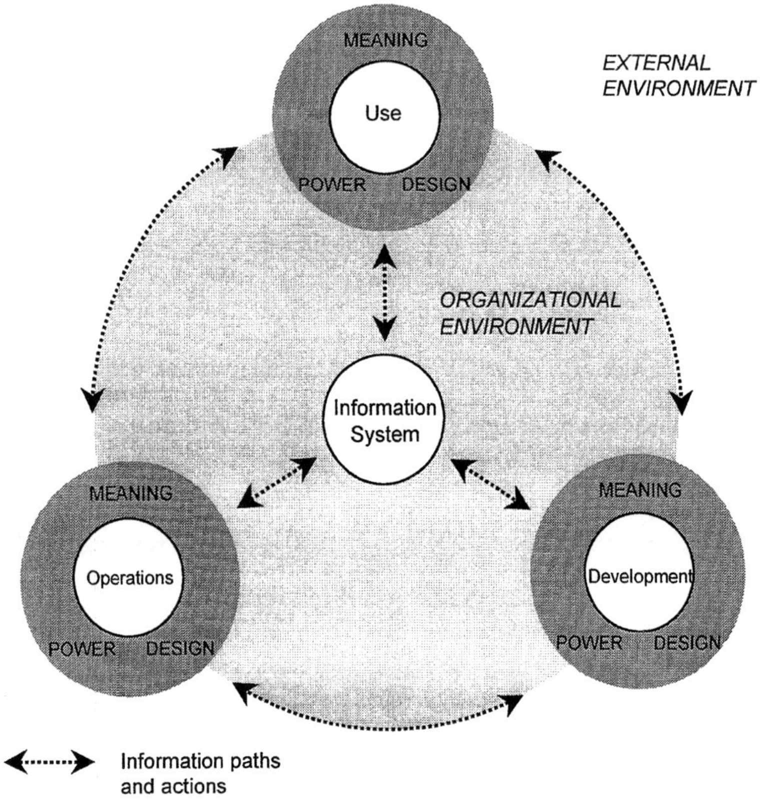

Figure 2: Fluidity and Interpenetration of Information System and Environment

acknowledges the mutuality, fluidity and interpenetration between its elements: both internally and at the nexus with the external environment. This recognizes Tricker's (1992: 15) criticism of Ives *et al's* (1980) original model: this being that "... the environment of an information system defines the purposes of, the constraints on, and the resources available for the information system. It does not see the information system as a fundamental part of the organizational model itself". Lastly, we stress the dynamism underlying the process, with individuals and collective concerns changing constantly.

Let us now further our explanation by considering how negative concerns may be formed. Since the widespread touting of the 'software crisis' (Pressman, 1994), systems development has increasingly been seen in terms of increased control and the widespread adoption of formalized systems

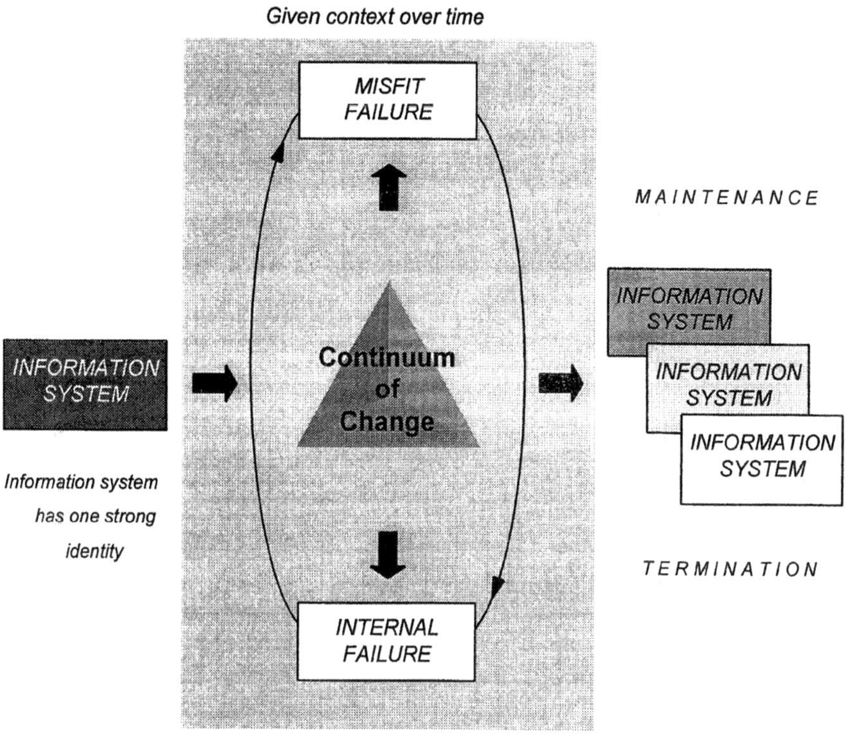

Figure 3: Identity Loss

development methodologies (Grindley, 1986; Hirschheim et al, 1995; Fitzgerald, 1996). Though these may be argued to be weak or 'retrospectively constructed' in practice (see Baskerville, 1996; Fitzgerald, 1996), the stalwart of all major approaches is the *specification of requirements*. Thus, we would argue, an *identity* is placed upon a formal information system from the moment a decision is made to put one in place. Current design approaches strive to maintain this identity and, though they may allow for iteration and evolution in the design process, they fail to allow: (1) for any shifts that may occur in the business context; and (2) for any shifts in individual or collective expectation (both with regard to the relative utility of the system and information 'needs').

Identity loss allows us to explain this. Information systems inhabit a time continuum from their inception to their final demise - intentional or otherwise. If we combine the passage of time with the dynamism of our previous model, the contextual change that results has serious implications for the identity of an information system - it erodes. The concept of identity loss is illustrated at Figure 3 in the previous page.

On the left side of the figure the system has the *strong identity* imposed upon it by the specification of requirements. The second stage in the figure illustrates a *given context over time*. This subsumes the previous model herein and thus contains the environments and circuits previously discussed. Change - realized through the interplay of individuals, environments and circuits - can take any, or a combination, of the following forms: desirable/undesirable, gradual/sudden and temporary/permanent (Kanellis *et al.*, 1996). However, it is this 'contextual change' that has a destabilizing effect on an information system that has no adequate response for it.

With this in mind, we argue that these phenomena can be explained by the following propositions: (1) that the system no longer meets its perceived design objectives (*internal* failure); or (2) that the system objectives are no longer perceived to meet the information needs (*misfit* failure). These two types of failure are not seen as mutually exclusive, both are products of contextual change. A successful business is constantly adapting to change within its environment and, following the argument of mutuality, so should its information systems. However, as has been argued, the 'exacting' identity given to the system inhibits its ability to adapt to shifts in the business context - resulting in misfit failure. Likewise, perceived flaw in the execution of the design, or shifts in individual or collective expectation (either during design or when the system is in use) results in internal failure. Clearly, this is a *mutual* relationship, with contextual factors affecting expectation and vice versa. This takes us to the final stage of Figure 3, which shows the effect of contextual change - the information system iteratively losing its identity. Once this state is reached, there are two options available to the stakeholders affected by the situation: (1) to maintain the system and thus restore its identity; or (2) to terminate it.

In developing the identity loss model, we have purposely sought to avoid producing a model that is prescriptive - i.e., one, which can be used to diagnose the risk of failure and to plan stakeholders' action. However, the interested reader can find empirical application of the philosophies contained herein in Kanellis *et al* (1998). Our aims here are: (1) to provide an understanding of a major theoretical mechanism that produces information systems failure (identity loss); and (2) to provide a fresh conceptual view regarding information systems development. With regard to the former point, the two types of failure that we have chosen to depict within the model are viewed as generic: we would propose that most types of failure that we have discussed would fall within one or the other of those shown. The latter point now forms the focus of our attention. The case study that follows offers an empirical example of the identity loss model and forces us to postulate that what is truly needed is a fundamental reconsideration of approach to the development of information systems.

5. THE CASE STUDY

In this section we present the results of a case study which was carried out over a period of eight months at National Power (NP). NP is a devolved organization operating within and outside the UK electricity sector. It is one of the world's largest international contenders in the fast – growing independent power market, and the biggest in the UK with an over $6 billion turnover. NP was moving from a period of relative certainty during the privatization process, to a much more uncertain time in the UK electricity market. This was coupled with an expansion into new, and unfamiliar, international markets.

The fact that it is only price that distinguishes NP's electricity from that produced by its competitors resulted in the company having to set new and clear objectives in addition to a rapid and radical reorganization. NP's information systems were put in place in 1990. Upon its establishment, the company was a 'green field', and the task of putting the IS into place was undertaken by a consulting firm. The classic 'big-bang' approach was adopted for their development using a proprietary methodology. Taking into account the continuing change that they have been experiencing post-privatization, we investigated how their main systems had fared. The rest of the present section offers an interpretation of the situational conditions resulting initially to information systems disappointment at NP, whilst at the same time making possible the emergence of true flexibility in an unorthodox way. The interested reader is referred to Kanellis (1996) for a description of the methodology followed regarding the collection of case study data and the synthesized framework used for the subsequent analysis.

The analysis of data indicated numerous instances of misfit failure being experienced at NP, leading to internal failure and back again in a circular fashion, as depicted in the identity loss model.. For the purpose of clarification, we have termed these as **structural misfit**, **processual misfit**, and **technological misfit**.

5.1 Structural Misfit

The systems at NP were built around the structure of the company, and either just after they were implemented or at the point that they were implemented, the company changed. A review was carried out in the three months to February 1992 of the suitability of the IS to operate following the devolution of business activities to power stations. The systems in question were mainly the Finance systems and PRISM (a work management system). The findings of the review were that the systems available were suitable for devolved use with some minor modifications. Those modifications represented only those aspects of the systems that could directly prevent devolution. It was also recognized that as those systems were designed prior to devolution, other changes could be usefully made to enhance effectiveness or efficiency. In the time space of almost three and a half years (February 1992 to May 1995), one would expect that the modifications would have been completed successfully, resulting to no misfit at all. However, evidence shows that this is not the case – the process of devolution made demands on the systems that could not be satisfied by simply maintaining them.

> The finance systems we put in, we set up for a particular structure, culture – whatever you want to say and that changed in the last couple of years tremendously. It was like trying to fit a square in a rounded hole, and the number of changes requests to the systems increased, and have been coming non-stop ever since.

Procurement for example, was a central activity that had specialist people dedicated to this task. Devolution meant that this task was now undertaken 'part-time' by non-specialist personnel, as people were required to be more flexible and to work on different job aspects. This meant that the task was now only four or five hours a week of an employee's time, resulting in a negative perception about the systems as being geared towards professionals, and hence too complicated and difficult to use.

> In the early days, we regretted some of the assumptions that we made, as we used to design systems to particularly reflect the structure of the organization, or the way people worked, and while it may have been true at the time, it wasn't always true in the longer term… and I think one of the major problem areas was in the procurement side of things, and still is…

The very clear division of the organization into distinct business units provides another example of structural misfit. The systems were designed to fit this structure, but in time the business cycle has come to cross all the function areas; the systems now fit the functional breakdown, but they do not fit the organization as one entity. In addition, systems are perceived as being too 'big' for what the organization needs for what it does now. This type of misfit has serious implications for the ways that development projects will be managed in the future. It indicates a change to the structure of the systems development units themselves, and poses a question as to how they will operate in the future. A senior developer explained:

> You cannot shrink the business continually and expect those projects of that size to remain unchallenged. So far as the changes concerned, the threat is that if the operation is reduced, we get to a particular financial level where the IS activity becomes disproportionately large in terms of operation. I think that is perhaps the single area where the greatest threat is.

5.2 Processual Misfit

This type of misfit refers to the inability of an information system to keep providing the same level of service to a business process. It would not be an exaggeration to say that no process has remained the same since the early stages of privatization; processes have not only changed but they have kept on changing. IS that support these kinds of business processes are the most vulnerable to change as they deal with voluminous and complicated data at the half-hour level. The systems at the Energy Management Centre (EMC) had to scrapped altogether and a new breed of systems based on the concept of data warehousing had to be developed to account for the changed processes. A senior manager commented:

> The part of the systems that you can define – that you know it has to be a deliverable – your interfaces, getting the data from the power stations and into your offer file – that is the easy part. What it is, it is the analysis of all that – the kind of thinking – the strategy point of view. It is all around the main deliverable for the EMC – that's what is continually changing. It is impossible to define or specify in advance a deliverable. It changes every day!

Processual misfit is also evident with other business units such as Fuel. One manager commented:

> I have seen a couple of instances where management IS have failed to cope with the pace of change and have caused the organization to make inappropriate decisions as a result, and we then had to run to catch up with the circumstances.

It is probably this type of misfit with 'intellectual' systems such as MIS and DSS, that hinges to a need for a different approach to development. One developer responsible for developing such systems for the Sales and Marketing and Strategy and Financial Planning units remarked:

> If everything is changing which it does do, then one thing that I have found is that it is actually quite difficult to alter the scope of an application whilst under development. You tend to fix your scope at the beginning, and you refine it into more and more detail, and by that stage it is quite difficult to stick your head above the parapet and see if you are still at the same place. Then you show it to the users for acceptance test, and they say "Oh! But that was all very well then – we do things differently now!"

What one might define as 'operational systems', and expect them to be stable, are in fact equally vulnerable to change. For example, although the process of work management might seem as fairly stable, it had changed in the sense that the way the work is done at power stations now is much different. For a start, there is not the same number of personnel that was available at one time, and there are no planning departments now, which there were before. There was a much greater emphasis on cost-benefit that determines the maintenance philosophy in deciding to change processes or operations. A manager from Generation provides some evidence for our argument:

> Some of the changes were never at the outset envisaged as being as extensive as they actually were, which resulted in us making more changes to the systems that we have otherwise had anticipated. It also meant that some of the more refined facilities of the systems have become less used. So yes, they have been inflexible in the sense that it would require a large amount of effort to change or add some functionality.

5.3 Technological Misfit

This type which is caused simply by advancements in technology, seemed to affect all the main systems at NP. As those were designed five years ago, they were character-based and with busy screen representation. In the sense of usability, they are perceived as not being up to current practice standards. This means that in order to use the systems, users have to get familiar with them for some time, and this is not always possible under the current situation – few employees, many tasks, little time. Users have now to be fairly able to switch from one system to another and perform various tasks at the same time. Technological misfit does not immediately mean that an existing process can be performed more effectively with new technology, in terms of the quality of information needed to make a decision. Indeed, managers commented that for many people at NP, that seems to be secondary, and they draw a parallel with the fashion world. They see however this desire to work with the most current and 'sexy' system as a natural thing – a progression, but at the same time they are also aware of the fact that it might lead to a diversion from what the business actually wants. Most managers, feeling powerless with this technological evolution have decided to consciously 'ride' along with it. What they are finding however, is that the line between 'going there because it is there', and 'going there because you know why you go there' is becoming more blurred, as the rate of this technological process increases.

In summary, the implications of the three types of misfit that follow are the result of information systems at NP that have not been designed to provide for change. These were:

- The quality of information provided limits the purpose which particular systems were designed to serve.
- Accessing the information is difficult. Users are asking for a lot of information but they do not know how to get at it.

- Users need the information in different ways and at the same time, the number of users who need this information is increasing. This demands a level of sophistication that existing systems cannot provide.
- The current level of integration between the systems hardly approximates the one required. As a result, the information flows suffer considerably.
- Management information has been neglected. Attempts to provide for it by combining systems or building on top of operational systems, has produced ones that are over-complicated and under-utilized.

The paper suggests that the identity of a system is bound up with the functionality that it displays. It can be argued that identity and functionality are quite different matters because a system can be successfully maintained, and hence its initial identify in functional terms may be totally lost without the system failing. Although we agree with this point of view, we want to stress out that in a dynamic environment, maintenance produces no results. Change here is the dependent variable, and the initiator of a dynamic process against a predetermined identity given to it and defined by the specification of its requirements. Because of change, repetitive identity loss will finally result to abandonment and termination – disappointment in the beginning and then failure. NP provides a good example of an organization where the rate of change has superseded all maintenance efforts resulting in systems that should be deemed failures in any of the categories defined by DeLone and McLean (1992) [system quality, information quality, use, user satisfaction and individual impact].

In turn, what differentiates the identity loss model of information systems failure from previous ones is the fact that those see 'maintenance' as a solution or accept it as a 'necessary evil' in information systems development. By rejecting this view, and realizing the vulnerability of information systems in turbulent environments, the value of the identity loss model rests in demonstrating that information systems research and practice should rather stop offering palliatives to combat the symptoms of information systems failure, and begin to reconsider its fundamental assumptions and approaches.

6. THE IMPLICATIONS OF 'IDENTITY LOSS' AND THE EMERGENCE OF TRUE FLEXIBILITY

Organizational impact, one of DeLone and McLcan's (1992) success variables refers to the extent of the effect that the systems can have on organizational performance. In the case of NP this gives rise to the following paradox: how, on one hand, is it possible for such a level of information systems misfit to exist, and yet an organization as heavily dependent on its systems, to be able to flex and adapt successfully to continuous environmental contingencies? Although there was a negative overall perception regarding the fit of the systems, with a large percentage of those not being used as they were supposed to – user activities and tasks did not seem to be disrupted in any way. One would expect otherwise, but we found that users were not tied down by the systems. What explains this phenomenon is perhaps the simple rule of survival: threatened by adverse circumstances, one has no choice but to adapt. One manager from Finance commented:

> You think that you have a financial accounting system, and you think you are producing the company's trading account, and one day you find that everybody is doing it in a different way by the spreadsheets. And you could say "You shouldn't do that! It is all there. It is a waste of time!" But people do not waste their time for the sake of it, do they? It is obvious then that they are doing it because there is some great hole in there.

The same phenomenon is evident in what a manager from Generation said:

> Systems have fallen away and people are not using them as much as they should. And just about everybody, everywhere, is taking data out of the main systems, and either re-keying it in, or use whatever method is available to them to get data into little applications, so that they can then move the data around and use it the way they want to, because they see that the system they access – the PRISM system – is inflexible. What we are trying to do now is to recognize that this is a key requirement, and just deal with the data – not to deliver them any systems.

The Sales and Marketing business unit makes heavy use of the Finance systems. This is what a manager there said:

> As changes occur in the business world, if you cannot get to change the system because the money or the project team has gone – they do it with a spreadsheet – they do not bother with the system that you have spend half of your life to develop – that's a hidden problem as well. I mean, we look at systems and say "Oh! We never change the system. It is a bloody success!" But really, what happens is that the buggers put a Lotus spreadsheet there to do their work with it. I mean our Finance systems are crap. If I wanna know how much money I have spend on contracts at the end of this month, I go and get a bloody spreadsheet. Walker cannot tell me – not in the way I wanna say it. So people do bits and bobs around the edges, don't they?

There were a number of conditions that made possible the development and existence of the above phenomenon. NP upon privatization put in place a number of IS; continuous change since then has practically crippled them with respect to what their initial purpose was; at the same time the policy of the company was such that it gave users almost complete autonomy and freedom with respect to meeting their own systems and informational needs; people used this freedom and have developed small applications of their own, and along with application packages have cannibalized the overarching systems to give themselves a system that is working by adapting it to their particular need. A truly flexible information system, but certainly not a planned or intended one.

Information Technology Services (ITS) even had a name for this situation. When we were asking for comments, they were referring to it as the 'Lotus Cult'. An appropriate name we thought – 'cult' signifying a kind of underground alliance – for the groups of users who have a disregard for the formal IS imposed on them, and in a way have taken control of their own 'fate'. We must note however, that this underground activity has come to be seen as essential even by the 'authorities' themselves. One member of the ITS team said that if one ever attempts to take this away, parts of NP would stop operating within a day, and the company would soon collapse.

7. THE NEED FOR LIVING INFORMATION SYSTEMS

The maintenance route, indicated in Figure 3, represents 'where we stand today' with regard to information systems that have to adapt to change. However, as Paul (1994: 392) notes, ". . . the very word maintenance suggests corrective action, as though somehow, the need for change could have been avoided if somehow, we had known better". It is this mentality that guides our current 'understanding' with regard to systems development and pushes us toward more control, rigour and formalization. This 'understanding' is expressed by Paul (1994: 391) in the 'mock' Fixed Point Theorem of Information Systems, this being that:

> "There exists some point in time when everyone involved in the system knows what they want and agrees with everyone else".

We have shown, through the development of the first model, that this is extremely unlikely. Unfortunately this understanding is exacerbated by the project-based nature of development (see Grindley, 1986) which, in the current paradigm, necessarily restrains development to a fixed time period. Thus we develop systems around a (hypothetical) point in time, which are then asked to operate across a time continuum. This time continuum, in turn, is characterized by our first model.

Identity is therefore 'lost' because it is static and exacting. That is not to say that identity is not important: it is very important, as it is the way that the stakeholder 'sees' the system. However, what this identity needs to exhibit is a 'plasticity' (see Maturana and Varela, 1973) - allowing the system to remain consonant with its context over time. For us, what is required for living businesses are living systems. These are systems that are not judged to 'right' or 'correct' but that are constantly undergoing change to meet changes in context, need and circumstance.

In retrospect, the concept of identity loss implies a paradigm shift in information systems development - to one where the systems designer will no longer be required to foresee every contingency or articulate every requirement of a design. Information systems will not be given a static identity, but will be developing their own - having been brought in existence as 'infants', with the ability to grow and adapt, as opposed to 'inflexible' adults. It is thus postulated that what is required is an architecture for information systems that is designed for breathing, and thereby adapt to inevitable and unknown change. Such an architecture has less to do with 'what is wanted', and more to do with the creation of a living space within the information system that enables the information system to live.

Our own research into the plausibility of such a development 'understanding' currently takes two forms. Firstly, through external-reference and external-modification: examining 'tailorable systems' as a way of giving stakeholders better 'real time' control over their particular part of an architecture. Secondly, through self-reference and self-modification: examining whether biological theories such as 'autopoiesis' (Maturana and Varela, 1973), in combination with genetic and evolutionary techniques, can provide better architectures for information systems.

8. CONCLUSIONS

We have used the concept of *identity loss* for two purposes: firstly, to draw together existing conceptualizations of failure; and secondly to highlight the static nature of the predominant information systems development paradigm. In addressing the former we have sought to offer a more complete conceptualization of: (1) the 'what' factors that should be considered as part of the explanation; (2) 'how' they interact with each other; and (3) 'why' the outcome of these relationships may produce flaws or, more seriously, termination. The 'what' and 'how' have been accounted for extensively through the concepts of mutuality, fluidity and interpenetration. Sauer's (1993) criticism of expectation failure - that it gives equal weight to all interests - does not apply here. The circuits of power, meaning and design are argued to have different values at different points in time for different groups of stakeholders. Their interrelationships allow that: (1) some stakeholders will have greater capacities than others; (2) some stakeholders expectations may be more reasonable than others; and (3) that they most certainly convey explicitly or implicitly some intention.

The 'why' rests on contextual change. Its projection through the notion of *identity loss* is what we believe differentiates our conceptualization from those that have gone before. We have not actively sought to produce a model that is prescriptive - i.e., one that can be used to diagnose the risk of failure and to plan stakeholders' action. Instead we have used our synthesis of the literature to point toward what we see to be a fundamental flaw in the way that information systems development is currently 'understood'. In addressing this, we have painted our own vision for the future. This rests on developing an understanding of 'living' information systems - that is, information systems that are able to adapt to context, needs and circumstance. However, we would venture that a major improvement in information systems development will only occur when many, if not most people involved, take on the paradigm shift necessary.

9. REFERENCES

Aldag, R. J., and Power, D. J. (1986). 'An Empirical Assessment of Computer-Assisted Decision Analysis'. *Decision Sciences*, **17** (4), pp. 572-588.

Bailey, J. E., and Pearson, S. W. (1983). 'Development of a Tool for Measuring and Analyzing Computer User Satisfaction'. *Management Science*, **29** (5), pp. 530-545.

Baronas, A. K., and Louis, M. R. (1988). 'Restoring a Sense of Control During Implementation: How User Involvement Leads to System Acceptance'. *MIS Quarterly*, **12** (1), pp. 111-123.

Baroudi, J. J., Olson, M. H., and Ives, B. (1986). 'An Empirical Study of the Impact of User Involvement on System Usage and Information Satisfaction'. *Communications of the ACM*, **29** (3), pp. 232-238.

Baskerville, R., Travis, J., and Truex, D. (1996). 'Amethodological Systems Development: The Deferred Meaning of Systems Development Methods'. , Department of Informatics and Management Accounting, Copenhagen Business School, Copenhagen.

Bell, J. (1984). 'The Effect of Presentation Form on the Use of Information in Annual Reports'. *Management Science*, **30** (2), pp. 169-185.

Benbasat, I., and Dexter, A. S. (1986). 'An Investigation of the Effectiveness of Color and Graphical Information Presentation and their Varying Time Constraints'. *MIS Quarterly*, **10** (1), pp. 59-83.

Benbasat, I., Dexter, A. S., and Masulis, P. S. (1981). 'An Experimental Study of the Human/Computer Interface'. *Communications of the ACM*, **24** (11), pp. 752-762.

Beynon-Davies, P. (1995). 'Information Systems 'Failure': The Case of the London Ambulance Service's Computer Aided Despatch Project'. *European Journal of Information Systems*, **4** , pp. 174-184.

DeBrabander, B., and Thiers, G. (1984). 'Successful Information Systems Development in Relation to Situational Factors Which Affect Effective Communication Between MIS-Users and EDP-Specialists'. *Management Science*, **30** (2), pp. 137-155.

DeLone, W. H., and McLean, E. R. (1992). 'Information Systems Success: The Quest for the Dependent Variable'. *Information Systems Research*, **3** (1), pp. 60-95.

Dickson, G. N., DeSanctis, G., and McBride, D. J. (1986). 'Understanding the Effectiveness of Computer Graphics for Decision Support: A Cumulative Experimental Approach'. *Communications of the ACM*, **29** (1), pp. 40-47.

Fitzgerald, B. (1996). 'Formalized Systems Development Methodologies: A Critical Perspective'. *Information Systems Journal*, **6** , pp. 3-23.

Fuerst, W. L., and Cheney, P. H. (1982). 'Factors Affecting the Perceived Utilization of Computer-Based Decision Support Systems'. *Decision Sciences*, **13** (4), pp. 554-569.

Goodhue, D. (1988). 'IS Attitude: Towards Theoretical Definition and Measurement Clarity'. *Database* (Fall/Winter), pp. 6-15.

Grindley. (1986). *Fourth Generation Languages: Volume 1, A Survey of Best Practice*, IDPM Publications Ltd., London.

Hamilton, S., and Chervany, N. L. (1981). 'Evaluating Information System Effectiveness - Part II: Comparing Evaluator Viewpoints'. *MIS Quarterly*, **5** (3), pp. 55-69.

Hiltz, S. R., and Turroff, M. (1981). 'The Evolution of User Behaviour in a Computerized Conferencing System'. *Communications of the ACM*, **24** (11), pp. 739-751.

Hirschheim, R., Klein, H. K., and Lyytinen, K. (1995). *Information Systems Development and Data Modeling: Conceptual and Philosophical Foundations*, Cambridge University Press, Cambridge.

Hirschheim, R., and Smithson, S. (1988). 'A Critical Analysis of Information Systems Evaluation'. *Information Systems Assessment: Issues and Challenges*, N. Bjorn-Andersen and G. B. Davis, eds., North Holland, Amsterdam, The Netherlands.

Ives, B., Hamilton, S., and Davis, G. B. (1980). 'A Framework for Research in Computer-Based Management Information Systems'. *Management Science*, **26** (9), pp. 910-934.

Ives, B., and Olson, M. H. (1983). 'User Involvement and MIS Success: A Review of Research'. *Management Science*, **30** (5), pp. 586-603.

Ives, B., Olson, M. H., and Baroudi, J. J. (1983). 'The Measurement of User Information Satisfaction'. *Communications of the ACM*, **26** (10), pp. 785-793.

Kanellis, P., Paul, R.J. and Crick, A. (1996) An Archetype for Researching Information Systems Flexibility. In the *Proceedings of the 5th International Conference on Information Systems Development*, Wrycza, S. and Zupancic, J. (Eds.), September 24-26, Gdansk, Poland, pp. 147-161.

Kanellis, P. (1996) *Information Systems and Business Fit in Dynamic Environments*. Unpublished PhD Dissertation, Department of Information Systems and Computing, Brunel University, UK.

Kanellis, P., Lycett, M. and Paul, R.J. (1998) An Interpretive Approach to the Measurement of Information Systems Success: From Concept to Practical Application. In *Information Systems Success Measurement*, Garrity, E.J. and Sanders, L.G. (Eds.), Idea Group Publishing, Harrisburg, P.A., U.S.A.

Keen, P. G. W. (1981). 'Value Analysis: Justifying Decision Support Systems'. *MIS Quarterly*, **5** (1), pp. 1-15.

Keen, P. G. W. (1991). 'Relevance and Rigor in Information Systems Research: Improving Quality, Confidence, Cohesion and Impact'. *Information Systems Research: Contemporary Approaches and Emergent Traditions*, H.-E. Nissen, H. K. Klein, and R. Hirschheim, eds., Elsevier, Amsterdam, The Netherlands, pp. 27-49.

Kim, E., and Lee, J. (1986). 'An Exploratory Contingency Model of User Participation and MIS Use'. *Information and Management*, **12** (2), pp. 87-97.

King, W. R., and Epstein, B. J. (1983). 'Assessing Information System Value'. *Decision Sciences*, **14** (1), pp. 34-45.

King, W. R., and Rodriguez, J. I. (1981). 'Participative Design of Strategic Decision Support Systems'. *Management Science*, **27** (6), pp. 717-726.

Land, F. F. (1992). 'The Information Systems Domain'. *Information Systems Research: Issues, Methods and Practical Guidelines*, R. D. Galliers, ed., Blackwell Scientific Publications, Oxford, UK.

Land, F. F., and Hirschheim, R. (1983). 'Participative Systems Design: Rationale, Tools and Techniques'. *Journal of Applied Systems Analysis*, **10** .

Land, F. F. a. K.-M. G., M. (1987). 'Information and Information Systems; Concepts and Perspectives'. *Information Analysis: Selected Readings*, R. D. Galliers, ed., Addison-Wesley, Wokingham, Berkshire, U.K, pp. 63-91.

Lucas, H. C. (1976). *The Implementation of Computer-Based Models*, National Association of Accountants, New York, NY.

Lucas, H. C. J. (1975a). 'Performance and the Use of Information Systems'. *Management Science*, **21** (8), pp. 908-919.

Lucas, H. C. J. (1975b). *Why Information Systems Fail?*, Columbia University Press, New York, NY.

Lucas, H. C. J. (1981). 'An Experimental Investigation of the Use of Computer-Based Graphics in Decision-Making'. *Management Science*, **27** (7), pp. 757-768.

Lyytinen, K., and Hirshheim, R. (1987). 'Information Systems Failures: A Survey and Classification of the Empirical Literature'. *Oxford Surveys in Information Technology*, **4** , pp. 257-309.

Mahmood, M. A., and Medewitz, J. N. (1985). 'Impact of Design Methods on Decision Support System Success: An Empirical Assessment'. *Information and Management*, **9** (3), pp. 137-151.

Markus, M. L., and Keil, M. (1994). 'If We Built it, They Will Come: Designing Information Systems That People Want to Use'. *Sloan Management Review* (Summer), pp. 11-25.

Maturana, H. R., and Varela, F. J. (1973). 'Autopoiesis: The Organisation of the Living'. *Autopoiesis and Cognition*, R. S. Cohen and M. W. Wartofsky, eds., D. Reidel Publishing Company, Dordrecht.

Melone, N. P. (1990). 'A Theoretical Assessment of the User-Satisfaction Construct in Information Systems Research'. *Management Science*, **36** (1), pp. 76-91.

Millman, Z., and Hartwick, J. (1987). 'The Impact of Automated Office Systems on Middle Managers and their Work'. *MIS Quarterly*, **11** (4), pp. 479-491.

Olson, M. H., and Lucas, H. C. (1982). 'The Impact of Office Automation on the Organization: Some Implications for Research and Practice'. *Communications of the ACM*, **25** (11), pp. 838-847.

Paul, R. J. (1994). 'Why Users Cannot 'Get What They Want''. *International Journal of Manufacturing Systems Design*, **1** (4), pp. 389-394.

Pressman, R. S. (1992). *Software Engineering: A Practitioners Approach*, McGraw-Hill, London.

Rivard, S., and Huff, S. L. (1984). 'User Developed Applications: Evaluation of Success from the DP Department Perspective'. *MIS Quarterly*, **8** (1), pp. 39-50.

Sauer, C. (1993). *Why Information Systems Fail: A Case Study Approach*, Alfred Waller, Henley on Thames, UK.

Scarborough, H., and Corbet, J. M. (1992). *Technology and Organization: Power, Meaning and Design*, Routlege, London, UK.

Strassmann, P. A. (1985). *Information Payoff: The Transformance of Work in the Electronic Age*, The Free Press, New York.

Swanson, E. B. (1974). 'Management Information Systems: Appreciation and Involvement'. *Management Science*, **21** (2), pp. 178-188.

Tricker, R. I. (1992). 'The Management of Organizational Knowledge'. *Information Systems Research: Issues, Methods and Practical Guidelines*, R. D. Galliers, ed., Blackwell Scientific Publications, Oxford, UK.

Walsham, G. (1995). 'The Emergence of Interpretivism in IS Research'. *Information Systems Research*, **6** (4), pp. 376-394.

Zanna, M. P., and Fazio, R. H. (1982). 'The Attitude-Behaviour Relation: Moving Toward a Third Generation of Research'. *Consistency in Social Behaviour: The Ontario Symposium (Vol.2),* M. P. Zanna, E. T. Higgins, and C. P. Herman, eds., Erlbaum, Hillside, NJ.

Zmud, R. W. (1979). 'Individual Differences and MIS Success: A Review of the Empirical Literature'. *Management Science*, **25** (10), pp. 966-979.

Comments on "Failure, Identity Loss and Living Information Systems" by P. Kanellis, M. Lycett, and R.J. Paul

Kalle Lyytinen

Department of Computer Science and Information Systems, University of Jyväskylä
P. O. Box 35, 40351 Jyväskylä, Finland
Email: kalle@jytko.jyu.fi

Information system (IS) failure is a pervasive phenomenon. Like the paper's introduction, common sense and statistics show information system failure is common and also important, because huge amounts of human effort and economic resources are spent without much gain. The issue of failure is also related to FRISCO report and the theme of the conference in two ways. First our concepts and ideas about information system and the nature of information system development can affect either positively or negatively our intellectual and technical capabilities to influence the likelihood of IS failure. Second, because information system definition forms one key concept and focus of the FRISCO report it may help achieve a common and more precise understanding of "what it is" that is failing.

The paper by Kanellis, Lycett and Paul delivers four distinct but interrelated results:

1) a definition / survey of IS success and a criticism of the prevailing positivistic accounts of the topic
2) a survey of IS failure literature and an attempt to develop a synthesis of the pertinent literature and conceptions of IS failure,
3) a proposal of a concept *identity loss* which is defined as the gap between the espoused functional whole (identity) and the actual

performance of that functionality w. r. t. environmental change. This change may result in loosing the identity in two different dimensions:

- in relation to environment i.e. a. k. a. misfit failure, and
- in relation to technical platform i.e. a. k. a. internal failure.

The concept is illustrated with a case study that demonstrates the validity of the use of the "identity loss" in relation to developing an internal accounting system for a large national company that is being privatised.

4) a call for a paradigm shift which defines Information systems as "living" systems based on the work of Maturana and Varela.

Overall I find the paper to be interesting and a fresh addition to the expanding discourse on IS failure. It offers a new and possibly exciting attempt to use concepts like identity and social construction of identity to understand the dynamics of legitimation and commitment creation in relation to IS development initiatives. It also points out the current weakness in the FRISCO report to understand second order change and the dynamic interactions between the IS and its environment.

Despite these positive observations I have a few critical observations and reservations to the approach adopted:

1) It is not really clear how the concept of identity loss synthesises previous failure concepts, and if so, what is the value added of this synthesis. Who could use it and for what purposes?

2) It is not clear how the concept leads to "web" like descriptions of failure (as alleged in the paper) in any way better than the past definitions of Lyytinen and Hirschheim or Sauer, and in what sense the resulting description is non-deterministic? If the description would be totally non-deterministic all failures would be totally random and no explanation would be possible, and needed. So, some sort of "intermediating" concept of causality is needed here which is lacking from the paper (like systemic dependencies, emergent features and path dependencies)

3) It is not clear how the paper would lead to a different type of failure analysis than in the past, and if this is the case, what would be those differences?

4) I found the concept of an identity loss at most vaguely defined. Clearly the concept of system here is not self-referential in the sense that the information system builds its own identity. Rather the identity is constructed by the stakeholders (which are not part of the system,

but in the environment) through social action and talk. Yet, how this attribution of the identity is accomplished, what mechanisms are used and by whom, is not discussed, though I find it critical for the whole concept of "identity". In this sense I do not see here much difference what is proposed from what a stakeholder based analysis would suggest.

5) The equation of identity with functionality is problematic. Normally identity during systems development is not defined by what the system is supposed do (i.e. its functions), because these may change or the actors do not know them. Rather it is defined by the goals (this is why we do this), the work units (this is how much we can spend and how long we can work on this), the contracts (this is what we agree to exchange with one another) etc. Therefore I would have expected a more detailed analysis of mechanisms of identity construction.

6) Instead of an identity loss (due to difficulties observed above) I would rather discuss information systems and their development and maintenance trajectories in Marchian terms as "Garbage-cans" that bundle together varying actors, interests, competencies, resources, and solutions over time. These can stay in the organisational landscape for long periods of time until no support (=interest) is available. Therefore an identity for such "garbage-can" is dependent on the mobilisation of bias i.e. on the attribution of something which is worth of building and using resources by some stake-holders.

I was puzzled by the claim that "living systems" is something new in the field. In fact there is nothing new here (for a detailed analysis see J. Porra, Information Colonies and Punctuated Prototyping, PhD Thesis, University of Jyväskylä, 1996). I would find it much more worthwhile to ask *why* do we need fixed requirements and a clear identity for the task units of systems development. Then we should start looking at agency-dynamics, task complexity and uncertainty and issues that deal with institutional regulation and evolution in complex organisational domains. In particular it is not clear how "living systems" would be different from what is currently accomplished with evolutionary designs and incremental development, interoperability, portability and enhancive maintenance.

An Ontological Evaluation of the OML Metamodel

Andreas L Opdahl[1], Brian Henderson-Sellers[2] and Franck Barbier[3]

[1] *Department of Information Science, University of Bergen, Norway; andreas@ifi.uib.no . Presently at the School of Computing Sciences, University of Technology, Sydney, Australia.*
[2] *School of Computing Sciences, University of Technology, Sydney, Australia; brian@socs.uts.edu.au .*
[3] *IRIN, Université de Nantes, France; Franck.Barbier@irin.univ-nantes.fr .*

Key words: Object-oriented modelling, Ontological analysis and evaluation, OPEN, OML, the BWW-model, FRISCO.

Abstract: The paper presents results of analysing and evaluating the OPEN Modelling Language (OML) metamodel in terms of the Bunge-Wand-Weber (BWW) model of information systems and the Framework of Information Systems Concepts (FRISCO). The analysis and evaluation has suggested several ways to improve the modelling constructs supported by OML and to improve how OML is defined and organised. It has also made it clearer how and why ontological models like the BWW-model and FRISCO can and should be used to improve and define object-oriented (OO) modelling languages. In particular, it has led to a template for defining OO modelling constructs in terms of what they represent in the problem domain during IS development. Finally, the analysis and evaluation has suggested ways to improve FRISCO as an analysis and evaluation tool for OO modelling languages.

1. INTRODUCTION

Object-oriented (OO) modelling languages have become widespread in recent years. However, some critics claim that object orientation is less well suited for modelling "real-world" problem domains during information systems (IS) development because object-oriented abstractions are tailored to represent software artefacts rather than things in or aspects of problem domains. For example, critics question whether OO-concepts such as message passing and encapsulation are really features of the real-world things that are represented and whether things really belong to fixed classes throughout their life-times (e.g., Jackson, 1995; Parsons and Wand, 1997b.)

To shed light on these problems and related ones, the paper presents results of using ontology to analyse and evaluate how well the metamodel of the OPEN[1] Modelling Language (OML; Firesmith et al., 1998) supports representation of "real-world" problem domains. The analysis and evaluation is anchored in the Bunge-Wand-Weber (BWW) model of information systems (e.g., Wand and Weber, 1995; Weber, 1997) and in the Framework of Information Systems Concepts (FRISCO; Falkenberg et al., 1998.) It is the result of systematically comparing more than 160 OML-constructs with 44 ontological constructs in the BWW-model and 98 constructs in FRISCO.

Since space does not permit a detailed discussion of each OML-construct, the paper instead discusses important outcomes in general. (1) The analysis and evaluation has suggested several ways to improve the modelling constructs supported by OML and to improve how OML is defined and organised. (2) It has made it clearer how and why ontological models like the BWW-model and FRISCO can and should be used to improve and define object-oriented (OO) modelling languages. (3) As a consequence, it has led to a template for defining OO modelling constructs in terms of what they represent in the problem domain of IS development. (4) Finally, the analysis and evaluation has suggested ways to improve FRISCO as an analysis and evaluation tool for OO modelling languages. Since detailed suggestions for improving OML will be presented elsewhere, the paper will focus on the latter three outcomes.

In what follows, Section 2 first introduces OML and the BWW-model along with the method of ontological analysis and evaluation. Also, this section explains why we have chosen OML as our object of study and why we have chosen ontological analysis and evaluation based on the BWW-model and FRISCO as our method of research. Section 3 then presents an outline of the analysis, before Section 4 gives an overview of our results. Finally, Section 5 concludes the paper and outlines paths for further work.

2. THEORETICAL BACKGROUND

This section will briefly present the OPEN Modelling Language (OML) and the Bunge-Wand-Weber (BWW) model of information systems. It will also explain our choices of study-object and research method.

The OML Metamodel. The OPEN[1] Modelling Language (OML; Firesmith et al., 1998; Firesmith and Henderson-Sellers, 1998; Henderson-Sellers and Firesmith, 1998) is an object-oriented modelling language which provides modelling constructs, diagram types, graphical notations and a metamodel for representing problem domains as well as logical and physical IS designs during all phases of IS development. This paper focusses on OML's metamodel.

Although it is an independent modelling language with a user-base of its own, OML is perhaps more important as a variant of the Object Management Group (OMG)'s standard Unified Modelling Language (UML; OMG, 1999.) In OML, more sophisticated and more formal concepts can be evaluated in theory and in practice (Henderson-Sellers et al., 1999.) It has been argued that OML is more "properly OO" than UML and provides a richer set of modelling constructs (Graham, 1998.) Also, OML has fewer modelling constructs and appears better organised than UML. We consider OML an appropriate object of study for the following reasons: (1) Improvements to OML also contribute to the further development of UML. (2) Since OML is a "proper" and rich OO modelling language, our results can be readily generalised to OO modelling in general. (3) Since OML's metamodel is small and well organised, it is a useful intermediate step before analysing and evaluating the larger and more complex UML. Based on the results and experiences from the present study, we have initiated such a study of UML.

Since space does not allow us to present the OML metamodel in detail, we will explain each OML-construct we have used when it is encountered in the text.

Ontological Analysis and Evaluation. Ontological analysis and evaluation has been proposed by Wand and Weber (e.g., Wand and Weber, 1993) as a method for assessing and improving IS modelling languages. The method applies philosophical ontology to analyse the meaning of modelling constructs and to evaluate whether the set of constructs provided by a language is appropriate or not. Philosophical ontology can be described as "the science concerned with the whole of reality" (Bunge, 1977, p.5) and is therefore an appropriate foundation for analysing and evaluating modelling languages which are meant to represent "real-world" problem domains. (Although it is considerably more specialised due to its closer adaptation to the IS field, this paper will also treat FRISCO as an ontology in this sense.)

The method proposed by Wand and Weber prescribes two *mappings* between an ontological model (such as the BWW-model and FRISCO) and a modelling language to be evaluated (such as OML's metamodel.) On the one hand, an *interpretation mapping* from the set of modelling constructs to the set of ontological constructs is carried out to identify (1a) *excessive* modelling constructs with no ontological counterpart, as well as (1b) *overloaded* modelling constructs with more than one counterpart in the ontology. The interpretation mapping also provides (1c) a precise definition of each modelling construct in terms of the ontological model. On the other hand, a *representation mapping* from the set of ontological constructs to the set of modelling constructs is carried out to identify (2a) *redundant* modelling constructs, several of which have the same counterpart in the ontology, and (2b) *deficits* in the modelling language because there are ontological constructs with no counterpart in the language.

Our analysis and evaluation focusses only on OML's support for modelling "real-world" problem domains during IS development. We must therefore distinguish between two groups of excessive OML-constructs. One group is "truly excessive" because the constructs are clearly meant to represent something in the problem domain, yet have no counterparts in the ontology. Another group of excessive constructs is instead "not oriented towards problem domains" because the constructs are not meant to represent anything in the problem domain but instead represent, e.g., a part or aspect of the proposed software system. Only a "truly excessive" modelling construct is a problem.

We consider ontological analysis and evaluation an appropriate research method for the following reasons: (1) The analysis and evaluation has suggested several concrete improvements to OML and FRISCO. (2) It has prepared for a later analysis and evaluation of the OMG-standard, UML, and has suggested several other paths for further work.

The BWW-model. In addition to FRISCO, our ontological analysis and evaluation is anchored in the Bunge-Wand-Weber (BWW) model of information systems. The BWW-model has been proposed by Wand and Weber (e.g., Wand and Weber, 1995; Weber, 1997) as an adaptation to the IS field of Mario Bunge's comprehensive ontology (Bunge, 1977, 1979.)

We consider the BWW-model and FRISCO appropriate for our ontological analysis and evaluation of OML since they are two among several ontologies that can and should be used to improve and better define existing OO modelling languages. Following (Wand and Weber, 1993), we also argue that the BWW-model is (1) better developed and formalised than competing ontologies, (2) based on concepts that are fundamental to the computer science and IS fields and (3) productive, in the sense that it has produced useful results already. Also, the BWW-model has already been used to analyse and evaluate several other modelling languages and frameworks (e.g., Wand and Weber, 1989; Weber and Zhang, 1996; Green, 1996; Weber, 1997; Green and Rosemann, 1999.) In addition, our analysis and evaluation is based on earlier work by Wand (Wand, 1989) which has proposed the BWW-model as a formal model of objects. This work has resulted in an object-oriented information systems model (Takagaki and Wand, 1991) and in analyses and discussions of object-oriented concepts (Parsons and Wand, 1997a, 1997b.) However, to our knowledge, the work described here is the first analysis and evaluation of an existing object-oriented modelling language using the BWW-model.

Since space does not allow us to present the BWW-model in detail, we will explain each BWW-construct we have used when it is encountered in the text.

3. OUTLINE OF THE ANALYSIS

Tables 1 to 3 show interpretation mappings of the 54 constructs in OML that are most important for representing problem domains. Since the full analysis is too large to be presented in detail, this section will instead present an overview and explain the OML-, BWW- and FRISCO-constructs we will use later. The next section will present and discuss the main results.

Objects and classes in OML. In relation to the BWW-model, OML-objects represent BWW-things and OML-classes represent BWW-classes of things. In relation to FRISCO, OML-objects represent FRISCO-predicated things and OML-classes represent FRISCO-populations thereof. Hence both ontologies contain constructs which underpin OML's objects and object classes. However, whereas BWW-things are "concrete" things in the problem domain, FRISCO-predicated things are "conceptions" in the minds of human actors. This is because the BWW-model is based on "metaphysical realism" whereas FRISCO is a "constructivist" ontology. As a consequence, the two ontologies lead to different interpretations of OML-objects and this difference in turn leads to similarly different interpretations of many other OML-constructs.

Characteristics and responsibilities in OML. OML's characteristics represent what an object "knows", what it "does" and which "rules" it obeys. In the BWW-model, the three kinds of OML-characteristics represent "regular" BWW-properties, to BWW-transition laws and to BWW-state laws, respectively. (BWW-laws are a kind of BWW-properties.) In FRISCO, the corresponding three constructs are FRISCO-predicators "in general", FRISCO-rules about permissible transitions and FRISCO-rules about permissible states.

An important distinction made in the BWW-model (Weber, 1997) is between BWW-*human* laws (e.g., traffic regulations, business policies) and BWW-*natural* laws (e.g., laws of physics.) Whereas the natural laws always hold, human laws are social constructs which can be broken. OML does not represent this distinction explicitly, although violations of human laws might be represented as OML-*exceptions*. The FRISCO report (Falkenberg et al., 1998) distinguishes between *rules* and *organisational norms*.

OML-responsibilities have no primitive counterparts in the BWW-model or in FRISCO and still need to be defined more precisely in relation to "real-world" problem domains.

Relationships in OML. OML defines a comprehensive set of relationships between objects and classes (Firesmith and Henderson-Sellers, 1998.) For example, OML distinguishes between *using* and *non-using* linkages between OML-objects. A *using* linkage is one used to invoke OML-operations in another object. OML-linkages represent FRISCO-relationships as well as BWW-*mutual* properties, i.e., BWW-properties that belong to more than one BWW-thing. OML-*using* linkages represent BWW-mutual properties which *couple* two BWW-events occurring in different things, so that one event *causes* the other because it changes the mutual property. There is no similar FRISCO-construct.

OML also defines several variants of whole-part relationships (Henderson-Sellers and Barbier, 1999.) In this respect, OML is more fine-grained than both the BWW-model's *whole-part relations* and FRISCO's *set membership*. (BWW-whole-part relations are also a kind of BWW-properties.) On the other hand, OML and FRISCO lack explicit distinctions like the one in the BWW-model between *resultant* and *emergent* properties of composite BWW-things.

Interactions, messages and scenarios in OML. An OML-interaction represents a FRISCO-message transfer and a *pair* of BWW-events which are coupled by a mutual property. However, in FRISCO there is no distinction which underpins the one in OML between normal and exceptional interactions and transitions.

An OML-scenario represents a "contiguous set of interactions" and has no primitive counterparts in the BWW-model or in FRISCO.

States and transitions in OML. Both ontologies comprise constructs which underpin OML's states and transitions. But whereas OML- and BWW-states are defined in terms of property values, FRISCO-states are composite objects.

4. DISCUSSION OF THE RESULTS

Whereas detailed clarifications of and suggestions of improvements to OML will be presented elsewhere, this section will give an overview of the results and focus in particular on how ontological models like the BWW-model and FRISCO can and should be used to improve and define OO modelling languages.

Suggested improvements to OML. The analysis and evaluation has identified several cases of *overloaded*, *redundant* and *genuinely excessive* OML-constructs, as well as few *deficits* in OML. Prominent examples of redundant constructs are the group of OML-constructs which represent

BWW-state laws and the group of constructs which represent *BWW-transformation laws*. In addition, there are several overlaps between constructs which deal with OML-interactions and -messages on the one hand and with OML-states and -transitions on the other. An example of a deficit is that OML lacks a clear distinction which represets the BWW-model's distinction between *human laws* and *natural laws.* In comparison to FRISCO, OML also lacks a counterpart to *transition structures* and to *goals* and *goal pursuing actors*.

Better definitions of OML-constructs. The analysis and evaluation has proposed definitions of the most important OML-constructs in terms of which things in and aspects of the problem domain each construct is meant to represent. At present, the OML-constructs are defined *both* in relation to the BWW-model *and* in relation to FRISCO. Below we suggest to align these two sets of definitions in the future.

A related suggestion is to redefine OML's *diagram types* to ensure that the diagrams used during the early phases of IS development only comprise OML-constructs that represent things in and aspects of problem domains.

The multiple roles of OML-constructs. The analysis and evaluation has identified four major roles and several sub-roles played by the modelling constructs in OML. Two of the major roles confirm the ones identified in (Wand, 1989; Parsons and Wand, 1997b.) The major roles are (a) representing things in and aspects of the problem domain, (b) representing things in and aspects of the development process, (c) representing things in and aspects of the final software system, and (d) contributing to and complying with the internal organisation of OML's metamodel. Whereas some OML-constructs play only one of these roles, others play two or more.

OML is one of the few OO modelling languages that has been developed with an explicit aim of representing "real-world" problem domains in addition to designs and implementations. Our study nevertheless indicates that many of its constructs are defined to compromise between these four roles and often at the expense of role (a). We therefore suggest that the four roles should be identified explicitly in the definition of each OML-construct. The internal organisation of OML's metamodel should be revised to reflect this.

Template for defining IS-modelling constructs. Our experience with interpreting and defining OML-constructs in terms of the two ontologies has lead to a *template* for defining modelling constructs in relation to "real-world" problem domains. We expect the template to be useful even for other modelling languages than OML, OO or otherwise.

The template is presently based on the BWW-model. In particular, it is based on the fundamental view inherent in the BWW-model that the world is comprised of *BWW-things* and their *BWW-properties*. Although the BWW-model introduces several other constructs, they all somehow emerge from temporal and other relations between these two fundamental ones. The template therefore requires each modelling construct to be defined by answering the following three questions:

1. Which class of things is the construct meant to represent?
2. Which property (or group of properties) is the construct meant to represent?
3. Which ontological category is the construct meant to represent?

The first question delimits each OML-construct in "thing space", i.e., with respect to which *kind of things* it is meant to represent. This question is answered by making explicit the *characteristic properties* of the BWW-class in question, i.e., the set of properties that is possessed by all the BWW-things in the class. For example, "OML-software external" is meant to represent BWW-things which are software artefacts and with which the proposed software system will interact. "OML-path", on the other hand, is meant to represent BWW-things which are systems of other BWW-things that are involved in some OML-scenario. In this way, different OML-constructs are meant to represent different classes of things in the problem domain. A group of very general OML-constructs, which includes "OML-class", "OML-object" and "OML-characteristic", are meant to represent *any* kind of BWW-things, regardless of their class.

The second question delimits each OML-construct further in "property space", i.e., with respect to which *aspects of things* it is meant to represent. When it is applicable to an OML-construct, this question is answered by making explicit the *actual BWW-property* or group of properties that the construct is meant to represent. For example, "OML-*using* linkage" is meant to represent BWW-mutual properties which *couple* two BWW-events that occur in different things. "OML-aggregation relationship", on the other hand, is meant to represent BWW-whole-part relations along with certain BWW-state laws that pertain to the whole and its parts. In this way, different OML-constructs are meant to represent different kinds of properties of things in the problem domain. Again, a group of general OML-constructs (which only includes "OML-characteristic") is meant to represent *any* kind of BWW-properties. For another group of general OML-constructs, the second question is *not applicable*. Constructs in this group, such as "OML-class" and "OML-object", are not meant to represent BWW-properties at all.

However, a modelling language may even provide *several* modelling constructs meant to represent the *same* group of BWW-properties (for example, mutual properties) for the *same* class of BWW-things (for example, human actors). Although these modelling constructs are identical with respect to questions 1 and 2, they may still differ because they represent *different* ontological phenomena (for example, the *values* of mutual properties of humans, or their *histories* over time, or the *events* that occur in them etc.) The third question therefore delimits each modelling construct further in "ontology space", i.e., with respect to which *ontological constructs* it is meant to represent. In OML, "interaction" and "*using* linkage" are identical in all respects except in ontology space.

The template has already been used successfully to propose definitions of all the 54 most important OML-constructs. However, there may still be some overlap between the second and third questions and we plan to explore the template further by using it on other modelling languages in addition to OML.

The relation between the BWW-model and FRISCO. The ontological analysis and evaluation has also put us in a position where we can compare the two ontologies we have applied. On the one hand, FRISCO appears more *coarse-grained* than the BWW-model in relation to *systems* and to *dynamic behaviour*. For example, FRISCO does not distinguish between resultant and emergent predicators of FRISCO-composite things and it has no constructs which match the BWW-distinctions between external and internal events and between stable and unstable states[2]. However, FRISCO is also more fine-grained than the BWW-model in a few areas. For example, it supports state transition structures (sequence, choice and concurrency) and it distinguishes between transitions as *general behaviour patterns* at the type level and transition *occurrences* at the instance level.

On the other hand, in other areas the BWW-model appears more *general* than FRISCO. For example, unlike FRISCO, the BWW-model lacks explicit constructs related to perceptions, conceptions, interpretations and representations. FRISCO also comprises several other specialised constructs which are relevant to the IS field, such as knowledge, models and modelling and which are not found in the BWW-model.

This explains our choice of the BWW-model, rather than FRISCO, as our starting point for defining the above template. The BWW-model is sometimes (but not always) more comprehensive than FRISCO in "ontology space", whereas FRISCO is more closely adapted to the IS field in "thing space." The BWW-model is therefore a better starting point because it can easily import FRISCO-constructs it lacks by simple specialisation in "thing space", whereas extending FRISCO with BWW-constructs it lacks in "ontology space" is more difficult.

Improvements to FRISCO. The ontological analysis and evaluation has so far suggested several improvements to and extensions of FRISCO. Concrete suggestions for extensions inspired by the BWW-model include FRISCO-constructs which distinguish between resultant and emergent predicators of composite things and constructs which distinguish between stable and unstable states as well as external and internal events. In addition, OML's metamodel and related work identify numerous useful distinctions between different kinds of whole-part and other relationships (Henderson-Sellers and Barbier, 1999; Firesmith and Henderson-Sellers, 1998.) Another challenging task is to clarify the semantics of *responsibilities* of human and other actors within FRISCO.

Our comparison has shown that the BWW-model and FRISCO each have their comparative advantages. Since the two differ in ontological coarseness and degree of adaptation to the IS field, an interesting path for further work is to reconcile the two, e.g., using the proposed template to define each FRISCO-construct in terms of the BWW-model.

This raises the question of how an ontology based on "metaphysical realism" such as the BWW-model can be reconciled with a "constructivist" framework such as FRISCO. We argue that this is possible because the BWW-model distinguishes between *properties* that are inherent in BWW-things and *attributes* that are *ascribed* to *models* of BWW-things. We only know things in the world through models we make of these things, and we ascribe attributes to model things in order to represent the properties we believe the real things have (Bunge, 1977, pp. 58–60; Weber, 1997.) Since an attribute is dependent on *both* the observer thing and the thing observed, it therefore turns out to be a *BWW-mutual property* of the two or a *BWW-emergent property* of the BWW-system of the two. We conjecture that all the FRISCO-constructs that are "conceptions" of "domains" can be analysed in terms of the BWW-model in this way. Similar ideas have been elaborated as part of the facet-modelling framework (Opdahl and Sindre, 1997) which may guide reconciliation of the BWW-model and FRISCO along the lines suggested here.

5. CONCLUSION AND FURTHER WORK

The paper has presented an ontological analysis and evaluation of the OPEN Modelling Language in terms of the BWW-model and FRISCO. The analysis and evaluation has made it clearer how and why ontological models like the BWW-model and FRISCO can and should be used to improve and define object-oriented (OO) modelling languages. As a consequence, it has led to a template for defining OO modelling constructs in terms of what they represent in the problem domain during IS development. The analysis and evaluation has also suggested ways to improve FRISCO as an analysis and evaluation tool for OO modelling languages. Although they have not been presented in this paper, the analysis and evaluation has also suggested several ways to improve the modelling constructs supported by OML and to improve how OML is defined and organised.

There are several paths for further work in addition to the ones mentioned already. For one thing, the analysis has only considered "conventional" OO-constructs — such as objects, classes, operations, etc. — which are already part of OML. An interesting further development is to extend OML with a broader spectrum of constructs from the requirements engineering field, where constructs such as agents, goals and obstacles are currently topical. The two research areas already overlap in their shared focus on scenarios, interactions, actors and roles.

Also, whereas this study has focussed on the *individual* modelling constructs in OML, another interesting path is to evaluate the seventeen *diagram types* it supports. Such an analysis could form the basis of an empirical study of how OML-diagrams are used in practice, along the lines suggested in (Green, 1996.)

Finally, we will follow-up this study by analysing and evaluating the Unified Modeling Language (UML; OMG, 1999) in a similar way and eventually compare the two languages.

ACKNOWLEDGMENTS

This is Contribution number 99/8 of the Centre for Object Technology Applications and Research (COTAR). Andreas L. Opdahl wishes to thank COTAR and the University of Technology, Sydney, as well as the Department of Commerce, University of Queensland where parts of this work was carried out.

NOTES

1. Object-oriented Process, Environment, and Notation (OPEN) is an integrated object-oriented information systems development methodology (Graham et al., 1997; Henderson-Sellers et al., 1998.)
2. *BWW-external event:* "An event that arises in a thing, subsystem or system by virtue of the action of some thing in the environment of the thing, subsystem or system." *BWW-internal event:* "An event that arises in a thing, subsystem or system by virtue of lawful transformations in the thing, subsystem or system." *BWW-unstable state:* "A state that will be changed into another state by virtue of the action of transformation in the system." *BWW-stable state:* "A state in which a thing, subsystem or system will remain unless forced to change by virtue of the action of a thing in the environment (an external event)" (Wand and Weber, 1995.)

REFERENCES

Bunge, M. (1977). *Treatise on Basic Philosophy: Vol. 3: Ontology I: The Furniture of the World*. Reidel, Boston.

Bunge, M. (1979). *Treatise on Basic Philosophy: Vol. 4: Ontology II: A World of Systems*. Reidel, Boston.

Falkenberg, E. D., Hesse, W., Lindgreen, P., Nilsson, B. E., Oei, J. L. H., Rolland, C., Stamper, R. K., Van Assche, F. J. M., Verrijn-Stuart, A. A., and Voss, K. (1998). *A Framework of Information System Concepts — The FRISCO Report (Web edition)*. IFIP.

Firesmith, D. and Henderson-Sellers, B. (1998). Upgrading OML to version 1.1: Part 1 — referential relationships. *Journal of Object-Oriented Programming (ROAD)*, 11(3):48–57.

Firesmith, D., Henderson-Sellers, B., and Graham, I. (1998). *OPEN Modelling Language — OML Reference Manual*. SIGS Reference Library. Cambridge University Press.

Graham, I. (1998). *Requirements Engineering and Rapid Development — An Object-Oriented Approach*. Addison-Wesley.

Graham, I., Henderson-Sellers, B., and Younessi, H. (1997). *The OPEN Process Specification*. Addison-Wesley, U.K. 314 pp.

Green, P. and Rosemann, M. (1999). An ontological evaluation of integrated process modelling. Proceedings of CAiSE*99, The 11th Conference on Advanced information Systems Engineering, Heidelberg/Germany, 14–18 June 1999.

Green, P. F. (1996). *An Ontological Analysis of Information Systems Analysis and Design (ISAD) Grammars in Upper CASE Tools*. PhD thesis, Department of Commerce, University of Queensland.

Henderson-Sellers, B., Atkinson, C., and Firesmith, D. G. (1999). Viewing the OML as a variant of the UML. To be presented at <<UML'99>>, Fort Collins/CO.

Henderson-Sellers, B. and Barbier, F. (1999). What is this thing called aggregation? In Mitchell, R., Wills, A. C., Bosch, J., and Meyer, B., editors, *TOOLS29*, pages 216–230. IEEE Computer Society Press.

Henderson-Sellers, B. and Firesmith, D. (1998). Upgrading OML to version 1.1: Part 2 — additional concepts and notation. *Journal of Object-Oriented Programming (ROAD)*, 11(5):61–67.

Henderson-Sellers, B., Simons, A. J. H., and Younessi, H. (1998). *The OPEN Toolbox of Techniques*. Addison-Wesley, U.K. 426 pp. + CD.

Jackson, M. (1995). *Software Requirements & Specifications — A lexicon of practice, principles and prejudices*. ACM Press/Addison-Wesley, Wokingham/England.

OMG (1999). *OMG Unified Modeling Language Specification*.

Opdahl, A. L. and Sindre, G. (1997). Facet modelling: An approach to flexible and integrated conceptual modelling. *Information Systems*, 22(5):291–323.

Parsons, J. and Wand, Y. (1997a). Choosing classes in conceptual modeling. *CACM*, 40(6):63–69.

Parsons, J. and Wand, Y. (1997b). Using objects for systems analysis. *CACM*, 40(12):104–110.

Sommerville, I. and Sawyer, P. (1997). *Requirements Engineering — A good practice guide.* Wiley, Chichester/England.

Takagaki, K. and Wand, Y. (1991). An object-oriented information systems model based on ontology. In Van Assche, F., Moulin, B., and Rolland, C., editors, *Object Oriented Approach in Information Systems*, pages 275–296, Amsterdam. Elsevier (North-Holland).

Wand, Y. (1989). A proposal for a formal model of objects. In Kim, W. and Lochovsky, F. H., editors, *Object-Oriented Concepts, Databases, and Applications*, chapter 21, pages 537–559. ACM Press/Addison-Wesley, New York/NY.

Wand, Y. and Weber, R. (1989). An ontological evaluation of systems analysis and design methods. In Falkenberg, E. and Lindgreen, P., editors, *Proceedings of the IFIP WG8.1 Working Conference on Information Systems Concepts: An In-Depth Analysis, Namur/Belgium*, pages 79–107, Amsterdam/The Netherlands. North-Holland.

Wand, Y. and Weber, R. (1993). On the ontological expressiveness of information systems analysis and design grammars. *Journal of Information Systems*, 3:217–237.

Wand, Y. and Weber, R. (1995). On the deep structure of information systems. *Information Systems Journal*, 5:203–223.

Weber, R. (1997). *Ontological Foundations of Information Systems.* Number 4 in Accounting Research Methodology Monograph series. Coopers & Lybrand, 333 Collins Street, Melbourne Vic 3000, Australia.

Weber, R. and Zhang, Y. (1996). An analytical evaluation of NIAM's grammar for conceptual schema diagrams. *Information Systems Journal*, 6:147–170.

Table 1 When OML-constructs are taken to represent concrete problem domains, they map onto BWW-constructs. When taken to represent conceptions of problem domains, they map onto the corresponding FRISCO-constructs. (Part 1 of 3.)

OML-construct	*BWW-construct*	*FRISCO-construct*
OML-object	BWW-thing	FRISCO-predicated thing which is *not* a predicator, relationship or state. (Referred to as FRISCO-"object" in this table.)
OML-actor		FRISCO-human actor
OML-external object	BWW-thing in a system's environment.	FRISCO-"object" in a system's environment.
OML-aggregate	BWW-system.	FRISCO-composite "object" which is a FRISCO-system.
OML-part (of an aggr.)	BWW-part thing of a system.	FRISCO-"object" which is a FRISCO-system component.
OML-group	BWW-composite thing, which in some cases is a BWW-system.	FRISCO-composite "object", which in some cases is a FRISCO-system.
OML-member (of a group)	BWW-part thing of a composite, and in some cases of a system.	FRISCO-"object" in an element set, and which in some cases is a FRISCO-system component.
OML-container		
OML-entry (in a container)		
OML-multiobject		
OML-object class	BWW-natural kind *or* BWW-class *or* BWW-property codomain.	*Related to* FRISCO-type and to FRISCO-population.
OML-role		
OML-instance-level characteristic	BWW-property *of a particular*	FRISCO-predicator of *or* FRISCO-relationship between "objects" *or* FRISCO-actand *or* FRISCO-rule.
OML-class-level characteristic	BWW-property *in general*	FRISCO-type of a predicator of *or* a relationship between "objects" *or* of a FRISCO-actand *or* of a FRISCO-rule.
OML-property	BWW-property which is not a law.	FRISCO-predicator of *or* FRISCO-relationship between "objects."
OML-attribute	BWW-intrinsic property which is not a law.	FRISCO-predicator of "objects."
OML-assertion	BWW-state law	FRISCO-rule.
OML-operation	BWW-transformation, BWW-transformation law.	FRISCO-action, FRISCO-action occurrence.
OML-invariant of an op.	*A kind of* BWW-state law.	FRISCO-rule which determines permissible FRISCO-actions.
OML-precond. of an op.	*A kind of* BWW-state law.	FRISCO-rule which determines permissible FRISCO-actions.
OML-postcond. of an op.	*A kind of* BWW-transformation law.	FRISCO-rule which determines permissible FRISCO-actions.

Table 2 When OML-constructs are taken to represent concrete problem domains, they map onto BWW-constructs. When taken to represent conceptions of problem domains, they map onto the corresponding FRISCO-constructs. (Part 2 of 3.)

OML-construct	*BWW-construct*	*FRISCO-construct*
OML-unidir. relationship		
OML-bi-dir. relationship		
OML-specialisation rel'ship	BWW-class/subclass relationship	
OML-partition		
OML-discriminant		
OML-association rel'ship	BWW-mutual property *in general*	FRISCO-type of a relationship between "objects."
OML-associative class		
OML-N-ary association	BWW-mutual property *in general* which is possessed by more than two things.	FRISCO-type of a relationship between more than two "objects."
OML-aggregation rel'ship	BWW-whole-part relation in a system.	FRISCO-set membership involving "objects" which form a FRISCO-system.
OML-membership rel'ship	BWW-whole-part relation in a composition, and in some cases in a system.	FRISCO-set membership involving "objects", which in some cases form a FRISCO-system.
OML-containment rel'ship		
OML-non-using link(age)	Binding BWW-mutual property.	FRISCO-relationship between "objects", which does not involve an actand.
OML-using link(age)	Non-binding BWW-mutual property.	FRISCO-relationship which involves an actand.
OML-interaction	When a BWW-event in one thing changes a binding BWW-mutual property and thereby induces a BWW-event in another thing.	FRISCO-message transfer
OML-message (interact.)	As for OML-interaction, when no BWW-law is broken.	FRISCO-message transfer, when no FRISCO-rule is broken.
OML-exception (interact.)	As for OML-interaction, when a BWW-law is broken.	FRISCO-message transfer, when a FRISCO-rule is broken.
OML-exception (property)	Binding BWW-mutual property which is changed so that a BWW-law is broken.	FRISCO-message which is transferred so that a FRISCO-rule is broken.
OML-state	BWW-state *or* set of BWW-states.	FRISCO-state (but defined differently from OML- and BWW-states) *or* set of FRISCO-states.
OML-atomic state	BWW-state.	FRISCO-state (but defined differently from OML- and BWW-states.)
OML-aggregate state	(Set of BWW-states.)	(Set of FRISCO-states.)

Table 3 When OML-constructs are taken to represent concrete problem domains, they map onto BWW-constructs. When taken to represent conceptions of problem domains, they map onto the corresponding FRISCO-constructs. (Part 3 of 3.)

OML-construct	*BWW-construct*	*FRISCO-construct*
OML-transition	BWW-transformation law *or* BWW-transformation *or* BWW-event.	FRISCO-transition *or* -transition occurrence.
OML-normal transition	As for OML-transition, when no BWW-law is broken.	As for OML-transition, when no FRISCO-rule is broken.
OML-exceptional trans.	As for OML-transition, when a BWW-law is broken.	As for OML-transition, when a FRISCO-rule is broken.
OML-trigger	(*A kind of* BWW-event.)	(*A kind of* FRISCO-transition *or* -transition occurrence.)
OML-guard condition	*A kind of* BWW-state law.	FRISCO-rule which determines permissible FRISCO-actions.
OML-scenario **OML-scenario class** **OML-path** **OML-uses relationship** **OML-invokes relationship** **OML-precedes relationship**		
OML-responsibility **OML-multiplicity**	(Various kinds of BWW-state law.)	(Various kinds of FRISCO-rule.)
Additional BWW- and FRISCO-constructs that are not directly covered in OML.	All the BWW-constructs related to state and event spaces. BWW-resultant versus -emergent properties. BWW-history, -stability condition, -corrective action. BWW-external versus -internal event. BWW-unstable versus -stable state. BWW-lawful versus -unlawful event. BWW–well-defined versus -poorly defined event.	FRISCO-transition structure. FRISCO-sequence, -choice, -concurrency. FRISCO-absolute time. FRISCO-goal, -goal pursuing actor. FRISCO-composite transition, -composite action, -co-action. Most FRISCO-constructs related to *perceptions*, *conceptions*, *interpretations* and *representations*. Most FRISCO-constructs related to *modelling*. FRISCO-constructs that describe various kinds of *systems*. FRISCO-knowledge, -information, -shared knowledge. FRISCO-information system, -information system denotation and -computerised information sub-system.

Comments on "An Ontological Evaluation of the OML Metamodel" by A.L. Opdahl, B. Henderson-Sellers and F. Barbier

Arne Sølvberg

Trondheim, Dept.Computer Science
The Norwegian University of Science and Technology (NTNU)
N-7491 Trondheim, Norway

The starting point of the paper is to analyse the constructs of the OPEN Modeling Language (OML) which is developed with one of the co-authors as the driving force. The analysis is done in terms of the FRISCO ontology (which is the subject of the ISCO conference series) and of the Bunge-Wand-Weber (BWW) ontology. The result of the analysis is summed up in four tables and is a comprehensive description of OML.

The discussion in the paper is not only about OML, but is also a discussion and comparison of the conceptual contents of FRISCO and BWW. For the latter discussion OML is used as a vehicle for discussing the relative merits of the two proposals for information systems ontologies. Both discussions (the OML clarification, and FRISCO vs. BWW) are interesting and useful. The latter, however, appears more as an afterthought than as having been planned for when the reported investigation started. For this reader the FRISCO vs. BWW discussion is the more interesting of the two, and would therefore like to see a continuation of the work beyond what is currently reported. The following remarks are to this end.

The OML analysis is verbal. The various OML constructs are compared to their FRISCO and BWW counterparts not through formal expressions but with words. FRISCO invites to a formal comparison through the formal definitions of its ontological constituents. A formal comparison between OML and FRISCO should be within reach. This is a difficult job, however, and is without precedent as far as I am aware of. It should nevertheless be done in order to remove the vagueness (implied by necessity) of a verbal comparison. The same goes for the FRISCO vs. BWW comparison. We have proceeded so far now in our deliberations on concept modeling that increased formality appears to belong to the next step in IS research.

There is disturbing vagueness in parts of the basis of BWW and FRISCO which should be straightened out. E.g., it is stated in the paper that BWW-things are "concrete" and FRISCO-things are "conceptions". What this really means is difficult to understand. The paper does also not offer much help in this respect. So we have to live with a corresponding vagueness in the analysis of OML, e.g., an OML-object is a BWW-thing, but may also be an FRISCO-instance, which is a conception and not a concrete thing (table 1, first entry).

There is no reason to give the authors full responsibility for the vagueness. It is unavoidable because of the inherent vagueness in either FRISCO, BWW or in both of the frameworks. Further research should remove such discrepancies. The authors of the current paper have shown that they may be able to contribute to this end. They are hereby encouraged to do exactly that in their future research.

Overviews of Models Defined with Charts of Concepts

Xavier Castellani

CEDRIC IIE (CNAM) research laboratory
18 allée Jean Rostand, F-91025 Evry Cedex, France
Phone: 33 1 69 36 73 34. Fax: 33 1 69 36 73 05
Email: castellani@iie.cnam.fr
http://www.iie.cnam.fr/~castellani/

Keywords: Charts of concepts, Metamodelling, Overviews of models.

Abstract: Models of analysis and design methods get more and more complex which makes it necessary to create overviews of these models both defined by selections of concepts and macro views of models. It is not easy to create overviews of models defined by texts and ER or OO metamodels. Hence, we propose to define models with charts of concepts which are directed graphs where nodes represent the concepts involved in a model, and arcs illustrate dependencies between definitions of its concepts. As charts of concepts are directed graphs, they easily permit when selecting concepts to see the concepts that must be selected with the chosen concepts and those that are not selected. A macro view of a model is a directed graph where nodes represent charts of concepts, and arcs illustrate macro dependencies between these charts. So, charts of concepts allow defining overviews of concepts of models both defined by selections of concepts and macro views of these models. We present charts of concepts of an overview of the UML.

1. INTRODUCTION

Models of analysis and design methods are more and more complex. Reasons for this greater complexity lay in the growing number of their concepts, and in the increasing interdependency between the definitions of concepts. Hence, it is very difficult for analysts, designers, and students to study all the concepts of analysis and design methods. Then, methodologists and teachers have to select concepts in the models of these methods and have to present global views of these models.

That is why the question this paper intends to answer is: how to make an abstraction of models of analysis and design methods? Our proposition is to create overviews of models. We consider that an overview of a model must be both defined by a selection of concepts and a macro view of this model. A macro view of a model is a view of its sub-models (or its groups of concepts), and of relationships between its sub-models.

1.1 Difficulties to Create Overviews of Models

Generally, models of analysis and design methods are defined with texts and metamodels defined with the entity-relationship model [7] or with an object-oriented model. For example, the metamodel of the UML [1] is modeled with the MOF (Meta-Object Facility) [10].

A lot of works are developed on metamodelling of analysis and design methods. Certain of these works allow comparisons of models of methods to evaluate them or to define core models of methods [11] [15]. The goal of other works is to define meta-case tools as MetaEdit [14]. Each case tool, such as GraphTalkMeta, Kogge, MetaEdit, MetaView, Mviews, ... , has its notation to define metamodels.

It is not easy to create overviews of models defined by texts and ER or OO metamodels for two reasons. First, it is difficult to select concepts in texts that define a model. It is also difficult to select concepts in a model defined with an ER or an OO metamodel because it is not easy to see concepts that are to be selected (because they are used to define the selected concepts), and those which are not selected. This difficulty results in particular from the fact that these metamodels are defined with several kinds of relationships: associations, specializations/generalizations or inheritances, aggregations, compositions. And second, it is difficult to create macro views of models defined by texts and ER or OO metamodels. That results from the fact that these representations do not allow defining easily views of sub-models (or groups of concepts) of models, and of relationships between sub-models.

1.2 Our Suggestion: Create Overviews of Models Defined with Charts of Concepts

As it is difficult to create overviews of models defined by texts and ER or OO metamodels, we advocate to create overviews of models starting from simple graphical representations of models. These representations must allow easily selections of concepts in models, and easily representations of macro views of models.

The simpler graphical representations of models are directed graphs such as each node represents a concept, and only one kind of relationship is defined between concepts. We call these relationships *definitional dependencies.* A definitional dependency is defined from a concept CPx to a concept CPy if CPx is used in the definition of CPy. We call *charts of concepts* these graphical representations of models [2] [3].

As charts of concepts are directed graphs, they easily permit when selecting concepts to see the concepts that must be selected with the chosen concepts and those that are not selected.

Macro views of models are also simple to be defined with directed graphs where nodes represent charts of concepts, and arcs illustrate macro dependencies between these charts.

As example, we present an overview of the version 1.1 of the model of the Unified Modelling Language (UML) [1]. We do not recall definitions of concepts of this model. The justifications of the definitional dependencies between concepts result from these definitions. These justifications are not specified in this paper for sake of conciseness. The reader could refer to definitions of concepts in [1].

1.3 Outline of this Paper

This paper is organized as follows. Charts of concepts of a model are defined in Section 2. Overviews of models defined with charts of concepts are described in Section 3; an overview of the UML is presented in this section (charts of concepts of this overview are in Appendix). A brief discussion on the interest of charts of concepts to create overviews of models is in the conclusion.

2. CHARTS OF CONCEPTS OF A MODEL

A definition of a concept of a model is given in Section 2.1. Definitional dependencies between concepts are specified in Section 2.2. The definition of a chart of concepts is given in Section 2.3. Precision on the notation used to represent charts of concepts is in Section 2.4.

2.1 What is a Concept of a Model?

For us, *a concept of a model is anything in this model that can be used by software analysts and/or designers to represent or to specify phenomena of the real world or technical phenomena*. A concept is identified by a unique name; there cannot be two concepts in a chart with the same name.

It is not easy to find concepts of a model. It is a classical problem whatever the model used to represent a metamodel, ER or OO for example.

It is the case for the model of the UML. The model of the UML is presented with texts and an OO metamodel. All concepts, or supposed to be, are not in this metamodel. We have studied glossaries and indexes of these documents to decide if notions represent or not concepts. We have also used our culture on the object-oriented approach to take decisions.

Examples taken in the UML:

We have taken into account as concepts notions of "Action associated to an entry transition" and "Action associated to an exit transition" used in statechart diagrams (of which the chart is in Figure 23 in Appendix), because these two notions are used to define the notion of "Point of execution of an operation". This last notion has also be considered as a concept.

We have not taken into account as concepts notions of "Cyclic activity" and "Sequential activity" in statechart diagrams by considering the little importance granted in the documents to these two notions.

2.2 Definitional Dependencies Defined between Concepts of a Model

The notation of charts of concepts settles on definitional dependencies between concepts.

Definitional Dependencies Between two Concepts

We create a definitional dependency from a concept CPx to a concept CPy if CPx is used in the definition of CPy. A such definitional dependency means that concept CPx must be presented before concept CPy.

Example: in Figure 1 is depicted the definitional dependency that exists from concept "Object" to concept "Message" of the basic concepts relative to objects of the model of the UML (the chart of the basic concepts relative to objects is in Figure 15 in Appendix).

Figure 1. Example of definitional dependency between two concepts

If there exists a definitional dependency from a concept CPx to a concept CPy and an inverse dependency from CPy to Cpx then a co-definitional dependency exists between these two concepts.

Example: in Figure 2 is depicted a co-definitional dependency that exists between concept "Conditional branching" and concept "Branching condition" of the sequence diagrams of the model of the UML (the chart of the sequence diagrams is in Figure 22 in Appendix).

Figure 2. Example of co-definitional dependency between two concepts

If a co-definitional dependency exists between two concepts, then a circuit of definitional dependencies exists between these two concepts.

Non Representation of Definitional Dependencies Resulting from Transitivity of Definitional Dependencies

If there exists a definitional dependency from a concept CPx to a concept CPy, and a definitional dependency from CPy to a concept CPz, then there is a transitive definitional dependency from CPx to CPz. To simplify charts of concepts we do not represent the definitional dependency that exists from CPx to CPz.

Example: in Figure 3 is depicted definitional dependencies that exist between three concepts of the basic concepts relative to objects of the model of the UML; the definitional dependency between the first one and the third one is not represented in the chart of the basic concepts relative to objects (this chart is in Figure 15 in Appendix).

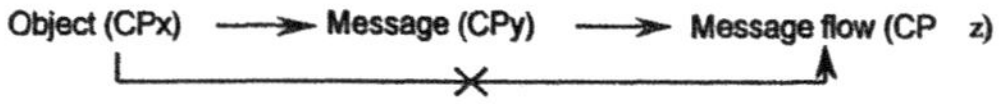

Figure 3. Example of non representation of a definitional dependency resulting from transitivity of definitional dependencies

Logical Expressions Between Definitional Dependencies

If dcfinitional dependencies exist respectively from a concept CPx to concepts CPy, CPz, ... , that means that CPx has been defined before CPy *and* CPz *and* ... These *and* are not represented in the charts of concepts.

Example taken in the chart of basic concepts relative to objects of the UML (chart which is in Figure 15 in Appendix): the graph in Figure 4 represents the fact that concept "Object" is used in the definitions of concepts "Key", "Object persistence", "Object flow", *and* "Message". Then, the concept "Object" must be presented before concepts "Key", "Object persistence", "Object flow", *and* "Message".

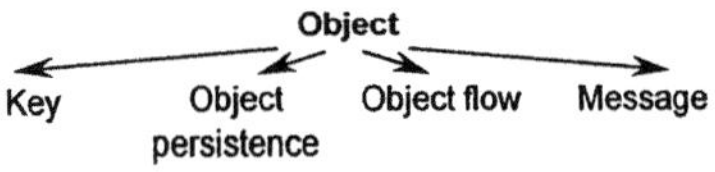

Figure 4. Example of definitional dependencies starting from a concept

If several definitional dependencies end to a same concept CPy, a logical expression mentioned on the graph specifies how concept CPy depends on the concepts beginning these definitional dependencies.

Example of logical expression defined with a simple *and* taken in the chart of concepts of the class diagrams of the UML (which is in Figure 20 in Appendix): concept "Sub-set constraint" depends on concept "Constraint", *and* on concept "Role".

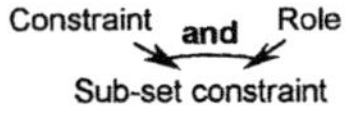

Figure 5. Example of definitional dependencies ending to a concept with an *and*

Example of logical expression defined with a simple *or* taken in the chart of concepts of the class diagrams of the UML (which is in Figure 20 in Appendix): concept "Constraint on an association" depends on concept "Sub-set constraint", *or* on concept "Constraint or".

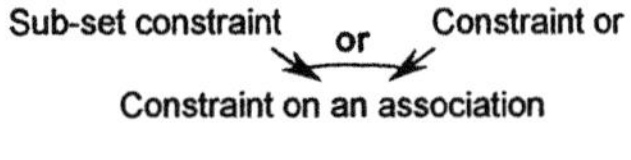

Figure 6. Example of definitional dependencies ending to a concept with an *or*

Example of logical expression defined with an *and* and an *or* taken in the chart of concepts of the sequence diagrams of the UML (which is in Figure 22 in Appendix): concept "Arrow of a sequence diagram" depends on concept "Message flow" *or* (on concept "Event", *and* on concept "Use case").

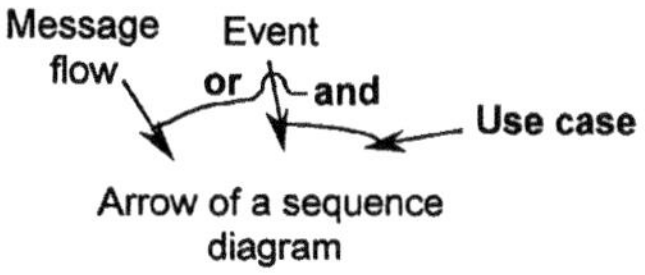

Figure 7. Example of definitional dependencies ending to a concept with an *and/or*

Root Concepts

A root concept of a model is a concept that is not defined using any other concept of this model. A root concept of a model has no ascendant in the charts of concepts of this model. A root concept is denoted by a small black triangle.

Example: in Figure 8 is depicted the concept "Identity" of the basic concepts relative to objects of the model of the UML, concept which is a root concept of this model (the chart of the basic concepts relative to objects is in Figure 15 in Appendix).

Figure 8. Example of root concept

Terminal Concepts

A terminal concept of a model is a concept such that no other concept definition of this model makes use of it. A terminal concept of a model has no descendant in the charts of concepts of this model. A terminal concept is denoted by a small black circle.

Example: in Figure 9 is depicted the concept "Key" of the basic concepts relative to objects of the model of the UML, concept which is a terminal concept of this model (the chart of the basic concepts relative to objects is in Figure 15 in Appendix).

Figure 9. Example of terminal concept

2.3 Definition of a Chart of Concepts. Precision on Charts of Concepts

Definition of a Chart of Concepts

A chart of concepts of a model is a directed graph where nodes represent the concepts involved in the model, and where arcs illustrate the definitional dependencies resulting from the definitions of the concepts.

Examples: Charts of Concepts of the Version 1.1 of the UML

Authors of the UML present concepts of its model in two categories of groups of concepts: basic concepts, and concepts which allow defining 9 types of diagrams. We defined charts of concepts for each of these groups of concepts.

. The basic concepts of the model of the UML are: basic concepts relative to objects, basic concepts relative to classes, auxiliary elements, extension mechanisms, and data types. Selected charts of concepts of these groups of basic concepts are in Appendix.

. The 9 types of diagrams of the model of the UML are: use case diagrams, class diagrams, object diagrams, collaboration diagrams, sequence diagrams, statechart diagrams, activity diagrams, component diagrams, and deployment diagrams. We do not recall definitions of these 9 types of diagrams. The reader could refer to their presentation in [1]. Selected charts of concepts of these diagrams are in Appendix.

Representation of Concepts of a Chart of Concepts Used in Another Chart of Concepts

Certain models are shared in sub-models or groups of concepts. It is the case of the model of the UML which is shared in parts that contain 5 groups of basic concepts and groups of concepts that allow the representation of 9 types of diagrams.

If a concept CPx defined in a chart of concepts CCi is used in a chart of concepts CCj, the name of the concept CPx is mentioned surrounded with an ellipse in the chart of concepts CCi. The three cases of surrounding or not surrounding a concept with an ellipse in a chart of concepts are explained in Figure 10.

For sake of clearness, we have not represented definitional dependencies from concepts that begin definitional dependencies and that end to concepts that belong to other charts.

If a concept of a chart is beginning of a definitional dependency that ends to a concept of another chart, this concept is not therefore terminal. So, it is not represented with the small black circle that would mean that it is terminal.

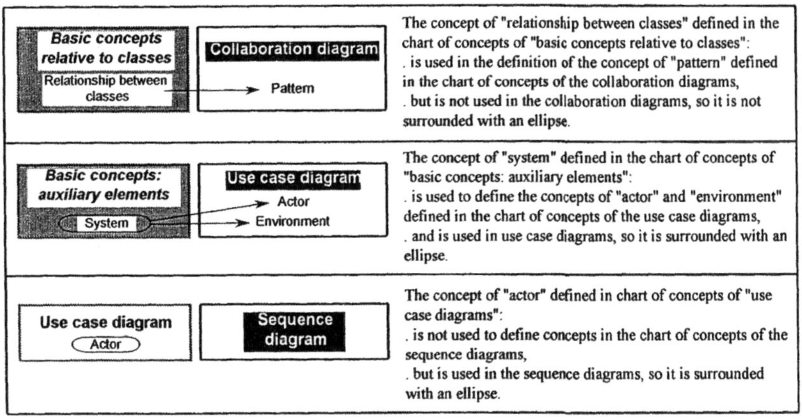

Figure 10. Examples of the three possible cases of surrounding or not surrounding a concept with an ellipse

Circuits Between Definitions of Concepts, and Non Connected Sub-graphs

It is very important to detect anomalies in a model. The definition of a model through text or through a ER or an OO metamodel does not permit to see easily circuits that can exist the definitions of some of the concepts. As charts of concepts are directed graphs, such circuits are very easy to find. Moreover, charts of concepts allow finding easily independent sets of concepts represented with non connected sub-graphs.

Circuits Between Definitions of Concepts. A circuit exists between concepts CPx, CPy, ..., CPz, if concept CPx is used in the definition of concept CPy, concept CPy is used in the definition of concept CPz, ... , and concept CPz is used in the definition of concept CPx.

The existence of a circuit between concepts of a model relates a default in definitions of these concepts because the presentation of one of these concepts necessitates the presentation of all concepts of this circuit. Then, the selection of one of the concepts of a circuit necessitates the selection of all concepts of this circuit.

Let recall that co-definitional dependencies define circuits between two concepts.

Examples: we found several circuits between definitions of concepts of the UML model; one of them is in the chart of basic concepts relative to objects which is in Figure 15 in Appendix; this circuit is in Figure 11.

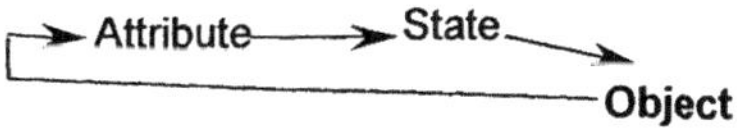

Figure 11. Example of circuit between concepts

Non Connected Sub-graphs in Charts of Concepts. Concepts of non connected sub-graphs between concepts of a model can be presented apart from the other concepts. Such concepts are not sufficiently integrated in a model.

Selections of concepts of a non connected sub-graph of a model are not concerned by selections of concepts that do not belong to this non connected sub-graph.

Examples: in charts of concepts of the UML, we found four non connected sub-graphs in the chart of concepts of sequence diagrams which is in Figure 22 in Appendix; one of them is in Figure 12.

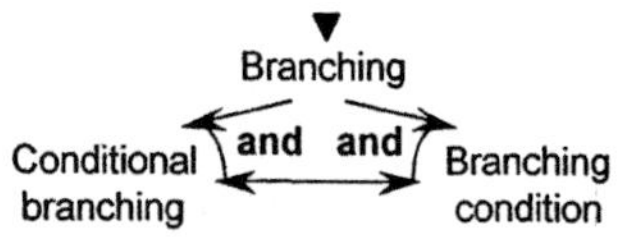

Figure 12. Example of non connected sub-graph

2.4 Precision on the Notation Used to Define Charts of Concepts

The notation used to represent charts of concepts is slightly different from the one of Sowa's conceptual graphs [13]. Conceptual graphs allow the use of different kinds of conceptual relationships. On the contrary, all the arcs used in charts of concepts have the same signification which is *"a definitional dependency is defined from a concept CPx to a concept CPy if CPx is used in the definition of CPy"*.

We do not consider that it would be interesting to permit the use of different kinds of definitional dependencies in metamodels defined with charts of concepts for two main reasons. First, it would be more difficult to create charts of concepts. And second, metamodels defined with charts of concepts would be more difficult to be used to verify models, to select coherent sub-sets in models, to create customized versions of models, to gradual learn models, to evaluate models, and to create overviews of models.

As charts of concepts are defined with only one kind of arcs, they can be considered as particular conceptual graphs. But with charts of concepts we can define logical expressions between definitional dependencies (cf. Section 2.2).

Many operations can be defined on conceptual graphs: copy, restriction, join, projection, specialization, generalization, simplification. With charts of concepts we can use an other operation: selection of parts of a model in its charts of concepts.

In the field of conceptual modeling, several authors have proposed relationships between concepts to build conceptual schemes. For example, Kangassalo [12], proposes a system and a methodology for conceptual modeling and information construction called COMIC. In this model, the basic epistemological relation between concepts is a relation of *"intentional containment"*. An intuitive explication can be given by saying that *"a concept CPy contains intentionally a concept CPx if the knowledge that forms the concept CPy contains the knowledge that forms the concept CPx"*.

In our charts of concepts, definitional dependencies are created from the definitions of the concepts. Therefore, we reckon that charts of concepts are more easily usable than COMIC diagrams to create representations of existing models.

Moreover, Kangassalo considers that in principle there is an infinite number of epistemological relations, and he mentions that the most commonly used are the aggregation, the generalization, and the value transformation.

We above explain how we consider that charts of concepts of metamodels are defined with only one kind of arcs. So, we do not consider that it would be interesting to specialize definitional dependencies in metamodels defined with charts of concepts.

It has to be pointed out that charts of concepts should not be confused with types lattices: a concept depending on another concept is not necessarily "A Kind Of" that concept, or does not inherit from that concept. So, the definitional dependencies have not the same power of semantics that these kinds of relationships because they are only defined by taking into account the fact that concepts are defined with others. A complementary study of the semantics of a definitional dependency can conclude to define "A Kind Of" relationship or an inheritance between the two concepts concerned.

The definitional dependencies are defined between concepts without taking into account possible values of these concepts. So, definitional dependencies should not be confused with dependencies such as associations defined with roles, aggregations, compositions, or dependencies from the relational model such as functional dependencies, multivalued dependencies, or inclusion dependencies [8] [9]. A complementary study of the possible values of two concepts linked with a definitional dependency can conclude to define one of these dependencies.

3. OVERVIEWS OF MODELS DEFINED WITH CHARTS OF CONCEPTS

Recall that we consider that an overview of a model is both defined by a selection of concepts and a macro view of this model. Selection of concepts in a model is presented in Section 3.1. The definition of a macro view of a model is presented in Section 3.2.

3.1 Selection of Concepts in a Model Defined by Charts of Concepts

A selection of concepts in a model defined with charts of concepts is an extraction of concepts in this model to create a restricted version of this model in which:
. the selected concepts are selected with their ascendants,
. a non selection of concepts implies the non selection of their descendants.

The mechanism of selection of concepts in a model is the following one. We associate to each concept CPy:
. a logical choice variable Cy: the value "true" means that the manager of software analysts and designers wants to select concept CPy;
. a logical function Fy of which arguments represent the selection variables of the antecedents of CPy, arguments joined by logical operators.

The logical selection variable of the concept CPy is: Sy = Cy and Fy; the concept CPy is selected if Sy is true.

The evaluation of the logical function Fy associated to the concept CPy depends on values of selection variables of its antecedents, which depend on values of selection variables of their antecedents, etc.

To select several concepts the selection mechanism above-mentioned to select one concept is repeated, and the selected concepts are marked.

Example: Selection of Concepts to Define an Overview of the UML

First of all we have to fix a goal and criteria to select concepts in the model of the UML; examples:
. goal: to initiate professionals working in computer science that are not familiarized with the OO approach in the UML.;
. selection criteria:
  . to only consider object-oriented concepts;
  . to take an interest to classes instead of objects, to conceptual and logical levels more than to the physical level, to static representations instead of dynamic representations.

<u>Selection of concepts in the charts of the basic concepts of the UML</u>. According to our goal and to our criteria to select concepts in the UML we obtain the selection of concepts in the charts of basic concepts in Figure 15

to 18 in Appendix. As no concept of extension mechanisms are selected, we do not select the chart of this group of concepts.

Selection of concepts in the charts of concepts of the 9 types of diagrams of the UML. According to our goal and to our criteria to select concepts in the UML we do not select concepts of the object diagrams, the activity diagrams, the component diagrams, and the deployment diagrams. Charts of concepts of the selected diagrams: use case diagrams, class diagrams, collaboration diagrams, sequence diagrams, and statechart diagrams, are in Figures 19 to 23 in Appendix.

Table 1 summarizes the numbers of concepts defined in charts of concepts of the complete model of the UML version 1.1, and of our selection of concepts. The number of concepts of the complete model is high (233). This number justifies the necessity to select concepts to present an overview of this model. The selected concepts of the proposed overview of this model contains 71 concepts. This number is reasonable for an overview. With our academic experience we consider that this overview can be presented in three or four days.

	Complete model	**Concepts of the overview of the UML**
Basic concepts		
Chart of basic concepts relative to objects	24	11
Chart of basic concepts relative to classes	8	7
Chart of basic concepts: auxiliary elements	12	3
Chart of basic concepts: extension mechanisms	8	0
Chart of basic concepts: data types	32	18
Total number of basic concepts	***84***	***39***
Diagrams		
Chart of concepts of use case diagrams	7	6
Chart of concepts of class diagrams	42	17
Chart of concepts of object diagrams	7	0
Chart of concepts of collaboration diagrams	9	3
Chart of concepts of sequence diagrams	23	2
Chart of concepts of statechart diagrams	33	4
Chart of concepts of activity diagrams	6	0
Chart of concepts of component diagrams	11	0
Chart of concepts of deployment diagrams	11	0
Total number of concepts of charts of diagrams	***149***	***32***
Numbers of concepts	**233**	**71**

Table 1. Numbers of concepts of the model of the UML version 1.1 and of the overview of this model presented in this paper

3.2 Macro View of a Model Defined with Charts of Concepts

We propose to represent *a macro view of a model with a directed graph where nodes represent the selected charts of concepts of this model, and where arcs illustrate the macro dependencies resulting from concepts of charts used to define concepts of other charts.* Macro dependencies between charts of concepts are presented hereafter. An example of macro view of the UML is given hereafter.

Macro Dependencies between Charts of Concepts of a Model

There exists a macro dependency from a chart CCi to a chart CCj if at least one concept of the chart CCi is used to define a concept of the chart CCj.

The fact that a macro dependency exists from a chart of concepts CCi to a chart of concepts CCj means that the chart CCi must be presented before the chart CCj.

We consider that a chart of concepts is a particular concept. So, the logical expressions between definitional dependencies, the non representation of definitional dependencies resulting from transitivity of definitional dependencies, and the root and the terminal concepts, can be applied to macro dependencies between charts of concepts.

Example: in Figure 13 is depicted the macro dependency that exists from the chart of concepts of collaboration diagrams to the chart of concepts of sequence diagrams of the UML.

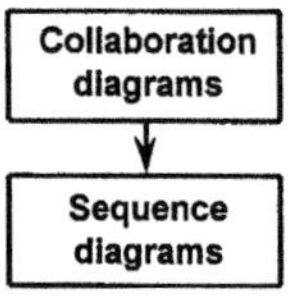

Figure 13. Example of macro dependency between two charts of concepts

Example of Macro View of Charts of Concepts of the UML

Example: according to our goal and to our criteria to define a selection of concepts in the UML (cf. Section 3.1), the macro view of the selected charts of concepts of this model is defined with the groups of concepts of which names are not hatched in Figure 14. Among the non selected groups of concepts are the object diagrams and the activity diagrams. Note that these two diagrams cannot be represented with the version 4 of the UML case tool Rose commercialized by Rational Software.

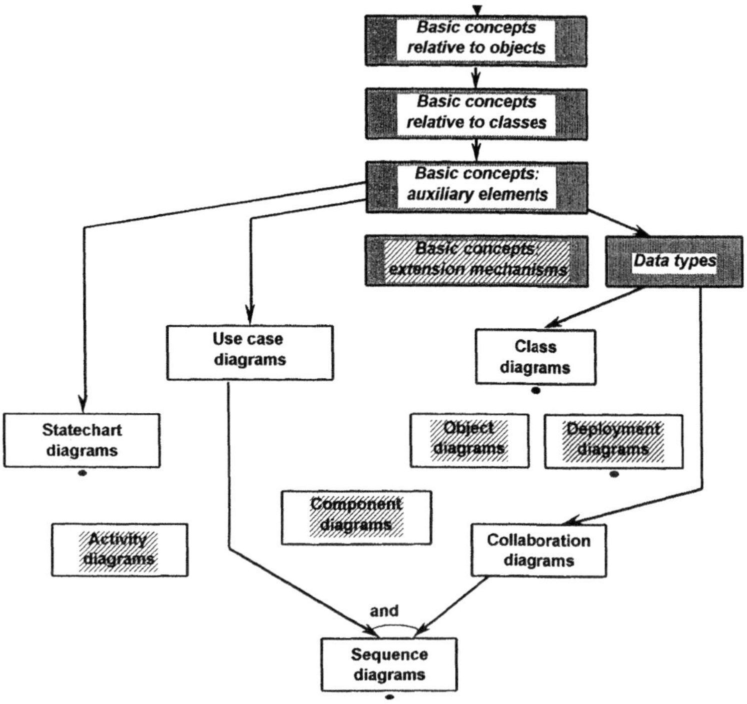

Figure 14. A macro view of charts of concepts of the UML model

4. CONCLUSION

We explain in the introduction why ER or OO metamodels do not easily allow creation of overviews of models both defined by selections of concepts and macro views of these models. We show in this paper how charts of concepts allow creation of overviews of models. As charts of concepts are directed graphs, they easily permit when selecting concepts to see the concepts that must be selected with the chosen concepts and those that are not selected. Macro views of models are simple to be defined with directed graphs where nodes represent the selected charts themselves, and arcs illustrate macro dependencies defined between them.

As example we present an overview of the UML. This selection of concepts in this model contains 71 concepts. It was easily obtained starting from the complete charts of concepts of the UML.

It is easy to delete concepts in a selection of concepts of a model by seeing the concepts that are deleted with the chosen concepts. It is also easy to add concepts in a selection of concepts of a model by seeing the concepts that must be selected with the new concepts.

This paper underlines the use of charts of concepts to create overviews of models. A work in progress is developed to map metamodels defined with an object-oriented model onto charts of concepts. Then it would be possible to map OO metamodels onto charts of concepts to create overviews of models.

The possibility to define selections of concepts in models is exposed in [3] with presentation of the version 1.0 of the UML. This application is developed and extended in [5], paper in which a core of the version 1.1 of the UML is presented. Charts of concepts allow creation of customized models, by easily selecting concepts, modifying definitions of concepts, and adding concepts in models because they are directed graphs [6].

For the same reason, charts of concepts easily allow evaluation of models with metrics usable to measure sizes, complexities, and anomalies in models such as circuits between concepts and non connected sub-graphs [4].

To summarize, the principal uses of charts of concepts are: verification of models, selection of coherent sub-sets in models, creation of customized versions of models, definition of overviews of models, and evaluation of models. So, the charts of concepts are a general proposal in the field of the method engineering [6].

That is why we think that charts of concepts would be a good tool to represent the information systems concepts of the FRISCO framework (anonymous ftp://ftp.leidenuniv.nl/pub/rul/fri-full.zip).

ACKNOWLEDGMENTS

I would like to thank Vincent Bataille, PhD student, and Hong Jiang, PhD in computer science, for their valuable remarks on this paper.

REFERENCES

1. Booch G., Jacobson I., Rumbaugh J., "Unified Modeling Language (UML), Version 1.1", Rational Software Corporation, Santa Clara, 1 September 1997.

2. Castellani X. "Méthodologie générale d'analyse et de conception des systèmes d'objets (MCO). L'ingénierie des besoins". Masson Editor, 1993.

3. Castellani X., *Cartes de concepts permettant de créer des versions personnalisées d'UML.* Journal Ingénierie des Systèmes d'Information (ISI), Volume 5, n° 5/1997, September 1997, Hermès.

4. Castellani X., *Evaluation of Models Defined with Charts of Concepts: Application to the UML Model.* CAISE'98/IFIP 8.1, Third International Workshop on Evaluation of Modelling Methods in Systems Analysis and Design (EMMSAD'98), Pisa, Italy, 8-9 June 1998.

5. Castellani X., Hamamouche N., *Definition of Customized Models: Application to Define a Core of the UML Model.* Tenth International Conference on Software Engineering and Knowledge Engineering (SEKE '98), San Francisco, USA, 18-20 June 1998.

6. Castellani X., Hamamouche N., *Model Engineering using Charts of Concepts: Application to the UML Model,* International Conference on Object-Oriented Information Systems (OOIS' 98), Paris, 9-11 September 1998, proceedings published by Springer-Verlag.

7. Chen P.P., *The entity-relationship model,* ACM transactions on database systems, Vol. 1, No. 1 March 1976.

8. Codd E.F., *A relational model of data for large shared data banks,* ACM, Vol. 13, No. 6, June 1970.

9. Codd E.F., "Further normalization of the data base relational model", Data base systems, Prentice Hall, Englewood Cliffs, New Jersey, 1972.

10. DSTC & CO-SUBMITTERS, Meta-Object Facility (MOF), Object Management Group, Inc (OMG), Framingham, USA - ad/97-08-14 - 1997.

11. Henderson-Sellers B. and Firesmith G., *COMMA: Proposed core model,* Report on Object Analysis and Design, Vol. 4, No. 1, 1997.

12. Kangassalo H., COMIC: A system and methodoly for conceptual modelling and information construction, Data & Knowledge Engineering, Vol. 9, No. 1, October 1992.

13. Sowa J.F., "Conceptual structures: Information processing in Mind and Machine", Addison-Wesley Publishing Company, 1984.

14. Tolvanen J.P., Marttiin P., Lyytinen K., Rossi M., Tahvanainen V.P. and Smolander K., *Modelling Requirements for Future CASE: Modelling Issues and Architectural Consideration,* Information Resources Management Journal, Vol. 8, No. 1, 1995.

15. Welke R.J., Kumar K., *Method engineering: a proposal for situation-specific methodology construction, in Systems Analysis and Design: A Research Agenda,* Cotterman and Senn(eds), Wiley, 1992.

APPENDIX: CHARTS OF CONCEPTS OF THE PROPOSED OVERVIEW OF THE UML

Charts of selected basic concepts and of selected diagrams of the proposed overview of the UML model are in this appendix:
. charts of selected basic concepts: basic concepts relative to objects, basic concepts relative to classes, auxiliary elements, data types (Figures 15 to 18);
. charts of concepts of selected diagrams: use case diagrams, class diagrams, collaboration diagrams, sequence diagrams, statechart diagrams (Figures 19 to 23).

The names of the non selected concepts are hatched in these charts of concepts.

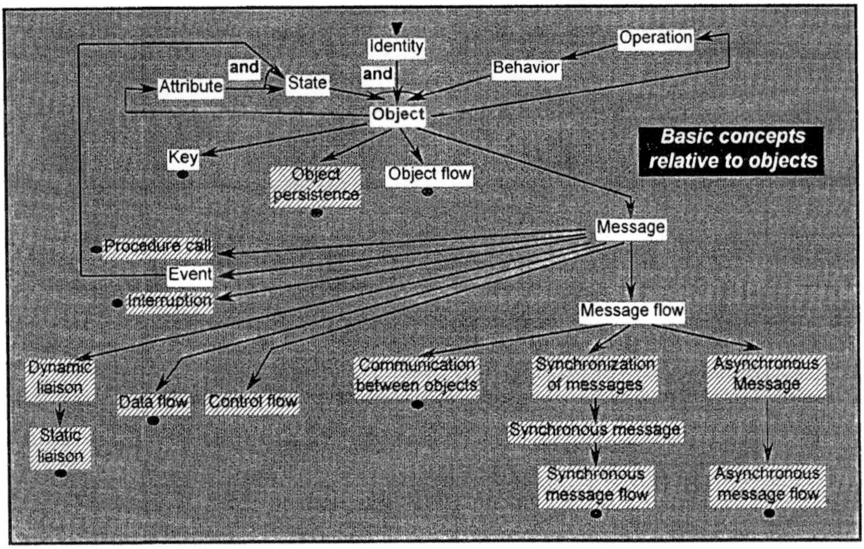

Figure 15. Chart of basic concepts relative to objects

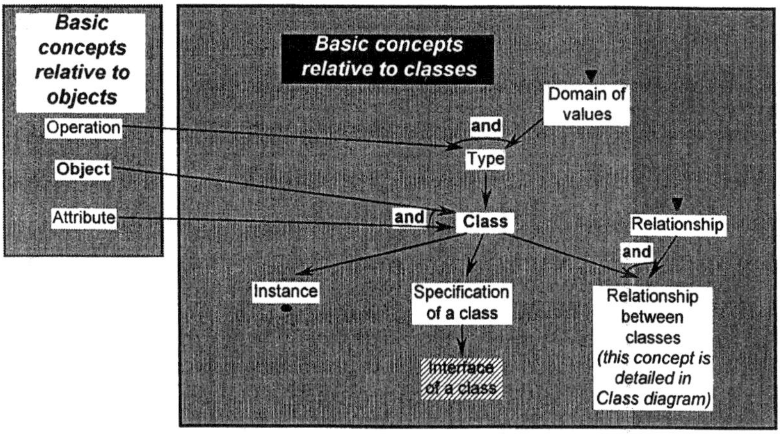

Figure 16. Chart of basic concepts relative to classes

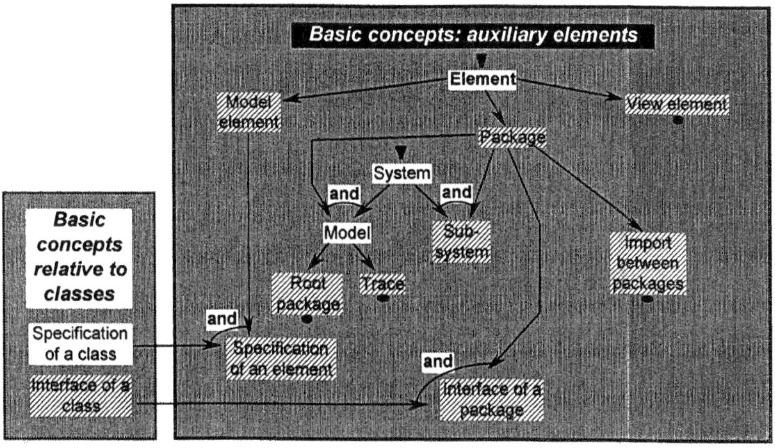

Figure 17. Chart of basic concepts: auxiliary elements

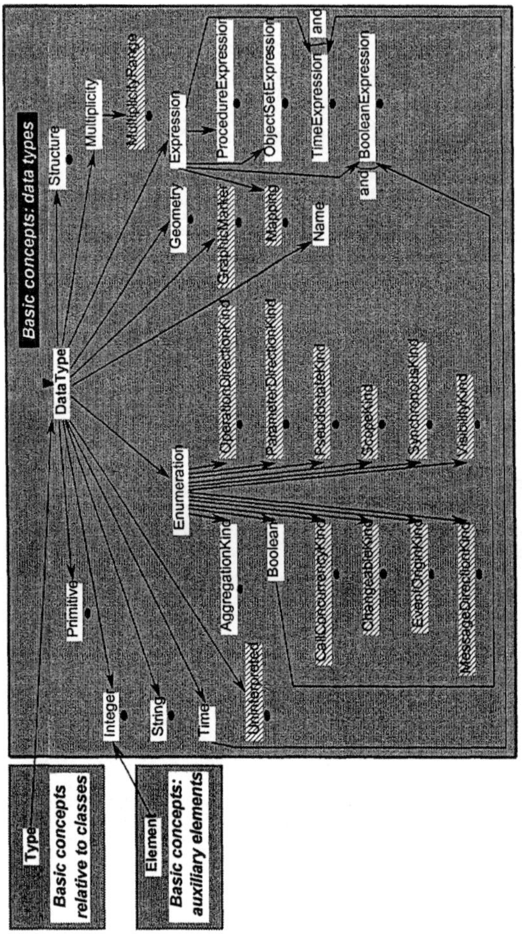

Figure 18. Chart of basic concepts: data types

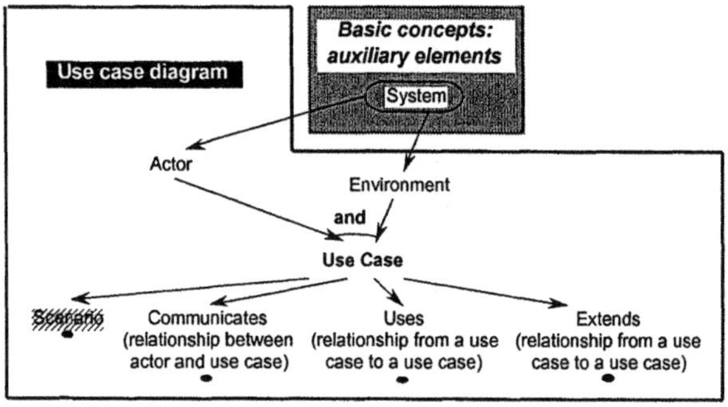

Figure 19. Chart of concepts of use case diagrams

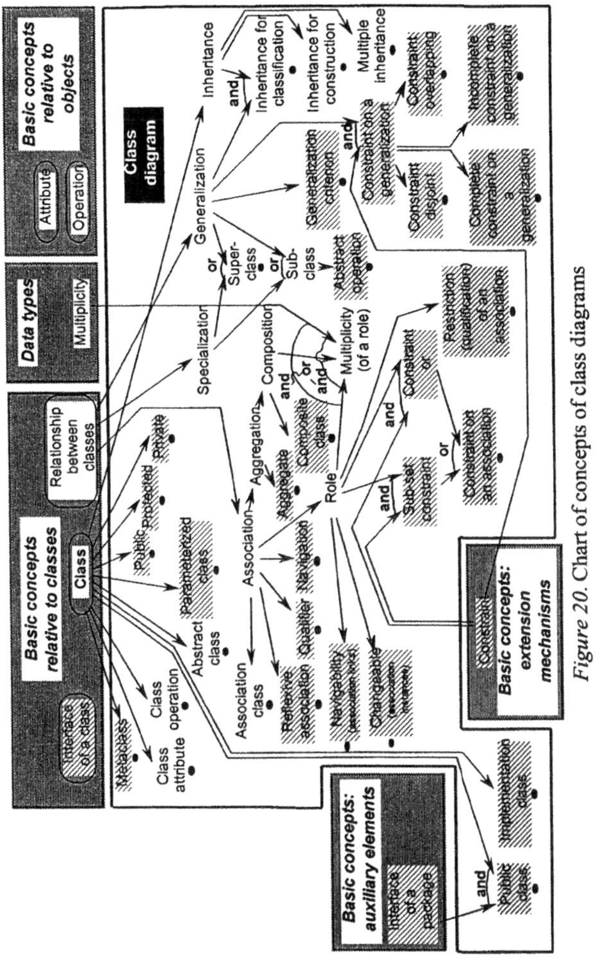

Figure 20. Chart of concepts of class diagrams

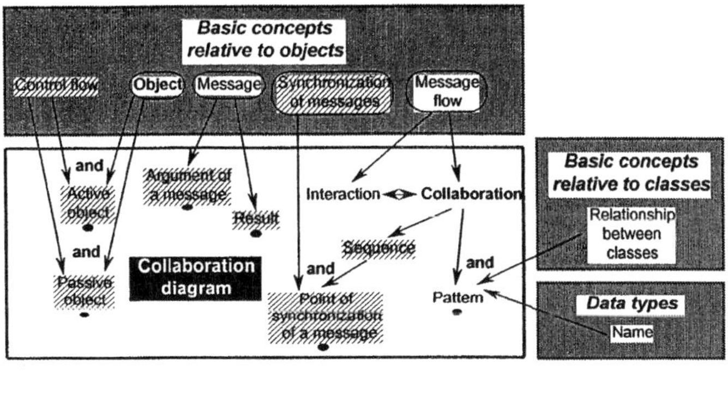

Figure 21. Chart of concepts of collaboration diagrams

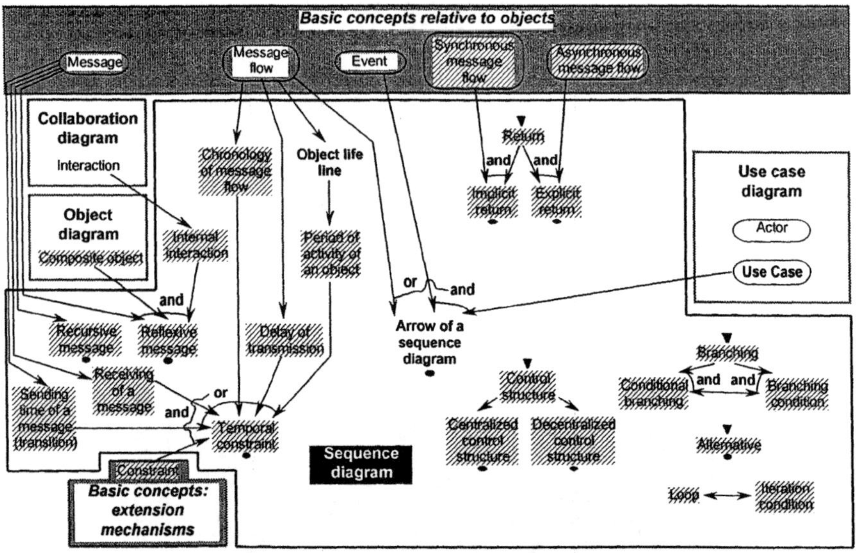

Figure 22. Chart of concepts of sequence diagrams

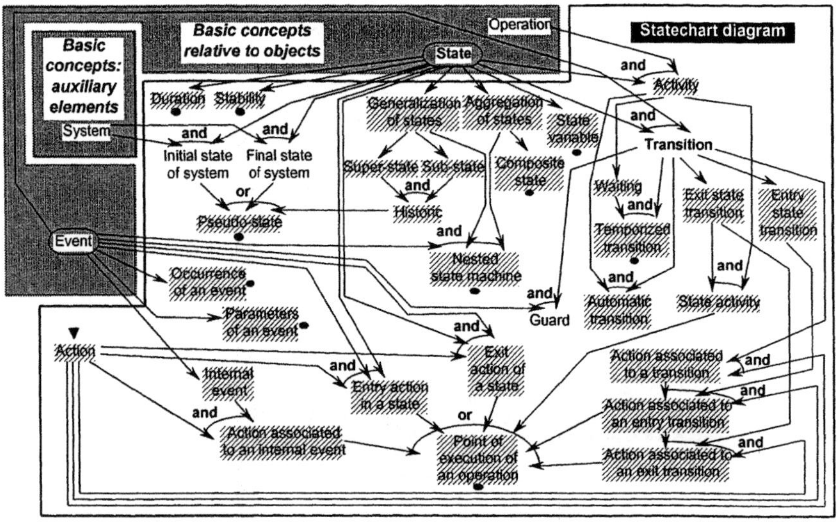

Figure 23. Chart of concepts of statechart diagrams

Comments on "Overviews of Models Defined with Charts of Concepts" by X. Castellani

Zheying Zhang

Department of Computer Science and Information Systems, University of Jyväskylä
P. O. Box 35, 40351 Jyväskylä, Finland
Email: zhezhan@cc.jyu.fi

This paper has introduced a simplified model for the representation of system development methods. The model forms charts of concepts. Different from other metamodels that are made to explain methods in details, the charts of concepts are to help understanding of the concepts of methods using graphic presentation.

With respect to the charts of concepts, the author introduced the models in details about its primary data types: concept and definitional dependency. A concept of a model is "anything that can be used by software analysts and/or designers to represent or to specify phenomena of the real world or technical phenomena". The definitional dependency defines the dependency relationship between the concepts. The author presented different representations of these two data types, such as root concepts, terminal concepts, and the logical expressions between definitional dependencies. It can be expanded to represent a macro view of a specific methodology. He also presented an overview of the models of UML modelling language by using charts of concepts model to demonstrate its applicability.

However, from my point of view, the usability-related issues are the most critical issues when designing such kind of conceptual models. Therefore, I would have appreciated to see a detailed discussion of e.g. the following aspects in the paper:

- Why overviews of models are needed, i.e. illustrate any application domains, such as improving reuse process in method construction, and so on?

- The author claimed that “the principal uses of concepts are: verification of models, selection of coherent sub-set in models, creation of customised versions of models, definition of overviews of models, and evaluation of models”. However, it remains unclear how the goals are achieved. I would like to see some concrete comparisons between this simple model and other semantic richness model such as GOPRR.

- What are the weaknesses and constraints of such models?

Meanwhile, the author mentioned in the paper, “a complementary study of the semantics of a definitional dependency can conclude to define “A Kind Of” relationship or an inheritance between the two concepts concerned”. The fundamental benefits from thc charts of Concepts are their simplified representation of the dependence relationship. Being enriched the semantics, it will be back to the same complex situation of ER metamodel or other OO metamodels and lose its worthy. Moreover, the work of identifying what the “concepts” are seems no different from other approached such as GOPRR. That is to say it is still a hard work.

To summarise, the paper makes a valuable conceptual contribution by proposing the charts of concepts model to ease the understanding of methodologies. On the other hand, the author needs to spend more time motivating the usefulness of this model.

Information System? Which One Do You Mean?

João Alvaro Carvalho

Information Systems Department, University of Minho, 4800 Guimarães, Portugal
Email: jac@dsi.uminho.pt

Key words: Information, System, Information system

Abstract: *Information systems and technology* is an emerging area of human knowledge that experiences some difficulties related to a lack of consensus about its more basic concepts and terminology. Instances of problematic terms are *information* and *information system*. Any person attending conferences or reading books and papers related to information systems will soon discover that there is more than one possible meaning for the term *information system*. In other words, people that talk or write about information systems aren't always referring to the same object. The distinctions among the different objects that can be viewed as information systems are not always clear because they have many aspects in common: they all deal with information; they all are somewhat related to organisations or to the work carried out in organisations; and they all are related to information technology, either because they can benefit from its use or because they are made with computers or computer-based devices.

In this paper it is claimed that a more elaborated view of the *system* concept might bring some light to this problem. Using a specific definition of *system*, it will be argued that: there are four different objects that, legitimately, can be considered information systems; all of these objects are interesting objects in the area of IST; each of them is useful for different professional activities. The four objects will also be associated with several definitions of information systems proposed in different works, including the definition proposed in the FRISCO Report.

1. INTRODUCTION

Browsing the literature in the area of *information systems and technology*[1] (IST) anyone quickly comes to the conclusion that there is no agreement on what an *information system* is! However, the problem is not related with a lack of consensus on an adequate wording for a definition. The problem is that the same term – information system – is being used to designate different things. And the distinction among the different information systems is not always clear because they have several aspects in common: they all deal with information, they all are somewhat related to organisations or to the work carried out in organisations, and they all are related to information technology, either because they can benefit from its use or because they are made with computers or computer-based devices.

Although some effort has been made to clarify the nature of information systems (e.g., [Falkenberg and Lindgreen 1989], [Falkenberg, et al. 1992], [Falkenberg, et al. 1996], [Weber 1997], [Checkland and Holwell 1998]) certain aspects aren't clear yet. A more elaborated view of the *system* concept might bring some light to this problem. Using a definition of *system* based on the work of Le Moigne [Le Moigne 1977], I will argue that: there are four different objects that, legitimately, can be considered information systems; all of these objects are interesting objects in the area of IST; each of them is useful for different professional activities.

The four objects will also be associated with several definitions of information systems proposed in different works, including the definition proposed in the FRISCO Report [Falkenberg, et al. 1996].

The objective is not to provide yet another definition for *information system* or to develop a taxonomy of information systems but to review and compare possible meanings for the term, and distinguish among several concepts hidden in the same designation.

[1] Often, the area is designated simply by *information systems* (e.g., [Buckingham, et al. 1987], [Mingers and Stowell 1997], [Checkland and Holwell 1998]). However, in order to avoid the use of the same term - information system - to designate both an object of scientific interest and the area of human knowledge about that object, we decided to use the term "information systems and technology" to designate the latter. Attending to the importance of information technology in the area, it can be argued that this designation is more adequate. Bacon and Fitzgerald [Bacon and Fitzgerald 1996] present an interesting argument to justify its adoption.

2. INFORMATION, SYSTEMS, AND INFORMATION SYSTEMS

It is important to start by defining the two basic concepts of *information* and *system*. The risk undertaken is that there isn't agreement either on the meaning of these two important terms. So, the definitions proposed herein might be rejected by some of the readers. However, the necessity of presenting these two definitions is undeniable.

System is a concept that is useful to study active objects, especially when they are complex. A system is the result of viewing the active world from a certain point of view. Any thing (and specially an active thing) can be viewed as being a system. A system (in general or in abstract) can be defined as an ***active*** (does something), ***stable*** (has a structure ...) and ***evolutionary*** (... that changes over time) thing or object that operates in an ***environment*** (it interacts with other things) with some ***purpose*** (from the point of the view of the modeller, there is a reason for the system to do what it does) [Le Moigne 1977]. It should be noted that the adoption of a less strict definition of *system* is frequent. To some authors (e.g., [Ackoff 1971], [Laszlo 1983], [Boulding 1985], [van Gigch 1991], [Bunge 1979], [von Bertalanffy 1975], [Jordan 1968]), a system is just something whose components are inter-related. The adoption of Le Moignes's definition in this work is justified by the richness it brings to the systemic study of an object.

Simple systems are mere active objects without self-control and with no cognitive capacities. More complex systems have some kind of control upon what they do. They are also able of learning and making decisions and they can reach a high level of autonomy, i.e., they might have independent existence, they are capable of governing them selves and surviving in a changing (and sometimes hostile) environment. In this case, systems need knowledge and perform several operations upon that knowledge[2]. In between it is possible to identify different levels of self-control.

It will be considered that an autonomous system (e.g., an organisation) can be sub-divided in three sub-systems: operational, managerial, and informational. The operational sub-system includes those activities that perform actions directly related to the system's purpose or mission (and perhaps some supporting actions). The managerial sub-system includes the

[2] Several authors recognise that systems can be more or less elaborate and propose classifications of systems according to the level of complexity and characteristics they possess (e.g., [Boulding 1956], [Boulding 1985], [Ackoff 1971], [von Bertalanffy 1975], [Jordan 1968], [Checkland 1981], [Bunge 1979], [Le Moigne 1978a], [van Gigch 1974], [Laszlo 1983]; a summary view of systems definitions and classifications can be obtained in [Skyttner 1996]).

activities that manage (organise, plan, control, coordinate, etc.) the operational activities. The informational sub-system establishes communication among the other two sub-systems. The necessity of the informational system is particularly clear when that communication is asynchronous and the existence of mechanisms that support the memorisation and retrieval of information is evident.

Figure 1 illustrates this view of autonomous systems. Although it can be considered as a simplistic view, it is considered to be useful to the purposes of this paper.

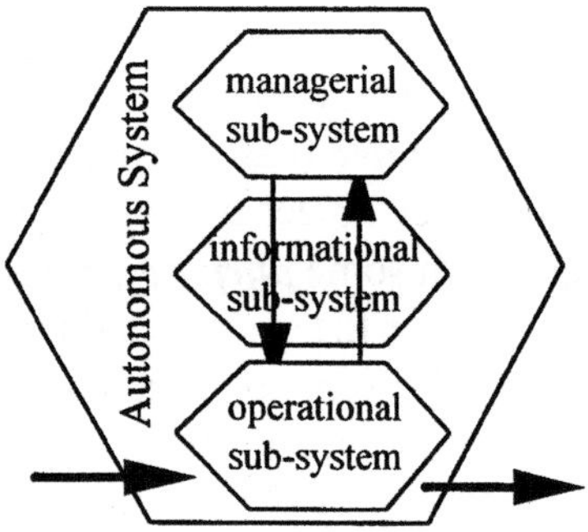

Figure 1. - Sub-systems of an autonomous system. The thicker arrows illustrate the modification produced by the system; the other arrows illustrate the communication between the operational and managerial sub-system; this communication is performed through the informational sub-system

The action of a system alters some other object(s). The altered object can be either passive (matter, energy or information) or active (in such case it can also be viewed as a system). In the first case, the alteration can change the object in its form, in space or in time. In the second case, the alteration modifies the structure of the object. Table 1 summarises the types of alterations that a system can produce and the types of objects that can be altered.

Table 1. Types of alterations that a system can produce and the types of objects that can be altered; the table shows some words normally used to refer to some of the alterations

changed objects		**form**	**space**	**time**
passive objects	**matter**	transformation	transportation	storage, stocks
	energy	conversion	transportation	accumulation
	information	processing	transmission	storage, memory
active objects	**system**	the alteration of a system addresses its structure		

Information is herein understood as symbolic objects[3] (opposed to material and energetic objects) deliberately built in order to enable communication and the formation of knowledge.

It should be noted that the criteria used to define information are related to the object's nature: matter, energy or information. This criteria is rather different from the one used in the FRISCO report, where information is defined as a form of knowledge ("the knowledge increment..."). FRISCO's definition of information is however too far from its usage in common language and this makes it very difficult to apply. This is perhaps a major inconvenient to its widespread adoption and use. FRISCO's concept of data ("... collection of representations...") is closer to the concept of information as defined in this work.

Sometimes, the term information is also used to refer to the act of informing i.e., the action of providing the means to the construction of knowledge (in this case, information is a noun that names an action). These two meanings for information are, however, inter-related: the latter refers to an action (to inform) and the former to the means used to achieve that action (symbolic objects or representations).

Based on the definitions of information and system provided in the previous paragraphs, it is legitimate to conclude that an **information system** is either: (i) an active object that deals with (processes) information; or (ii) an active object whose purpose is to inform.

The first interpretation focuses the nature of the processed objects. Information systems are systems that process only information, i.e., symbolic objects or representations. Material and energetic objects are not considered to be relevant. Processed objects can be affected in its form, space and time. In the case of information, the possible operations upon it might include: calculate, process, create, code, decode (form); collect, present, transmit (space); store, memorise (time). So, any active object that carries out any of these operations might be entitled to be considered an information system.

The second interpretation focuses on the purpose of the system. Information system is a system whose purpose is to inform, i.e., to contribute to someone's acquisition of knowledge. This knowledge is necessary to the execution of some action in some context.

It is also possible to consider that an information system is an active object that deals with (processes) symbolic objects AND whose purpose is to inform. This third interpretation is a combination of the other two. The existence of such a system is very plausible as a system that informs its

[3] As the symbolic objects are used to represent other things they can also be called *representations*.

clients/users has to deal with information. However, it should be noted that not all systems that deal with information have the purpose of informing. Insurance companies and banks are two examples of such systems.

3. FOUR OBJECTS ENTITLED TO BE CONSIDERED INFORMATION SYSTEMS

The criteria for identifying objects that can be considered information systems is now set. The identification of information systems within, or related to, organisations can be started at the level of the organisation itself. Organisations whose purpose is to provide information to their clients can be considered information systems:

> **IS1** - Organisations (autonomous systems) whose business (purpose) is to provide information to their clients. The following are some examples of objects that can be considered as IS1 information systems: libraries, information services, information brokers, newspapers, radio or TV stations.

Looking inside organisations, other information systems will emerge. In any organisation, viewed as an autonomous system (i.e., a system that is capable of governing itself) it is possible to identify a sub-system that assures the communication between the managerial and operational sub-systems of an organisation (cf. section 2). Such organisational sub-system is an information system:

> **IS2** - A sub-system that exists in any system that is capable of governing it self (autonomous system). The information system (IS2) assures the communication between the managerial and operational sub-systems of an organisation – that's its purpose. When this communication is asynchronous, a memory to store the messages is necessary. IS2 includes such memory.

IS2 makes extensive use of computer-based artefacts to support their functionality. Such artefacts process information, acting upon its form, space, or time: calculate, process, create, code, decode (form); collect, present, transmit (space); store, memorise (time). The purpose of these artefacts (systems) may vary according to the operations they actually perform and the intentions of their creators and users. However, the use of these artefacts in organisations is not restricted to the boundaries of IS2. They can be used to support or automate any organisational activities that deal with information irrespective of their "affiliation" to any of the three organisational sub-systems identified above: operational, managerial or informational. So, the third information system is the following:

> **IS3** - Any combination of active objects (processors) that deal only with symbolic objects (information) and whose agents are computers or computer-based devices – a computer-based system. IS3 can be used in organisations to support or automate any activities (organisational work) that deal with information, irrespective of their "affiliation" to the operational, managerial or informational sub-systems of an organisation). The purpose of these systems may vary according to the operations they actually perform [Carvalho 1998] and the intentions of their creators and users. Examples of IS3s include artefacts such as: transaction processing systems, data processing systems, management information systems, decision support systems, workflow management systems, data mining systems, environmental scanning systems, executive information systems.

The apperception that activities that deal with information exist all over an organisation (and are not restricted to its informational sub-system) leads to the identification of another information system:

> **IS4** - Any combination of active objects (processors) that deal only with symbolic objects (information). When applied to an organisation, this view corresponds to all organisational activities excepting those that deal with materials or energy.

In certain cases, an IS4 may coincide with the whole organisation, or at least be very close to it. One such case is when the organisation is an IS1. Another case is when the organisation, despite not having the purpose of informing its clients, deals solely with symbolic objects. Examples of such organisations are banks, insurance companies, software houses, architecture offices, etc.

IS4 poses a problem from the point of view of a systemic analysis: ***purpose***. IS4s have no purpose in themselves! An IS4 is perhaps more adequately described as a *sub-set* [4] of an organisation that includes any information handling activities, irrespective of being carried out within the operational, the managerial, or the informational sub-system. Another way of describing IS4 would be as *abstractions* of organisations that include the activities that deal with information. This view leads to the conclusion that most of an organisation is an information system.

[4] Sub-set is used to call the attention to the fact that IS4 is not identified as a sub-system whose purpose is necessary to achieve the purpose of its supra-system (the organisational system). IS4 is identified as anything, within the organisational system, that deals with information.

Using Le Moigne's definition of system, introduced in section 2, it is difficult to consider IS4 as a system because it is not possible to ascribe it a purpose. However, it should be recognised that Le Moigne's definition of system is more restrictive than other common definitions of system. So IS4 might only be considered a system, if a definition of system less restrictive that Le Moigne's is adopted. In spite of that, in the remainder of this paper, this fourth object will be called an information system.

The four information systems are schematically depicted in figure 2.

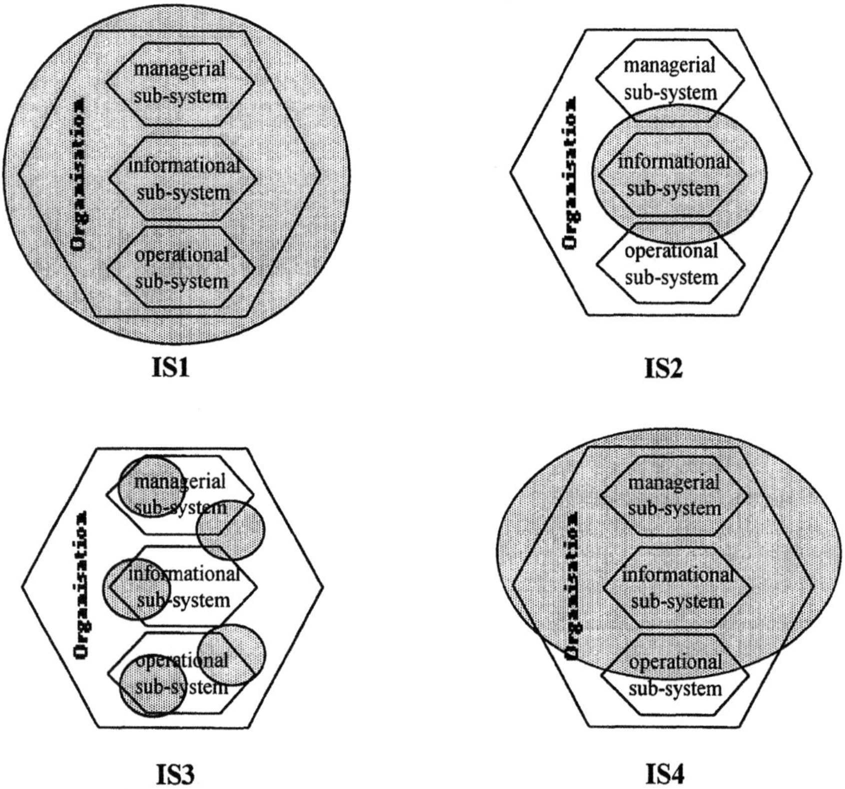

Figure 2. Schematic representation of four different objects that can be considered information systems: IS1 is an organisation whose purpose is to inform its clients; IS2 is an organisational sub-system that supports communication between the operational and the managerial sub-systems. Such sub-system exists in any autonomous system (i.e., a system capable of self-govern); IS3 is any artefact that uses computers and computer-based devices to perform information manipulation activities; IS4 is a *sub-set* of an organisation that encompasses all information manipulation activities; if the organisation deals only with information, IS4 includes all the organisational activities; however, it is distinct from an IS1 information system as, in a IS4 there is no reference to purpose (each IS is delimited by a circle).

Table 2 summarises the characteristics of the four objects that can be considered information systems according to some features derived from the system view presented in section 2.

Table 2. Summary of the characteristics of IS1, IS2, IS3 and IS4 information systems

	IS1	**IS2**	**IS3**	**IS4**
i) Processed objects	Information	Information	Information	Information
ii) Operations upon the processed objects	Some or all the possible operations	Some or all the possible operations	Some or all the possible operations	Some or all the possible operations
iii) Purpose of the system	To inform	To inform (assure communication between the operational and managerial sub-systems	Is normally related to some support to information manipulation activities	**No purpose can be ascribed**
iv) Nature of the agents that perform the operations:				
- Humans	yes	yes	no	yes
- Non-computer-based information technology	yes	yes	no	yes
- Computers and computer-based devices	yes	yes	yes	yes
v) Environment of the system:				
- Context	The organisational environment	The other organisational sub-systems: operational and managerial; the organisational environment	People that use the system (or benefit form its existence) and their work context;	The organisation and its environment
- Clients/users	The organisation's clients	Organisational agents belonging to the managerial and operational sub-systems	People that "handle" the system (normally called "users")	Organisation agents and a sub-set of the organisation's environment

Table 2 (cont.) Summary of the characteristics of IS1, IS2, IS3 and IS4 information systems

	IS1	IS2	IS3	IS4
vi) Degree of self control	Autonomous system	Normally it doesn't have any kind of self-control. But it is a necessary sub-system in any autonomous system	Normally, an IS3 system is a system without any kind of self-control, even thought that an IS3 system can automate the control function within a system.	As it is not possible to ascribe it a purpose, it doesn't make sense to talk about self-control[5].

The features are the following[6]:

i) nature of processed objects (information, material, energy)[7];

ii) operations upon those objects; the operations processing information upon its form space and time and might include: calculate, process, create, code, decode (form); collect, present, transmit (space); store, memorise (time);

iii) purpose of the system;

iv) nature of the agents that carry out the operations; the agents might be: humans, non-computer-based information technology (e.g., paper, microfilms, photocopying machines, telephones, fax, etc.); or computers and computer-based devices;

v) the environment within the information system operates; in what concerns the environment, it might be useful to distinguish the context and the clients/users of the information system;

vi) degree of self control; whether the system is autonomous or, at least, has any kind of self control.

[5] As an IS4 consumes resources, it is however possible to associate it with some sort of resource management function.

[6] The features used to compare the different objects that might be considered information systems include most of the elements considered by Checkland [Checkland 1981] in the definition of a system: Clients, Actors, Transformation, Weltanschauung, Owner, Environment (CATWOE). Clients and Environment are grouped in item v). Actors are included in item iv) although only their nature is considered to be relevant. Transformation is somewhat considered in item ii) and iii).

[7] Although this will be a constant in all information systems, this aspect is central to the issue in discussion.

Features i) and ii) are common to the four ISs. Focusing only on these two features it is possible to formulate a definition that is suitable to fit all the four ISs. However, the four ISs are very different in what relates to the remainder features, supporting the argument that they really are different systems. Table 3 provides some examples for each IS.

Table 3. Examples of IS1, IS2, IS3 and IS4

IS	Examples
IS1	CNN; EU's Cordis; a weather service
IS2	The following are part of the IS2 information system: data base; procedures manual; accounting books
IS3	A transaction processing system; a computer based data base; a decision support system; an expert system
IS4	Any organisation can be viewed as an IS4 information system[8]

4. INFORMATION SYSTEM DEFINITIONS: PRESENTATION

Considering the existence of four different things that can be considered information systems, an interesting question to raise is which IS (or ISs) might fit different definitions of information system.

The definitions considered in this section have been searched in the IST literature especially in introductory textbooks or in books and papers that address the question of what is an information system. Any intention of being exhaustive or systematic was soon abandoned when it became evident that there are too many different definitions and that many authors do not bother to define the concept. This isn't always problematic, as it's normally easy to recognise the assumptions about information systems underlying the statements being made.

Several authors acknowledge the existence of different definitions, difficult to conciliate, and present and discuss some of those definitions (e.g., [Avison and Wood-Harper 1986], [Avison and Fitzgerald 1988], [Amaral 1994]). Normally they end up by selecting the definition, which they consider being more useful to their intentions and to the subject they intend to develop.

Some authors deeply discuss the concept of information system but they do not attempt to provide a short definition for it. This happens, for example,

[8] In the case of organizations that deal only with symbolic objects the information system will coincide with the organization. This doesn't mean that the IS4 coincides with an IS1 system. An insurence company is an example of such a situation where the IS4 system encompasses the whole organization but that cannot be considered as an IS1 information system.

in the books from Weber [Weber 1997] and Checkland and Holwell [Checkland and Holwell 1998]. Other authors avoid the issue of what an information system is by providing an enumeration of its components (e.g., [van Griethuysen 1982], [Kroenke and Dolan 1987], [Rolland, et al. 1988]).

Table 4 presents some definitions and assertions about information found in the literature systems (ordered chronologically by year of publication) and associates to each one the ISs that, in the author's opinion, correspond to the definition or fit the assertion. The association established between each definition and one or more IS depends on the personal interpretation of the author for each definition found. This brings a subjective dimension in the study but is unavoidable due to the nature of the human language and of the learning process. It should also be noted that terms such as *information* might be used with different meanings in different definitions.

Table 4. Some definitions of information system and the corresponding ISs

Reference	Definitions	ISs encompassed
[Davis 1974]	"... an integrated man/machine system for providing information to support the operations, management and decision making functions in an organisation. The system uses computer hardware, software, manual procedures, management and decision models and a data base."	IS2, IS4; IS3 are considered as being part of the system
Le Moigne[9] 197?	"... can in effect be considered as the memorisation system of the organisation: the system which permits it to keep in memory: its transactions with its environment; the events in its environment which it wishes to recall easily for some period; the common rationale which its members gladly share, or those which are imposed by its environment"	IS2
[van Griethuysen 1982], pp. 1-5	"... as consisting of a conceptual schema, an information base, and an information processor".	The elements described can exist in IS1, IS2, IS3 or IS4
[Avison and Wood-Harper 1986]	"a system to collect, process, store, transmit, and display information"	IS1, IS2, IS3, IS4

[9] This definition is presented in a document whose origin and date hasn't been possible to trace. It is a chapter of a book. The chapter is entitled "The FOUR-FLOWS MODEL as a Tool for Designing the Information System of an Organization" and corresponds to the pages 324 to 341. At the end of the chapter, there is an abstract in German. The same view of information system is present in other documents produced by Le Moigne (e.g., [Le Moigne 1985], [Le Moigne 1977], [van Gigch and Le Moigne 1990], [Le Moigne 1978a], [Le Moigne 1978b], [Le Moigne 1979a], [Le Moigne 1979b].

Table 4 (cont.) Some definitions of information system and the corresponding ISs

Reference	Definitions	ISs encompassed
[Buckingham, et al. 1987], pp.18	"... a system which assembles, stores, processes and delivers information relevant to an organisation (or to society), in such a way that the information is accessible and useful to those who wish to use it, including managers, staff, clients and citizens. An information system is a human activity (social) system which may or may not involve the use of computer systems"	IS1, IS2, IS4; IS3 are considered as being part of the system
[Kroenke and Dolan 1987]	"an information system consists of five components: hardware, programs, data, procedures and people	The elements described exist in IS1, IS2 or IS4; IS3 includes all but one - people
adapted from [Rolland, et al. 1988]	"... a set formed by: data; rules that define the informational function; set of procedures to collect, store, transform, retrieve, and communicate information; set of human resources and technical means, integrated within a system, that cooperate and contribute to its function and to achieve its purpose"	The elements described exist in IS1, IS2 or IS4; IS3 includes all but one - human resources
[Parker 1989], pp.10	"... any system that provides to people with either data or information relating to an organisation's operations."	IS3; can also fit IS2 and IS4;
[Ein-Dor and Segev 1993], pp. 167	"... any computerised system with a user or operator interface [...] provided the computer is not physically embedded".	IS3
[Wand, et al. 1995], pp. 287	"... represents a perceived real-world system."	This definition can be applied to part of the information IS1, IS2, IS3 and IS4 deal with
[Hirschheim, et al. 1995], pp. 11	"structural perspective: a collection of people, processes, data, models, technology and partly formalised language, forming a cohesive structure which serves some organisational purpose or function. functional perspective: technologically implemented medium for the purpose of recording, storing and disseminating linguistic expressions as well as for the supporting of inference making"	The elements described in the structural perspective exist in IS1, IS2 or IS4; IS3 includes all but one - human resources; The functional perspective fits IS1, IS2, IS3 and IS4

Table 4 (cont.) Some definitions of information system and the corresponding ISs

Reference	Definitions	ISs encompassed
[Alter 1996], pp. 2	"... a system that uses information technology to capture, transmit, store, retrieve, manipulate, or display information used in one or more business processes."	IS3; IS1, IS2 and IS4 might be included if they most rely on computers and computer-based devices
[Falkenberg, et al. 1996], pp. 74, 211 (FRISCO Report)	"... is a sub-system of an organisational system, comprising the conception of how the communication- and information-oriented aspects of an organisation are composed (e.g., of specific communicating, information-providing and/or information seeking actors, and of specific information-oriented actands) and how these operate, thus describing the (explicit and/or explicit) communication-oriented and information-providing actions and arrangements within that organisation."	Attending to the FRISCO's definition of information, fits a sub-set of IS4; Includes IS2; IS3s are designated in the FRISCO report as *computerised information system*

5. INFORMATION SYSTEM DEFINITIONS: DISCUSSION

The first conclusion to draw from the previous section, is that most of the times, authors do not distinguish among the four things presented in section 3 as candidates to be considered information systems.

None of the definitions presented in the previous section, addresses IS1 in particular. This is not surprising, attending to the tradition in the IST area. IS1s are perhaps interesting to library science or other areas concerned with the creation of information services. However, things might be changing. The emergence of IT based information services is demanding that more attention is paid to the study of such services as information systems.

Only one definition addresses explicitly IS2. In fact, the view underlying IS2 has not been very exploited within the IST area. This view of information systems, based on the cybernetic and systemic approaches, provides an interesting basis to understand organisations as learning and acting systems, thus providing a promising framework to support the study of knowledge management. This view is also important to the general activity of organisational design and to other activities related with organisational design such as business process reengineering or even the determination of the information needs of organisational agents (either managers or operators).

IS3 and IS4 are often mixed in such a way that it is difficult to separate them. The only feature that can be used to distinguish among them is whether or not they include human agents. This "fusion" of IS3 and IS4 is perhaps due to the fact that IST people like to emphasise that they are not interested in just IT applications - IS3 systems. IT applications are interesting when studied in their context which includes the people that use them and the activities where they are used. Davis' definition [Davis 1974], for example, suggests this interpretation. It is normally used by those involved in the development of information systems (which is commonly understood as covering the earlier steps of software engineering projects, including the determination of requirements for computer-based systems) and (computer-based) database design. It is present in many textbooks about systems analysis and design, database design and information systems development (e.g., SAD [Yourdon 1989]; SSADM [Downs, et al. 1992], [Cutts 1991]; MULTIVIEW [Avison and Wood-Harper 1990]; OOA [Coad and Yourdon 1991]; [Hoffer, et al. 1999]). The problem with this view of information systems is that it dilutes the separation between IS3 and IS4. Very often, there is no explicit reference to the fact that it is necessary to study a wider information system (an organisational system that deals with information) in order to decide which kind of IT support can be provided to that system (computer-based information systems). In fact, there are two different types of systems (both can be considered to be information systems) and it isn't always advantageous to view them as just one system. The separation between the two types of systems is stressed by Checkland and his collaborators ([Checkland and Holwell 1998], [Winter, et al. 1995]) who refer to the relationship between IS3 and IS4, as a *serving* and a *served* system. It becomes clear that the study of serving system demands the study of the served system, i.e., both systems have to be dealt with. But it doesn't mean that both systems should be considered as just one.

Few authors use the term information systems to refer solely to IS3 without mixing them with IS4 (e.g., [Ein-Dor and Segev 1993]), although IS3 are sometimes identified as sub-systems of IS4 (e.g., FRISCO computerised information systems).

Among the definitions related to IS4 it is possible to identify two streams, distinguished by a subtle difference. The first one stresses that information systems <u>must</u> include information technology. This view underlies Davis' definition and perhaps Alter's as well (Alter's definition seems to be more focused on IS3s but it doesn't exclude completely IS4s). The other stream rather emphasises that the use of computer-based technology is incidental. Information systems are viewed as independent from the nature of their agents, i.e., independent from the technology used to implement them. Such view is suggested by the definitions of [Buckingham, et al. 1987], [Rolland, et al. 1988], [Hirschheim, et al. 1995], [Falkenberg, et al. 1996]. Other authors also seem to share this view (e.g., [Stamper 1997], [Carvalho and

Amaral 1993]). It is interesting to note that the first stream can be associated to an American tradition while the second corresponds to a European tradition.

The IS4 view is very useful in another context - the professional activity of planning, deploying and maintaining (i.e., managing) the technological infrastructure for the information handling activities of an organisation. This activity is similar to the activity of managing other infrastructures for things such as water, electricity, air-conditioning, vapour, or sewage. The IT infrastructure of an organisation includes: transmission network (cables, sockets, infra-red or radio receptors and emitters, rooters, servers, etc.); storage servers; processing servers; workstations; information collection devices, printers and other presentation devices. The IS4 view is adequate to these activity, because it provides a "blueprint" of the information handling activities where the IT requirements of each activity can be mapped and where the connections among different devices can be outlined.

The IS4 view is also adopted to support business process reengineering (BPR) projects, specially when they are motivated by intentions of IT adoption. However, BPR projects could benefit from combining this view with an IS2 view, as this one enforces the importance of control mechanisms necessary in any process.

Table 5 summarises the professional domains where each of the IS views might be useful.

Table 5. Professional domains where each IS view is useful

IS	Professional domain
IS1	Devising and management of information services
IS2	Organisational design; determination of information needs of managers and operators; knowledge management; business process reengineering
IS2 & IS3	Determination of requirements for computer-based systems; information systems development; data base design
IS3	Design and construction of computer-based systems
IS3 & IS4	Information systems development; data base design; determination of requirements for computer-based systems
IS4	Information systems planning; business process reengineering (IT driven); design and management of the IT infra-structure

All the professional domains listed in table 5 are normally recognised as being strongly related to the IST area and dealing with information systems. However, they focus on different types of systems. This is often hidden under definitions of information systems which are broad enough to encompass all the four ISs identified in section 3 but that fail to alert to the existence of different types of systems, whose deep understanding relies in knowledge borrowed from quite different disciplines.

6. CONCLUSIONS

Any definition of information system is inevitably a general statement that can fit different instances. The situation in the IST area is that the existing definitions do not allow to properly identifying the objects that are in the mind of their proponents. The main reason to this seems to be related with some freedom on the use of the concept *system*.

The use of a more strict definition of system contributed to the identification of four different types of objects that can legitimately be considered as information system. The differences among them were stressed, the importance of distinguishing among them was referred, and their applicability and usefulness was discussed. Some of the assertions made about the role of certain IS views in some professional activities still demand confirmation. For example, the usefulness of an IS2 view in activities such as knowledge management or business process reengineering is not evident. Further research work pursuing this suggestion should first be accomplished.

An analysis of some information systems definitions found in the IST literature confirmed that they can correspond to more that one object. Although in some cases this is not harmful, in other situations it leads to confusion about what is the object of interest of a professional activity or a scientific domain. Moreover, this confusion contributes to the difficulty on establishing a terminology consensus in the IST discipline, which then contributes to the difficulty on establishing a shared core to the discipline.

7. REFERENCES

Ackoff, R.L., "Towards a Systems of Systems Concepts", *Management Science*, 17, 11 (1971), 661-671.

Alter, S., *Information Systems: A Management Perspective*, The Benjamin/Cummings Publishing Company, 1996.

Amaral, L.A.M.d., *PRAXIS: Um referencial para o Planeamento de Sistemas de Informação*, Tese de Doutoramento, Universidade do Minho, 1994 (in Portuguese).

Avison, D.E. and G. Fitzgerald, *Information Systems Development: Methodologies, Techniques and Tools*, Blackwell, 1988.

Avison, D.E. and A.T. Wood-Harper, "Multiview - An Exploration in Information Systems Development", *The Australian Computer Journal*, 18, 4 (1986), 174-179.

Avison, D.E. and A.T. Wood-Harper, *MULTIVIEW: An Exploration in Information Systems Development*, Blackwell Scientific Publications, 1990.

Bacon, C.J. and B. Fitzgerald, *The Field of IST: A Name, a Framework, and a Central Focus*, Research Report, 1996.

Boulding, K.E., "General Systems Theory: The Skeleton of Science", *Management Science*, 2, 3 (1956), 197-208.

Boulding, K.E., *The World as a Total System*, Sage Publications, 1985.

Buckingham, R.A. R. Hirschheim F.F. Land and C.J. Tully, "Information Systems Curriculum: a Basis for Course Design" in Buckingham, R.A. R. Hirschheim F.F. Land and C.J. Tully, *Information Systems Education: Recommendations and Implementation*, Cambridge University Press, 1987., 1987.

Bunge, M., *A World of Systems*, D. Reidel Publishing Company, 1979.

Carvalho, J.A., "Using the Viable System Model to Describe the Role of Computer-Based Systems in Organisations" in Callaos, Nagib, Linda Holmes and Rodolfo Osers (Eds.), Proceedings of the SCI'98 - World Multiconference on Systems, Cybernetics and Informatics, July 12 - 16, Orlando USA, Volume 4, 1998.

Carvalho, J.Á. and L. Amaral, "Matriz de Actividades: Um Enquadramento Conceptual para as Actividades de Planeamento e Desenvolvimento de Sistemas de Informação", *Sistemas de Informação*, 1 (1993), 37-48 (in Portuguese).

Checkland, P. and S. Holwell, *Information, Systems and Information Systems: Making Sense of the Field*, John Wiley & Sons, 1998.

Checkland, P.B., *Systems Thinking, Systems Practice*, John Willey & Sons, 1981.

Coad, P. and E. Yourdon, *Object-Oriented Analysis*, Yourdon Press/Prentice-Hall, 1991.

Cutts, G., *Structured Systems Analysis and Design Methodology*, Blackwell, 1991.

Davis, G.B., *Management Information Systems: Conceptual Foundations, Structure, and Development*, McGraw-Hill, 1974.

Downs, E. P. Clare and I. Coe, *Structured Systems Analysis and Design Method*, Prentice Hall, 1992.

Ein-Dor, P. and E. Segev, "A Classification of Information Systems: Analysis and Interpretation", *Information Systems Research*, 4, 2 (1993), 166-204.

Falkenberg, E. W. Hesse P. Lindgreen B.E. Nilssen J.L.H. Oei C. Rolland R.K. Stamper F.J.M.V. Assche A.A. Verrijn-Stuart and K. Voss, *FRISCO: A Framework of Information Systems Concepts*, IFIP WG 8.1 Task Group FRISCO, 1996.

Falkenberg, E.D. and P. Lindgreen (Eds.), *Information Systems Concepts: An In-depth Analysis,* North-Holland, 1989.

Falkenberg, E.D. C. Rolland and E.-S.N.-E.-.D. El-Sayed (Eds.), *Information Systems Concepts: Improving the Understanding,* North-Holland, 1992.

Hirschheim, R. H.K. Klein and K. Lyytinen, *Information Systems Development and Data Modelling: Conceptual and Philosophical Foundation*, Cambridge University Press, 1995.

Hoffer, J.A. J.F. George and J.S. Valacich, *Modern Systems Analysis and Design*, Addison-Wesley, 1999.

Jordan, N., *Themes in Speculative Psychology*, Tavistock Publications, 1968.

Kroenke, D. and K.A. Dolan, *Business Computer WSystems: An Introduction*, Mitchell Publishing, 1987.

Laszlo, E., *Systems Science and World Order: Selected Studies*, Pergamon Press, 1983.

Le Moigne, J.-L., *La Théorie du Système Général: Théorie de la Modélisation*, Presses Universitaires de France, 1977 (in French).

Le Moigne, J.-L., "Towards New Epistemological Foundations for Information Systems", *Systems Research*, 2, 3 (1985), 247-251.

Le Moigne, J.L., *La Théorie du Système d' Information Organisationnel*, 1978a (in French).

Le Moigne, J.L., *La Théorie du Système d' Information Organisationnel: 2 La Définition Fonctionelle du SIO*, 1978b (in French).

Le Moigne, J.L., *La Théorie du Système d' Information Organisationnel: 3 La Définition Génétique du SIO*, 1979a (in French).

Le Moigne, J.L., *La Théorie du Système d' Information Organisationnel: 4 La Définition Organique du SIO*, 1979b (in French)

Mingers, J. and F. Stowell (Eds.), *Information Systems: An Emerging Discipline?*, McGraw-Hill, 1997.

Parker, C.S., *Management Information Systems: Strategy and Action*, McGraw-Hill, 1989.

Rolland, C. O. Foucault and G. Benci, *Conception des Systèmes d' Information: La Méthode Rémora*, Editions Eyrolles, 1988 (in French).

Skyttner, L., *General Systems Theory: An Introduction*, Macmillan Press, 1996.

Stamper, R., "Organisational Semiotics" in Mingers, J. and F. Stowell (Eds.), *Information Systems: An Emerging Discipline?*, McGraw-Hill, 1997., 1997.

van Gigch, J.P., *Applied General Systems Theory*, Harper & Row Publishers, 1974.

van Gigch, J.P., *System Design Modeling and Metamodeling*, Plenum Press, 1991.

van Gigch, J.P. and J.-L. Le Moigne, "The Design of an Organisation Information System: Intelligent Artefacts for Complex Organisations", *Information & Management*, 19, (1990), 325-331.

van Griethuysen, J.J. (Eds.), *Concepts and Terminology for the Conceptual Schema and Information Base, Report ISO TC97/SC5 - N 695 from the ISO working group ISO TC97/SC5/WG3 - Conceptual schema,* 1982.

von Bertalanffy, L., *Perspectives on General Systems Theory: Scientific-Philosophical Studies*, George Braziller, New York, 1975.

Wand, Y. D.E. Monarchi J. Parsons and C.C. Woo, "Theoretical Foundations for Conceptual Modelling in Information Systems Development", *Decision Support Systems*, 15, 4 (1995), 285-304.

Wand, Y. and R. Weber, "An Ontological Evaluation of Systems Analysis and Design Methods" in Falkenberg, E.D. and P. Lindgreen, *Information Systems Concepts: An In-depth Analysis*, North-Holland, 1989.

Wand, Y. and R. Weber, "An Ontological Model of an Information System", *IEEE Transactions on Software Engineering*, 16, 11 (1990), 1282-1292.

Wand, Y. and R. Weber, "On the Ontological Expressiveness of Information Systems Analysis and Design Grammars", *Journal of Information Systems*, 3, (1993), 217-237.

Wand, Y. and C.C. Woo, *Object-Oriented Analysis: Is it Really Simple?*, Faculty of Commerce and Business Administration, The University of British Columbia, 1996?

Weber, R., *Ontological Foundations of Information Systems*, Coopers & Lybrand, Australia, 1997.

Winter, M.C. D.H. Brown and P.B. Checkland, "A Role for Soft Systems Methodology in Information Systems Development", *European Journal of Information Systems*, 4, (1995), 130-142.

Yourdon, E., *Modern Structured Analysis*, Prentice-Hall, 1989.

Comments on “Information System? Which One Do You Mean?” by J.A. Carvalho

John Lindsay

Reader in Information Systems Design, Kingston University
United Kindom
Email: lindsay@kingston.ac.uk

1. BROWSING

ABI, Inspec, ISI, LISA, DAI, URL?

I could have spent my ten minutes just on the first word of this paper. Where did the browsing happen? What were the terms browsed? "Information", or "systems", or "information and systems"?

If "information" was used, there would be thousands of hits, if "system" similarly, if a logical and then a much smaller number, but the relation between the words and the concepts means that all sorts of stuff might not have been recalled?

If the author didn't use those words in the title of the document, or the abstractor didn't use them in the abstract, or the controlled vocabulary didn't recognise them, then we don't know what would have been retrieved.

In practice the browsing could have been to cast an eye along the bookshelves; in which case if I did the same, there would be some correspondence and much difference.

It says something about the organisation of knowledge in our discipline that we have no shared compendium, collection or encyclopaedia or form of knowledge organisation.

2. SYSTEM :: HOLISM

bus ;; transport ;; city

The paper discusses first the properties of a system, as a consequence of surveying some of the literature which follows the browsing exercise. There seems to me one important missing concept; that of holism: that the property of a system is that it exhibits a property not present in its components. From the perspective of a designer the important issue is whether this component is the one intended in the design? In other words, does intention produce effect? So a bus is a system which is not just engine, chassis, seats; a transport system is not a conglomeration of buses; and a city is not just a transport system plus housing and employment.

3. ACTION (TO INFORM) :: ACTION (INTENT, EFFECT)

The paper goes on to discuss the nature of information and suggests that it is an action (to inform). This seems to me no where near enough. It has to have added to it that the action to inform is with the intent of producing an effect, another action, in the person (or thing) informed, and that information has happened only if the effect is that intended.

4. IS 1 - 4

Classical classification

Then is developed a classification scheme in four parts for dividing the authors and possibly their concepts into groups with certain properties.

It would take much more space than here available to consider this with the many others in order to decide their usefulness. Here only to remark that in classical classification we have the concepts of taxis, genera, symmetry, entaxis and parataxis, and we might look at this scheme with that framework.

5. IST + C + ASSYRIA =/ TD

The author goes on to suggest what might dangerously approach a technological determinism with his IST, and he leaves out communication, which is not the same as computation, though it might use a computer. In ancient Assyria the land taxation system was build of person, land parcel, good, output, tax level, and the accounts were constructed by reordering the clay tablets. This efficient system had an effect on the society, but deciding the relation between the society and the system gives us the same set of problems we have today.

6. EXAMPLES

FX, Postcode, barcode. UDC, ATA, Read code, Grid reference

There are then a few examples of "systems" and how they fit into the classification. At this point I add a paragraph I didn't say during the discussion for I left a couple of minutes to allow discussion of the list I put here, yet there was none. The list of acronyms at the top I thought some people would know and others not, but this list I suspected contained some which would be uncommon. From the absence of question I draw a conclusion.

7. KM, TQM, BPR, BSE

Then there is a discussion of frameworks like FRISCO, which have been fashionable at various stages to which perhaps could be added knowledge management, total quality management, perhaps Checkland, UML, XML, Zackman, SSADM, RAD, DSDM, Multiview to see whether the classification stands up?

We seem still to me to be addressing the problem of whether information systems design has information as the dominant planet with systems, science, management, etc as moons; information and systems as dipoles or logical ands; system as the planet with information as a moon along with transport, logistical, operational, etc; or information systems as a new thing in the way water does not contain the properties of hydrogen and oxygen.

It is what I call our version of BSE, mad cow disease: do we regard information systems design as a business, a science or engineering, and of which do we use the proof protocols?

The 'Information' Concept in FRISCO Compared to Empirical Studies of Information in Decision Making

Jens Kaasbøll

Department of Informatics, University of Oslo

Key words: Human behavior, Decision-making processes, Information in organizations, Relevance of information

Abstract: The Framework of Information System Concepts has been based on assumptions of rationality. Three findings from studies of people's use of information in organizations are presented: expertise, cognitive illusions, and information as signal and symbol. FRISCO with a few extensions could be used for describing these phenomena. When defining concepts concerning social affairs, each choice may bring in assumptions that influence how system developers used these concepts. Discussing different precise definitions of the same concepts may bring up preconceptions that otherwise might have hidden issues in a development project.

1. INTRODUCTION

FRISCO (1996) constitutes probably the most comprehensive attempt at building a conceptual platform for the subject of information systems. This subject was grounded on use of computers for administrative purposes and production control in companies. The inclusion of both human and computer issues has prevailed, and in recent years development of computer systems and organisations has merged to a greater extent than ever before.

Various debates have emerged over the issue of whether to base the subject in the scholarly worlds of computer science or in a humanistic discipline, and theories from both areas have been considered, without any one standing out as the obvious core of an information systems discipline.

An early IFIP-definition defines "information" as "... the meaning that a human assigns to data by means of the known conventions used in its representation." (IFIP-ICC, 1966). This definition points to a core of the discipline, being the relation between people and computers. Lots of research on information has been carried out since then, and the concept seems to remain a core one, since also FRISCO has put effort into its definition.

At least two reasons point to the need for precise definitions in our field. First, if the concept is going to be implemented on the computer, e.g., "entity," "object" and "data," precision is required. Regarding information as something on people's minds, this reason does not apply. Second, the way people express themselves during system development may influence the design of the application. For instance, when a system developer asks whether a described system design satisfies a user's need for information, both the developer and the user operate on the basis of their preconceptions of what information is and for what purpose it is going to be used. The developer assumes that information is an entity of which a user can know her or his needs, and the user who accepts the system description assumes that information is something that a computer system can provide. If any of these preconceptions are incorrect, the design process may provide a less desirable result. Therefore, clarifying assumptions behind central concepts may help system developers so that they avoid some sources of misunderstanding. "Information" seems to be such a basic concept in the discipline of information systems.

This paper will briefly review the current conception of information and data used in routine operations, and then present some empirical findings on information use. The material will be used for discussing FRISCO's concept of information and the more general problem of bridging the worlds of rational ideals and descriptions of information use in the information system discipline.

2. SEMANTICS

The basic view that information is people's interpretation and data is in the realm of computers has survived and been elaborated since the IFIP definition from 1966. Langefors (1966) emphasized the relation between data and its use in control of business operations. His ideas were operationalized in methods, put into practice in system development projects, and elaborated by many researchers. In a recent contribution in Langefors's tradition, Goldkuhl (1995) regards data in a communicative setting with sender and receivers and with semantic and pragmatic aspects. The semantic aspect captures the fact that information is about something, and this aboutness requires the appropriate context and conventions for interpretation.

FRISCO's definition is

Information is the knowledge increment brought about by a receiving action in a message transfer, i.e. it is the difference between the conceptions interpreted from a received message and the knowledge before the receiving action.

This seems to be in line with the view of information being a result of data being interpreted, while the aboutness is not explicitly mentioned. Nesting up FRISCO's definition of underlying concepts, we see that a conception is an interpretation of a perception, which is the result of observing a domain, which comprises parts or aspects of the world. A reasonable interpretation of this is that "information in the FRISCO sense is about parts or aspects," hence the aboutness is established.

3. INFORMATION FOR FORMALIZABLE DOMAINS

Goldkuhl (1995) argues that the main use of information in business is that a sender intends the receivers to act in some way on the basis of the information received, such that the sender should refer to the same semantic contents as the receiver. Information should therefore be considered both at the sender and the receiver ends of communication. Nilsson's reflection in the FRISCO report points to the same need.

FRISCO places information at the receiver end of communication only. In its model of communication, the term "conception of message" (p.71) is used where Goldkuhl uses "information."

Information systems have for long supported routine operations in business. In a work process one person completes her or his operation and enters this into the computer system. Others will be informed by reading the data and carrying out the appropriate task. When the domain is easily formalizable, as e.g., in simple cases of trade, companies successfully let the computer system transfer information by which business operations are controlled.

FRISCO defines:

An **organisational system** is a special kind of system, being normally dynamic, active and open, and comprising the conception of how an organisation is composed (i.e. of specific actors and actands) and how it operates (i.e. performing specific actions in pursuit of organisational goals, guided by organisational rules and informed by internal and external communication), where its systemic properties are that it responds to (certain kinds of) changes caused by the system environment and, itself, causes (certain kinds of) changes in the system environment.

An "information system" is subsequently defined as a sub-system of an organisational system. Since the super-system of an information system is operating by pursuing goals guided by rules, information systems are assumed to operate the same way. This seems to be well aligned with information systems for easily formalizable domains.

4. EXPERT INTUITION

When people have become experts at interpreting data and making decisions, the relation between data and information may become unintelligible for others. This section will present empirical evidence of expert behaviour, and discuss FRISCO's concepts in relation to these.

Psychology has found that for learning to occur, feedback has to be immediate, unambiguous and consistent (Balzer et al, 1989). Another relevant finding is that when learning concepts and classification, and hence prediction, learning cannot surpass theoretical knowledge for constructing well-defined categories.

Consider the following example by Perby (1987). The meteorologists at an airport base their work on observations, weather maps, satellite pictures, conversations with pilots and glances out of the window. From these different sources of data, they compile the "notion of the weather development in all three dimensions of the atmosphere over a period of time which stretches into the future" (p.217) which they call the "inner weather picture."

Concerning the conditions for learning, the time period between making of the forecast and the actual weather conditions prevents an immediate feedback on the forecast itself. When the period is down to half an hour, the delay may be short enough for the meteorologists to remember their forecast and adjust their method of forecasting if necessary. The observation of the local weather is immediate, unambiguous and consistent through continuous local observations and looking out of the window. The categories used for local forecasting do not differ from those of the science of meteorology. The conditions for learning seem therefore mostly to be fulfilled. An indication that the meteorologists actually learn making better forecasts is found in a quotation where one of them speaks of a more experienced colleague: "It strikes me repeatedly that he knows more about the prevailing weather than he has really been informed about—and he is right." (Perby, 1987, p.219).

From the point of view that information is what people who interpret data cognise, the inner weather picture seems to constitute the meteorologists' information of the weather. Also considering information as the basis for decisions, inner weather picture constitutes the information upon which decisions concerning forecasts are made, if not to say that the information also includes these decisions. The relation between data and information seems to be only for the expert meteorologists to establish and impossible to describe such that others can interpret the data in the same way.

Having established that some experts have the exclusive ability to establish some relations between data and information, system developers cannot describe the way these relations are made up. The conceptual basis for information systems should therefore allow the such relations to occur.

The core of FRISCO's information concept is a knowledge increment, i.e., an alteration of the person's mind. This knowledge increment is a result of receiving a message and the person's knowledge before the receiving. A message is data transmitted by a sender and intended for others to receive. Data is again representations of knowledge expressed in a language.

First, in the meteorologist case, reading the observations, maps, satellite pictures and talking to pilots seem to constitute receptions of messages, which again are representations of knowledge communicated to the meteorologist. These actions of receiving therefore seem to be covered by the information concept in FRISCO.

Second, the meteorologists need their expertise in receiving the data in order to obtain their inner weather pictures, and this prior knowledge is also mentioned in the FRISCO definition.

Third, FRISCO does not assume any specific relation between data and information, thus also catering for the meteorologists' way of doing it.

Forth, the meteorologists also look directly at the weather outside the window when building up their inner weather picture. This action of direct observation does not involve any reception of messages from another human being. Other studies of work (e.g., Benner, 1984; Kaasbøll, 1985; Wynn, 1979) have reported similar findings of people being informed also through observation without any communication taking place.

In summary, FRISCO's concept of information seems to cater for experts' information, except that the concept should also include actions of perception.

Considering that FRISCO includes "information" and "knowledge," there can be little reason to keep the concept of learning away from the framework. Since this section concerns learning taking place under the conditions mentioned above, the following definition is suggested, based in FRISCO's concepts:

Expertise is knowledge based on theoretical types (="categories" in FRISCO terms), gained through repeated feedback in the forms of message reception or perception, which followed immediately after actions based on the knowledge was carried out, such that the feedback could be interpreted unambiguously and consistently.

This definition will be used in the next section.

5. COGNITIVE ILLUSIONS

Often the conditions for learning referred in the previous section are not met. In these cases, people use their general cognitive skills, which are strictly limited in a number of ways. Decades of psychological experiments unanimously point to weaknesses of people's cognitive abilities, called "cognitive illusions" (von Winterfeldt and Edwards, 1986). These are defined as follows.

- **A formal rule specifies how to determine a correct answer.**
- **A judgement is made without the aid of physical tools.**
- **There exists a systematic discrepancy between the correct answer and the judged answer. Random errors do not count**

The systematic errors that people make include: ignoring information that seems less relevant, ignoring underlying statistical distributions, overestimating events that are easily recalled, ignoring sample size, underestimating combinatorial explosion and exponential growth, changing mind slower than data indicates, having overconfidence in covariance, exaggerating what could have been anticipated and exaggerating the quality of one's own predictions (Kahneman et al, 1982).

When making decisions in organizations and the criteria for learning are not met, people confronted with a large number of data make the cognitive illusions errors. The information they obtain becomes dysfunctional for the decisions they are going to make. Decisions made through simple calculations based on the two or three most relevant predictors would have yielded better results (Dawes et.al., 1989). E.g., when admitting students, selections made on the basis of previous exams outperform selections where individual interviews and letters of recommendations are taken into consideration.

Since the myth of the human intellectual capacity over calculations in this respect seems to flourish in organizations, we will find numerous and systematically created cases where people's information are erroneous or at least of inferior quality.

When considering the information concept, cognitive illusions trigger the need for separating a descriptive concept of people's information from a normative concept of what information people should have had. FRISCO mentions "false information" in note under the definition of information, but false information covers deliberate lies, while cognitive illusions are unintended.

Information systems are often created with the aim of improving the bases for decision making, which seems to be in line with FRISCO's assumptions. Whether a framework of information system concepts should cater for descriptive versus normative accounts of information is a question of how far one will go in pursuing issues relating to information quality.

Except for its motivation, the process of change of information systems seems to be outside the scope of FRISCO. Given the complexity of such processes, their conceptual framework would have been as voluminous as the FRISCO one. However, since the point of the work of information system specialists often is changing systems, an extension of the framework to include concepts for separating between existing and planned information system qualities could be beneficial. Then we could say, that the current information in the system is cluttered, while a planned change supports decisions made on the basis on the most relevant data.

The concepts "decision" and "relevance" seem necessary to include to cope with cognitive illusions. FRISCO mentions that information is used by the receiver, and rational decisions constitute the normal aim for information. The concept "decision" can be defined with reference to other FRISCO concepts:

> A **decision** is the choice amongst alternative <u>actions</u>, based on <u>knowledge</u>.

"Relevance" of knowledge for a decision can be defined based on its effect on the quality of decisions or on the way this knowledge has come to existence. The former introduces the need for evaluating quality of decisions, which may be an impossible target. The latter can refer to the two ways of providing the knowledge described in the current and the previous sections. With this background, the definition may go:

> The **relevance for decision** of <u>knowledge</u> is its degree of significance as found through either <u>expertise</u> or research.

The rcference to research leaves the issues of the degree of significance to the merits of the research methods employed.

6. INFORMATION FOR DECISION MAKING

The kind of business operation outlined in the previous sections may correspond to the major bulk of day-to-day operations of a company. Studies of information use in non-routine decision making reveals that decisions are made on grounds that may be all but rational and formalizable. In a survey of a large number of studies of decision making in organizations, Feldman and March (1981) summarized information use:

1. Much of the information that is gathered and communicated by individuals and organizations has little decision making relevance.
2. Much of the information that is used to justify a decision is collected and interpreted after the decision has been made, or substantially made.
3. Much of the information gathered in response to requests for information is not considered in the making of decisions for which it was requested.
4. Regardless of the information available at the time a decision is first considered, more information is requested.
5. Complaints that an organization does not have enough information to make a decision occur while available information is ignored.
6. The relevance of the information provided in the decision-making process to the decision being made is less conspicuous than is the insistence on information. (p.174)

Feldman and March provide some instrumental and some cultural for these findings. The instrumental ones are summarized here:

- **The cost of collecting information is underestimated, because collecting usually occurs in other parts of the organization than where cost is accounted for.**
- **It is safer for decisions makers to have information that is not needed than not to have information that might be needed.**
- **Organizations are monitoring their environment for surprises, which could constitute new alternatives or changes in the world. The gossip gathered is often irrelevant, and the relevance cannot be specified in advance.**
- **Communication in organization happens in a context of conflicts and with consciousness of possible decision consequences. Actors produce information for persuading others, and competition turns persuasion into a contest in most unreliable information.**

The two former reasons given do not indicate information use that transcends FRISCO's definition of knowledge increment through message receiving. The third reason points to that the act of actively collecting information is at least as abundant as that of passively being informed.

These three reasons indicate that relevance of information is a concept that often has to be used, and that much information is irrelevant regardless of decisions, and that degree of relevance often cannot be determined or at least can only be determined after the decisions has been made.

The latter reason given indicates that FRISCO's note concerning false information and dis-information may deserve more attention in a conceptual framework where the information concept is a central one.

In the ongoing power games in organizations, people try making sense of what is happening in their own ways (Weick, 1995). Being in power is related to producing the most convincing information, based on the situation that people recognise. This points to the problematic side of labelling some information true and other false. People may be convinced that information that they had considered intentionally false or unlikely actually constitutes the most appropriate information concerning a particular subject.

More important than the instrumental reasons are, according to Feldman and March, the symbolic and signalling values of information. Referring to information symbolizes intelligent choice, and this there is no value closer to the core of Western civilizaton than this which symbolizes correct behaviour. Information also signalizes legitimacy of decisions.

Feldman and March do not tell precisely whether by the term "information" they mean data or "information in the head." If meaning data, and assuming that much of this data has been interpreted, their explanations nevertheless have the same substance.

The symbolic and signalling values of information pose the same challenge to information relevance as mentioned under the instrumental reasons above.

For the FRISCO concepts of information and data, one question raised is whether FRISCO concepts can be used to say that "information" and "data" can symbolize competence, status, wealth, power, etc. Looking at FRISCO's concepts, nothing seems to prevent that anything can represent, or symbolize, anything else. The relation between the representation and its meaning is determined by the person interpreting the representation.

7. THE BEHAVIOURISTIC ARGUMENT

The finding from cognitive illusions that data in addition to the two to three most relevant ones clutters up information, points to another challenge for FRISCO. Since information is defined as a cognitive quality, the unreliable method of introspection must be used in order to get hold of it. When people who read "Singh: Age 38" respond to the question of what information they received, and they respond: "Singh is 38 years," introspection may seem pretty OK. However, if the age constituted the fourteenth factor that the receiver added to her or his knowledge when considering admitting Singh for a Master's program, the receiver may have much more trouble explaining how this fact altered her or his aggregate impression of the candidate. According to the findings of cognitive illusions, the receiver would be well beyond the level of sensemaking, although she or he would probably try to express her or his impression in a perfectly rational manner.

Similar shortcomings can be found in the realm of non-routine decisions. Few people would admit that they collect information in order to strengthen their status and power.

The shortcoming of introspection has also been noted by Stamper in his reflections in FRISCO, and he refers to an alternative approach. Behaviouristic alternatives can be found in psychology, pedagogy and other social sciences.

A problem with purely behaviouristic descriptions is that they often become superficial, while when dealing with people and information systems, system developers have to come as close as possible to an emphatic understanding of other people.

Material phenomena and behaviour can be observed and measured. This gives an outside view of cultural phenomena. (Pike, 1967). Knowledge of intentions, meanings, values, rules, etc., has to be inferred from the behavioural patterns. The way to test whether or not an outside description is adequate, is to relate it to observations of people's behaviour, without asking them about their own opinion of the descriptions. When studying behaviour as seen from persons inside the culture, the researcher has to interact with the people in the culture, in order to learn about their own accounts of their plans, goals, values, meanings, etc., and their own explanations of their behaviour (Pike, 1967, p.37, Harris, 1990, p.53). The evaluation of whether an inside description of people's thoughts is adequate and accurate depends on the opinion of the people themselves (Harris, 1975, p.159). The combined inside and outside perspectives provides a richer picture of users' knowledge than if only using one of the two perspectives (Kaasbøll, 1995). Whether this richness provides valuable insight or clutters up clear information remains to be seen.

8. DEFINING INFORMATION

Including the option that people get informed both by receiving messages and by observing the world, FRISCO's information definition can be extended to cover this:

Information is the knowledge increment brought about by a receiving action in a message transfer or by perception, i.e. it is the difference between the conceptions interpreted from a received message or from a perception and the knowledge before the receiving action.

Expertise was defined in section 5. Based on the definition of information suggested above, it may be redefined as:

Expertise is knowledge based on theoretical types, gained through repeated information, which followed immediately after actions based on the knowledge was carried out, such that the information was obtained unambiguously and consistently.

Building further on FRISCO's definitions, rational decision making could also be easily catered for. This indicates that FRISCO can be easily extended as long as the domain covered corresponds to FRISCO's basic worldview.

The empirical studies referred point to two levels of ambition for defining information. First, information can be defined regardless of its quality and use. This corresponds to FRISCO's stance, where the definition relies on the way information came about. Second, qualities of the information can be regarded, including the relation between information and what it represents and the purposes and use of the information.

8.1 Introspective inquiry into information

For information systems to add value, the systems have to respond to people's requests for data, so that their needs for information are be satisfied. The concepts of data provision and information needs could therefore also be included in FRISCO.

Since the definition of information in FRISCO is based on people's previous knowledge and what they receive or perceive, each person will be informed in her or his own way, and there is no way of knowing how others get informed. The definitions of information and expertise do therefore not point to any easy ways of determining needs for data when designing computer systems.

Another way of determining which data to support through computerization is to supply data to people and ask whether they get informed according to their needs for information. An operational way of defining needs is therefore:

Information need is a human actor's knowledge of her or his lack of information.

Satisfaction of information needs occur when human actors state that their needs are satisfied by the data provided.

Data provision is the sum of data available to a human actor.

Satisfaction of data provision occurs when human actors' information needs are satisfied.

A practical consequence of these definitions is that people do not have to state their intentions and use of information when determining whether their needs are satisfied. Considering people's decision making behaviour and power struggles, being able to state needs without revealing reasons may ease the acceptance of computer systems and also support the existing behaviour. The cognitive illusions are also given ample opportunities when people already receiving lots of irrelevant and disturbing data are determining their needs for more.

This way of defining and operationalizing information through introspection helps the system developers to understand people's needs for information. Even so, when avoiding requesting their reasons for their needs, people's information behaviour can be preserved.

8.2 Information as a social entity

The consequence of the definition of information needs above points to the option of defining information needs based on socially available characteristics, e.g., tasks to be performed or status to be achieved. The definition could be

Information need is the socially accepted knowledge of the lack of information of those who have to use this information for achieving their socially known goals.

By stating that information needs should be derived from socially known goals, people would be required to discuss goals and intentions that they unlikely reveal. This requirement would therefore probably make the discovery of information needs very difficult, except for goals rooted in organizational tasks. If information needs stemming from goals like power games or culturally unrecognised goals were considered, people have a tendency to fake reasons that are more aligned with the organizational culture.

9. CONCLUSION

FRISCO defines information as a conceptual event which takes place when people receive messages from others. Information is therefore not going to be implemented at any computer system, so no precise definition is needed for this reason.

The other reason for considering the concept is that getting to know people's needs for information is of central concern when developing information systems. FRISCO was extended in two attempts so that it also covered need for information. On the one hand, basing information needs on people's subjective conceptions without requiring insight into their goals will hide people's poor ability to judge their needs when they already have too much information. On the other hand, having to state goals make people fake rational reasons when their goals are likely to be judged as anti-social, counter-productive or otherwise not acceptable.

Discussions of central concepts may be effective in order to increase the awareness of future system developers on such issues. Instead of refraining from attempts at defining the concepts precisely, the implications of different definitions need to be considered. Developers may realize more of their prejudices when being confronted with choices which are based on different assumptions and have implications on the fulfilment of their tasks.

10. REFERENCES

Balzer, W.K.; Doherty, M.E.; O'Connor, R. (1989) Effects of cognitive feedback on performance. *Psychological Bulletin,* 106, 410–433

Benner, P. (1984*) From Novice to Expert: Excellence and Power in Clinical Nursing Practice.* Addison-Wesley, Menlo Park, Cal.

Dawes, R.M.; Faust, D.; Meehl, P.E. (1989) Clinical Versus Actuarial Judgement. *Science,* 343, 1668–1674

Falkenberg, E.D. et al (1996) *FRISCO: A Framework of Information System Concepts.* The IFIP WG 8.1 Task Group FRISCO http://www.wi.leidenuniv.nl/~verrynst/frisco.html

Feldman, M.S. and March, J.G. (1981) Information in Organizations as Signal and Symbol *Administrative Science Quarterly* 26, 171–186

Goldkuhl (1995) Information as Action and Communication. In Dahlbom (ed.) *The Infological Equation: Essays in honour of Börje Langefors.* Gothenburg Studies in Information Systems. Report 6

Harris, M. (1975) *Culture, People, Nature: An introduction to general anthropology,* Second Edition, Thomas Y. Crowell, New York. First edition

Harris, M (1990) Emics and Etics Revisited. In T.N. Headland, K.L. Pike, and M. Harris (eds.) *Emics and Etics: The Insider/Outsider Debate,* Sage Publications, Newbury Park, California, 48–61

International Federation for Information Processing and International Computation Centre, Joint Technical Committee on Terminology (1966) *Vocabulary of Information Processing.* North-Holland, Amsterdam, 1966

Kaasbøll, J. (1985) Observation of Human Information Processing as a Technique in System Development. In Lassen and Mathiassen (eds.) *The Eight Scandinavian Research Seminar on Systemeering.* University of Århus

Kaasbøll, J. (1995) Knowledge from the inside and outside in participative development and research on participative development. In G. Pervan and M. Newby (eds.) *6th Australasian Conference on Information Systems* Curtin University, Perth, 413–429

Kahneman, D.; Slovic, P.; Tversky, A. (1982) *Judgement under uncertainty: Heuristics and biases.* Cambridge University Press, Cambridge

Langefors, Börje (1966) *Theoretical Analysis of Information Systems.* Fourth Edition, Auerbach Publishers, Philadelphia, Pa., 1973. First published by Studentlitteratur, Lund, Sweden, 1966

Perby, Maja-Lisa (1987) Computerization and the Skill in Local Weather Forecasting. In Bjerknes, Ehn, and Kyng (eds.) *Computers and Democracy: A Scandinavian Challenge,* 213–229

Pike, K.L. (1967)*Language in Relation to a Unified Theory of the Structure of Human Behaviour* Second, revised edition, Mouton & Co, The Hague. Preliminary edition, 1954. First edition, 1959

Weick, K.E. (1995) *Sensemaking in Organizations.* Sage Publications, Thousand Oaks, CA

von Winterfeldt and Edwards (1986) *Decision analysis and behavioural research.* Cambridge University Press

Wynn, E.H. (1979) *Office Conversation as an Information Medium.* University of California, Berkeley

Comments on "The 'Information' Concept in FRISCO Compared to Empirical Studies of Information in Decision Making" by J. Kaasbøll

Deborah Bunker

Deborah Bunker, School of Information Systems, Technology and Management, University of New South Wales, Kensington, NSW 2052, Australia.
d.bunker@unsw.edu.au

The author's discussion of FRISCO, and its approach to "building a conceptual platform for the subject of information systems" raises many interesting issues for our field of research and practice. The need for "precise definitions" in our field, is highlighted due to the nature of the technology which supports information systems (IS). This point raises the issue of the many different perspectives, users of a single computer based IS (CBIS) might have, and how these can be accommodated in its design and creation. The idea of "rational ideals and descriptions of information use" is supported by the characteristics of an IS and the supporting technology, but are the ideals and descriptions of CBIS use purely rational?

There are many participants within an organisational framework who are not only required to make decisions but also act out cultural, political and social agendas. The author feels that "clarifying assumptions behind central concepts" is the way forward for more successful system design, and this idea is also a key motivation for FRISCO, however, cultural, political and social differences (all of which affect what each individual means by information) also need to be addressed as part of an overall systems building approach [Baskerville [1995]].

A way forward for the author's ideas and the FRISCO approach might be to look at the way we use language as a symbolic representation of culture [Young [1971]]. The author states that "a sender [of information] intends the receivers to act in some way on the basis of the information received, such that the sender should refer to the same semantic contents as the receiver". Language and the values, beliefs and norms on which it is based, therefore, shape information and the system that delivers it. The tools we use both physically/conceptually to create and use CBIS are also passed from one generation to the next through the use of the language [Young [1971], Bunker[1998]]. FRISCO can be seen, therefore, as a conceptual tool based on certain cultural underpinnings (use of language) which need to be understood for diffusion purposes.

The author also looks at the role of information, data, the relationship between them and how expertise, learning and observation affect perception, action, knowledge and interpretation. The cultural aspects of expertise (experts versus generalists), learning (polychronic/cyclical versus mono-chronic/linear) and observation (revealed truth versus experimentation) are all areas that the IS discipline needs to address with some rigor in order to ensure that tools, such as FRISCO, are well understood and applied in the most effective way [Hofstede [1998], Schein [1984]].

The author states that "Knowledge of intentions, meanings, values, rules, etc, has to be inferred from behavioural patterns." Do CBIS tools force us into a certain method of operation which infers certain behavioural patterns? If we consider, that even though we know that it is possible to create Web sites that are non-English language based, the origin, history and nature of the Internet and its use as a means of globalisation, necessitates the use of the originator's own cultural symbolic communication (language) as the communications "protocol" [Pargman [1998]].

In reading this paper there appears to be two specific areas that may be appropriate topics for further research. What are the values, norms and beliefs which underpin FRISCO? Understanding the motivation and assumptions on which FRISCO is based, will ensure that it is used appropriately. What are the values, norms and beliefs which underpin CBIS? It is only in understanding what these tools are attempting to represent, that we can create and use them in an effective manner [Bunker [1998]]. Too many systems have been created, promising success, which have then gone onto fail while consuming a vast amount of organisational resources.

In conclusion the author discusses the FRISCO approach and how attempts at applying it highlight the richness of social phenomona, thus limiting its applicability. This is by no means a negative statement. FRISCO's strength lies within the detailing of the values, norms and beliefs on which it is based. The articluation and understanding of these assumptions should ensure that it is used appropriately. Let us consider part of FRISCO's motivation. Why is there the need for such a framework? We have seen that historically we have had little success in the creation and design of systems and also there have been issues relating to the legitimisation of the IS "discipline". FRISCO provides us with an example of a well constructed and documented tool to utilise and study within our disciplinary area, thus giving us an opportunity to gain insight and knowledge.

References

Baskerville, R. [1995] "Structural entropy model of technology transfer" in Kautz, K., Pries-Heje, J., Larsen, T. & Sorgaard, P. (Eds), Proceedings of the First IFIP TC8 Working Conference on Diffusion and Adoption of Information Technology, October, 14-17,1995, Leangkollen, Oslo, Norway. Conference Notebook.

Bunker, D.J. [1998] "A Philosophy of Information Technology and Systems (IT & S) as Tools:Tool Development Context, Associated Skills and the Global Technical Transfer (GTT) Process." MIS – shaped or misshaped ? Emerging issues in the new global arena. Proceedings of IFIP WG 8.7 Working Conference, Helsinki, Finland, 1998.

Hofstede, G. [1998] 'Attitudes, Values and Organisational Culture: Disentangling the Concepts' Organisation Studies, 19/3.

Pargman, D. [1998] "Reflections on Cultural Bias and Adaptation" from C. Ess and F. Sudweeks (eds), Proceedings of Cultural Attitudes Towards Communication and Technology '98, University of Sydney, Australia.

Schein, Edgar H. [1984] *Coming to a New Awareness of Organisational Culture*, Sloan Management Review, Winter.

Young [1971] *An Introduction to the Study of Man*, Oxford, Clarendon Press.

Keynote Address: Formal and Informal Aspects of Intelligent Agent-based Systems

John-Jules Ch. Meyer

Utrecht University, Department of Computer Science,
Intelligent Systems Group,
P.O. Box 80099, 3508 TB Utrecht,
The Netherlands

email: jj@cs.uu.nl

Key words: Intelligent agents, Agent-oriented programming, Modal logic, Multi-agent systems

Abstract: Recently on the borderline between computer science, software engineering and artificial intelligence the subject of *intelligent agents* has become in the limelight very much, cf. [WJ94]. Interestingly much work has been done on both the foundations and practical applications of agent technology. However, as yet there remains a big gap between these two in the sense that it is not obvious at all how the foundational work on agent logics and other formalisms relate to the practice of designing and implementing agent-based systems for such applications as the web and other user assistants more in general, but also for the control of hardware entities such as intelligent robots. In this paper we will discuss some of the work that has been done on the foundations of agents as well as the problems that remain to 'bridge the gap' between theory and practice.

1. INTRODUCTION

The area of intelligent agents is an emerging technology which is aimed at constructing more 'intelligent' software in the sense that such software does not merely react to a user but is also supposed to anticipate on its user's needs and interests [Mae95]. A key concept here is that of *autonomy*. Agent software should possess a certain degree of autonomy in order to be able to fulfil the requirement of being *proactive* instead of merely *reactive*. In the literature many words are spent (or spilt as some people would say) on the definition of an agent, not unlike the endless discussions one or two decades ago on the definition of an object in the object-oriented programming paradigm.

In this paper I will not attempt to try and give yet another definition of what an agent is, nor do I intend to repeat the many definitions from the extensive literature on this topic. Rather I like to focus on a few aspects concerning the concept of an intelligent agent. Viewed from a distance it is of course quite interesting to see a community searching for the 'right' definitions and concepts concerning a new technology, and I myself think it is certainly not a waste of time to think about this carefully and make an inventory of the possibilities. On the other hand the field should not be blocked by this activity, since there is already a lot of interesting things to be done employing partial definitions or by maintaining various distinct variants of definitions / notions. As an aside we remark that Lakatos [LM70] argued for the rationale of the practice of having multiple distinct theories available in the methodology of the exact sciences. In the case of agent technology I believe this is even more rational since it is quite possible that in the end there will be several kinds of intelligent agents. For example, it is not *a priori* evident at all that agents that will be designed for obtaining information from the Web will have the same characteristics as those that will be employed for controlling pieces of hardware like e.g. intelligent robots.

What in my opinion makes an agent interesting from a scientific point of view is that in order to display some kind of autonomy it will have to be endowed with several *attitudes* for which some kind of 'mental state' of the agent is a convenient metaphor. Of course, one can now engage in very troublesome discussions as to the nature of such a mental state, and if / how it relates to human mental states, but for the purpose of this paper I will not discuss this in much depth since in my view the use of a mental state as a metaphor is already a very potent means for describing and specifying (the behaviour of) intelligent agents. This is especially so since in philosophy there has been done much work on several of these mental or cognitive aspects from a perspective of *logic*. The notions that are arising from this work are particularly fit to be used for a foundation of intelligent agents since these abstract away from the human / psychological aspect, so that they are in principle amenable to artifacts as well. In robotics this has been realised recently in a new subarea called *cognitive robotics* ([D98]).

The logic referred to in the last paragraph is known under the name *modal logic*, the logic of *modality*. In this context by modalities are meant things like knowledge, belief, time, desires, goals, intentions, obligations, etc., in fact quite a range of distinct notions that have to do with the mental or cognitive state of an agent.

Interestingly, although these are all formal logics in the strict sense of the word, the notions they describe are still rather vague or abstract in the sense that still many more concrete instances of these notions are captured by them, and no particular choice is made. I regard this 'vagueness' as a feature rather than as a bug: as argued before this enables us to use these logics for describing the mental states of agents in an abstract way which allows for a non-human implementation of these mental states. This is what I mean by the metaphoric use of these mentalistic concepts: they allow us to structure the architecture of the systems we like to build without having to look too much at implementations as they occur in nature (such as the human brain).

On the other hand, unfortunately the abstract notions of the modalities as defined by modal logic also cause in some sense the problem of 'bridging the gap' between (logical) theory and practice, since by their very abstract nature they do not give much indication as to how these notions should be implemented into a real system. However, as I shall argue in the sequel this problem might be overcome by means of the use of a modal logic that is close to the notion of programming (viz. dynamic logic [Har84]).

2. MENTAL STATES AS SYSTEM STATES

A very important notion when considering systems — whether artificial or not — is that of a (system) state. Since the beginning of computer science this has been realised, and one encounters states in e.g. automata theory and the semantics of programming languages. Usually there is also some notion of state transition capturing how computation proceeds stepwise by means of executing a program, for example. In the semantics of programming this idea has given rise to the formal notion of a transition system which is a formal system by means of which one can derive transitions of the system / program at hand.

In programming agents or agent-oriented programming, as it is called since [Sho91, Sho93], the notion of a state also occurs naturally, but whereas in traditional programming the state typically involves such matters like the values of variables, here things are a bit more involved. Using the mentalistic metaphor one arrives at the concept of a *mental state* of an agent [HS93], which evolves over time. So what kind of things should we think of when talking about an agent's mental state? Well, it depends on the application and the particular kind of agent one needs for this. Generally one can say that in order to display some kind of autonomy the agent needs to have the disposal of *information* and, perhaps more controversially, *motivation*. So the agent has to maintain certain *knowledge* about the environment it is to work in (or perhaps rather *beliefs*, since the information maintained may not be actually true of the world / environment; for instance it may be outdated or just obtained erroneously by means of a faulty communication or sensor device). But in order to be proactive and anticipate on things that happen in its environment it is also necessary to equip an agent with some motivational attitudes, such as the maintenance of goals and commitments. These things should all be recorded in the agent's mental state. So we have to find some means to express this in a precise and formal way.

3. MODAL LOGIC

As said before, for this we may resort to work in philosophical logic, and *modal logic* in particular. Modal logic is a very elegant and general framework to express the modalities as mentioned above [Che80]. It is an extension of classical logic by a special operator $\Box$ (or multiple of these) denoting some kind of 'modality'. Typical examples of modalities concern the notions of knowledge and belief, but also time, action, obligation, desires and intentions. Therefore modal logic seems an excellent tool to be used for describing and specifying intelligent agents. A 'neutral' reading of the $\Box$ operator is 'necessarily', but depending on the application it can also be read as 'it is known / believed that', 'always in the future it holds that', 'after performance of the action it holds that', 'it is obligatory / desired / intended that'. Of course, the operator will enjoy different properties for these different readings, but there are some properties that are common to all. The most prominent among these is a property called (K):

$$\Box(\varphi \to \psi) \to (\Box\varphi \to \Box\psi)$$

or equivalently

$$(\Box(\varphi \to \psi) \wedge \Box\varphi) \to \Box\psi)$$

which expresses that if is necessary that φ implies ψ, then if it is necessary that φ then it also necessary that ψ. For knowledge we additionally have the following properties:

$\Box\varphi \to \varphi$ *'knowledge is true'*
$\Box\varphi \to \Box\Box\varphi$ *'knowledge is known'*
$\neg\Box\varphi \to \Box\neg\Box\varphi$ *'ignorance is known'*

The last property is rather controversial. Philosophers generally deny this property while computer scientists normally adopt it. Although the reasons for this adoption by computer scientists of this third property, called *negative introspection* varies, one might for simplicity's sake think of situations in computer-based systems like databases where the knowledge ascribed to the system is finitary, so that in principle it becomes possible for such a system to infer that something is *not* known (see further [MH95], [FHMV95]).

For belief we have similar properties (the negative introspection is deemed even more acceptable in this case, also for philosophers!). However, it is not reasonable that beliefs are true, so the first property is replaced by a weaker one (called (D)):

$$\neg\Box\bot \quad \textit{'belief is not inconsistent'}$$

For deontic and intentional notions like desires and goals mostly not many properties beyond the basic ones like (K) is assumed. Obligations and goals generally are taken to satisfy (D).

4. MENTAL STATES IN MODAL LOGIC: EPISTEMIC STATES ETC.

While states in traditional (imperative) programming contain information about such things as the values of programming variables, in agent-oriented programming we need to store / represent more sophisticated information. Models for modal logic are suited very well for this. These Kripke models as they are called [Kri63] consist of a set of so-called *possible worlds*, which can be taken to represent situations in which the 'world' (the environment of the system, or the system as a whole) can be. Formally this is reflected by a truth assignment function π which assigns truth-values to atomic formulas per possible world. But, most importantly, these models contain a relation R on the set of possible worlds, called the *accessibility relation* R(w, w') indicates that world w' is accessible from world w. Thus Kripke models for this basic kind of modal logic are of the form $\langle W, \pi, R\rangle$, where W is a set of possible worlds, π is a truth assignment function, and R is an accessibility relation.

It depends on the reading of the modal operator how the accessibility relation should be interpreted. For instance, for knowledge the relation yields so-called epistemic alternatives of a world: if R(w, w') holds it means that for an agent in world w the world w' might be considered an alternative. This must be viewed in the following sense: the agent considers on the basis of his/her knowledge (or rather the lack of it) the world w' as a possible state of the world. The interpretation of the modal operator is given by means of this accessibility relation: in a model M and a world w in that model it holds that the formula $\Box\varphi$ is true, if φ is true for every R-accessible world from w. More formally,

$$M, w \models \Box\varphi \text{ if and only if } M, w' \models \varphi \text{ for every } w' \text{ such that } R(w, w')$$

For knowledge the relation R is generally taken to be an equivalence relation. One can show that this choice has as a consequence that the three properties of knowledge that we gave above hold with respect to the models thus obtained. This gives rise to a natural notion of an epistemic state of an agent, viz. an equivalence class of worlds, all considered equally possible from the perspective of the agent. We can generalise this idea to mental states more in general by considering a world in a Kripke model together with the R-related worlds as the representation of the mental aspect associated with the modality under consideration. In the case of an obligation, for instance, the accessible worlds represent so-called deontic perfect alternatives in which all obligations are fulfilled (cf. [MW93]).

5. SPECIFYING AGENTS BY MEANS OF MODAL LOGIC

Now we know how we can model mental states of agents by means of the technique of modal logic we can specify the (intended / desired) behaviour of agents by means of this logic. To distinguish between the various modal operators we write the operators as K, B, D, ... for knowledge, belief, desires, ... So, for example $K\varphi$ means that φ is known. In general, we thus obtain a multi-modal logic, a modal logic with several distinct modal operators. Models for multi-modal logics have accessibility relations for each of the modal operators. Now a 'multi-modal mental state' of an agent is represented by a world and all the worlds that are accessible from this world by some of the accessibility relations.

Examples of such multi-modal logics are the well-known BDI logic proposed by Rao & Georgeff [RG91], in which the modalities belief, desire (in the form of goal) and intention are combined with a (branching-time) temporal logic. As said before, also time itself can be viewed as a modality and its associated accessibility relation is time-accessibility (the flow of time) (cf. [Eme90]). Although this idea sounds simple, the logic becomes rather technically involved, so that we will not go into any details here. Although thinking of agents in terms of BDI has also given rise to more or less concrete (BDI) architectures of agent systems, it remains a problem to relate agent programs with BDI logic. The logic is in some sense too abstract or 'ungrounded'. Another problem is that the properties of agents, although abstract in the sense that they are implementation-independent, are sometimes nevertheless regarded as 'too ideal'. The very basic property (K) of modal logic is an example of this: it states that modalities are closed under logical implication. For modalities such as knowledge, belief and certainly intentions / goals this is not very realistic. For instance, if it is intended to go to the dentist, but it is necessarily so that this will result in having toothache, closure under logical implication yields that it is then also intended to have toothache! For knowledge and belief this problem is called the *logical omniscience problem* [MH95]. By its very nature of being at the core of modal logic, it is hard to circumvent if one would like to (mostly by looking at a non-standard Kripke-style semantics, which complicates matters further, or introducing additional non-modal operators).

An attempt to remedy these problems is our own KARO logic [Lin96, LHM96, DMWK96, HLM98] where we base the attitudes of agents on a well-known logic of *action* (rather than time), viz. *dynamic logic*, which is then enriched with such notions as knowledge, belief, desires, goals and commitments. In this way we get a BDI-like logic which is founded on the agent's performance of actions rather than just the flow of time. In our view this renders a formalism that is better equipped to specify agent programs, since there is a direct and obvious relation between such programs and the actions of agents! In other words, unlike the original BDI logic, the KARO logic is grounded in the actions of agents.

6. AGENT-ORIENTED PROGRAMS AS MENTAL STATE TRANSFORMERS

In computer science and the semantics of programming languages in particular programs are often viewed as state transformers. Shoham [Sho93] extends this idea to viewing agent programs as *mental state transformers*. So, one can regard as the meaning / semantics of an agent program the way how mental states are transformed. One might think of an agent's performing of an observation resulting in a different epistemic state reflecting the update of the agent's beliefs about his/her environment. Another example is the agent's committing to do some action resulting in a change of the 'motivational / intentional' state of the agent. An elegant technical tool of treating these state transitions in a formal way is that of a *transition system* developed in the area of semantics of programming languages ([Plo81]). This idea is directly connected to the idea of agent programs as (mental) state transformers: a transition system can be used to derive transitions

$$<P, s> \rightarrow <P', s'>$$

representing a transition from state s to s' under the (partial) execution from (agent) program P to (remaining program) P'. We have used transition systems for giving formal semantics to agent-oriented languages [HBHM].

7. FROM AGENTS TO MULTI-AGENT SYSTEMS

Most researchers in the field agree that the biggest promise of agent technology lies in building and applying multi-agent systems (MAS), collections of more or less autonomous intelligent agents that are co-ordinated in some way as to be able to solve problems and perform involved tasks in a distributed manner. The applications seem to be endless: from e-commerce where agents representing companies negotiate contracts with each other to concrete multi-robotic systems used for transport and military purposes.

In order to describe such systems we need (at least) to extend our agent logics with the possibility to distinguish distinct agents. So we may use modal operators K, B, D,..., now marked with an index to indicate the agent concerned. For example $K_i\varphi$ means that agent i knows that φ, etc. Models for these logics now contain accessibility relations R_i for every agent-indexed modality $\Box_I$. But this is not all. In a multi-agent context it is also natural to consider notions of shared / distributed knowledge, common knowledge, joint intentions etc., group variants of the notions that are associated with individual agents. There has already been done quite some work on this, especially on the group notions of knowledge ([FHMV95], [MH95], [HLM99]). For example, there is the notion of *distributed knowledge* within a group. Intuitively, something is distributed knowledge within a group of agents, if by 'pooling' knowledge the group could conclude that it is the case. Formally one can define a modal operator D, where $D\varphi$ is read as φ is distributed knowledge, and gets a formal semantics by means of an accessibility relation R_D which is obtained by taking the intersection of all accessibility (knowledge) relations for the individual agents in the group: $R_D = \cap_i R_i$. An obvious property of distributed knowledge is

$$K_i\varphi \rightarrow D\varphi$$

expressing that if some agent knows φ then φ is also distributed knowledge in the group. A subject that has obtained much attention is that of *common knowledge*. Something is common knowledge if it not only the case that everyone knows it, but also everyone knows that everyone knows it, and everyone knows that again, *ad infinitum*. This notion plays an important role in game-theoretical situations but also in the analysis of communication protocols among agents where the communication channels are faulty and unreliable. A typical axiom for common knowledge, denoted by the operator C, is the following:

$$C\varphi \rightarrow EC\varphi$$

expressing that when something is common knowledge then everyone knows that it is. Here $E\varphi$ stands for 'every agent knows that φ', formally defined as (n is the number of agents):

$$E\varphi \leftrightarrow K_1\varphi \wedge \ldots \wedge K_n\varphi$$

Recently also some work has been done already on motivational attitudes in MAS, such as *obligations* in MAS (e.g. [Kro95, DL96]) and *joint intentions* of a group (e.g. [DDV99]), but much more need to be done here.

Clearly *communication* plays an important role in MAS, and indeed this topic has also attracted much attention. There are even (semi-) standard agent communication languages (ACLs) proposed like KQML [FMFM94] and FIPA-ACL [FIPA97], together with a more or less formal semantics using some kind of modal logic and speech act theory. Although in our opinion it seems a bit early for standards, this indicates the need for communication primitives for agents together with a well-defined meaning. However, also the 'formal' semantics that is provided [LF94] is not yet quite satisfactory: it still contains a lot of imprecision and moreover it seems to be too abstract from a computational point of view, cf. [EBHM99, HBHM99]), so that we have tried to give a computation-based semantics using the concept of a *transition system* as we have mentioned above. In [EBHM99] we have been able to adapt ideas of modelling communication in 'classical' concurrent programming languages as Hoare's CSP [Hoa78] to the context of agent communication where instead of sending mere values more involved information is communicated. For details we refer to the aforementioned paper.

Another problem with multi-agent systems is that concerning the *ontology* used, or rather the ontologies used, since in general for autonomous agents there is no reason why they should talk the same language. Obviously some assumptions should be made here for a fruitful communication to work. Some approaches take certain (fixed) translators into account, but in our opinion at least some part of the translations between agent languages should be made adaptable (cf. [EBHM99]).

8. CONCLUSION AND OUTLOOK

Agent technology, and especially the use of multi-agent systems, is an enormously promising area. It has many potential applications, several of which are already in advanced state of realisation (see e.g. [PAAM'97, PAAM'99]). Examples are (see [JW98]):

•industrial applications such as process control, manufacturing, air traffic control

•commercial applications such as information management, electronic commerce, business process management

•medical applications such as patient monitoring, health care

•applications for entertainment such as games, interactive theatre and cinema

For these non-trivial applications, particularly those involving human lives and huge financial consequences, it should be very desirable to have formal methods around to verify them in the sense that one can prove analytically that the agents devised behave in a desired and specified manner. It would also be very helpful if one could systematically (and perhaps even to some extent automatically) construct agent systems from formal specifications.

Although agent logics like BDI logic have helped to think about agent concepts, there are as yet no methods available to 'derive' agent programs from specifications in these logics, nor are there as yet formal ways to verify agent programs. Within the area of 'traditional' software engineering there has been done a lot of work on the development of formal methods in order to obtain correct software from formal specifications. This work has to be extended towards agent-oriented software as well, where the main challenge is to cater for the much more intricate notion of state as we have seen above. I believe that in principle it is possible to extend traditional logic-based methods to the agent-oriented paradigm employing the agent logics discussed as well as a formal semantics of agent programming languages in a style as above, but it is obvious that this will take quite some years of intensive research to come. In view of the many future applications of agent technology this will be worth the effort.

References

[Che80] B.F. Chellas, *Modal Logic. An Introduction*, Cambridge University Press, Cambridge, 1980.

[D98] G. De Giacomo, Cognitive Robotics, Papers from the 1998 AAAI fall Symposium, Orlando, Techn. Report FS-98-02, AAAI Press, Menlo Park CA, 1998.

[DDV99] F. Dignum, B. Dunin-Keplicz and R. Verbrugge, Dialogue in Team Formation, *in Proc. IJCAI'99 Workshop ABS-2 on Agent Communication Languages* (F. Dignum & B. Chaib-draa, eds.), Stockholm, 1999, pp. 39-50.

[DL96] F. Dignum and B. van Linder, Modelling Social Agents: Communication as Action, *Intelligent Agents III — Proceedings of the 3rd International Workshop on Agent Theories, Architectures, and Languages (ATAL-96)* (J. Müller, M. Wooldridge and N. Jennings, eds.), 1996, pp. 83-93.

[DMWK96] F. Dignum, J.-J.Ch. Meyer, R.J. Wieringa and R. Kuiper, A Modal Approach to Intentions, Commitments and Obligations: Intention plus Commitment yields Obligation, in: *Deontic Logic, Agency and Normative Systems* (M.A. Brown and J. Carmo, eds.), Springer-Verlag, 1996, pp. 80--97.

[EBHM99] R.M. van Eijk, F.S. de Boer, W. van der Hoek & J.-J. Ch. Meyer, Operational Semantics for Agent Communication Languages, *in Proc. IJCAI'99 Workshop ABS-2 on Agent Communication Languages* (F. Dignum & B. Chaib-draa, eds.), Stockholm, 1999, pp. 89-103.

[Eme90] E.A. Emerson, Temporal and Modal Logic, in: *Handbook of Theoretical Computer Science, Vol. B* (J. van Leeuwen, ed.), Elsevier, 1990, pp. 995-1072.

[FHMV95], R. Fagin, J.Y. Halpern, Y. Moses and M.Y. Vardi, *Reasoning about Knowledge*, MIT Press, Cambridge MA, 1995.

[FMFM94] T. Finin, D. McKay, R. Fritzson and R. McEntire, KQML: An Information and Knowledge Exchange Protocol, in: *Knowledge Building and Knowledge Sharing* (K. Fuchi and T. Yokoi, eds.), Ohmsha and IOS Press, 1994.

[FIPA97] Foundation for Intelligent Physical Agents, FIPA'97 Specification Part 2 - Agent Communication Language, October 1997.

[Har84] D. Harel, Dynamic Logic, in: *Handbook of Philosophical Logic, Vol. 2* (D.M. Gabbay and F. Guenthner, eds.), D. Reidel, Dordrecht, 1984, pp. 497-604.

[HBHM99] K.V. Hindriks, F.S. de Boer, W. van der Hoek & J.-J. Ch. Meyer, Semantics of Communicating Agents Based on Deduction and Abduction, *in Proc. IJCAI'99 Workshop ABS-2 on Agent Communication Languages* (F. Dignum & B. Chaib-draa, eds.), Stockholm, 1999, pp. 105-118.

[HBHM] K.V. Hindriks, F.S. de Boer, W. van der Hoek & J.-J. Ch. Meyer, Agent Programming in 3APL, *Int. J. of Autonomous Agents and Multi-Agent Systems*, to appear.

[Hoa78] C.A.R. Hoare, Communicating Sequential Processes, *Comm. ACM* 21(8), 1978, pp. 666-677.

[HLM98] W. van der Hoek, B. van Linder and J.-J. Ch. Meyer, An Integrated Modal Approach to Rational Agents, in: M. Wooldridge and A. Rao (eds.), *Foundations of Rational Agency*, Applied Logic Series 14, Kluwer, Dordrecht, 1998, pp. 133-168.

[HLM99] W. van der Hoek, B. van Linder and J.-J. Ch. Meyer, Group Knowledge Isn't Always Distributed (Neither Is It Always Implicit), *Mathematical Social Sciences* 38, 1999, pp. 215-240.

[HS93] J. Horty and Y. Shoham (eds.), Reasoning about Mental States: Formal Theories & Applications, Papers from the 1993 AAAI Spring Symposium, Stanford CA, Techn. Report SS-93-05, AAAI Press, 1993.

[JW98] N.R. Jennings & M.J. Wooldridge (eds.), Agent Technology, Foundations, Applications, and Markets, Springer, Berlin, 1998.

[Kri63] S. Kripke, Semantic Analysis of Modal Logic, *Zeitschrift für Mathematische Logik und Grundslagen der Mathematik* 9, 1963, pp. 67-96.

[Kro95] C. Krogh, Obligations in multiagent systems, in: *SCAI'95 —Fifth Scandinavian Conference on Artificial Intelligence* (A. Aamodt and J. Komorowski ,eds.), IOS Press, 1995, pp. 19-30.

[LF94] Y. Labrou and T. Finin, A Semantics Approach for KQML - A General Purpose Communication Language for Software Agents, in: *Proc. 3rd Int. Conf. on Information and Knowledge Management (CIKM'94),* 1994.

[LM70] I. Lakatos and A. Musgrave, *Criticism and the Growth of Knowledge,* Cambridge Univ. Press, Cambridge, 1970.

[Lin96] B. van Linder, Modal Logics for Rational Agents, Ph.D. Thesis, Utrecht University, 1996.

[LHM96] B. van Linder, W. van der Hoek and J.-J. Ch. Meyer, Formalising Motivational Attitudes of Agents: On Preferences, Goals and Commitments, *Intelligent Agents Volume II — Agent Theories, Architectures, and Languages* (M. Wooldridge, J.P. Müller and M. Tambe, eds.), LNAI 1037, Springer-Verlag, 1996, pp. 17-32.

[Mae95] P. Maes, Intelligent Software, *Scientific American* 273(3) (Special Issue on Key Technologies for the 21st Century), 1995, pp. 66-68.

[MH95] J.-J. Ch. Meyer and W. van der Hoek, *Epistemic Logic for AI and Computer Science*, Cambridge University Press, 1995.

[MW93] J.-J. Ch. Meyer and R.J. Wieringa, Deontic Logic: A Concise Overview, in: *Deontic Logic in Computer Science* (J.-J. Ch. Meyer and R.J. Wieringa, eds.), John Wiley & Sons, 1993, pp. 3-16.

[PAAM'97] *Proceedings of the First Int. Conf. on the Practical Applications of Intelligent Agents and Multi-Agent Systems*, London, 1997.

[PAAM'99] *Proceedings of the Fourth Int. Conf. on the Practical Applications of Intelligent Agents and Multi-Agent Technology,* London, 1999.

[Plo81] G. Plotkin, A Structural Approach to Operational Semantics, Techn. Report DAIME FN-19, Aarhus University, 1981.

[RG91] A.S. Rao and M.P. Georgeff, Modeling rational agents within a BDI-architecture, in: *Proc. 2nd Int. Conf. on Principles of Knowledge Representation and Reasoning (KR'91)* (J. Allen, R. Fikes and E. Sandewall, eds.), Morgan Kaufmann, 1991, pp. 473-484.

[Shoh91] Y. Shoham, Implementing the Intentional Stance, in: *Philosophy and AI: Essays at the Interface* (R. Cummins and J. Pollock, eds.), MIT Press, Cambridge, MA, 1991.

[Sho93] Y. Shoham, Agent-Oriented Programming, *Artificial Intelligence* 60, 1993, pp. 51-92.

[WJ94] M. Wooldridge and N.R. Jennings, Intelligent Agents: Theory and Practice, *The Knowledge Engineering Review* 10(2), 1995, pp. 115-152.

Conceptual Foundations of Information Systems

Report on Workshop 1

Wolfgang Hesse

FB Mathematik und Informatik, Philipps-Universität Marburg,
D-35032 Marburg/Germany, email: hesse@informatik.uni-marburg.de

Key words: Information systems, Conceptual framework, Semiotics, Conceptual modelling, System theory

Abstract: This memorandum reports on the first workshop of the ISCO 4 conference which had the "Conceptual Foundations of Information Systems" as its topic. A total of nine contributions of workshop participants addressed the general FRISCO goals, scope and position in the scientific world. In particular, it comprised a thorough review of the FRISCO report, including its target groups, purpose, line of reasoning, structure and particular concept definitions. The last section addresses the future of FRISCO including concrete suggestions for a possible revision of the report.

1. INTRODUCTION

This memorandum reports on the first workshop of the ISCO 4 conference which had the "Conceptual Foundations of Information Systems" as its topic. In the introductory section, the goals and participants of the workshop are listed and a brief overview of its agenda and its course is given. The main part (sections 2 and 3) deals with the central issue of the workshop, a review of the FRISCO report, its goals, structure and contents and discussions on possible revisions. The last section addresses the future of FRISCO including suggestions for concrete actions to be taken.

Goals of the workshop

Originally, the following goals of the workshop had been formulated::

(1) Review the scope, targets and achievements of the FRISCO work in general

(2) Review the FRISCO line of reasoning

(3) Review the structure and contents of the FRISCO report - including particular concepts and definitions

(4) Clarify the relationship of FRISCO to adjacent fields like Conceptual Modelling, Natural Language-based modelling and contemporary modelling methodologies and notations

(5) Suggest concrete actions to be taken to disseminate and further develop the FRISCO achievements

Workshop participants

The following persons participated at the workshop:

- El-Sayed Abou-Zeid (Concordia University, Montreal, Canada)
- Hubert v. Braun (ASG München, Germany)
- João Carvalho, (Universidade do Minho, Portugal)
- Felice Cardone, (Università di Milano-Bicocca, Italy)
- Samuel Chong (Staffordshire University, UK)
- Eckhard Falkenberg (Germany)
- Wolfgang Hesse (Philipps-Universität Marburg, Germany):
- Anastasia Pagnoni Holt (Università di Milano-Bicocca, Italy)
- Bart-Jan Hommes (TU Delft, Netherlands)
- Hannu Kangassalo (Univ. of Tampere, Finland)
- Christian Kop (Univ. Klagenfurt, Austria)
- Andreas L Opdahl (Univ. of Bergen, Norway)
- Yair Wand (Univ. of British Columbia, Vancouver, Canada)

Workshop agenda

The agenda of the workshop was as follows:

- *First session:*
  - Short review of the workshop goals
  - Presentations of workshop participants
- *Second session:*
  - Discussion on FRISCO in general and review of the FRISCO report
  - Discussion on the future of FRISCO and suggestions of concrete actions

The workshop took place according to the agenda. Initially, the workshop goals were approved - with the limitation that goal (4) could certainly not be achieved in this breadth during the workshop. There was an agreement that the review of the FRISCO report and discussion of its future should be given highest priority.

There were nine presentations of workshop participants. They had been brought into an order roughly following the structure of the FRISCO report (addressed topics and chapters of the report are indicated below by an → arrow).

List of presentations

- A. Holt: FRISCO and its relation to Human Organisation (→ FRISCO in general, Ch. 2)
- Heinrich C. Mayr, Christian Kop (presented by Ch. Kop): Natural language as a basis for information systems concepts (→ FRISCO basis and NL relationships, chs. 2 & 3)
- Y. Wand: General observations on IS foundations (→ FRISCO basis, chs. 2 & 3)
- H. v. Braun: Logic of language and relationship types in the FRISCO conceptual structure (→ FRISCO basis, ch. 3)
- W. Hesse: Towards a better structure of the conceptual framework (→ FRISCO report structure, including particular concepts and definitions, chs. 3 & 4)
- E. Falkenberg: Comments on the FRISCO report structure and particular definitions (→ chs. 3 & 4)
- J. Carvalho: Comments on FRISCO and system theory (→ chs. 2, 3 & 4)
- A. Holt: Remarks on the Japan Wines Example and the purpose of a case study (→ FRISCO sample application, ch. 5)
- El-Sayed Abou-Zeid: What is missing in the FRISCO report (→ all chapters, in particular chs. 2 & 3)

The presentations were followed by a discussion on FRISCO at present and in the future, its scope and localisation in the scientific field. This point will be further addressed in section 2.

2. FRISCO AT PRESENT AND IN THE FUTURE

There was an unanimous consent that the FRISCO group has undertaken a fairly difficult task, has reached many of its goals and has produced a comprehensive report which cannot fulfil everyone's expectations but, as a whole, forms an important (one participant called it even "tremendous") step towards a well-founded theory of the IS field. All participants affirmed the suggestion that the work done so far deserves to be continued and concluded with the goal to produce a (physically available) book. This should be based on the achieved results but present them in a reasonably modified and better recognisable form.

FRISCO goals

The overall goals of the FRISCO approach can be summarised as follows "FRISCO helps to understand the basic concepts of IS better than before. This implies in particular to understand the relation of symbols to reality better than before." (H. Kangassalo). A method is sometimes characterised as a notation together with a process (e.g. UML & RUP - Rational's Unified Modelling Language & Process). However, there is a third (kernel) part: the *basic concepts and their foundations*. One FRISCO goal is to provide this kernel part for the field of Information Systems.

FRISCO target groups

A brief review of the target group of the FRISCO report resulted in the suggestion to focus on its *primary target groups* - advanced students (on the master's or Ph.D. level), researchers, methodologists - without loosing track of the idea to support system developers who beyond their daily work activities are interested in the foundations and fundamental principles of their working area.

A careful review of the report (including possible rewriting of some sections) following these general goals was suggested.

FRISCO scope

There was a debate on the scope of the FRISCO report, in particular on the question whether it is too narrow and should be extended in some way. Possible extensions were suggested in the position statements of some participants as well as in the general debate. The latter focussed on the question how far modelling aspects and, in particular, relationships to former CRIS work and to UML should be covered. At present, the FRISCO authors consider the report to be a common basis for various methodologies (including UML-related ones) but it does neither cover methodological aspects of modelling in detail nor elaborates on links and relationships to particular method and method-specific concepts.

An argument for extending the FRISCO report in this direction was that it might get more attention by such an extension. The counter-argument was that this would imply a major effort and that this field cannot be covered in an encompassing way by a small group like FRISCO.

Particular suggestions for possible extensions will be addressed in the section 3.3 (omissions and gaps).

3. REVIEW OF THE FRISCO REPORT

The review was based on the FRISCO report in its final form published on the Web (cf. [FHL+ 98]). Due to time constraints, most of the discussions could neither address their themes in full depth nor come up with definitive conclusions. Insofar, many of the reported results are to be understood rather as suggestions and hints for further investigation than as final decisions.

The review results are structured according to the following topics:

- Strengths and merits
- Errors and open problems
- Omissions and gaps
- Over-definitions (material which should be left out)
- Changes of the report structure
- Further remarks and suggestions

3.1 FRISCO strengths and merits

In the following respects, the FRISCO report is considered to have made essential achievements which should be kept (modulo suggested modifications in some details), further developed and, if necessary, used for better "selling" FRISCO:

- Its profound philosophical anchoring, the constructivist view adopted in the baseline definitions,
- the fact that FRISCO brings the philosophical basis to the forefront (admitting that this may be a problem for "selling" it in North America),
- its independence from particular methods or methodology schools,

- its effort in testing the informally presented concepts by a formalised counterpart in chapter 4 (which should, however, be presented in a better readable form in the revised report),
- the overall approach to build a layered framework and follow a systematic construction plan rather than to build just a glossary of terms,
- the uniqueness of FRISCO in filling the gap between reality and modelling concepts, in yielding a first summary of the ontology we use.

The last point was in particular addressed by the presentation of Y. Wand. He formulated eight principles concerning our human approach to reality (which is to be reflected by IS analysis and design methods). One key point is the role of the observer: "Reality" is always "viewed" by people, knowledge is created by humans through their experience, reflections and reasoning and it is shared through human communication. Foundations for such an approach are: cognitive sciences, linguistics, speech act theory, formal languages. This conforms well to the overall FRISCO approach and, in particular, to its philosophical foundation.

3.2 FRISCO errors and open problems

Some participants pointed out that - besides its well-acknowledged strength and merits - the FRISCO report in its present form contains some errors (in particular: circular definitions) and raises some problems which should be corrected or removed in a possible future book edition. The following errors and problems (listed according to the present report structure) were addressed in the position statements and/or discussed in the workshop plenary:

- Chapter 2: The notion of "added value" (addressed by A. Holt).

  In chapter 2, the report suggests that "value" can be measured in an unambiguous, objective way and ignores the relativity of any "value system". In fact, different people, groups and societies have different priorities on "values" and this is a frequent reason for disputes and even fights. According to E. Falkenberg, the FRISCO report tacitly assumes a specific sort of value, e.g. making the organisation more prosperous. According to E. Abou-Zeid, a value in the FRISCO sense might be "some common (shared) understanding of all members on the organisation's welfare". This should be clarified in the corresponding paragraphs of chapter 2.

- Chapter 3: The use of standard relationship types in the basic definitions, e.g. of the "is-a" relationship (addressed by H. v. Braun)

  As is commonly known, "is-a" might be interpreted in various ways, for example as "is-subset-of" or as "is-element-of" - the first being a transitive relation, but not the latter. To give an example from chapter 3:

  (1) "a predicator is a thing" and
  (2) "a thing is a conception"

  If these relationships are considered to be transitive, then one can say that

  (3) "a predicator is a conception"

  which will possibly cause problems within the semiotic triangle context.

- Chapter 3: Logic of language (addressed by H. v. Braun)

  Is *conception* a predicator (according to FRISCO) or rather a meta-predicator (according to the logic of language)? What impact would the latter notion have - if applied - on the FRISCO line of reasoning? This point addresses the overall structure of the framework and was further discussed in a broader context (see section 3.5 below).

- Chapter 3 and 4: The treatment of "conception" and "thing" (addressed by H. v. Braun, W. Hesse and other participants)

  The "explanatory definition" of *conception* in chapter 3 (which has caused much debate in the FRISCO community) should be revised and more focused on its social aspects (in the sense of "shared knowledge"). The explanation using *perceptions* might be reduced to some introductory remarks (explaining how individual conceptions are formed) - or even skipped at all. If *conception* is considered a base level concept (see section 3.5 below) the corresponding (axiomatic) "definitions" in chapter 4 could (and should) be dropped

  The relationship of the two concepts of *conception* and *thing* should be clarified. A constructive proposal addressing these issues can be found in [BHA+ 99]. The *thing* concept seems to be particularly overloaded which is, for example, reflected in the many (and very heterogeneous) examples.

- Chapters 3 and 4: Circular definitions and the need for a clearly layered structure of concepts (addressed by W. Hesse)

  Chapters 3 and 4 follow the general principle to build a layered conceptual framework where concepts on higher layers may depend on those of lower layers but not vice versa. This principle is acknowledged since it reflects the overall hierarchical structure of the framework and prevents from errors like circular definitions.

According to W. Hesse, chapter 3 in its present form hurts this principle at some places which leads to circular definitions - some of which are considered to be quite harmful - but can be removed by a better layering. An example of such a circular definition can be found if definitions E1, E13-E15 and E20 of chapter 3 are considered in connection:

Roughly spoken,

- a *conception* is explained as a (special) *actand* using the *actor* concept (def. E20),
- an *actor* is explained as a (special) *thing* (def. E13),
- an *actand* is explained as a (special) *thing* (def. E15), and
- a *thing* is explained as a (special) *conception* (def. E1).

This (double) loop can be resolved

- by a better definition and separation of the framework layers (see below), and
- by splitting the *actor* into two concepts:

  (1) the general "world observer" (from now on to be called *observer*) addressed in the assumptions at the beginning of chapter 3 and in the explanations of FRISCO's constructivist view

  (2) the actor involved in the development or use of an IS (still to be called *actor*). Such a split would also help to clarify "self-reflection" processes by distinguishing the *subject* and *object roles* of the self-reflecting person.

  The presence of definitional circularities was objected to by E. Falkenberg. He pointed out that some loops in the explanatory presentation of chapter 3 in the FRISCO report are inherent to the complex nature of the overall subject. Its section 3.2 it was attempted to clarify the "explanatory loops" by pointing out the different contexts for the definitions in question. However, in the axiomatically oriented chapter 4, circularity is (formally) avoided by choosing "thing" as the most primitive concept and exempting the link between "conception" and "thing" from formalisation.

- Chapter 5: The "Japan Wines Inc." sample application (addressed by A. Holt)

A. Holt reported that he expected to find an introductory example and that this one did not motivate him at all. It should be more operational and, for example, start with the "problems" to be solved. E. Falkenberg pointed out that this example was not meant to be a modelling exercise at all. Its only purpose was to demonstrate the most important FRISCO concepts using a coherent example.

3.3 FRISCO omissions and gaps

The contributions to this topic are ordered in a top down way, stepping from the more general to the more specific ones:

- "Localisation" of FRISCO in the science landscape, its relation to Computer Science, System Science and other related areas (addressed by J. Carvalho and other participants).

  It was suggested to better illuminate these relations in the introductory chapters. The FRISCO inclusion that the Information System be a part (or subset) of Organisational System was questioned. It should be reviewed, e.g. with respect to inter-organisational or world-wide IS. Furthermore, system dynamics would need more attention.

- Motivation of the potential FRISCO "clients" (addressed by A. Holt)

  There should be more and better motivation for the approach as a whole. For example, it might be explicitly shown how members of the FRISCO target groups can profit from the results. (See also the above section on FRISCO goals)

- The identity and evolvability of IS (addressed by El-Sayed Abou-Zeid)

  Like organisations, IS have an "identity" but evolve over time. Which are its stable and its changing parts? The evolvability of IS should be covered by FRISCO, including the role of communication in IS evolution. El-Sayed alludes to the "fractal nature" of IS and recommends an "autopoietic view" to them (further detailed in his conference contribution [A-Z 99]).

- The role of the computer in Information Systems (addressed by A. Holt)

  There are strongly opposed positions with respect to this point. A. Holt claims that in the FRISCO report, "almost nothing" is said about the computer. On the other hand, Ronald Stamper (in various other sessions of the conference) repeatedly expressed his disappointment that - as far as he can see - the technical view excessively dominates the social view. In a revised version of the report, FRISCO's position should be clarified.

- Dependency chart of FRISCO definitions

  It was suggested to supply in a revised version a dependency chart of all concepts defined by FRISCO. Hints for that and an example application on UML concepts can be found in X. Castellani's contribution to this conference [Cas 99].

3.4 "Over-definitions" (to be removed from the FRISCO report)

- Set membership (addressed by W. Hesse)

  In chapter 3 (def. E4, p. 38) "set membership" is introduced as a FRISCO concept, which is in conflict to the use of (mathematical) set theory underlying the whole definitional framework (for more details cf. the appendix of [BHA+ 99]). "Set membership" should be used in the traditional mathematical sense only, without being subject to a definition as such. This position is to be clarified early on (accompanied by the customary caution to avoid self-reference and other potential paradox causing statements). Thus, it can be freely used for defining a number of concepts in the framework, as recommended by E. Falkenberg. On the other hand, concepts such as "composition" (or "decomposition") and "aggregation" might be introduced for enhanced expressiveness.

- Overloaded "thing" concept (addressed by W. Hesse)

  The definition for "thing" (ch. 3, def. E1) should be narrowed - which would make some of the examples in the report obsolete. According to E. Falkenberg, any narrowing would result in a less powerful meta-model.

3.5 Changes of the report structure

❑ Overall report structure

It was generally agreed that the report would gain by a number of structural changes. In particular, it was suggested

- to merge chapters 1 and 2 into one introductory chapter (where parts of chapter 2 might be shifted to later chapters) and
- to replace the present "vertical" structure of the central chapters 3-6 by a "horizontal" one according to the layers of the framework.

Each new chapter would correspond to one layer and contain a series of concepts. Each concept is described by

- an introducing textual definition (adopted from old chapter 3),

- a corresponding formal definition - as far as necessary (based on old chapter 4)

- explanations by examples, preferably using a common, continued case study like the Japan Wines example, cf. old chapter 5)

- further material elaborating on the concepts (optional, e.g. to be taken from old chapter 6).

❑ Layered structure of the framework (addressed by W. Hesse and other participants)

Many of the problems identified might be remedied by restructuring the framework (reflecting any changes in the corresponding chapters). Specifically, a clearer and more rigid separation of layers is recommended: Concepts defined in a higher layer may depend on or derive from those defined in lower layers but not the other way around. The following layers were proposed (for more details cf. the appendix of [BHA+ 99])

▪ Base level: Containing the *philosophical background* (constructivist view, the *observer* - to be distinguished from *actor*), *basic ontology* (assumptions), *semiotics, linguistics* (language, predicators etc.), *perceptions* (if still needed) and *conceptions*. Set theory is assumed to belong to the underlying basic knowledge like any other used concepts of mathematics, logic or philosophy.

▪ Kernel level: Starting with *thing* and containing the main part of sections 3.1 -3.5 of the FRISCO report, but without the semiotics part (section 3.4*), per/conceptions, set membership* and with the *actor* reduced to his role in def. E13 (p. 43).

▪ System level: Containing all system- and organisation-related concepts. This is the contents of sections 3.6-3.10 of the original FRISCO report.

3.6 Further remarks and suggestions

- FRISCO's relationship to Natural Language (NL) (addressed by Ch. Kop):

Natural Language is considered an important tool for the early phases of system analysis and modelling (called "pre-design"). NL-based analysis applies filtering techniques to NL-documents like requirements catalogues and leads to a (systematic and coherent) glossary describing the application domain. Glossary entries may be associated to (and in fact:

are instances of) concepts which can be mapped to FRISCO concepts, i.e. FRISCO provides a possible meta-model for such glossaries. This correspondence might be used for a possible test of the FRISCO concepts.

4. CONCRETE ACTIONS

Based on the consensus that the FRISCO work should be continued and its results should be made better accessible in the future, suggestions for concrete actions to be taken were gathered and debated. In the following paragraphs, these are listed following an order from short-term to long-term actions.

- Actions for better dissemination of FRISCO-related material:
  - Do more advertising on FRISCO results - the report, conference proceedings and contributions.
  - Write and publish journal articles reporting on the FRISCO approach and the work so far done.
  - Publish a series of articles on particular FRISCO issues (which might eventually together form a book).
- Actions for revising the FRISCO report:
  - Form a small group responsible for a thorough revision of the report according to the above suggestions (and including re-structuring). The result should be a (printed) book and be published not later than 2001.
  - Rewrite the FRISCO report to form a textbook for advanced academic courses. (This would require more work than just a revision but probably find better acceptance by the publishers.)
- Actions for further development in the FRISCO field:
  - Form a successor task group which takes the FRISCO achievements as a baseline and starts with new goals (to be formulated by the group itself) as e.g. extending FRISCO for modelling tasks, merging the results of FRISCO and CRIS task groups, building a bridge from FRISCO to UML.

Acknowledgement

I wish to thank Hubert v. Braun, Eckhard Falkenberg and Alex Verrijn-Stuart for careful reading this memorandum and for their helpful comments and suggestions.

5. REFERENCES

[A-Z 99] El-Sayed Abou-Zeid: An autopoietic view on the concept Information System. See this issue.

[BHA+ 99] H. v. Braun, W. Hesse, U. Andelfinger, H.B. Kittlaus, G. Scheschonk.: Conceptions are social constructs - Towards a solid foundation of the FRISCO approach. See this issue

[Cas 99] X. Castellani: Overviews of models defined with charts of concepts. See this issue

[FHL+ 98] E. Falkenberg, W. Hesse, P. Lindgreen, B.E. Nilsson, J.L.H. Oei, C. Rolland, R.K. Stamper, F.J.M. Van Assche, A.A. Verrijn-Stuart, K. Voss: FRISCO - A Framework of Information System Concepts - The FRISCO Report. IFIP WG 8.1 Task Group FRISCO. Web version: *ftp://ftp.leidenuniv.nl/pub/rul/fri-full.zip* (1998)

Innovation and Standardization in the Information Systems Field

Report on Workshop 2

T. William Olle

T. William Olle Associates
email: Bill_Olle@Compuserve.com

Key words: Information systems, Standardization, Innovation

Abstract: This report presents the findings of a workshop which was held as part of the IFIP Working Group 8.1 working conference held at the University of Leiden, The Netherlands, 20-22 September 1999

1 INTRODUCTION

Participants:

Chair:	T. William Olle,	T. William Olle Associates, Surrey, UK (email Bill_Olle @ Compuserve.com)
Members:	Deborah Bunker,	University of N.S.W., Sydney, Australia
	Hungjung Lee,	National Computerization Agency, Korea
	John Lindsay,	Kingston University, UK
	Kalle Lyytinen,	University of Jyväskylä, Finland
	Zheying Zhang,	University of Jyväskylä, Finland
	Per Zaring,	Borås University, Sweden

Title:

The original title of the workshop ("*Innovation and Standardization in the Information Systems Field*") was accepted by the opening meeting of the workshop.

2 KEY QUESTIONS

The five key questions as formulated in the Call for Participation were reviewed carefully. After some discussion, it was agreed to a revised formulation of the first four questions. It was noted that the first two questions were concerned with standardization. The third question was concerned with the FRISCO report and standardization. The fourth and fifth key questions as formulated addressed innovation in the information systems. It was agreed that the fourth question should be revised and the fifth question merged into the fourth question.

As a result of this, the participants are on the following formulation of the key questions:

1. In what way does standardization impact innovation?
2. What are the benefits and risks of standardization in the information systems field?
3. Should FRISCO serve as a basis for a standard set of information systems concepts?
4. Is there a need for the following:
   a. new kinds of information system;
   b. new approaches to understanding, designing and building IS;
   c. new user interfaces to IS?

3. INITIAL THOUGHTS ON KEY QUESTIONS

3.1 Impact of standardization on innovation

It was noted that standardization may either be pre-emptive or post hoc. In the former case, the standard tries to pre-empt the market and create a way of doing things before any approach emerges as accepted. In the post hoc case, the standardization work is based on accepted practice and may have to choose among several approaches. There can be major problems with both pre-emptive and post hoc standardization.

A second dimension to standardization is that its scope of applicability may be any of the following:

a. organization (with a division or a company);
b. sectoral (manufacturing, geomatics, health);
c. national or supra-national (France, Canada, European Community, North American Trade Federation);

d. international;
e. cross sectoral.

A third dimension to standardization is the following:

a. related to potential commercial products
b. profession standards relating to the competence of persons
c. ethical relating to the behaviour of persons
d. education and qualifications relating to the training required by persons.

A final dimension to the standardization concept is that some standards are developed and approved by the official international body ISO (International Standards Organisation) which is a federation of more than 100 national standards bodies. In the field of information systems, most standards are international rather than national. Such standards are referred to as "de jure" standards, in other words having some legal standing. However, there is usually no legal enforcement of information technology standards in most countries. Legal enforcement of safety standards which are designed to protect lives is very common.

It is noted that there are frequent problems with "de jure" standardization work. With the current rapidly increasing rate of technological development, procedures adopted by ISO have had to be revised in a number of ways. For example, ISO now recognizes the concept of "publicly available specifications" which may be submitted to a fast track approval procedure.

In addition, there have been various consortia established (frequently supplier dominated) to develop specifications ostensibly more rapidly that has proved possible within ISO. Their developments means that there is a clear requirement to disseminate research results more quickly.

Standardization can also be regarded as a "way of viewing the world" so that the imposition of standards may also be a way of imposing a particular "world view" on ways of doing business. For example, the Internet is dependent on technology and infrastructure standards that enable businesses to globalise. It is noted that some countries and some individuals that do not have access to the Internet. This could mean that they unable to participate in the global marketplace and hence their ability to innovate is constrained.

There are many organizations interested in standardization apart from the aforementioned official international and national bodies. Examples of such are the following:

a. equipment suppliers (including software suppliers)
b. major users of products based on the standards
c. academics who have to be aware of important standards when teaching
d. consortia of suppliers and users usually formed to develop pre-emptive standards which they hope will become de facto and then de jure standards

It was noted that, in the information systems field, equipment suppliers are frequently the most heavily involved .

The reason for broadening the question from "in which way does standardization inhibit or stimulate innovation" to the wording used in this report was because it was felt that there were potential impacts other than "stimulate" and "inhibit". Examples of such possible impact were given as "help developing countries" and "improve the quality of life threatening systems" such as air traffic control and data protection.

3.2 Benefits and risks of standardization

One of the earliest benefits of standardization to be recognized was that referred to as "portability". In the early days a computer programme developed for one model of computer would not run on another model - even if that model was from same manufacturer. This lead to the standardization of the early programming languages such as Fortran and Cobol.

Another advantage to be recognized early was that of making it easier for educators to train student in skills which could have a wider degree of applicability.

It was also noted that standardization is in itself a kind of technology convergence in a specific technical area; standardization can enable technology convergence between separate technical areas.

One of the most important potential benefits of standardization was felt to be in enabling the inter-operability of information systems constructed on heterogeneous platforms. This should have the effect of reducing the risk in new investment, and hopefully reducing the price.

An important beneficial role of some of the more fundamental standards is that they can be enabling. Examples of such standards are character sets, measurement systems and coding systems. Such standards will become even more important in the future due to inter-operability and e-commerce requirements.

On the other hand, two noteworthy risks of standardization to businesses are as follows. The time to bring new applications and architectures to market is effectively shortened as these are now easily copied and emulated by competitors. For example, e-commerce publishing activities are easily copied, plagiarised and inappropriately linked

The security of systems is difficult and expensive to ensure, due to common operating platforms and the integration of value chain activities across these platforms.

3.3 FRISCO report as a basis for standard set of information system concepts

A number of questions arise when considering this question the first of which is "how can the some of the concepts spelled out and defined in the report be related to those already in use?" Another question is "is it too late for the carefully defined FRISCO concepts to have an impact on the broad practitioner world of information systems.

Given the importance of teaching in the information systems field, how would teaching FRISCO concepts contribute to a student's understanding of the skills needed to work in the information systems field?

The FRISCO report is essentially an attempt to derive a standard framework which can be used as a basis for understanding and communicating information systems concepts. This is a positive but also problematic activity as it helps to establish a "world view" which is invaluable in building and teaching information systems. It may also form a barrier, however, or inhibit the systems building activities of those countries and individuals that understand information systems in a slightly or totally different way.

The standardization of concepts such as those in the FRISCO report does not make sense. It is possible to standardize notions and procedures but in a democratic society it is not possible to standardize the way people think. The impact of the FRISCO report should be in the shaping of textbooks and associated teaching.

3.4 Need for news kinds of information systems approaches

3.4.1 New kinds of information system

There have been considerable advances in recent years in the kinds of information which can be handled by information systems. From the early days of structured data and formatted text, it is now possible to handle graphics, audio and video. Since it is now technically possible to digitize odours (and presumably tastes), it should also be soon possible to recreate the original form from the digitized form. This could be useful in distributing samples of perfumes and other fragrances as well as foodstuffs.

E-commerce technological developments and the associated use of standards (e.g. TCP/IP) have together seen inter-organisational systems become much more important (Extranets). Utilisation of information technology (IT) to integrate and automate value chain activities has meant that multi-business systems platform integration needs to be addressed for e-commerce to work effectively.

Furthermore, it is clear that new kinds of information system will surely be needed to ensure that public transport functions more safely and more effectively. The information systems used to support and drive e-commerce must be seen to reduce the risk of error.

3.4.2 New approaches to designing information systems

There appear to be almost as many ways of designing information systems as there are people trying to do it. Whether any given approach can be designated as "new" at any time is open to question – although an approach may be "new" to the person using it. Because it is so easy to develop an approach to information systems design, everyone does it. Some years ago, the use of CASE tools was widely advocated, only to fall into some disrepute because the results achieved did not match those suggested as possible in the marketing hype. The skill needed to design information systems does not scale easily. It may seem easy enough to develop smaller systems. The skills level required to design more complex systems does not increase linearly and this problem cannot be solved by using more people.

The trend, understandably enough, has been towards more multi-option, shrink wrapped (or pre-packaged) systems. This means that the user environment has the responsibility for deciding which options it wants at the time the system is installed and not at the time it is designed. Certain options required by the environment may not be provided in the shrink-wrapped package and these omissions can be serious.

Another aspect of this sub-question is the increasing need for the information systems to be able to inter-operate. This is particularly important in the business to business scenario of electronic commerce.

With the rise in importance of inter-organisational systems, there does not seem to have been a corresponding rise in inter-organisational systems building approaches and methods. There have been some frameworks developed for identifying opportunities for E-commerce within a business but serious systems building methods have been somewhat neglected. Work is required in this area.

It should also be clear from experience during the past three or four decades that an information system which is designed and built to meet a set of business requirements at a given point in time will invariably have to be modified at a later point in time. If the need (in general terms) to meet evolving requirements is recognized initially, then the modification can usually be effected more speedily and at lower cost. The concepts of "design for change" and "living systems" are clearly relevant here.

3.4.3 Need for new kinds of user interface to information systems

The world of "point and click" has been here for some time and can be clearly identified as a de facto standard for a user interface. The associated use of pull down menus (which is certain circumstances may be customized by the user) is an important element in the world of point and click.

Other user interfaces of importance include the QWERTY keyboard and voice recognition.

The QWERTY keyboard is clearly very basic to the extent that "point and click" is really a supplement to the keyboard in most situations. There are several standards for keyboard layouts, the multiplicity being governed by the many alphabets in world wide use.

Use of voice recognition is growing in acceptance as the technology improves and it is difficult to speculate on whether it will ever replace rather than merely supplement the duo of mouse and keyboard.

In short it does not seem as if there is a need for new kinds of user interface to information systems at least in the sense discussed above.

However, in another sense, the question merits further consideration. There are two broad classes of interaction between persons and information systems. There are firstly the prescribed types of interaction (including retrieval of information from the system and changing the information content of the information system).

Secondly, there are the types of interaction, which cannot be prescribed by an information systems designer. One example of such an interaction is an ad hoc query, which hopefully can be formulated by a user using some kind of query language.

On the subject of user interface, there is considerable room for improvement in the matter of structuring user levels so that the lowest level of user (in terms of complexity of requirements) is not confronted with options which he does not understand, does not wish to use, and probably should not try to use anyway.

Over the years, there has been a lot of research on "user satisfaction". The type of appropriate systems interface developed has been one of the subsets of this research (e.g. Human Computer Interaction). Just as e-commerce has affected the importance of inter-organisational systems development, it has also affected the importance of the customer as the system user. The customer is set to become a new class of system user as the Internet and web–based system design and creation become more commonplace. It seems that more activity and research needs to be focussed on the customer/user.

4. WHY THIS REPORT IS NOT A MANIFESTO

There was some feeling expressed in the workshop that a manifesto is needed on the subject of responsibility for information systems. The argument for this is that information systems professionals in general and those participating in IFIP working groups in particular need to comment publicly on the economy and effectiveness of the processes of standardization and innovation.

The was a feeling expressed that the process is sometimes a conspiracy to defraud, sometimes a series of design errors and sometimes a political process where different parties acting in different ways can make a difference. The well known situation relating to OSI, X500 and TCP/IP is felt to be an example of this.

This leads to the proposal that this report should constitute a manifesto indicating the responsibilities for IFIP Working Group 8.1.

Although the issue being raised is clearly of paramount importance, it is also clear that this report does not constitute such a manifesto. It is not clear that the questions posed to the workshop at its inception were of a nature to steer its deliberations in that direction.

Information System Concepts in Practice

Report on Workshop 3

Willem Hengeveld and Alexander A. Verrijn-Stuart

Deloitte Touche Bakkenist and Technical University Delft, The Netherlands
email: w.hengeveld@sepa.tudelft.nl

Department of Computer Science, Leiden University, The Netherlands
email: alexander.verrynstuart@wxs.nl

Key words: Information systems (IS), Concepts, Modelling, Practice, Information systems engineering (ISE), FRISCO

Abstract:

The main question addressed is how information system concepts influence the practice of designing and implementing information systems. We argue that this happens only indirectly, through methods and education. Vice-versa, the practitioner's information system concepts are limited to those encountered in practical experience, in particular via commercial tools and methods, and frameworks such as UML. This situation often leads to unwitting adoption of concepts that are not necessarily optimal for the task. In this connection, the FRISCO Report only plays a moderate role, primarily in academic circles, but not in any practice dominated environment. Information system glossaries that provide coherent explanations may be very important for new developments in the coming years, given the fast developments of the field and the large number of new staff that will not have a formal education in the discipline. In response to this, the Internet may be a suitable medium for the academic world to get stakeholders involved and committed.

1 INTRODUCTION

The original title of the workshop ("*How do our concepts shape our practice and vice-versa?*") was considered a good starting point but also somewhat restrictive. As to the second half of the implied question, one observes that practitioners [1] mostly make implicit use of the concepts that underlie the information system design and construction tools that are available to them. Conscious and explicit use of concepts mainly appears to result from earlier education and training. Thus, the members of the workshop felt that their task should cover the entire range of concepts appropriate to the field. In particular, the question was posed to which extent the FRISCO framework and other research in information system concepts might provide a beneficial influence on the various sectors of what is called 'practice'.

2 NEW TRENDS (requiring attention):

The growth and increasing variety of systems, changes in the practice of use, and emerging research developments will cause the research into information system concepts (ISCO) to look to new principles and hence concepts. The traditional way to look at information systems as a system for an organisation that should support business processes is long gone. New developments in Information Systems Engineering (ISE) should be reflected in research into information system concepts if that research aims at being relevant for practitioners.

The following trends in ISE are considered to be important (the possible and probable consequences for research into ISCO is being marked by a ☛):

- The future will show a predominance of **multi-media** systems over purely **administrative** systems.
  ☛ This shift involves different processes and requires a *changed emphasis* on various possible *conceptual structures*.
- The emergence of **very large size distributed systems** that may require an approach in terms of 'packages' or components.
  ☛ When dealing with prefabricated components instead of constructing those oneself, *new methods and tools* will be required.
- **E-commerce** and **Internet** are there to stay and seem to have their own concepts. ☛ This development not only changes the practical use of systems, but also triggers *new areas of research into concepts* (*conversations*, *agents*, etc.).
- **Workflow** especially in an **inter-organisational** context will pose new challenges.
  ☛ This changing context demands *inter-organisational involvement*, which, in turn, means that increased *conceptual clarity* will be needed.
- **Business needs and requirements** are gradually becoming more important than programmers' needs (because of increasing sophistication of users and their systems).
  ☛ This change in emphasis gives rise to an associated *shift of support needs*.

Finally, one encounters clear *standardisation* challenges, such as UML, etc., that need to be addressed (addressed by Workshop 3, "Inovation and Standardization in the Information Systems field", elsewhere in these Proceedings).

3 THE FRISCO REPORT: analysis of its applicability

The FRISCO Report offers a 'line of reasoning' intended to improve the dialogue between IS users and IS specialists. In practice, attention may well centre on its 'glossary' of IS terms. This may result in a neglect of its fundamental basis (a coherent set of assumptions, from which a reasoned list of definitions follow, and which imply a set of guidelines for analysing the conceptual structures). This would be regrettable and should be overcome by suitable educational effort.

However, the open explanatory style of the "overview" chapter has led to some doubts regarding the consistency of the list, in that a certain definitional circularity is perceived. Thus, a revision of the report that clarifies such problems would be of great value.

The main message of the FRISCO Report is considered to be of great value, by both information system researchers and practitioners. For instance, it was remarked that the FRISCO line of reasoning and definitions imply (even if not explicitly expressed) ways of thinking about: ER, forms, flow of signals, codes and so on. This may in turn lead to clearer specifications and designs. Furthermore, opportunities may exist for comparing different models or even (in the future) translating them via meta-modelling. Unfortunately, such options have not yet been proven in practice.

The general conclusion, however, is that the FRISCO Report should be revised, such that the coherence of assumptions and the consequent views on meta-modelling and the significant concepts stand out more clearly for and that the credibility is enhanced with practitioners.

4 WHAT THE PRACTITIONERS' WORLD EXPECTS

The requirements of 'practitioners' naturally depend on their positions and tasks: senior executives, middle management, operational and clerical staff take very different perspectives regarding 'information systems' and its use. Similarly, there is a wide range of responsibilities among IS specialists, who may be designers and builders of information systems, and hence concentrate on other aspects than the 'users', but who will tend to be more practical in outlook than IS researchers. Thus, the expectations of the user and specialist categories (as opposed to the researchers) include answers to the following questions and wishes:

- How one gets from the real world to models that represent the appropriate information systems, is a question that is important for the designer of Information Systems. Moreover, a specific desire is often to change existing business practice by using new information systems that change sub-optimal processes (in a favourable direction). Information systems in the broader sense thus also include procedures, organisational structures etc.; these should be further elaborated to make FRISCO operational.

- Modelling of IS should be supported by implementation tools: thus, the design and implementation roles are to be rolled into one integral activity. Methods to obtain requirements from users and put them in models and verify user wishes, while simultaneously (or at least in one single sweep) arriving at the corresponding computer system are now expected from IS tools and methods developers. For using Information System Concepts by practitioners easy accessibility and making concepts fit for use is highly important. Credibility however comes first.

- Information systems concepts often merely derive from tools and languages that practitioners use – hence, one would wish to be provided with a (reasonably) all-embracing framework. Clear problems at the moment are how to find the borders around IS. Elaborated semantics of models should lead to comparison of different models to bring one model in the form of another model (automatically).

Given these expectations from the practitioners' world, we might try to sketch the relationship between the world of the practitioners and the research and IS-method developers. This is illustrated somehow in Figure 1. The figure summarises the relationship of the worlds of practitioners and researchers, as linked by their varied concepts. Practitioners predominantly base their views on 'common sense' and the nature of the tools available to them.

Researchers, on the other hand, are expected to come up with 'uncommon sense' (i.e. innovative ideas). So far, research has been primarily theoretical (i.e. based on the researchers' perception of the practitioners' environment) and was aiming in particular at researcher themselves (this is indicated with the "thick arrow"). More empirical research into explicit and implicit usage of concepts ought to be conducted. The combined results of 'theoretical' and 'empirical' research might well lead to improved methods. The influence on method developers, therefore, could be significant, on practitioners somewhat less, on IS users only indirect.

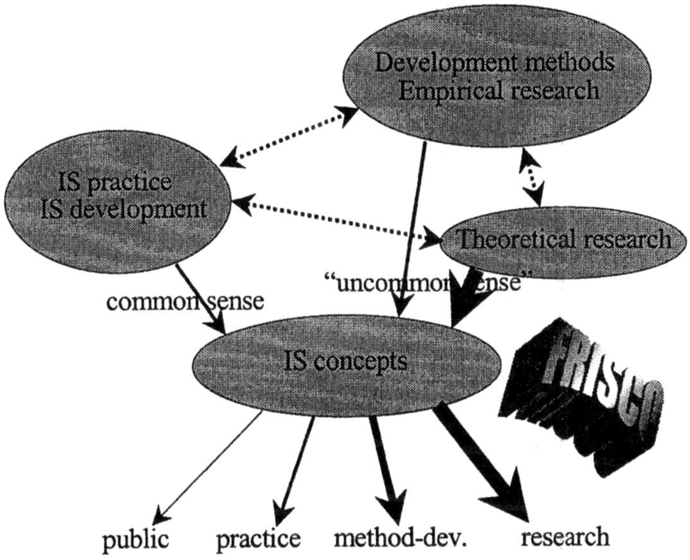

Figure 1. The current and future links between theory and practice

The dotted arrows denote the new (or so far insufficiently stressed) interactions that could be beneficial for both the IS research and the practitioners world:

- mutual consideration of theory and practice;
- empirical research into the practical significance and applicability of concepts;
- evaluation of new development methods in the light of the above.

It is important that such new approaches – including an update and/or extension of the FRISCO Report – be conducted in an effective manner, that tries to keep up with the pace of developments and that includes beforehand mechanisms to involve practitioners. A possible approach to do so is included in the following section.

5 A ROADMAP FOR ACTION

The tacit assumption is that IS research and in particular research associated with concepts ("ISCO") will yield interesting results, that might be useful in practice. The question is under what conditions and with what ambition one may come to sensible research lines (that can be taken up in the context of e.g. a follow up on FRISCO). The following recommendations and ideas express the conclusions of the workshop:

- It is essential to ***inform stakeholders*** about ISCO results. This should be pursued indirectly through [continuous] education and by dissemination in the form of papers in scientific and applied journals. Examples of journals that might be interested in the FRISCO Report and its extensions are the MIS Quarterly and the Journal of Information Systems. Additionally, 1-day training courses, a book for educational situations, an IFIP or more specific "FRISCO" web site should be aimed for in addition to the more traditional means of delivering research results.

- An ***extension of the glossary*** like the one of FRISCO is not only useful, but also necessary. Several new concepts need to be put in perspective. The list of topics to be addressed was given above. Furthermore the (perceived) significance FRISCO should be extended beyond its present glossary. It should be enhanced with ***educational information***, the personal views (chapter 7) might be brought forward so as not to be buried under the precise but boring detail of the earlier chapters, and concepts in the 'social' step of the semiotic ladder – such as norm, rule, responsibility – should be emphasised. Moreover the credibility and consistency of the report should be carefully reviewed.

- Important is the question how to define feasible ***empirical research programmes***. This research should aim at investigating how IS concepts used by practitioners in, discussions, designs, programs, implementation tools, and how they may contribute to some benefit.

- IS ***method developers*** will give ISCO research more attention when the clear added value is shown. This could be done by showing how e.g. UML can be described in terms of information system concepts **and *how FRISCO relates to other IS concept framework studies***, such as those conducted by Bubenko, Loucopoulos and others.

- As indicated at the beginning of this report, practitioners benefit from concept frameworks mainly indirectly; hence the need is to ***address*** the next generation of "developers", i.e. ***students***, as well as the responsible ***knowledge managers*** within the ICT industry.

All in all, the main conclusion from the above is that Information Systems Concepts research needs a clear redirection and refocusing of the work which has been dominant in this area. It also means that research lines need to be developed that are being performed by practitioners and researchers together. Furthermore, it is clear that less traditional means of disseminating research results is necessary, in order to benefit optimally from the necessary changes in this field.

6 PARTICIPANTS

The workshop was attended by a diverse group of representatives from the academic world and industry. Some of the participants are professionally involved in both worlds. The participants were: Alistair Barros (Australia), Vincent Bataille (France), Xavier Castellani (France), Samuel Chong (United Kingdom), Pim Hengeveld (Netherlands), Sue Holwell (United Kingdom), Jens Kaasbøll (Norway), John Krogstie (Norway), Kecheng Liu (United Kingdom), Paul Mallens (Netherlands) , Arne Sølvberg (Norway) , Ronald Stamper (NL and UK) , Alex Verrijn-Stuart (Netherlands) and others.

The workshop was chaired by prof. dr W. Hengeveld from Delft University of Technology with the assistance of prof. dr A.A. Verrijn Stuart of Leiden University. This report is their sole responsibility.

References:

A Framework of Information System Concepts: The FRISCO report, E.D. Falkenberg et al., eds, © IFIP 1998; ISBN 3-901882-01-4 (Web edition: ftp://ftp.leidenuniv.nl/pub/rul/fri-full.ftp)

The Unified Modeling Language User Guide (The Addison-Wesley Object Technology Series) by Grady Booch, Ivar Jacobson, James Rumbaugh, Addison-Wesley Pub Co; ISBN: 0201571684

Uml Distilled : Applying the Standard Object Modeling Language (Addison-Wesley Object Technology Series) by Martin Fowler, Kendall Scott (Contributor), Ivar Jacobson, Addison-Wesley Pub Co; ISBN: 0201325632

UML in Action, Comm. ACM **42** (October 1999, Number 10), Grady Booch, guest ed. (articles by Cris Kobryn, Grant Larsen, Bran Selic, Alex E.Bell/Ryan W. Schmidt, Jim Conallen), pp 26-71.

Further information on *UML*, in general, see: http://www.omg.org

The reference to proposals to profile *UML* with enterprise models is:

http://www.omg.org/techprocess/meetings/schedule/UML_Profile_for_EDOC_RFP.html

This relates to the point that conceptual models are now being used as executable artifacts. The proposals define enterprise sub-models as well as their automatic, non-normative mappings through distributed middleware technologies (in this case Corba).

Various frameworks:

- P. Loucopoulos, P. McBrien, F. Schumaker, Theodoulidis, V. Kopanas and B. Wangler, *Integrating database technology, rule based and reasoning for effective information systems*, Journal of Information Systems **1** (Feb 1991) 129-152.
- D.E. Avison and A.T. Wood-Harper, *Information Systems Development Research: An Exploration of Ideas in Practice*, The Computer Journal **34** (2) 98-112, April 1991.
- A.T. Berztiss and J.A. Bubenko, *A software process model for business reengineering*, Proceedings of the IFIP WG8.1 Working Conference Information Systems Development for Decentralized Organizations (ISDO95), Trondheim, Norway, August 1995, pp 184—200, Chapman & Hall, 1995.

'Practitioners': persons involved in design, implementation and/or use of information systems, as opposed to researchers (academic) whose primary interests are foundations, formalisms, languages, tools and the applicability thereof; method and tool designers often straddle the divide.

INDEX OF CONTRIBUTORS

KEYWORD INDEX

9 780792 378068

GPSR Compliance

The European Union's (EU) General Product Safety Regulation (GPSR) is a set of rules that requires consumer products to be safe and our obligations to ensure this.

If you have any concerns about our products, you can contact us on ProductSafety@springernature.com

In case Publisher is established outside the EU, the EU authorized representative is:

Springer Nature Customer Service Center GmbH
Europaplatz 3
69115 Heidelberg, Germany

Batch number: 10755284

Printed by Printforce, the Netherlands